More Than a
Historian

More Than a Historian

The Political and Economic Thought of Charles A. Beard

Clyde W. Barrow

Transaction Publishers
New Brunswick (U.S.A.) and London (U.K.)

Library of Congress Catalog Number: 00-037391
ISBN: 0-7658-0027-6
Printed in the United States of America

Library of Congress Cataloging-in-Publication Data

Barrow, Clyde W.
   More than a historian : the political and economic thought of Charles
   A. Beard / by Clyde W. Barrow.
      p. cm.
   Includes bibliographical references and index.
   ISBN 0-7658-0027-6 (alk. paper)
      1. Beard, Charles Austin, 1874-1948— Political and social views.
   2. Beard, Charles Austin, 1874-1948—views on economics. I. Beard,
   Charles Austin, 1874-1948. II. Title.

JC212 .B37 2000
320.51'3'092—dc21   00-037391

Dedicated to the late Richard Ashcraft,
With respect and admiration

Contents

List of Figures

Abbreviations

AAA	Agricultural Adjustment Act
AHA	American Historical Association
APSA	American Political Science Association
BMR	Bureau of Municipal Research
BOSAP	Board of Strategy and Planning
CRA	Capital Reserve Account
EIS	Export-Import Syndicate
NEC	National Economic Council
NIRA	National Industrial Recovery Act
PSQ	*Political Science Quarterly*
SIA	Social Insurance Account

Acknowledgments

There are several people whose good will and support advanced this project at critical points when it would have been easier to abandon the manuscript. I owe an enormous debt to the late Richard Ashcraft, my dissertation advisor and mentor for nineteen years. Richard Ashcraft's contributions to the new historicism in political theory have played an important role in my conceptualization and execution of the project. Ashcraft insisted that political theorists must not only read texts carefully, but must also be serious historians and competent sociologists, if they are to interpret textual meanings in a way that is relevant to a contemporary audience. Ashcraft's method of interpreting political theory had its epistemological origins in Marx's theory of ideology, while its methodological foundation was based in Karl Mannheim's sociology of knowledge. Anyone familiar with those works will recognize their influence on this book.

However, it was Professor Eldon Eisenach at the University of Tulsa who first took a serious interest in my work on Charles A. Beard. After delivering a paper on Beard (Chapter 4) at the Southwestern Political Science Association in 1985, Eldon encouraged me to continue my work at a time when most political theorists regarded *American* political thought as something less than "political theory," evidently on the assumption that political theory is a peculiarly European art. At each major juncture in the development of the book, I sought Eldon's advice and the book would not have been completed without his encouragement, although he is exonerated from its shortcomings, because I did not always take his advice.

I was also fortunate, at the earliest stages of this project, to receive assistance from Jerome Mileur, the former editor of *POLITY* and a political theorist at the University of Massachusetts Amherst. Professor Mileur patiently worked with me in responding to scholarly reviewers, and portions of this work appeared in that journal more than a decade ago. Karen Orren, co-editor of *Studies in American Political Development*, also provided a forum for the publication of two exceptionally long articles on Beard (Chapter 4 and Chapter 6) that would never have been published in less historically oriented political science journals.

As always, the University of Massachusetts Dartmouth librarians spent several years tracking down obscure publications by Charles A. Beard and other authors associated with him. My thanks to Jo-Ann Cooley, Linda Zeiper, and Erika Pereira. Robert Mauro, my former research assistant, spent innumerable hours over a three-year period retrieving interlibrary loans and tracking down bibliographical references, while his own initiative brought several articles to my attention. Importantly, his own enthusiasm for the work forced me to return to it again and again, particularly at those points when I just wanted to be finished with it.

Finally, the author gratefully acknowledges the following publishers:

1. Chapter 2 was published originally as "From Marx to Madison: The Seligman Connection in Charles Beard's Constitutional Theory," *POLITY* 25 (Spring 1992): 379-97. Chapter 5 was published originally as "Building a Workers' Republic: Charles A. Beard's Critique of Liberalism in the 1930s," *POLITY* (Fall 1997). Both articles are reprinted (with revisions) with the permission of *POLITY*.
2. Chapter 4 was published originally as "Beyond Progressivism: Charles A. Beard's Social Democratic Theory of American Political Development," *Studies in American Political Development* 8 (Fall 1994): 231-81. Chapter 6 was published originally as "The Diversionary Thesis and the Dialectic of Imperialism: Charles A. Beard's Theory of Foreign Policy Revisited," *Studies in American Political Development* (Fall 1997): 248-91. Both articles are reprinted (with revisions) with the permission of Cambridge University Press.

Preface

My first encounter with Charles A. Beard was a casual one, but it sparked a curiosity about his work that has lasted more than twenty years. In 1976, while an undergraduate at Texas A&M University at Kingsville, I was sitting in a professor's office waiting for him to retrieve some print-outs from the university computer center. As students often do in these situations, I began perusing the professor's bookshelves and almost immediately my eyes fixed on Charles A. Beard's *An Economic Interpretation of the Constitution of the United States*. I opened the book and began reading what I now know was the introduction to the 1935 edition. I was already fascinated by Marx and Marxism so I found it puzzling that Beard denied being a Marxist. I quickly drew the same conclusion as many previous readers: of course, Beard was a Marxist, but he was writing about the United States for an American audience so he had to deny it. Although I read no more than ten pages of the introduction before the professor returned to his office, the book's author, title, and thesis were always returning to my thoughts. Having grown up in south Texas, where every aspect of life was determined by the price of cattle or the price of oil, Beard's economic interpretation of history seemed like a self-evident proposition to me.

In graduate school at UCLA, I finally purchased my first copy of Beard's classic work on the Constitution and I noticed that other graduate students were constantly drawn to the book on my shelf. Everyone had heard of Charles Beard, everyone knew the title of the book, but everyone was amazed that I had actually read it. Beard's book on the Constitution seemed to exert some magical power that was both compelling and repelling to everyone who approached it. I always intended to write a seminar paper on Beard, but it was not until after graduate school that I finally sat down and wrote a paper on *An Economic Interpretation of the Constitution of the United States*. The paper was subtitled: "Is the Debate Really Over?"

My survey of the literature on Beard's *Economic Interpretation* concluded that it was premature to consign Beard to the dustbin of history and that, indeed, many of the so-called refutations of Beard's best-known work were directed at a straw man constructed explicitly for ideological purposes during the 1950s and 1960s. When I submitted the article to a leading political science journal, I received the answer to the question posed in my subtitle. The first referee was enthusiastic about publishing the manuscript and asked the editor to solicit rejoinders from well-known Beard critics, with the expectation that I would reply to those critics. The second referee submitted a terse two-sentence review stating that Beard was irrelevant to contemporary political theory and that it was unfathomable that anyone in political science could still be interested in his work. A third reviewer admitted that he had never read Beard and would, therefore, defer to the evaluation of the other referees. Confronted with a split decision, the journal's editor chose to reject the manuscript. When I submitted the same manuscript to a second major journal in political science, it met with *exactly the same result*!

I have grown accustomed to split decisions on Beard since that time. No American scholar in the twentieth century has provoked sharper or more widespread academic and public disputes through his written work. For this reason, a few comments on my method of interpretation and style of presentation are necessary to clarify my approach to Beard's writings. First, anyone who attempts to reconstruct Beard's political and economic thought enters a wide-ranging and intense debate that is littered with secondary interpretations and even tertiary interpretations of interpretations. Beard was an unusually prolific writer who published dozens of books, hundreds of articles and book chapters, and scores of book reviews. In turn, this immense and controversial corpus, which extends over five decades (1898 to 1948), has generated a secondary literature that is certainly no less voluminous than one would find over a comparable period of time for any of the so-called "great" political theorists.

Moreover, Beard has entered the pantheon of thinkers that most scholars no longer read, but only *read about* through secondary and tertiary sources. Beard is one of those thinkers that everyone claims to know so well that it is no longer necessary to even read him. Thus, to actually read Beard is to cut through a dense thicket of secondary interpretation, preconception and misconception, disdain, and even eight decades of continuing ad hominems. The book has been structured as a polemic against the dominant strains of interpretation and critique, although I must confess that trying to reach Beard through this thicket of unsupported assumptions has been the equivalent of hacking one's way through a rainforest with a pocket knife.

Notwithstanding the difficulty of reaching Beard through the heavy undergrowth of secondary interpretation, and unlike many of my colleagues in contemporary political theory, I am still convinced that one can discover and understand the real Charles Beard and that doing so is a worthwhile intellectual activity. By referring to the "real" Charles Beard, I am claiming that in a universe of finite available evidence, it is certainly possible to discard certain interpretations of Beard's work as incorrect, because they are incompatible with the preponderance of textual, biographical, and contextual evidence, not the least of which are the actions and statements of the author with regard to his own intentions and meaning. Similarly, it is possible to cast doubt on otherwise plausible interpretations to the extent that they are unable to account for significant actions and statements of the author with regard to his own intentions and meaning. Thus, I am claiming that it is possible, based on the weight of the available evidence, to construct an interpretation that is more plausible than competing alternatives, that is consistent with the actions and statements of the author with regard to his own intentions and meaning, notwithstanding the fact that no individual, including Beard, is perfectly rational, completely transparent, or unambiguous to subsequent observers. This interpretive principle is particularly important to my understanding of Beard's economic and political thought, because a large proportion of previous commentaries depend on assertions that Beard was dissembling, disingenuous, confused, or constantly prone to polemical exaggeration and posturing.[1] Hence, many of the most influential interpretations of Beard's work refuse to accept his own statements about his meaning and intentions seriously.

For this reason, the book is footnoted extensively, perhaps even excessively, and I have sometimes been criticized by reviewers and colleagues for this apparent peculiarity. However, there is first of all a sound methodological reason for my compulsion to footnote every quote, to document every biographical claim, to cite a source for every context, and to reference every statement of fact. It may seem presumptuous to elevate footnotes to the status of a methodological principle, but in the course of writing this book, I have been astounded by the number and range of unsubstantiated claims that scholars and politicians have made about the content of Beard's work, its ideological implications, and the author's intentions in writing certain books. Many of the most important critical claims about Beard have remained unchallenged and unsubstantiated for several decades; each book or article building on a previous myth, assuming a fact not in evidence, or taking for granted someone else's imputed meaning for a text. My radical response to this intellectual practice is to specify my sources for reconstructing Beard's political and economic thought in as much detail as possible. Multiple citations from Beard are used as a check on my own interpretation, and they are also used to document the consistency of Beard's theoretical claims across time.

Second, footnotes allow one to reconstruct the meanings and intentions of a particular author through his own language. J. G. A. Pocock has demonstrated admirably that the meanings of concepts are deeply embedded in the linguistic conventions of intellectual paradigms.[2] Therefore, if a contemporary author is to capture the intellectual context of a period, to convey a flavor for the language, conventions, usages, and meanings of a period, it is necessary to reconstruct an author's meanings through his own words, and those of his contemporaries, so far as possible. Otherwise, there is a tendency to impute contemporary meanings to archaic concepts or to impute unintended meanings to a political idea. At critical junctures in the Beard debates, misguided presentist imputations have made a significant impact on how contemporary scholars understand Beard's work. By remaining as close to Beard's texts as possible, and then supplementing those texts with intellectual and political context, it is my intention to offer a reconstruction of Beard's political and economic thought that stays as close to his own meanings and intentions as possible.

Specifically, my reconstruction of Beard is aimed at dispelling the idea that he was either a dissembling Marxist who was unwilling to embrace socialism publicly or that he was merely a disenchanted New Deal liberal. In contrast to these widely held views, I argue that Beard's intellectual underpinnings were the Hegelian philosophical tradition (i.e., the German historical school), institutional economics, and non-Marxian revisionist socialism. These strands of thought were all widely diffused among American scholars prior to World War II and, in Beard, they were synthesized into a highly original metanarrative of American political development. This metanarrative provides critical insights into the crisis of the American welfare state that point to a post-Marxian socialist political theory.

A second methodological principle has guided my interpretation of Beard's political thought. It is important to note that I have no significant quarrels with Beard's intellectual biographers, Ellen Nore and Thomas C. Kennedy, who in my estimate provide fairly definitive biographical treatments of Beard's life. I have relied heavily on these works for biographical insights that are pertinent to my treatment of Beard. Consequently, my interpretive quarrel on this front is more with the method of intellectual biography which is often bogged down in the minutiae of daily life and therefore it is a method profoundly preoccupied with the sequence of day-to-day responses to current events.

As a new historicist, I consider biographical and historical context to be important and relevant factors in the interpretation of any author's political thinking, but I am now convinced that the problem of how to use this biographical and historical evidence is terribly problematic for anyone attempting to interpret the political thought of someone who wrote after the nineteenth century. The texts and other evidence left behind by a Plato or Aristotle is relatively finite and manageable, but as one moves forward into the twentieth century authors no longer leave behind a few important books, articles, and original unpublished manuscripts. Contemporary authors leave behind all of these things as well as magazine articles and interviews, hastily written personal letters, conference proceedings, quotes in newspapers, transcripts of radio broadcasts, and speeches, and these outlets do not exhaust the many forms of communication in the contemporary world. Likewise, the development of modern bureaucracies, libraries, and archives mean that a much larger range and volume of biographical, historical, and other evidence is available for consideration.

Importantly, the practical difficulty of drawing on such evidence is likely to be even more problematic one hundred years from now given the plethora of new technologies and media available for preserving every minor action and idea of a particular individual. One wonders, for example, if any remarkable insights might have been gleaned from backup tapes of John Locke's electronic mail (instead of his letters) or from his monthly Visa Card statements (instead of his expense ledger); or would such records merely divert us into a litany of trivia where political theory is reduced to tabloid journalism? In other words, if it was necessary to include everything about Beard, it would not be possible to say anything significant about Beard without losing it in the minutiae of historical and biographical analysis.

In writing the book, I have chosen to deal with this problem in two ways. Given the amount of published primary and secondary sources by and about Beard, in some ways it is fortunate that Beard did not leave many unpublished manuscripts or other fragments behind him for the quibbling of future scholars.[3] Beard purposely destroyed many of these items shortly before his death, because he wanted to be judged only on the basis of his published works and "not on the basis of what he ate for breakfast." Beard was deeply dissatisfied with the emergence of academic political theorists whom he dismissed as dust sifters sifting through the dust of other dust sifters. Beard swept his own floor clean by destroying most of his personal records, correspondence, and unpublished manuscripts shortly before his death. Hence, while some political theorists and intellectual historians may criticize my historicist interpretation for failing to delve deeper into archival records, I am consistent with Beard's intentions by having concentrated almost exclusively on his published writings.

However, even this narrower focus, defended from a historical and intentionalist standpoint, does not fully resolve the problems of interpretative selection given the magnitude of Beard's published *oeuvre*. After twenty years, I believe that I have read everything Beard ever published and almost everything written about him. Nevertheless, as the book developed over many years, I became convinced that it is not necessary to cite every minor article, book review, or letter to the editor simply to impress other scholars. A great deal of Beard's writings have been accurately described as excursions into history unfolding. Unlike the majority of contemporary scholars, who are hesitant to make flash judgments, Beard was always ready to speculate for an admiring public. He took jabs at political leaders, corporate executives, and other academics and many times his commentary was unmercifully sarcastic.

These articles, editorials, radio addresses, and newspaper quotes were not necessarily put into the public arena with a concern for the logical consistency of a theoretical system, but were hasty interventions into the day-to-day tumult of politics. Sometimes Beard's remarks are a conscious application and extension of his historiography to unfolding events. Sometimes Beard was just plain angry. Sometimes Beard was just plain wrong. In dealing with this embarrassment of sources, I became increasingly dissatisfied with the growing tendency among the new historicists to accord equal weight to every article, every letter, and every off-hand utterance as if it should be accorded the same interpretive weight as the statements in a 1,200 page book written over several years with great care and consideration.

This is exactly the problem Beard tried to eliminate by destroying his personal records, but it cannot be avoided entirely, since he left behind a large number of hastily written articles, flippant remarks to newspaper reporters, and angry retorts in various public media. As someone committed to the interpretive principles of the new historicism,[4] I have continued using these minor sources, but I use them primarily where they document the overall continuity and consistency of Beard's thinking, clarify ambiguities in important concepts, or where they fill gaps in the conceptual structure of Beard's political and economic thought.[5]

Notes

1. Arthur MacMahon, "Charles Beard, the Teacher," in Howard K. Beale, ed., *Charles A. Beard: An Appraisal* (Lexington: University of Kentucky Press, 1954), p. 224.
2. J. G. A. Pocock, *Politics, Language and Time* (New York: Atheneum Press, 1973), Chap. 1.
3. The main repository of the Charles and Mary Beard papers is the Archives and Special Collections, Roy O. West Library, DePauw University. There is also correspondence from Beard and other items of interest in the papers of various individuals scattered throughout the country. See, Ellen Nore, *Charles A. Beard: An Intellectual Biography* (Carbondale: Southern Illinois University Press, 1983), pp. 285-87.
4. The interpretive principles and concepts of the new historicism are identified primarily with Quentin Skinner. See, James Tully, ed., *Meaning and Context: Quentin Skinner and his Critics* (Princeton: Princeton University Press, 1988). However, my methodological approach is deeply influenced by Richard Ashcraft, "On the Problem of Methodology and the Nature of Political Theory," *Political Theory* (February 1975): 5-25; Richard Ashcraft, "Political Theory and the Problem of Ideology," *Journal of Politics* (August 1980): 687-705; John G. Gunnell, "American Political Science, Liberalism, and the Invention of Political Theory," in James Farr and Raymond Seidelman, eds., *Discipline and History: Political Science in the United States* (Ann Arbor: University of Michigan Press, 1993), pp. 179-97; John G. Gunnell, *The Descent of Political Theory: The Genealogy of an American Vocation* (Chicago: University of Chicago Press, 1993). The new historicism is identified more broadly in my application of it with Karl Mannheim, *Ideology and Utopia* (New York: Harcourt, Brace, Jovanovich, Inc., 1936).
5. For example, Merle Curti, "Beard as Historical Critic," in Beale, ed., *Charles A. Beard: An Appraisal,* p. 185, observes that Beard authored at least 150 book reviews during his career, beginning when he was a graduate student at Columbia University. Curti finds that "a careful reading in chronological sequence of Beard's reviews illuminates many controversial questions about his intellectual development" (p. 186). Based on such a reading, Curti concludes that "Beard's historical thinking did not undergo any abrupt or radical shifts. It is equally clear that it was anything but static" (p. 212).

1

Charles A. Beard

The Historian as Public Intellectual

Contemporary scholars typically judge each other's success by the length of their curriculum vitae and, particularly, by the length of their publication list. By this standard, Charles A. Beard (1874-1948) was a prodigious scholar whose publications in history and political science consist of forty-two books, thirty-five co-authored books, thirty chapters in edited collections, twenty-five prefaces or introductions to books, 330 articles, 150 book reviews, and numerous letters to major newspapers and magazines.[1] By the end of his life, Beard's history books alone (i.e., not including political science) had sold more than 11.3 million volumes in the United States due primarily to his authorship of basic textbooks and to his large popular audience.[2] Following his death in 1948, scholars were virtually unanimous in their evaluation of Beard's intellectual impact on the historical disciplines.

Peter R. Levin suggests that "Beard was perhaps the most influential American historian of his time."[3] Howard K. Beale ranked Beard "among the most significant historians of the first half of the twentieth century."[4] According to Cushing Strout, no other scholar in his time has "written with more authority and influence" than Charles A. Beard.[5] Alvin Johnson acclaimed Beard "the greatest historian of his time—and, indeed, of all American time."[6] In one of the earliest effort's to evaluate Beard's legacy to American scholarship, an impressive group of historians and political scientists concluded that "in all of American history, only one other—Bancroft—has at the same time enjoyed an

1

outstanding reputation among scholars and been so 'popular' in his own day and so widely read by laymen."[7] Beard's writings continue to receive critical attention from historians and his work is still a standard citation in introductory textbooks on American Government.[8]

Beard's legacy to American history and social science is strongly identified with his method of economic interpretation. In many ways, the development of his thought can be traced through the pathbreaking books he managed to write in this genre in each of five decades. As an undergraduate student at DePauw University (1894-1898) and as a graduate student at Oxford University (1898-1902), Beard received an extensive education in modern history, political economy, and socialist theory.[9] Drawing on this background, Beard was convinced by the turn of the century that the classical age of laissez-faire capitalism was nearing its end. In his first book, *The Industrial Revolution* (1901), Beard predicted that laissez-faire capitalism was gradually self-destructing through the inner logic of its own development and was being replaced by a rationalized system of consolidated finance and industry based on the modern corporation. Beard surmised that the new corporations would establish the economic foundation for rational planning of production. As an effect of the new corporate economy, Beard hinted vaguely that "technological rationality" would be projected into every sphere of social, political, and cultural existence.

Beard was already convinced by this time that the most important question facing modern democracies was not whether there would be industrial and economic planning, but only whether planning would be conducted by private corporations, a state technocracy, or some democratically accountable form of economic governance. In other words, the twentieth century would offer a limited range of macropolitical choices that consisted of a retrograde form of corporate feudalism, a statist command economy, or some type of industrial democracy. These were the major alternatives inherent, respectively, in classical liberalism, Marxian socialism, and social democracy. It is no exaggeration to suggest that Beard's entire written *ouevre* is an effort to record the historical details of that process and to explore its theoretical implications for contemporary politics as they developed over the next forty-seven years.

Beard did not believe that any one of these alternatives was a foregone conclusion. Given his own commitment to industrial democracy, Beard never limited himself to writing books, but was an engaged public intellectual throughout his adult life. The youthful Beard of *The Industrial Revolution* was a leader in the new workers' education movement in Great Britain. Along with the American socialist, Walter Vrooman, Beard founded Ruskin College (1898) at Oxford University as the first labor college in Great Britain.[10] Ruskin College was a full-time resident institution described by its founders as a school of citizenship and public administration created for "workers endeavoring to elevate their class and not to rise out of it."[11] In fact, Beard wrote *The Industrial Revolution* for use as a text in economic history at Ruskin College and for use at other labor colleges being formed throughout Great Britain at this time.

As part of what became a life-long foray into the workers' education movement, Beard traveled throughout England's major industrial cities encouraging workers to contribute funds to the movement, to assist in the creation of new labor colleges, and to prepare themselves for a dominant role in the new industrial order. Beard sipped beer and argued with small groups of trade unionists in pubs and he lectured before large audiences of workers throughout the Midlands. Beard buttonholed Tory reformers for money, met with suffragettes and socialists, and hobnobbed at Labour Party councils.[12] By all accounts, Beard was a spellbinding speaker, whether delivering his message in a university classroom, a union hall, or a political assembly.[13] Beard was so popular among English workers that officials in the new Labour Party asked him not to return to the United States, since Ramsay Macdonald wanted Beard to be a Cabinet minister in the future Labour government, which many anticipated was on the near horizon.[14]

Charles Beard returned to the United States in 1902, where he completed an innocuous dissertation at Columbia University describing the origins and development of the justice of the peace in England (1904).[15] During his three years as a doctoral candidate, Beard so impressed senior members of the faculty that he was appointed to the history department after completing his dissertation. At Columbia University, Beard inhabited an academic world populated by past and future luminaries such as John W. Burgess, John Dewey, James Harvey Robinson, E. R. A. Seligman, Frank Goodnow, Harry Elmer Barnes, and many other scholars at the forefront of the new historical and social sciences. Beard's early years at Columbia University included an intense collaboration with James Harvey Robinson, who was then formulating the principles of a "new history" in the United States.[16]

The new history was "new" in four respects. First, the new history emphasized modern and contemporary history over ancient and medieval history. Second, the new history emphasized the underlying structural determinants of history—such as economic and social change—in contrast to the "surface events" described by most political and military historians. Third, the new history focused on the theoretical interpretation of history in contrast to the dull chronicling and archival fact-gathering of positivist or "scientific history."[17] Finally, the new historians insisted that history is always written from the standpoint of some interest in the present and is meaningful to the present only if it sheds some light on the underlying determinants and trajectory of contemporary events. These principles resulted in a historical approach that necessarily blurred into the emerging discipline of political science.[18]

Beard and Robinson introduced the new history to students and scholars with a series of introductory textbooks on European and American history published between 1906 and 1914.[19] However, as Robinson drifted into intellectual history, Beard's interests moved deeper into economics and its relationship to the development of political institutions. Thus, while Robinson became a founder of intellectual history and academic political theory as it is now practiced in the United States,[20] the culmination of Beard's effort was his publication of *An Economic Interpretation of the Constitution of the United States* (1913). Robinson's early book on intellectual history was received politely in academic circles. Beard's book was politically charged, first, because it overtly adopted a method of economic interpretation and, second, because it identified the origins of the U.S. Constitution as a class struggle between capitalistic and agricultural interests.

According to Beard, capitalistic interests had dominated the constitutional convention and, consequently, they authored a founding document that appealed "directly and unerringly to identical interests in the country at large."[21] Beard's new book became a powerful weapon in the hands of populists, progressives, liberals, socialists and, later, even communists, who would all cite his book as evidence that the Constitution was of the capitalists, by the capitalists, and for the capitalists.[22] Against the recent backdrop of the Populist Revolt, the meteoric rise of the Socialist party in 1912, and the various progressive movements, Beard's book set off a political firestorm inside and outside of academia. Beard's *Economic Interpretation of the Constitution* was unquestionably the most controversial historical work of his generation.[23]

E. S. Corwin, a leading Constitutional historian, denounced the work immediately as "bent on demonstrating the truth of the socialistic theory of economic determinism and class struggle."[24] Albert Bushnell Hart, a Harvard political scientist and constitutional scholar, considered the book "little short of indecent."[25] However, as with all of Beard's significant writings, the controversy was never confined to scholarly journals and professional conventions. Beard's book challenged the certainties of constitutional formalism and in doing so it offended the American plutocracy and the judicial establishment, both of whom quickly realized that one of their best kept secrets had been exposed to the restless masses. Thus, as opposed to the many scholarly reviews that one might cite, it is Beard's reception outside academia that tells one most about his impact as a public intellectual.

In one instance, an outraged committee of the New York Bar Association summoned Beard to defend his book at a formal hearing, and when he rejected their demand, its officers issued a summons to Beard as if he was in contempt of court.[26] On another occasion, Beard accepted an invitation to speak at the New York Republican Club. After discussing his book with the hostile audience, a friend whispered: "Beard, you know why these fellows despise you?" A deflated Beard queried back: "But why should anyone despise a poor professor on his way from obscurity to oblivion?" The answer: "Because you have shown them that the Fathers of their country were just like themselves."[27]

A newspaper reporter asked the recently retired ex-President William Howard Taft what he thought about Charles Beard's book on the Constitution. The future Chief Justice of the U.S. Supreme Court replied that he thought the facts in the book were true enough, "but why did the damn fool print it?" he asked. The *Marion Star*, a newspaper owned by Warren G. Harding, was not so kind in its assessment of Beard's scholarship. The newspaper attacked the book as "libelous, vicious, and damnable in its influence" and went on to urge "every patriotic citizen of the United States...to condemn him [Beard] and the purveyors of his filthy lies and rotten perversion." Senator William E. Borah of Idaho was equally harsh in calling Beard "a hyena" scavenging on the remains of the Founding Fathers. Amid the controversy, reporters queried Nicholas Murray Butler, the president of Columbia

University (and Taft's Vice-Presidential running mate in 1912), whether he "had read Professor Beard's last book." Butler's grim response was: "I hope so."[28]

Charles' wife, Mary Ritter Beard, recalls that he "was fairly flooded with abuse" for having published *An Economic Interpretation*. Beard always relished the polemical controversy that accompanied his writings, but it meant that academia was never an ivory tower of peaceful reflection for him. The story was often circulated that a student had entered Beard's office amidst the public turmoil surrounding *An Economic Interpretation* and found him sitting silently with his head in his arms. The student asked if anything was wrong and Beard replied: "I'm trying to collect my ideas; and if I do, I'll be accused of unlawful assembly."[29] On the other hand, Eric F. Goldman (also a student of Beard's in 1941) recalls that Beard's *Economic Interpretation of the Constitution* would later become a Bible to thousands of young academics in the 1930's: "There were bread lines outside, and smug men, hurrying by them, said that something or another in the Constitution blocked making moves against poverty. *An Economic Interpretation* hammered the Constitution down into the arena of material interests and broke open a way to make sure that democratic constitutionalism included jobs and bread."[30]

Despite the controversy, and against Nicholas Murray Butler's wishes, Beard planned to write a series of economic interpretations dealing with each major period in United States history. He never got past the second volume of the series, entitled *Economic Origins of Jeffersonian Democracy* (1915). Instead, Beard spent the following two decades collaborating with his wife on the *magnum opus* that was to solidify his reputation as an icon of the new history. In 1927, the Beards published the first two volumes of *The Rise of American Civilization*, a general history which extended his earlier thesis by interpreting the course of American political development in terms of its transition from an agricultural era (1620-1877) to an industrial era (1877-present). A dialectical clash between agricultural interests (Jeffersonianism) and capitalist interests (Hamiltonianism) had been the engine of American political development during this time. A decade later, the Beards published a third volume, *America in Mid-Passage* (1939), which developed a theme introduced in the last chapter of *The Rise* where Beard predicted that the United States was on the verge of transition to a new phase of social and industrial democracy.[31]

In contrast to the controversy surrounding his *Economic Interpretation of the Constitution*, the *Rise of American Civilization* became one of the most highly praised books of the century and it is probably the most successful large-scale synthesis in American historical writing.[32] The book captured the front pages of book sections in magazines and newspapers and, accordingly, the Beards' pictures were displayed widely in popular publications. The book's regular edition sold 71,000 copies and another 62,000 copies were distributed as Book-of-the-Month-Club selections.[33] Horace M. Kallen, a psychology professor at the New School for Social Research, suggested that as the author of one of the last great monuments to general history: "Charles Beard has a claim to be counted as an outstanding figure in the line of great philosopher-historians writing great history."[34] Max Lerner remembers "that Beard's *Rise* permeated downward and outward; it affected professional historians, students, and laymen; it left its imprint on a whole generation" to the extent that many of his former heresies "were close to establishing new orthodoxies" by the early 1930s.[35] John Patrick Diggins notes that "in the years between the two world wars, Beard's reputation was so firmly established that the adjective 'Beardian' was not only considered a compliment but denoted a respected school of thought."[36]

The *aufheben* of Beard's dialectic was the idea of social and industrial democracy, which Beard presented as a grand historical synthesis of Hamiltonian and Jeffersonian principles. Beard published another significant work, *The Open Door at Home* (1934), where he outlined this synthesis in his most systematic tract on political economy. In *The Open Door at Home*, Beard challenged the conventional economic assumption that the Great Depression had been caused by overproduction. Instead, Beard drew heavily on the institutional economists, who were at the apogee of their influence during the first New Deal, to argue that the business cycle was the effect of income inequalities produced by "maladjustments" in the distribution of wealth and property rights. Beard's solution to the business cycle was to pursue an "open door at home" policy, in contrast to developing export markets and pursuing military adventures to create an open door in China. Beard's policy of institutional restructuring called for extensive public and worker ownership of industry as well as the strong hand of "federalist" state planning. However, Beard observed that every thrust toward fundamental economic reform in the United States had run up against a solid wall of capitalistic interests. By the late 1930's, Beard concluded that New Deal liberals did not have the stomach for hand-to-hand combat with the capitalist class.

Consequently, Charles Beard's last significant book, *President Roosevelt and the Coming of the War, 1941: A Study in Appearances and Reality* (1948) was a bitter assault on the liberal President whom he accused of betraying the New Deal to pursue foreign adventurism and global empire-building. Beard's *President Roosevelt* relied on extensive quotations from the published statements of leading political figures, congressional debates and hearings, and press releases to contrast what he called the appearance of Roosevelt's commitment to peace and neutrality with the realities of secret deeds and utterances intended to provoke war with Japan. Beard argued that Roosevelt had conducted a systematic disinformation campaign aimed at dragging the United States into a Pacific and European war after major provisions of the first New Deal imploded or were declared unconstitutional. Beard charged that when a series of un-neutral acts (e.g., the Lend-Lease Act and repeal of the Neutrality Act) failed to incite Hitler into declaring war against the United States, the Administration provoked Japan into attacking the Pacific Fleet at Pearl Harbor.[37]

Beard was no stranger to criticism, but he was not prepared for the bitter controversy provoked by his last important book. Conservatives had waged war on *An Economic Interpretation of the Constitution*, but it was friends and allies who were the most vicious critics of this book. Liberals had been admiring fans when Beard directed his trenchant wit against the conservative icons of American politics and history, but in the afterglow of the New Deal and global military dominance, liberals found his attacks on Roosevelt outrageous. Despite a torrent of nasty and condescending reviews, Beard's *President Roosevelt* went through five printings in its first year and it stayed on the best-seller lists for several weeks. [38]

The Political Scientist as Public Intellectual

Despite a return to history by political scientists, and a return to the state by historians, contemporary scholars still think of Beard more as a historian than as a political scientist or a political theorist.[39] Yet, in welcoming the return to history by contemporary political scientists, William E. Leuchtenberg observes that as a freshman at Columbia

University in 1939 "it altogether seemed natural for political science to have a historical dimension."[40] Beard authored or co-authored twenty-eight books in political science ranging across every sub-field of the discipline: American government, municipal government, public administration, public policy, political theory, political economy, comparative politics, and foreign policy. In fact, Beard's reputation as a political scientist was sufficient to secure his election as president of the American Political Science Association (1926), well before he was elected president of the American Historical Association (1934).

Beard's approach to political science was historical, but he also had deep disciplinary roots in constitutional law and political economy. Prior to his association with James Harvey Robinson, Beard was a student of John W. Burgess, a professor of comparative constitutional law, who played a major role in founding the political science discipline.[41] It was the historical economist E. R. A. Seligman, and the political scientist Frank Goodnow, who first turned the young Beard away from narrative descriptions of institutional development and toward a theoretical consideration of economic factors and class struggle in history.[42]

Beard first became involved in the infant discipline by serving as editorial assistant to Seligman while he was editor of the *Political Science Quarterly* (PSQ).[43] At the time, PSQ was the nation's most prestigious scholarly journal in political science and political economy.[44] Although Beard was initially appointed to Columbia University's Department of History, he transferred to the Department of Public Law in 1907, with Burgess' and Seligman's support, to become an Adjunct Professor of Politics. In 1910, Beard was promoted to the newly created rank of Associate Professor and, in 1915, he became a full Professor of Politics.

Beard's new appointment to the Department of Public Law brought considerable changes to the department at Columbia University, and over the next twenty years Beard would play a pioneering role in creating the political science discipline.[45] In his course on politics, for example, Beard moved the emerging discipline away from its foundations in constitutional formalism and moral philosophy toward a dynamic understanding of political development anchored in the new history.[46] Beard's explicit emphasis on party conflict and its relation to underlying economic interests was to become a hallmark of his numerous books on government and politics.[47]

At Columbia University, Beard single-handedly developed the introductory course on American Government and Politics that is now commonplace on college campuses. The discipline embraced Beard's model for the introductory course on American government in 1913, when a committee of the American Political Science Association (APSA) recommended it as the "basic course" for departments of political science. His introductory course was also the basis for a trailblazing textbook, *American Government and Politics* (1910), which went through ten editions, the last in 1948, to become the standard text in this course for the next forty years.[48] Beard's text on American Government standardized the introductory course in American colleges and universities by dominating the field it helped to create.[49]

Beard's pedagogical influence was not confined to university-level classrooms. Beard authored and co-authored more than a dozen textbooks on American history, civics, and social studies for high school and junior high school students that sold approximately six million copies between 1914 and 1948.[50] Beard was also a member of several educational commissions during the 1930s, and these provided significant opportunities to influence the core curriculum of American junior high and high schools. The most notable effort was his participation on the Commission on the Social Studies of the American Historical Association (1929-1934) where Beard authored key volumes such as *A Charter for the Social Sciences* and *The Nature of the Social Sciences*. In the 1940s, Beard contributed to a report on Theory and Practice in Historical Study for the Social Science Research Council in conjunction with Merle Curti, Thomas C. Cochran, and Alfred G. Vagts (Beard's son-in-law), among others.[51] Consequently, it is hardly surprising that a textbook content analysis conducted during this period found that Beard's economic interpretation of the U.S. Constitution had achieved "orthodox status" in history and civics textbooks throughout American colleges, high schools, and junior high schools.[52]

Beard also continued his efforts to extend higher education beyond the walls of the traditional schoolhouse. In collaboration with Walter Vrooman, Beard established a branch campus of Ruskin College at Trenton, Missouri in 1902. He also attended meetings of The X Club (1903-1917), which consisted of New York literary figures, university professors, social reformers, and numerous people Morris Hillquit described as "just socialists."[53] The group included Socialist Party notables such as W. J. Ghent, Morris Hillquit, William English Walling, and Lincoln Steffens, as well as progressives like Walter Weyl and John Dewey. The group met every two or three weeks to discuss current topics ranging from politics to religion, to literature and art, until it split over the war issue in 1917. Beard's association with New York City Socialists in The X Club took him off the Columbia University campus on many occasions.

The idea of workers' education that Beard initiated at Ruskin Hall continued to inspire him. He joined with members of the American Socialist Society to establish the Rand School of Social Science in 1906. The original purpose of the school was to train Socialist Party officials, union and party organizers, labor journalists, and civil servants in socialist theory and applied social science. Beard served on the School's original board of directors and he donated his services on and off until 1921.[54] Beard never had a formal affiliation with any political party during his life, but early in his career Beard campaigned door-to-door for the Socialist Morris Hillquit during his unsuccessful congressional campaigns on New York's Lower East Side (1906 and 1908). Beard attempted to interest others in the American labor movement and, for a while, he and his wife Mary went from house to house collecting funds to support strike campaigns and legal defense funds.[55]

However, in contrast to the majority of American Socialists, Beard allied himself with an opposition group of moderate social democrats, who supported Woodrow Wilson's decision to enter World War I. As early as the autumn of 1914, Beard delivered a speech at the City College of New York so critical of the Central Powers that the college president banned Beard from speaking at the campus on the war issue. When America entered the Great War, Beard joined the Division of Civic and Educational Publications, a branch of George Creel's Committee on Public Information.[56] The World War was a disaster for the American Socialist Party. Afterwards, Beard spent the 1920s attempting to promote the workers' education movement, while tending his dairy farms in Connecticut or touring Europe and Asia as a consultant on modernization and urban reconstruction.

Beard made another foray into adult and workers' education when he joined with Robinson, Barnes, Dewey, and Thorstein Veblen to found the New School for Social Research in 1921. Many of the School's founders had taught at the Socialist Party's Rand School during the previous decade. Beard's brief tenure at the New School for Social Research brought him into direct contact with Herbert Croly,

Harold Laski, Thorstein Veblen, Wesley C. Mitchell, and other progressive luminaries. Beard was in charge of the New School's early planning committee, while James Harvey Robinson was elected chair-man of the faculty. Herbert Croly headed the New School's Labor Research Center, which provided research support to labor unions, government, and other organizations. The original faculty soon disagreed over the direction of the School and Beard was approached to replace Robinson as chairman of the faculty. Persistent acrimony among faculty members, especially with Herbert Croly, caused Beard to leave the New School, but not before his next venture in workers' education was already underway.[57]

In 1921, Beard attended the first meetings of the Workers' Education Bureau (WEB). The Workers' Education Bureau was initially a coalition of predominantly socialist trade unionists, political activists, and academic intellectuals organized "to cooperate and assist in every possible manner the educational work now carried on by the organized workers; and to stimulate the creation of additional enterprises in labor education throughout the United States."[58] Beard donated $2,000 to the fledgling organization, served as a member of the WEB Executive Board, and chaired a citizens' group that raised funds for the Bureau. Spencer Miller, Jr., a former student and protégé of Beard's, became Director of the WEB. During the 1920s, Charles Beard also served as chairman of the Editorial Board of the Workers' Bookshelf Series, which the WEB published as a series of short, inexpensive textbooks for use in labor colleges and workers' education classes. However, after the WEB was absorbed by the more conservative American Federation of Labor, Beard began teaching his course on the "Economic Basis of Politics" at the Workers' (Communist) School (1926 to 1929) in New York City.[59]

Beard's impact on the political science discipline also went beyond introductory American Government and political theory to the more applied sub-fields of public administration and public policy. Beard always believed that the struggle for social democracy would be won or lost in the details of public policy and in the minutiae of public administration. Thus, Beard became a leader and a founder of the rising field of public administration, beginning with one of the first graduate courses and textbooks on municipal government.[60] Beard joined the New York Bureau of Municipal Research (BMR), a privately funded agency that was founded in 1907 by Frederick A. Cleveland, a specialist in municipal accounting; William Allen, a social worker; Henry Bruere, a Socialist attorney; E. R. A. Seligman, a tax economist; and Frank Goodnow, a political scientist. The BMR was the first agency of its kind in the United States and was created to help improve the performance of municipal government. The BMR sought to make municipal government more accountable by promoting its simplification and by providing the public with accurate information about the activities and budgets of city departments.[61]

In 1914, Beard was appointed director of the BMR's new Training School for Public Service and, in 1918, he accepted the BMR directorship after resigning from Columbia University in his now infamous dispute with the Columbia University Board of Trustees.[62] During his affiliation with the Training School, Beard helped institute and popularize the idea of public administration internship; and he pushed the political science discipline to grant academic credit for field or observation work in government and administration, because he considered this work "fundamental to any real advance in training for public service."[63] In addition to general competencies in public budgeting, accounting, municipal politics, and public law, Beard insisted that graduates of the Training School specialize in functional areas of public administration, such as fire and police management, highway administration, or engineering.

Beard was also a staunch critic of "bureaucratese" at the BMR. Beard always preferred plain language to obfuscation and he persistently emphasized to students that administrative reports and management surveys would not have any impact unless they could be understood by elected officials and the general public. During his association with the BMR, Beard directed a number of major state and municipal surveys, including a 1915 report on the New York State Constitutional Convention, a 1918 study that led to the reorganization of Delaware state government, and a 1919 report on municipal reorganization for Newark, New Jersey.

Luther Gulick, a student who succeeded Beard as BMR director in 1920, observes that "Beard's views on the economic foundations of national politics found further confirmation in the realm of urban politics where landowners, possessors of franchises, recipients of tax favors, bondholders, municipal bankers, private utilities, favored contractors, and liquor, gambling, and vice rings, as well as the politics-for-profit city machines, were struggling to keep and expand their political power because without it their economic enterprises would disappear." Many of the municipal surveys prepared under Beard's direction challenged one or more these entrenched special interests, but the best example is his report on the New York City "traction crisis" (i.e., mass transit/rails). Beard recommended that "the way must be cleared for applying municipal ownership to the surface and elevated lines on definite terms and conditions as to acquisition and financing when and if such a step is desired by the people of the city."[64] Beard devised a detailed plan for municipalizing the rail transit system (modeled after the Prussian railway nationalization), and the plan played an important part in the eventual unification and municipalization of the system in 1940.

Beard's reputation as an urban modernizer eventually carried him across two oceans during the 1920s. Following the catastrophic Tokyo earthquake of 1922, Viscount Shimpei Goto, the Mayor of Tokyo, invited Beard to Japan to conduct an educational campaign among university faculty and city officials and to assist in the reconstruction of Tokyo. The purpose of the educational campaign was to promote the modernization of city government and to physically rebuild Tokyo as a model progressive city.[65] Beard accepted the invitation, and while in Tokyo he advised municipal officials on reorganizing the city and assisted in establishing Tokyo's Institute of Municipal Research. Beard spent the winter of 1922-1923 preparing a massive report for Goto on all aspects of municipal government, which was published as the *Administration and Politics of Tokyo* (1923). It is considered the culmination of Beard's thinking about municipal administration in modern cities.

Beard proposed that the entire metropolitan area be consolidated under the control of one city government with jurisdiction over fire, police, taxation, borrowing, public utilities, and building regulations. In making these recommendations, Beard pointed to London, Berlin, Paris, and New York to exemplify his claim that if a city does not control its suburbs, it will not be able to generate revenue from the individuals who use its streets, conduct business in its offices, and enjoy the other benefits of a major city. Yet, Beard left Japan discouraged because his modernization plan was rejected by entrenched local officials and it was actively opposed by Tokyo real estate interests.[66]

In 1927, Beard's reputation as a modernizer resulted in an invitation from the American-Yugoslav Society to assess the postwar

Yugoslav regime created by the Treaty of Versailles. Over a four-month period, Beard examined government documents, interviewed officials, attended sessions of the Yugoslav Parliament, met with interest group representatives (including rebel leaders), and toured the countryside.[67] Beard's report was published in 1929 as *The Balkan Pivot*. Beard applied his characteristic economic analysis by arguing that the main hope for Yugoslavia was to become a more urban industrial country, since "a normal politics" could not exist in the nation until an urban party, based on industry and commerce, was strong enough to do battle with the dominant agrarian party. Beard suggested that Yugoslavia's primitive economic base of handicrafts and agriculture supported a reactionary attachment to pre-modern ethnic and religious rivalries, while the little national cement in Yugoslavia was created by economic interactions in the cities. Beard concluded that commercial economic development was necessary to support modernization and prevent its regression into pre-modern conflicts.

After his adventurous travels in the 1920s, Beard retreated to his dairy farm in New Milford, Connecticut, where he adopted a semi-settled way of life.[68] No longer directly connected to university life, and increasingly peripheral to the New York intellectual scene after leaving the New School, Beard was partly insulated from the drift toward behavioralism that began as early as the 1920s.[69] Nevertheless, Beard remained in close touch with political events. He was not only an avaricious reader of newspapers and current events magazines, but during the 1930s, he spent most winter seasons in Washington, D.C., acting as an informal adviser to Cabinet Secretaries and delivering testimony to Congressional committees.

The Political and Economic Thought of Charles A. Beard

Beard's work has been the object of extensive criticism over the last half century, so one is justified in asking if there is more than a purely antiquarian reason for reconsidering Beard's political and economic thought. I suggest that many of the same reasons that are leading political scientists to reconsider historical methods generally warrant a new look at key elements of Beard's thinking. In particular, Beard's political and economic thought makes an original and still relevant contribution to our understanding of: (1) the methodological problems of historical institutionalism, (2) the epistemological problems of historical relativism, and (3) the dialectic of American political development and the crisis of the welfare state.

The New Institutionalism

The new institutionalism in political science was first advanced in the mid-1980s with an explicit (though vague) theoretical objective to "specify more closely the complex patterns of state-society relations."[70] The new institutionalists proposed a research agenda designed to employ historical studies of institutional and policy development as the basis for constructing dynamic middle-range hypotheses considered inaccessible to more abstract theories of the state. More than a decade later, questions about its meager *theoretical* contribution to the discipline are typically met with cavalier rejoinders that the new institutionalism is not a theory, but a frame of reference.[71] I suggest that when compared to Beard the new institutionalism in political science has made very little theoretical headway.[72] The new institutionalism has produced a plethora of interesting historical case studies, but as March and Olson observe, "the relevant theoretical work remains to be done."[73] Similarly, in a widely cited application of the new approach, Evans, Rueschemeyer, and Skocpol conclude that the new institutionalists "have not ended up with a new overall theory of the state—not even with a complete set of hypotheses."[74] Regardless of whether one accepts Beard's method of economic interpretation, he does at least articulate an actual *theory* of state-society relations and he uses it to construct a systematic and coherent interpretation of American political development.[75]

Beard's method of economic interpretation has often been identified incorrectly as Marxist. Chapter 2 reconstructs Beard's method of economic interpretation to distinguish it conceptually from Marx's historical materialism. I argue that Beard's method of economic interpretation relied on the American school of institutional economics (which originated in the German historical school) and that his concept of state-society relations (i.e., a theory of the state) was in fact derived from his reading of Madison's *Tenth Federalist*.

Marx claimed that class struggle was a structural effect of the exploitation of the propertyless by the propertied (i.e., the extraction of surplus value) and, therefore, Marx identifies the end of class struggle with the abolition of private property. In contrast, Beard theorizes the fundamental economic basis of political development as the struggle between classes for recognition and protection of asymmetrical rights in different forms and degrees of property. Therefore, Beard concludes that there is no permanent solution to class struggle; but as an alternative to Marx's abolition of private property, Beard suggests that "labor" be recognized as a form of property with the same constitutional protections as land and capital. In a manner similar to the institutional economists who explain historical development as the effect of a dichotomy between institutions and technology, Beard located the economic basis of political development in the struggle between classes for rights in property.[76] In this respect, Beard's new history establishes the foundation for a post-Marxist theory of the state, although it relies on a method firmly attached to the analysis of economic relations of production and to a historical conception of American capitalist development.

Historical Relativism

The new historicism in American political theory can trace its institutional origins directly to Beard's and Robinson's new history. The new historicism in political theory proposes a research agenda that evaluates the meaning and development of political ideas in terms of their relationship to authorial intentions and, especially, in relation to their specific historical contexts (i.e., economic, political, and intellectual).[77] By historicizing "great books," the new historicists have advanced a movement to decentralize and democratize political theory by documenting its ideological effects and origins in "minor" works, newspaper and magazine articles, personal letters, art and literature, government documents, popular pamphlets, etc. Thus, the new historicists are attempting to reconstruct political theory on a historical terrain that defies the nomological ambitions of behavioral social science and the universalistic moral claims of analytic political philosophies.[78]

Beard's economic interpretation of history insisted that political theories are a combination of ideas and interests embedded in everyday social relations, collective actions, and institutionalized patterns of behavior.[79] Consequently, the method of economic interpretation and the new historicism are both intertwined with epistemological debates about the nature of objectivity and science. Beard was hardly an epistemologist or philosopher, but during the 1930s he was both esteemed and reviled as a leading proponent of "historical relativism" in the social sciences. Beard's presidential address to the American Historical Association (1934), "Written History as an Act of Faith," was an epistemological jihad, which explored the implications of historical relativism for historians with respect to the political and ideological controversies of the day. Merle Curti concludes that by articulating the crude rudiments of a historical sociology of knowledge Beard dealt "a severe blow to the older assumption that the writing of history is merely an objective matter."[80] Beard's historical relativism continues to draw fire from neo-conservatives, who implicate him in the nation's cultural retreat from transcendent moral values.[81]

Beard's rudimentary forays into the theory of historical knowledge are examined in Chapter 3. Beard struggled to articulate a theory of historical knowledge that would bridge the intellectual terrain between Hegel's dialectical idealism and Marx's dialectical materialism with a concept of "realistic dialectics." In striving to formulate his concept of dialectical realism, Beard's thought wandered from G. W. F. Hegel (1900s) to Karl Marx (1910s), from Marx to Benedetto Croce (1920s), and from Croce to Max Scheler and Karl Mannheim (1930s). Beard settled on a highly selective appropriation of Scheler's and Mannheim's sociologies of knowledge, because each of them constructed a historical sociology that drew heavily on Hegel's phenomenology, but which avoided the radically subjectivistic strains of idealism (e.g., Croce) and the naive objectivism of most social scientists (e.g., positivists and Marxists).

Beard's contribution to historical theory is often criticized by contemporary historians and philosophers as a derivative contribution to epistemology and the philosophy of history. Nevertheless, I suggest that Beard was engaged in a highly original intellectual undertaking and that his work at least opens a window on the vibrant neo-Hegelian school that flourished in American political theory until after World War II and the behavioral revolution. Likewise, despite its philosophical limitations, Beard's conception of dialectical realism still poses a critical challenge to both the dominant strains of post-modern philosophy (subjectivistic relativism) and to the absolutist epistemologies assumed by most contemporary social scientists and political philosophers.

Beard claimed that our understanding of social and historical reality is never absolutely certain or complete, but that common sense could still establish numerous facts which were more than merely individual opinions or beliefs. Thus, even though it is possible to construct competing interpretations of an incomplete historical reality (i.e., metanarratives), not all interpretations are equally plausible given the known and accepted facts, nor are they equally consistent with the dominant developmental tendencies in history at any given time. Consequently, in emphasizing the relation between historically defined interests and written history (i.e., ideas), Beard poses a direct challenge to the subjectivist and individualistic claims of postmodern theory, particularly its debunking of historical metanarratives. Beard challenges the post-modernist rejection of historical metanarratives, first, by having constructed a dialectical metanarrative of American political development and, second, by adopting a phenomenological conception of meaning. In particular, Beard insists that it is impossible to conceive of history or human existence without a meaningful teleological referent (i.e., some conception of the purpose and meaning of history) even if that referent is a negative metaphysics of chaos. Indeed, Beard documents historically that philosophies of history resting on notions of decay, disorder, and chaos are nothing new or exceptional, but are themselves an ideological effect of institutional and social decay (or merely social change depending upon one's location in the economic and social structure).

American Political Development and the Crisis of the Welfare State

Beard considered the process of political development a bridge between social science and political theory, because he accepted the Hegelian proposition that the collective values of a society—the spirit of a people—are expressed through the social conflicts and political organizations crystallized in its institutions and constitution. Chapter 4 reconstructs Beard's theory of American political development (i.e., his metanarrative) on the philosophical and methodological foundations established in the two previous chapters. My objective is to emphasize Beard's role as a political theorist, rather than as a historian. Thus, unlike a chronologically structured intellectual biography, I have sought to capture the underlying *conceptual structure* of Beard's political thought, rather than his passing thoughts on this or that particular event. Yet, if one accepts the Crocean proposition, as Beard does, that such a history *is* philosophy, then one will not find an analytically constructed Beardian political philosophy of the sort that scholars now associate with the alienation of political theory.

American political theory, in particular, and social science generally, have become solipsistic activities isolated within the walls of academia. Indeed, the on-going concern with reexamining the historical and institutional foundations of modern social science is an explicit attempt to assess how social science and political theory reached this state of affairs.[82] In contrast to alienated political theory, Beard's political theory emerges "from within" real historical events and, therefore, its immanence in history directly implicates and engages this political theory in political action.

Beard's general history of American political development is structured around the dialectical clash of agricultural interests (Jeffersonianism) and capitalist interests (Hamiltonianism), which supply the engine of American political development until the twentieth century. Beard eventually extended his conception of realistic dialectics by proposing that the United States was on the verge of a transition to social and industrial democracy. In terms of his own political commitments, Beard was an early critic of the New Deal and the liberal welfare state. His intellectual biographers have described him as an adherent of Eduard Bernstein's evolutionary socialism. Beard is actually very difficult to pigeonhole ideologically, but I follow the biographers' lead and argue that Beard was a socialist whose political and economic thought was derived from a dialectical (but exceptionalist) conception of *American* historical development.

Most of the previous commentators on Beard's political thought have accepted Richard Hofstadter's assertion that Beard's reputation as a radical "is not sustained by his writings."[83] I have accepted Hofstadter's challenge to actually read Beard's writings. It is clear that the dominant interpretation of Beard stands in sharp contrast to Beard's promise to British workers in 1900 that he would never stop agitating "till the workers who bear upon their shoulders the burden of the world should realize the identity of their own interests and rise to take possession of the means of life."[84] Hofstadter suggests that the force and persistence of this "early 'socialism' has sometimes been exaggerated" by sympathizers and critics alike, but when Beard was asked to describe his vision for America more than thirty years later, he still answered: "It is a workers' republic."[85]

In Chapter 5 and Chapter 6, Beard's conception of American economic and political development is clarified as the basis for his critique of New Deal liberalism and American imperialism. Chapter 5 focuses on Beard's writings on political economy and economic planning to elicit his conception of the workers' republic. The chapter documents that Beard's concept of a workers' republic emerges out of his dialectical conception of American political development. The most widely accepted interpretations of Beard's political thought identify him as a progenitor of interest group liberalism whose political writings provide the basis for a liberal theory of the state. However, this chapter documents that Beard was well to the left of New Deal liberalism, particularly on the issue of wealth redistribution and economic restructuring. Beard was a sharp critic of the New Deal and by 1939 he was dismissing the welfare state as a minor gain for the American working class.

Ultimately, Beard's main critical concern, in both domestic and foreign policy, was the New Deal's failure to attack the underlying institutional structures that generate inequalities in income, status, and power: namely, wealth distribution and the legal construction of property rights. Interestingly, as a socialist, Beard anticipated many of the neo-conservative criticisms of the liberal welfare state with his speculations that the dole would turn the American Republic into a new Rome. He openly suggested that liberal welfare entitlements would damage the moral fiber of its recipients and, ideologically speaking, prove incompatible with the republican ideals of the American working class. Beard proposes full-employment socialism as the left alternative to entitlement liberalism. Moreover, in contrast to the model of a direct command economy, Beard proposed an early version of indicative economic planning along with a redistribution of wealth through a redefinition of the concept of property and property rights. He proposes an institutionalist solution to the contradictions of the welfare state and to the failures of Marxian state socialism. In other words, Beard proposed a genuine workers' republic that involves a deep restructuring of economic and political institutions, but one that is compatible with the American traditions of republican constitutionalism.

However, in Chapter 6, Beard's theoretical conception of American history plays itself out in a tragic cycle of imperialism and diversion that left him a disenchanted realist. In Beard's political thought, a dialectic of economic class interests propelled American political development forward, but at each crucial juncture concerted efforts at domestic reform are always diverted into international conflicts as popular leaders back down from the enormous political struggle entailed by a head-to-head confrontation with the capitalist class. Against a solid wall of capitalist opposition, a President must work within a federal constitutional system where power over domestic policy is diffused among several states and where competing special and local interests make it difficult for any President to press forward on economic reconstruction. The Supreme Court has often been an additional obstacle in promoting domestic economic reform.

Beard concludes that each time a reform-minded President fails to achieve decisive breakthroughs in domestic economic and social policy, the constitutional structure itself deflects them into foreign policy adventures. Foreign policy becomes the avenue for rebuilding public confidence, after domestic policy failures, because a President's constitutional powers in foreign policy are much greater than in domestic policy. Beard argued that American foreign policy is always an extension of *domestic* economic policy and, in particular, a result of the *failures* of domestic economic policy. As business assaults on the New Deal escalated in the mid- to late-1930s, Beard was increasingly concerned that Franklin D. Roosevelt would abandon the New Deal and divert national energies into a war with Japan just as Woodrow Wilson had diverted the New Freedom into the Great War. To avoid a repetition of this scenario, Beard proposed a continentalist foreign policy that relied heavily on managed trade and the creation of a hemispheric trading bloc to remove the United States from European and Asian conflicts.

In addition, Beard had begun to see a cycle in which modern warfare and imperial expansion drains the domestic economy of the military victors, while freeing defeated nations from imperial obligations. Consequently, even though a single nation might establish temporary global dominance (e.g., Spain, France, Britain, United States), the tangible costs of empire gradually erode the economic basis of their imperial dominance. Thus, regardless of the immediate outcomes of a second world war, Beard predicted that a discernible drift toward three regional trading blocs would continue over the long-term: a European bloc anchored by Germany's economic and political muscle, a Pacific bloc centered in Japan's emerging power, and a Western

Hemispheric bloc led by the United States. Importantly, the overarching goal of Beard's continentalism was to reduce America's involvement in international trade rivalries and warfare through domestic economic restructuring, rather than a realignment of global trade relations, international diplomacy, or military confrontation.

Because we now live in a political environment dominated by free-market neo-conservatives and pro-market neo-liberals, many scholars will question the value of re-examining Beard's socialism. However, it is that context which makes this re-examination meaningful and useful to contemporary political theory. In many respects, American politics has returned to the doctrinaire faith in free markets and the same naive anti-statism that Beard confronted in the early twentieth century. It was exactly this same historical context that led Beard and other social democrats to advance a relentless critique of capitalism. Following in the footsteps of the institutional economists, Beard admonished scholars, statesmen, and citizens that free markets do not always work effectively or efficiently, nor do they automatically guarantee a distribution of wealth and income compatible with a republican form of government. Beard advanced a forceful and confident critique of capitalism that is often missing in a democratic left paralyzed with self-doubts about "the end of history." Beard articulates an engaged social democratic political theory, which is post-Marxist in its philosophical and economic foundations, but that poses a fundamental challenge to neo-conservatism and neo-liberalism.

Notes

1. Ernest A. Breisach, *American Progressive History: An Experiment in Modernization* (Chicago: University of Chicago Press, 1993), p. 24. For bibliographies, see Jack Frooman and Edmund David Cronon, "Bibliography of Beard's Writings," in Beale, ed., *Charles A. Beard*, pp. 265-286; Thomas C. Kennedy, *Charles A. Beard and American Foreign Policy* (Gainesville, FL: University Presses of Florida, 1975), pp. 169-91; Nore, *Charles A. Beard*, pp. 285-313.

2. Howard K. Beale, "Beard's Historical Writings," in Beale, ed., *Charles A. Beard*, pp. 255-312. Many of these books were translated into German, Spanish, Portuguese, Japanese, and Braille.

3. Peter R. Levin, "Charles A. Beard: Wayward Liberal," *Tomorrow* 8 (March 1949): 36-40.

4. Howard K. Beale, "Charles Beard: Historian," in Beale, ed., *Charles A. Beard*, p. 115.

5. Cushing Strout, "In Retrospect: Charles Beard's Liberalism," *New Republic* 133 (October 17, 1955): 17.

6. Alvin Johnson, "A Born Politician," *New Republic* 130 (May 3, 1954): 20.
7. Beale, "Charles Beard: Historian," in Beale, ed., *Charles A. Beard*, p. 116.
8. Morton White, *Social Thought in America: The Revolt Against Formalism* (Boston: Beacon Press, 1957. Reprint edition. Published originally by The Viking Press in 1949), pp. 107-27, 220-35; Henry Steele Commager, *The American Mind: An Interpretation of American Thought and Character Since the 1880s* (New Haven, CT: Yale University Press, 1950), pp. 293-309; Eric F. Goldman, *Rendezvous With Destiny: A History of Modern American Reform* (New York: Alfred A. Knopf, 1952), pp. 108-19; Cushing Strout, *The Pragmatic Revolt in America: Carl Becker and Charles Beard* (Ithaca, NY: Cornell University Press, 1966. Reprint edition. Published originally by Yale University Press, 1958); Harvey Wish, *The American Historian: A Social-Intellectual History of the Writing of the American Past* (New York: Oxford University Press, 1960), pp. 265-92; Marcus Cunliffe and Robin W. Winks, eds., *Pastmasters: Some Essays on American Historians* (New York: Harper and Row Publishers, 1960), Chapter 4; John Higham, ed., *The Reconstruction of American History* (London: Hutchinson & Co., Ltd., 1962), pp. 157-79, passim; John Higham, Leonard Krieger, and Felix Gilbert, *History: The Development of Historical Studies in the United States* (Englewood Cliffs, NJ: Prentice-Hall, 1965), passim; Robert Allen Skotheim, *American Intellectual Histories and Historians* (Princeton, NJ: Princeton University Press, 1966); Richard Hofstadter, *The Progressive Historians: Turner, Beard, Parrington* (Chicago: University of Chicago Press, 1968); John Higham, *Writing American History: Essays on Modern Scholarship* (Bloomington: Indiana University Press, 1970), pp. 130-37; David Marcell, *Progress and Pragmatism: James, Dewey, Beard, and the American Idea of Progress* (Westport, CT.: Greenwood Press, 1974), pp. 258-319; Morton G. White, *Philosophy, The Federalist, and the Constitution* (New York: Oxford University Press, 1987), Chapter 5; Breisach, *American Progressive History*, Chapters 9 and 17.
9. Nore, *Charles A. Beard*, Chap. 1; Merle Curti, "A Great Teacher's Teacher," *Social Education* 31 (October 1949): 263-66; Clifton J. Phillips, "The Indiana Education of Charles A. Beard," *Indiana Magazine of History* 55 (March 1959): 1-15.
10. Harlan B. Phillips, "Charles Beard, Walter Vrooman, and the Founding of Ruskin Hall," *South Atlantic Quarterly* 50, 2 (April 1951): 186-91; Burleigh J. Wilkins, "Charles A. Beard on the Founding of Ruskin College," *Indiana Magazine of History* 52 (September 1956): 277-84. For background, see Marius Hansome, *World Workers' Educational Movements: Their Social Significance* (New York: Columbia University Press, 1931).
11. Arthur Gleason, *Workers' Education: American and Foreign Experiments* (New York: Bureau of Industrial Research, 1921), p. 47; Clyde W. Barrow, "Pedagogy, Politics, and Social Reform: The Philosophy of the Workers' Education Movement," *Strategies: A Journal of Theory, Culture, and Politics* 2 (Fall 1989): 45-66.
12. Goldman, *Rendezvous With Destiny*, p. 116.
13. Matthew Josephson, "Charles A. Beard: A Memoir," *Virginia Quarterly Review* 25 (1949): 586.
14. Goldman, *Rendezvous With Destiny*, p. 116.
15. Charles A. Beard, "The Office of the Justice of the Peace in England in Its Origins and Development" (Ph.D. Dissertation, Columbia University, 1904).
16. For background, see Luther V. Hendricks, *James Harvey Robinson: Teacher of History* (New York: King's Crown Press, 1946); Higham, Krieger, and Gilbert,

History, Chap. 2. Most scholars emphasize Robinson's influence on the young Beard, but Alvin Johnson, *Pioneer's Progress: An Autobiography* (New York: Viking Press, 1957), p. 156, recalls that "Beard was making it his mission to compel his chief, James Harvey Robinson, to read [Jean] Jaures' vast *Histoire Socialiste*, a work that awakened Robinson out of his academic slumber and gave us the Robinson all liberals love." For Beard's highly favorable review of Jaures' work, see, Charles A. Beard, "A Socialist History of France," *Political Science Quarterly* 21, 1 (March 1906): 111-20.

17. Breisach, *American Progressive History*, Chapters 1-2; Gertrude Himmelfarb, *The New History and the Old: Critical Essays and Reappraisals* (Cambridge, MA: Harvard University Press, 1987), esp. pp. 1-12, Chap. 1.

18. For a comprehensive overview of the new history, see Harry Elmer Barnes, *The New History and the Social Studies* (New York: The Revisionist Press, 1972).

19. Charles A. Beard, *An Introduction to the English Historians* (New York: Macmillan Co., 1906); James Harvey Robinson and Charles A. Beard, *The Development of Modern Europe: An Introduction to the Study of Current History*, 2 Vols. (New York: Ginn and Co., 1908); James Harvey Robinson, *The New History* (New York: Macmillan Co., 1912); Charles A. Beard, *Contemporary American History, 1877-1913* (New York: Macmillan Co., 1914).

20. James Harvey Robinson, *An Outline of the History of the Intellectual Class in Western Europe*, 2 vols. (New York: Marion Press, 1914).

21. Charles A. Beard, *An Economic Interpretation of the Constitution of the United States* (New York: Free Press, 1913), p. 188

22. Eric F. Goldman, "A Historian at Seventy," *New Republic* 111 (November 27, 1944): 696.

23. Hofstadter, *The Progressive Historians*, p. 181.

24. E. S. Corwin, "Review of Economic Interpretation of the Constitution of the United States, by Charles A. Beard," *History Teachers' Magazine* 5 (February 1914): 65-66.

25. Beard, "Introduction to the 1935 Edition," *Economic Interpretation of the Constitution*, p. viii.

26. Ibid., p. viii.

27. Hubert Herring, "Charles A. Beard: Freelance Among the Historians," *Harper's Magazine* (May 1939): 644.

28. Goldman, *Rendezvous With Destiny*, pp. 118-19; Josephson, "Charles A. Beard: A Memoir," p. 595.

29. Mary Ritter Beard, *The Making of Charles A. Beard* (New York: Exposition Press, 1955), p. 22.

30. Eric F. Goldman, "Charles A. Beard: An Impression," in Beale, ed., *Charles A. Beard*, p. 5.

31. It is well established that the Beards maintained a strict division of labor in writing *The Rise of American Civilization*. Charles authored the sections and chapters dealing with economic and political history. Mary authored the sections and chapters dealing with cultural and intellectual history, see Nore, *Charles A. Beard*, p. 112; Nancy F. Cott, "Two Beards: Coauthorship and the Concept of Civilization," *American Quarterly* 42, 2 (June 1990): 274-300.

32. Beale, "Charles Beard: Historian," in Beale, ed., *Charles A. Beard*, p. 263. Likewise, Max Lerner, "Charles Beard: Civilization and the Devils," *New Republic* (November 1, 1948): 21, characterizes *The Rise* as "the most creative general history written in the American field." Bernard Borning, *The Political and Social Thought of Charles A. Beard* (Seattle: University of Washington

Press, 1962), p. xxii, concludes that "this work perhaps more than any other securely established his reputation as one of America's foremost historians." Likewise, Nore, *Charles A. Beard*, p. 112, identifies *The Rise* as Beard's masterpiece.

33. Nore, *Charles A. Beard*, p. 124; Beale, "Beard's Historical Writings," in Beale, ed., *Charles A. Beard*, p. 311.

34. Horace M. Kallen, "In Remembrance of Charles Beard, Philosopher-Historian," *Social Research* 18 (June 1951): 243.

35. Max Lerner, "Charles Beard's Stormy Voyage," *New Republic* (October 25, 1948): 20.

36. John Patrick Diggins, "Power and Authority in American History: The Case of Charles A. Beard and His Critics," *American Historical Review* 86 (October 1981): 701-02.

37. Kennedy, *Charles A. Beard and American Foreign Policy*, p. 144.

38. Ibid., pp. ix-x., 152; Beale, "Beard's Historical Writings," in Beale, ed., *Charles A. Beard*, p. 311.

39. Ira Katznelson, "The State to the Rescue?: Political Science and History Reconnect," *Social Research* 59 (Winter 1992): 719-37; William E. Leuchtenberg, "The Pertinence of Political History: Reflections on the Significance of the State in American," *Journal of American History* 73 (December 1986): 585-600; Donald T. Critchlow, "Is Political History Dead?," *Clio: Newsletter of Politics and History* 5 (Spring/Summer 1995): 2-3; Martin Shefter, "History and Political Science," *Clio: Newsletter of Politics and History* 7 (Fall/Winter 1996-97): 1, 14.

40. William E. Leuchtenberg, "The Uses and Abuses of History," *History and Politics Newsletter* 2 (Fall 1991): 6-7.

41. R. Gordon Hoxie, *A History of the Faculty of Political Science, Columbia University* (New York: Columbia University Press, 1955); Gunnell, *The Descent of Political Theory*, pp. 36, 54-56.

42. Nore, *Charles A. Beard*, p. 30.

43. Johnson, *Pioneer's Progress*, p. 155.

44. Hoxie, *A History of the Faculty of Political Science*, p. 87.

45. Ibid., p. 264.

46. Irwin Edman, *Philosopher's Holiday* (New York: Viking Press, 1937), p. 130; Goldman, *Rendezvous With Destiny*, p. 116.

47. Charles A. Beard, *Politics: A Lecture Delivered at Columbia University in the Series Science, Philosophy, and Art*, February 12, 1908 (New York: Columbia University Press, 1912).

48. Hoxie, *A History of the Faculty of Political Science*, p. 265; Borning, *The Political and Social Thought of Charles A. Beard*, p. xix; Arthur W. MacMahon, "Charles A. Beard," *American Political Science Review* (December 1948): 1209.

49. APSA report quoted in Arthur MacMahon, "Charles Beard, the Teacher," in Beale, ed., *Charles A. Beard*, p. 226.

50. Beale, "Beard's Historical Writings," pp. 311-312.

51. Lawrence J. Dennis, *George S. Counts and Charles A. Beard: Collaborators for Change* (Albany, NY: SUNY Press, 1989) observes that "this facet of his [Beard's] work has been virtually omitted" from the intellectual biographies. Dennis' short book rectifies this omission by documenting Beard's role in the Commission on the Social Studies and, in the process, Dennis provides "a behind-the-scenes look at some of the activities and interests of the so-called left-wing group of the educational progressives" (p. 9). Also see, Raymond A. Ducharme, Jr., *Charles A. Beard and the Social Studies* (New York: Teachers College Press, 1969).

52. Maurice Blinkoff, *The Influence of Charles A. Beard Upon American Historiog-*

raphy, University of Buffalo Monographs in History, Vol. 12, 1936; Richard Hofstadter, "Charles Beard and the Constitution," in Beale, ed., *Charles A Beard*, pp. 75-80; Robert E. Brown, *Charles Beard and the Constitution* (Princeton, NJ: Princeton University Press, 1957), pp. 5-23.

53. Nore, Charles A. Beard, p. 39.
54. John L. Recchiuti, "The Rand School of Social Science During the Progressive Era: Will To Power of a Stratum of the American Intellectual Class," *Journal of the History of the Behavioral Sciences* 31 (April 1995): 149-61.
55. Nore, *Charles A. Beard*, p. 39. George S. Counts, "Charles Beard, the Public Man," in Beale, ed., *Charles A. Beard*, pp. 236-37.
56. Kennedy, *Charles A. Beard and American Foreign Policy*, p. 29; Carol Gruber, *Mars and Minerva: World War I and the Uses of the Higher Learning in America* (Baton Rouge: Louisiana State University Press, 1975).
57. Nore, *Charles A. Beard*, p. 90; Johnson, *Pioneer's Progress*, pp. 276-81. See William B. Scott and Peter M. Rutkoff, *New School: A History of the New School for Social Research* (New York: Macmillan, 1986).
58. Spencer Miller, Jr., "Workers' Education—Its Achievements and Its Failures," *American Federationist* (December 1922): 885-86.
59. Clyde W. Barrow, "Counter-Movement Within the Labor Movement: Workers' Education and the American Federation of Labor, 1900-1937," *Social Science Journal* 27 (October 1990): 395-417.
60. MacMahon, "Charles Beard, the Teacher," p. 228; Charles A. Beard, *American City Government* (New York: The Century Co., 1912).
61. Jane S. Dahlberg, *The New York Bureau of Municipal Research: Pioneer in Government Administration* (New York: New York University Press, 1966); Martin J. Schiesl, *The Politics of Efficiency: Municipal Administration and Reform in America, 1800-1920* (Berkeley and Los Angeles: University of California Press, 1977), p. 129.
62. Nore, *Charles A. Beard*, pp. 53-92, passim; Kennedy, *Charles A. Beard and American Foreign Policy*, pp. 29-38; Hoxie, *A History of the Faculty of Political Science*, pp. 106-08.
63. Charles A. Beard, "Methods of Training for Public Service," *School and Society* 2, 52 (December 25, 1915): 905-06.
64. Beard quoted in Luther Gulick, "Beard and Municipal Reform" in Beale, ed., *Charles A. Beard*, p. 52; Nore, *Charles A. Beard*, p. 92.
65. In 1918, Viscount Goto had visited the United States to observe the management of American cities and to see how public administration and urban planning were being taught in the United States. As part of the tour, he visited the New York Bureau of Municipal Research where he first met Beard. See Nore, Charles A. Beard, pp. 104-06. Some documents and speeches pertaining to this trip are in Beard, *The Making of Charles A. Beard*, Part II.
66. Kennedy, *Charles A. Beard and American Foreign Policy*, p. 50 fn31.
67. Nore, *Charles A. Beard*, p. 130. Some documents and speeches pertaining to this trip are in Beard, *The Making of Charles A. Beard*, Part III.
68. Hofstadter, *The Progressive Historians*, p. 289.
69. Charles E. Merriam, "Recent Advances in Political Methods," in James Farr and Raymond Seidelman, eds., *Discipline and History: Political Science in the United States* (Ann Arbor: University of Michigan Press, 1993), p. 131, observed as early as 1923 that the influence of history on political science was steadily being "supplanted by processes of actual observation and of psychological and statistical analysis."
70. Karen Orren and Stephen Skowronek, "Editors' Preface," *Studies in American*

Political Development, Vol. 1 (New Haven, CT: Yale University Press, 1986), p. vii, describe the new institutionalism as "a research agenda which seeks to use the work of the recent past as a new point of departure from which to specify more closely the complex patterns of state-society relations." Its major theoretical claim is "that institutions have an independent and formative influence on politics," while methodologically it emphasizes history "as the dimension necessary for understanding institutions as they operate under varying conditions." Similarly, Katznelson, "The State to the Rescue?" pp. 719-37; Philip Ethington and Eileen McDonagh, "The Eclectic Center of the New Institutionalism: Axes of Analysis in Comparative Perspective," *Social Science History* 19 (Winter 1995): 467-77.

71. Theda Skocpol, "Bringing the State Back In: Strategies of Analysis in Current Research," in Peter Evans, Dietrich Rueschemeyer, and Theda Skocpol, eds., *Bringing the State Back In* (Cambridge: Cambridge University Press, 1985), p. 8.

72. Clyde W. Barrow, *Critical Theories of the State: Marxist, Neo-Marxist, Post-Marxist* (Madison: University of Wisconsin Press, 1993), Chapter 5.

73. James G. March and Johan P. Olsen, "The New Institutionalism: Organizational Factors in Political Life," *American Political Science Review* 78 (1984): 747; James G. March and Johan P. Olsen, *Rediscovering Institutions: The Organizational Basis of Politics* (New York: Free Press, 1989).

74. Peter B. Evans, Dietrich Rueschemeyer, and Theda Skocpol, "On the Road toward a More Adequate Understanding of the State," in Evans, Rueschemeyer, and Skocpol, eds., *Bringing the State Back In*, p. 355.

75. Charles A. Beard, *The Economic Basis of Politics and Related Writings* (New York: Vintage Books, 1958).

76. Cf. L. De Alessi, "Development of the Property Rights Approach," in Eirik G. Furubotn and Rudolf Richter, eds., *The New Institutional Economics* (College Station: Texas A&M University Press, 1991), pp. 45-53; John L. Campbell and Leon N. Lindberg, "Property Rights and the Organization of Economic Activity by the State," *American Sociological Review* 55 (October 1990): 634-47; Marc R. Tool and Warren J. Samuels, ed., *State, Society, and Corporate Power*, 2nd Edition, Completely Revised (New Brunswick, NJ: Transaction Publishers, 1989), Part I.

77. Quentin Skinner, "Meaning and Understanding in the History of Ideas," *History and Theory* 1 (1969): 3-53; Quentin Skinner, "Motives, Intentions, and the Interpretation of Texts," *New Literary History* (Winter 1972): 393-408.

78. Richard Ashcraft, "The Changing Foundations of Political Theory," *Political Power and Social Theory*, Vol. 6 (Greenwich, CT: JAI Press, Inc., 1987), pp. 27-56.

79. *Gunnell, The Descent of Political Theory;* Raymond Seidelman, *Disenchanted Realists: Political Science and the American Crisis 1884-1984 (Albany: State University of New York Press, 1985);* Richard Ashcraft, "German Historicism and the History of Political Theory," History of Political Thought 8 (Summer 1987): 289-324.*

80. Merle Curti, *The Growth of American Thought*, 3rd Edition (New York: Harper and Row Publishers, Inc., 1964), p. 554.

81. Allan Bloom, *The Closing of the American Mind* (New York: Simon and Schuster, 1987), pp. 147-48. Similarly, as early as 1954, Beard was criticized on the grounds that "his philosophy of history has taken an historical starting point outside of Christianity," Thomas O'Brien Hanley, "Christian History for America,"

Catholic World 178 (February 1954): 326-31.

82. On history and the social sciences, Mary O. Furner, *Advocacy and Objectivity: A Crisis in the Professionalization of American Social Science, 1865-1905* (Lexington: University of Kentucky Press, 1975); Thomas Haskell, *The Emergence of Professional Social Science: The American Social Science Association and the Nineteenth-Century Crisis of Authority* (Urbana: University of Illinois Press, 1977); Dorothy Ross, *The Origins of American Social Science* (Cambridge: Cambridge University Press, 1991). On the political science discipline, see Seidelman, *Disenchanted Realists*; David Ricci, *The Tragedy of Political Science* (New Haven, CT: Yale University Press, 1984). On political theory specifically, see Gunnell, *Descent of Political Theory*.

83. Hofstadter, *The Progressive Historians*, p. 181.

84. Quoted in Phillips, "Charles Beard: The English Lectures, 1899-1901," p. 456; Also, Beard, *The Industrial Revolution*, p. xvi-xvii.

85. Charles A. Beard, "The World As I Want It," *Forum and Century* 91 (June 1934): 333-34.

2

The Method of Economic Interpretation

During the last fifty years, American scholars have uncritically accepted and reinforced many of the confusions of Beard's own generation about his viewpoint.[1] Beard's relation to Marx has become especially jumbled with the confusion beginning immediately after he published *An Economic Interpretation of the Constitution* in 1913. The notable E. S. Corwin denounced the work in an early review as "bent on demonstrating the truth of the socialistic theory of economic determinism and class struggle."[2] Corwin's objective was to dismiss the book as partisan ideology. Despite similar denunciations, the *Economic Interpretation* was soon embraced by American scholars, and by the mid-1930s, Beard's interpretation was considered so mainstream it was frequently reproduced in high school civics textbooks.[3] Consequently, in 1935, Theodore Clark Smith, the president of the American Historical Association, considered it necessary to reiterate that Beard's volume was a partisan use of history "which has its origins, of course, in the Marxian theories."[4]

Given such claims, it is no surprise that Beard's work was the object of relentless criticism by historians and political theorists during the 1950s. Richard B. Morris welcomed the rising tide of Beard critiques because his "economic formulation heartened the gathering host of American Marxists."[5] Yet, in the waning years of the Cold War, the specter of Beard's economic interpretation was still so haunting to American conservatives that Robert Eldon Brown considered a renewed counter-offensive against Beard vital to combating communism.[6] Indeed, following the subsequent decade of political turmoil on American campuses, Ernest Earnest found it necessary to admonish another generation of young scholars that "Beard's unexpressed basic premise was essentially the Marxist one of class conflict."[7] Finally, even amidst the neo-conservative victories of the 1980s, Allan Bloom was claiming that "Marxist debunking of the Charles Beard variety" was directly responsible for having weakened "our conviction of the truth or superiority of American principles." Bloom argues that the practice of calling the Founders racists, promoters of Indian genocide, and representatives of class interest "began in Charles Beard's Marxism."[8]

Clearly, much of the effort to link Beard with Marx has been part of an on-going polemical strategy designed to exclude Beardian historiography from the realm of serious political theory by dismissing it as mere ideology. There is good reason to make this connection because American Marxists have frequently turned to Beard's *Economic Interpretation* for their historical critique of the U.S. Constitution. American Marxists have often viewed Beard's *Economic Interpretation* as compelling empirical and historical evidence that the U.S. Constitution was essentially a capitalist document. As early as 1914, Allan L. Benson, a New York Socialist Party legislator was citing Beard's *Economic Interpretation* as evidence that the Founding Fathers "all were capitalists or the attorneys of the capitalist class" who had met in 1787 to create a government "by the rich for the rich."[9] Joseph Freeman, an early Socialist Party journalist, observed that members of the Party routinely invoked Beard whenever they were pressed for evidence to prove that the U.S. Constitution served the interests of the capitalist class.[10] Theodore Draper found a similar pattern among leaders of the early communist parties in America.[11]

Beard never denied that he was conversant with the theories and writings of Marx at the time he wrote *An Economic Interpretation of the Constitution*.[12] Yet, he steadfastly rejected the assertion that "the economic interpretation of history or my volume on the Constitution had its origin in Marxian theories."[13] Beard cited E. R. A. Seligman's, *The Economic Interpretation of History* (1902), and not Marx, as a general methodological reference in his own *Economic Interpretation*.[14] However, Beard's reference to Seligman befuddled conservative critics and radical supporters alike, because Seligman, a moderate reformer, was well known in political circles for his virulent attacks on socialism.[15]

Beard further confused any neat ideological categorization of his work by claiming that his application of the method of economic interpretation was based on the political science of James Madison.[16] When this claim was met with incredulity, Beard challenged his ideological critics with an essay on "The Intellectual Origins of Economic Interpretation," that was delivered as a lecture at Amherst College in 1916 and published in 1922. Beard points out that "the great political philosophers, with few exceptions, have regarded property as the fundamental element in political power, and have looked upon constitutions as a balance of economic groups."[17] Beard discusses the contributions of Aristotle, Machiavelli, Harrington, Locke, and Montesquieu to the development of economic interpretation, but he devotes a greater portion of the essay to Madison's thought than to that of any other single theorist. In fact, Beard considered the development and application of the method of economic interpretation to be the greatest contribution of American political thought to the Western intellectual tradition.[18] Two decades after publishing *An Economic Interpretation,* Beard was still insisting that the role of "economic interests as forces in politics and in the formulation of laws and constitutions....was expounded by James Madison, in Number X of the *Federalist*...long before Karl Marx was born." Beard persistently admonished critics that the "Fathers of the American Constitution were well aware of the idea [of economic interpretation], operated on the hypothesis that it had at least a considerable validity, and expressed it in numerous writings."[19]

Nevertheless, scholars have generally responded to Beard's disclaimers in one of two ways. Some critics assert that Beard underestimated the effect of Marxism on his *Economic Interpretation* and that he failed to understand the theoretical origins of his own thinking about American history and politics. Max Lerner suggests that even if one concedes that the proximate source of Beard's approach lay in the American tradition "that does not prevent its import from being Marxian."[20] Similarly, Morton White argues that Seligman's *Economic Interpretation of History* was "a forthright academic defense of Marx's theory of history." White suggests that "even if Beard had not been familiar with Marx and Engels at first hand, he did acknowledge the influence of a reasonably accurate secondhand version of their ideas." Thus, White concludes that "there is something irrelevant about Beard's protest."[21]

However, the more frequent response has been that Beard's disclaimers, and particularly the references to Seligman and Madison, were decisions made "on purely tactical grounds in order to confound the professional patrioteers."[22] Morton White considers Beard's references as "quite superfluous" and finds "nothing attractive about this appeal to the flag."[23] Likewise, Douglass G. Adair asserts that Beard cited Madison rather than Marx as a "device quite self-consciously adopted of wrapping himself in the American flag."[24] Hence, the American left has often criticized Beard for studiously avoiding the Marxist stigma, while the political right has criticized him as a Marxist masquerading behind the visage of James Madison.

In one sense, both accounts offer an adequate explanation of Beard's puzzling disclaimers, but only to the extent that one accepts *ad hominems* as political theory. The objective of this chapter is to suggest an alternative interpretation, in some respects the most obvious interpretation: namely, that Beard was neither a Marxist, nor was he engaged in an attempt to deceive his political detractors. The most consistent understanding of Beard's methodological standpoint and its implications for a theory of American political development is one that takes the intentional statements about his own writings seriously.[25]

Thus, just as Beard claimed, I suggest that E. R. A. Seligman's *The Economic Interpretation of History* is the key that unlocks Beard's understanding of the method of economic interpretation and, in particular, its distinction from the politics and theory of Marxism. If one goes back to Seligman's original work, it not only clarifies Beard's understanding of his methodological relation to historical materialism, but it also suggests a clear path to Madison as the foundation of Beard's constitutional theory. However, the second point has generally been obscured by the tendency to read Beard's *Economic Interpretation* as an isolated text instead of as one component in a theory of American political development. Indeed, Beard's theoretical commitment to the idea of American exceptionalism and his critical awareness of its implications for social democratic politics led him to make a number of significant conceptual departures from Marxism in his theory of American political development.

Beard and Marx

When Beard cited E. R. A. Seligman as a methodological reference for his *Economic Interpretation of the Constitution*, scholars and other critics immediately dismissed Beard's citation as an ideological smokescreen. Seligman was the son of a wealthy New York banker, a founder of the American Economics Association, and a member of the historical school that dominated the fledgling economics discipline.[26] There are at least two reasons for accepting the claim that Seligman had a significant influence on Beard's method of economic interpretation. First, the professional relationship between Seligman and Beard had been close for more than a decade by the time *An Economic Interpretation* was published in 1913. As Ellen Nore has emphasized, Seligman emerged as one of the dominant influences on Beard's intellectual development soon after he arrived at Columbia University as a graduate student.[27] Beard was not exceptional in this respect, because at Columbia University many future scholars were learning the economic interpretation of history in Seligman's political economy classes.[28]

Second, a point that is casually ignored in the rush to denounce Beard is that Seligman was a leading academic Marxologist among American university scholars until the mid-1920s. Seligman's influence on American Marxology was primarily the result of a three-part article published in the *Political Science Quarterly* during late 1901 and early 1902.[29] In this article, Seligman's theoretical objective was to supply a general statement of the economic interpretation of history while demonstrating specifically that "socialistic doctrines of labor and surplus value have in their essentials nothing to do with the economic interpretation of history."[30]

This distinction has been lost on contemporary scholars, but it was widely acknowledged at the time, particularly among historians and economists in Great Britain and Europe.[31] The first actual usage of the term "economic interpretation" is by James E. Thorold Rogers (1823-1890), who published *The Economic Interpretation of History* in 1888.[32] Rogers was a political economist at Oxford University who had authored an early and well-received college textbook on political economy.[33] Rogers was a Liberal member of Parliament from 1880 to 1886, where he became a follower of Richard Cobden and advocated labor reform legislation as an *alternative* to socialism. He edited John Bright's and Richard Cobden's speeches, which helped popularize the Manchester School of economics.[34] In *The Economic Interpretation of History*, Rogers explained British political development in terms of a class struggle between the landed aristocracy, the capitalist class, and the laboring class over the distribution of income among the three factors of production (i.e., land, capital, and labor).

Significantly, Eduard Bernstein was aware of Rogers' *Economic Interpretation* when he wrote his 1899 essays on evolutionary socialism. Bernstein rejected the labor theory of value as a norm for deciding the justice or injustice of the distribution of income and he praised Rogers as one of a group of British writers who first grasped the institutional importance of trade unions in negotiating the distribution of income in a democracy. However, Bernstein observes that Rogers' economic interpretation of politics had "little in common with the materialist conception of history."[35]

Similarly, in his 1904 essay, "The Protestant Ethic and the Spirit of Capitalism," the liberal sociologist Max Weber distinguishes between "the more naïve historical materialism," which he rejects (Marx), and the economic interpretation of history, which he views favorably. Despite his polemic against "vulgar Marxism," Weber indicates that he considers "the influence of economic development on the fate of religious ideas to be very important." Thus, Weber laments that the economic interpretation of history was often confused with the materialistic interpretation of the Marxists.[36] In fact, prior to World War I, the distinction between Marxian historical materialism and the economic interpretation of history was generally recognized by scholars familiar with the German, British, and French debates on liberalism and revisionist socialism.

Quite simply, by the time Seligman was writing in the early 1900s, economic interpretation was a term used mainly by liberals and non-Marxian socialists seeking to separate themselves from the economics, the historical determinism, and the revolutionary socialism of Marx's *Das Kapital*. Seligman and Beard both acknowledge Rogers' work in their own writings, and Beard explicitly acknowledges his debt to Bernstein, so it was impossible for either of them to draw any necessary logical relationship between Marxism and the method of economic interpretation. They were both aware of an extensive contemporary literature in which many scholars adopted the method of economic interpretation, while explicitly rejecting socialism.

It should also be noted as a matter of historical context that the *Political Science Quarterly* was one of the earliest political science journals in the United States, predating the *American Political Science Review* by a decade. It was published by Columbia University and edited by Seligman, partly with Charles Beard's assistance. However, not only was *PSQ* one of the only journals defining the new field of academic political science, but in this particular case the high demand for reprints of Seligman's article resulted in its publication as a small book by Macmillan Press in 1902. When the first run of Seligman's *Economic Interpretation of History* sold out in less than six months, it was republished the following year and then went through seven more printings by 1924.

Seligman's general statement of the economic interpretation of history, and the particular passage cited by Beard, is as follows:

> The existence of man depends upon his ability to sustain himself; the economic life is therefore the fundamental condition of all life. Since human life, how-ever, is the life of man in society, individual existence moves within the frame-work of the social structure and is modified by it. What the conditions of maintenance are to the individual, the similar relations of production and con-sumption are to the community. To economic causes, therefore, must be traced in the last instance those transformations in the structure of society which themselves condition the relations of social classes and the various manifesta-tions of social life.[37]

Beard explicitly cites this passage in *An Economic Interpretation of the Constitution* and he reiterates this passage in numerous writings over the next two decades.[38] Seligman's elaboration of the general method of economic interpretation engaged many of the same questions that preoccupied German historiography and social science. This is not surprising because American scholarship was widely infused with the influence of the German historical school until World War I, primarily because most American research scholars had received their own training in German universities.[39] Thus, it is worth noting that Seligman received his own graduate education in Germany and was familiar with a vast expanse of Marx's and Engels' extant works, including their personal correspondence and unpublished manuscripts. In addition, Seligman was well versed in German historiography, con-temporary Marxist political economy, and European economic his-tory.

There is every reason to believe that Seligman (and through him Beard) was quite familiar with the debates about Marx that were currently raging in the Second International and especially among German scholars. Indeed, in his *Economic Interpretation of History*, Seligman introduces two sets of theoretical innovations that reinforce this presumption. The first set of conceptual innovations is designed to distance the economic interpretation of history from what was commonly called vulgar Marxism or economic reductionism. Seligman's second set of theoretical innovations is then designed to separate his reconstruction of the method of economic interpretation from *Marxian* economics.

Seligman's first innovation was to reconstruct the method of economic interpretation "chiefly in the words of Marx himself" in order to defend the method against its reduction to *vulgar* Marxism.[40] Thus, Seligman polemically reconstructs a sophisticated Marxism that is distinguished from vulgar Marxism at three points: (1) its analytic conception of the economic; (2) its analytic conception of the role of superstructure; and (3) its rejection of a totalizing historicism. In defining the analytic meaning of the economic in Marx, Seligman chastised vulgar Marxists for reducing the concept to merely "technical or technological modes of production" in such a way as to imply a doctrine of technological determinism. On the contrary, Seligman proposed a more expansive concept of economic relations which included "the technical processes of extracting the raw material and of fashioning it into a finished product, but also the technique of trade and transportation, the technical methods of business in general, and the technical processes by which the finished product is distributed to the final consumer."[41] Moreover, Seligman introduced an additional modification that presaged Beard's integration of the Turner thesis into his work on American political development.

Seligman argues that as an analytic concept economic relations must also include physical factors such as geographical conditions because these often establish "limits within which the methods of production can act." In this respect, Seligman and Beard both saw geography as an economic factor that could obstruct the adoption of certain types of production and distribution (e.g., the absence of navigable waterways) or could naturally facilitate and promote other techniques/modes of production (e.g., seaports, fertile soil, native ores). Beard would later criticize American historians who emphasized the importance of sectional divisions to American political development, but who failed to explain whether the term section "meant a segment of physical geography or a set of social and economic arrangements within a geographic area, conditioned by physical circumstances."[42] The conceptual relation between geography, section, and economic divisions was well established among German historians and their followers in the United States, who considered the geographical interpretation of history, which traces its origins to Montesquieu, an integral component of the economic interpretation of history. [43]

A second distinction between Marx and vulgar Marxism was the explanatory role of superstructures. Seligman's argument was that economic relations of production, distribution, and consumption provided one with a theory of structure and real interests from which to *interpret* political actions, religious movements, or currents of thought. Nevertheless, in his view, economic relations rarely provided one with a theory of concrete action or motivation. From Seligman's perspective, the major error of vulgar Marxism was its attempt to draw a direct correlation between economic relations and individual or collective motives for historical action. Seligman accepted the claim that social classes do act occasionally out of direct economic motivations but he emphasized at the same time that neither Marx nor Engels "ever meant to claim an absolute validity for economic considerations to the exclusion of all other factors."[44]

For Seligman, economic relations determine the most important *actors* in society. Yet, he did not think that economic *interests* supplied the sole (or often even the most important) motivation for collective action, nor did it deterministically "cause" classes to organize their actions in a particular way. Seligman insisted that to understand the motivational and organizational factors involved in class mobilization, one had to examine actual history and to make these judgments on a case by case basis. However, Seligman did offer two methodological rules to guide such research. First, one could hypothesize for purposes of investigation that development and changes in economic relations were the preponderant though not exclusive influence in the historical impetus to political and social change. Second, this influence was always mediated by the actual form of organization which itself "is often determined by political, legal, philosophical and religious theories and conceptions." Consequently, Seligman's central historical thesis was that "the whole structure of society is modified by the relations of social classes, and how these relations are themselves dependent on antecedent economic changes."[45] The cycle of determination and conditioning hypothesized by Seligman is illustrated in Figure 2.1.

Finally, Seligman also sought to divorce the interpretive concepts of determination and conditioning from the positivist concept of causation in the explanation of historical events. Seligman's major objec-

FIGURE 2.1
The Method of Economic Interpretation

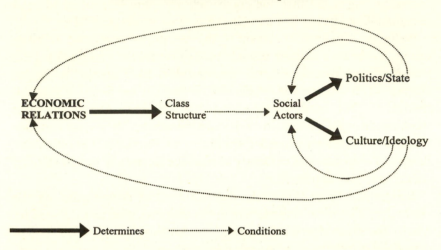

tive on this count was to inject a greater degree of historical contingency into the economic interpretation. This enabled Seligman to argue (as against vulgar Marxism) that *the meaning of history* was open-ended and neither predictable nor inevitable in its outcomes (e.g., socialism). Seligman insisted that the meaning of history was internally structured by class conflicts but that the outcome of those conflicts was open-ended and contingent upon the actions of real historical actors. The meaning of history is determined by economic relations in the last instance, but it is caused by real actors.[46] Beard also distinguishes the method of economic interpretation from Marxian historical materialism on grounds that the former "is not a closed system."[47]

On these points, Seligman's elaboration of the economic interpretation of history closely parallels the revisionist Marxist historiography emerging in Germany at this time. For example, one will no doubt observe a strong similarity between Seligman's general statement of the method of economic interpretation and Marx's equally synoptic, if more famous, statement on historical materialism in *A Contribution to the Critique of Political Economy* (1859).[48] In this vein, it is interesting to note that only four years previous to Seligman's work, Eduard Bernstein had cited the same passage from Marx as presenting "the general features of his [Marx's] philosophy of history." Therefore, Bernstein argued that this one passage should be taken as a general definition of the materialist conception of history. On this basis, Bernstein suggested that one could strip the pure science of Marxist socialism from its applied parts in the various writings of Marx.[49]

Seligman's general statement of the method of economic interpretation thus bears a striking resemblance to Bernstein's methodological revisionism. Likewise, several commentators have pointed to the influence of Bernstein's *Evolutionary Socialism* on Beard's political thought.[50] Yet, even to the extent that Seligman and Beard were working through a Marxian-revisionist paradigm, their own methodological conclusions exceeded the limits of Bernstein's revisionism. Seligman's agenda was evidently to advance Bernstein's methodological critique one step further.

Seligman, unlike Bernstein, was not content with separating the method of historical materialism from its particular applications by Marx. The final stop on Seligman's methodological itinerary was to separate the method of economic interpretation from historical materialism. The basis for this separation was Seligman's argument that Marxist revisionists still made the error of equating the *method* of economic interpretation with a specific economic *theory*. For Seligman, historical materialism was the specific philosophy of history that resulted from fusing the method of economic interpretation with Marxian economic theory.

Seligman maintained that historical materialism might be a necessary result of combining the method of economic interpretation with Marxist economics, but what revisionists failed to recognize is that it was not necessary to introduce Marxist economics into the equation in the first place. Thus, Seligman argues that economic interpretation is not only independent of specific applications of economic theory to history, it is in principle independent of particular economic theories. In other words, one might substitute some other economic theory for Marxist economics and end up with a very different conception of historical development.[51] In principle, there were as many economic interpretations of history possible as there were economic theories. Seligman observed that the chief evidence for this claim was that Neo-Marxists were beginning to diverge among themselves over how to apply Marxist economic theory to history, mainly because "we find many different versions of the theory."[52]

However, Seligman made it clear that he held an unfavorable view of Marxist economic theory. For Seligman, the essence of Marxian economics was the doctrine of surplus value. This concept supplied the foundation for Marx's theory of exploitation and class struggle. Marx's entire theoretical conception of capitalism and historical development hinged on the concept of surplus value. As a historical economist, Seligman considered the concept of surplus value defective but concludes that Marx's failings as an economist have "no bearing on the truth or falsity of his philosophy of history," i.e., on the method of economic interpretation. The result was that Seligman preempted Lukacs by twenty years with the claim that "even if everyone of Marx's economic theories was entirely false, this fact alone would not in any degree invalidate the general doctrine of economic interpretation."[53] According to Seligman, the method of economic interpretation was not reducible to the Marxist economic interpretation or to any one variant of Marxist economics.

On the contrary, the method of economic interpretation did not presuppose any specific economic theory or any specific set of historical economic relations. Hence, Seligman could insist that "the specifically socialistic doctrines of labor and surplus value...have in their essentials nothing to do with the economic interpretation of history." Unfortunately, Seligman observed, the relationship between the method of economic interpretation and Marxian economics has been confused historically by "the accidental fact that the originator of both theories happened to be the same man," i.e., Marx.[54] On the other hand, if one made this separation, Seligman concludes:

> We might agree that economic factors primarily influence progress; we might conclude that social forces, rather than individual whim, at bottom make history; we might perhaps even accept the existence of class struggles; but none of these admissions would necessarily lead to any semblance of socialism.[55]

The end result is that Seligman could note approvingly that "wherever we turn in the maze of recent historical investigation, we are confronted by the overwhelming importance attached by the younger and abler scholars to the economic factor in political and social progress."[56]

At the time, Seligman's book was considered the definitive statement of the method of economic interpretation among American scholars. In fact, Charles Merriam observes that the method of economic interpretation gained wider and wider acceptance among historians and political scientists in the early twentieth century after Seligman distinguished it from Marx's historical materialism.[57] By the 1920s, Harry Elmer Barnes considered it virtually self-evident that the economic interpretation of history "may be carried on without any adherence to the socialistic theory of economic reconstruction which Marx postulated." Barnes observes that "the most important work done in this field has been the product of writers...some of whom are leading critics of orthodox Marxian doctrine."[58] Melvin M. Knight, a professor of economics at the University of California, cited Beard's writings in 1929 as the most widely read example of a "frankly economic view of American history" that is "far from embracing the rigid determinism of the Marxians."[59]

Beard and Madison

Beard was no doubt one of the younger and abler scholars Seligman praised in his *Economic Interpretation of History*. Yet, unlike his mentor, Beard said very little about Marxism except to deny that he was a Marxist. As a result, Marxist scholars such as Eugene Genovese have found in Beard's work the "paradox of an economic interpretation of history without a dominant economic theory."[60] On the contrary, the explanation for Beard's silence is that he (1) considered the basic questions of historical methodology settled by Seligman and (2) viewed the core concepts of Marxian economic theory as simply irrelevant to American political development.

On the first point, it has already been noted that Beard continually answered critics that the economic interpretation of history "as a type of empirical realism was falsely ascribed to Karl Marx."[61] Notably, however, Beard made a positive reply to Walter Lippman who criticized Beard in a 1922 article for failing to examine "the metaphysics of the relations between economics and politics." Beard's answer to Lippman was that "on that point there is nothing better than Professor Seligman's very clear and interesting *Economic Interpretation of History*." Beard went on to recount how he "long ago planned to write a book tracing the social implications of economic forces, but in the search for materials I found much speculation and very few facts." Consequently, instead of replicating Seligman's "very clear and interesting" statement, Beard decided to spend his career "engaged in *the analysis of concrete historical and economic situations* than in the metaphysics of the matter."[62]

On the second point, Beard once complained of the absence of a Marxist interpretation of U.S. history, lamenting that Marxists in the United States were so factious that their most adept scholars "devoted more energy...to the denunciation of one another than to the application of their scheme of thought to the American scene."[63] Yet, Beard's reluctance to accept Marxian economics as a foundation for American historiography went deeper than his unwillingness to be engulfed by the intellectual chaos of the American left. Rather, if one reads Beard's *Economic Interpretation* in the light of Seligman's methodological work, then one can identify the ways in which Beard's approach departs from Marxist historiography.

First, Beard did not accept the analytic conception of economic relations developed by Marx in *Capital*. It is already well-known that Beard rejected Marxian economic theory on the same grounds as Seligman, even though unlike Seligman he accepted class struggle as an inevitable component of every social order.[64] Beard did not find Marx's concept of surplus value compelling and, hence, he rejected the entire matrix of theoretical implications carried by that concept. Most importantly, it led Beard to throw out Marx's theory of exploitation as the *explanation* for class struggle.[65] Consequently, Beard's dilemma was to find a theory of class struggle, rooted in economic relations, that could substitute for Marxian economics.

Importantly, Beard was struggling with a dilemma only partly defined by the specific concerns of Seligman's *Economic Interpretation of History*. As a prominent historical economist, Seligman belonged to an ideologically diverse school of economists that included Richard T. Ely, John R. Commons, and Simon Patten on the left and Arthur T. Hadley, among others, on the right. What these economists shared in common was the effort to construct an economics discipline that rejected many of the basic concepts and assumptions of both classical and Marxian economics. This school of historical and institutional economists was dominant in the United States from the 1880s until World War I, and they continued to exert considerable influence until the end of the first New Deal (1933).[66] Charles Beard was exposed to historical and institutional economics no later than 1896, as an undergraduate, when he first met John R. Commons, who became a lifelong friend.[67]

In contrast to the neo-classical assumption that market exchanges take place as frictionless and cost-free events between individual rational actors, historical and institutional economists were arguing that real world exchanges take place between business firms that must initiate, organize, and manage difficult and costly transactions. Economic transactions between real individuals and business firms, as opposed to abstract market exchanges, incur a variety of transaction costs involved in finding suppliers and consumers, negotiating and enforcing contracts, and gaining access to labor and product markets, among others. [68] For historical and institutional economists, this meant that the concept of private property could not be assumed as a conceptual *a priori*, because it is a historical institution that has to be constructed, defined, and enforced as a legal right. Similarly, transactions involve the negotiation and enforcement of contracts and, thus, the market requires a non-market institution (i.e., the state) to enforce these voluntary arrangements. In other words, the state was integral to historical and institutional economics, because without property and contract there could not be orderly transactions.[69] Despite the central importance of state theory to historical and institutional economics, the economists themselves did very little to construct a theory of the state.[70]

Beard found the rudiments of this theory in Madison's *Federalist* No. 10. The passages that Beard cites are quite familiar ones to contemporary scholars. One of the most important is Madison's observation that:

> the most common and durable source of factions has been the verious and unequal distribution of property. Those who hold and those who are without property have ever formed distinct interests in society. Those who are creditors, and those who are debtors, fall under a like discrimination. A landed interest, a manufacturing interest, a mercantile interest, a moneyed interest, with many less interests grow up of necessity in civilized nations, and divide them into different classes, actuated by different sentiments and views.[71]

Madison argues that in all modern societies there are always *three* possible axes of class struggle: (1) the propertyless vs. the propertied; (2) debtors vs. creditors; and (3) conflicts between those owning different kinds of property (e.g., land vs. capital). While each of these axes frequently intersect the others, no axis is wholly reducible to any other axis of class conflict. Furthermore, no one axis of class conflict can claim a prior analytic weight greater than the other axes. Finally, Madison relates this matrix of economic relations to the state, observing that "the regulation of these various and interfering interests forms the principal task of modern legislation."[72] Beard's concept of the state is rooted in this Madisonian thesis, which also provides a bridge to the institutionalist economics that anchor Beard's theory of American political development.[73]

For example, in *The Rise of American Civilization* (1927), Beard argues that American political development should be understood in terms of the political conflicts generated within and between two distinct economic eras. Beard characterized the first phase of American development as an agricultural era extending from colonization until 1860. A second industrial era had been launched in the womb of the first by the Hamiltonian political economy that was made possible by the U.S. Constitution. The industrial era launched by Hamilton and the Constitution was consolidated during the Civil War and then nurtured to dominance as the last bastions of American agrarianism were subdued over the next three decades. Finally, Beard envisioned twentieth century politics in the industrial era as a painfully slow movement "towards social democracy" in which labor was a rising social, political, and intellectual force.[74] Thus, for Beard, the historical phases of modern political development were underpinned by the shifting relations between the factors of production agreed upon by most economists: land, capital, and labor. In each case, political development and constitutional change was the result of deepening contradictions between this shifting economic base and the political superstructure.

According to Beard, the historical relation between economic base and political superstructure was supplied by "the interests" of different classes in particular types of constitutions. This interest was primarily determined by their need to obtain from government rules and policies that promote, or at least do not undermine, the larger economic relations which sustain their position as owners of a particular kind of property. Beard maintained that these interests can either be safeguarded by a structure of fundamental law which preserves them as rights, or the members of a particular class must directly control the organs of government and public policy.[75] It was Beard's thesis that this dilemma was always the problem of prime importance under any system of government where political power is shared by a large portion of the population. This is because particular propertied interests usually cannot be assured of maintaining instrumental control of the state, especially where they constitute a minority of the enfranchised population. Insofar as this conflict of rights and interests is resolved to the advantage of *specific* propertied interests, constitutions facilitate their dominance by virtue of the special protections, privileges, and rights that such groups enjoy within the framework of government.[76]

Beard distinguishes his own position from that of Marxists in two ways. First, he reconceptualizes the dynamics of class struggle in terms of the conflict between competing rights in property and constitutional office. Consequently, Beard is able to abandon the metaphysics of value theory in favor of a concept of class struggle grounded in *historical* claims to competing political and economic rights, rather than in a concept of exploitation. Thus, Beard argues that there is "a vital relation between the forms of property and the distribution of property, revolutions in the state being usually, the results of contests over property."[77]

Constitutional change plays a central part in this struggle because constitutions independently structure rights over long periods of time as particular state forms (e.g., as a capitalist or socialist state). In fact, Beard had already advanced this principle in rudimentary form as early 1908 with the observation that "changes in the form of the state have been caused primarily by the demand of groups for power, and in general these groups have coincided with economic classes which have arisen within the political society."[78] In addressing the proponents of American exceptionalism, Beard observes that "if government here [i.e., in the United States] is different from government in other times and places it is mainly because the forms and distribution of property are different." [79]

Second, on this point as well, Beard dismissed structuralist arguments (which persist even today) that constitutions could inherently guarantee the dominance of particular propertied interests. Instead, Beard saw constitutions as a framework of rules, offices, powers, and limits on power which *if used properly* would more readily facilitate the dominance of one class as opposed to others. Constitutions establish asymmetrical structures of right, privilege, and representation, but he notes that the process of government is set in motion and kept going by political parties and thus can not operate independently of them.[80] Or as Madison put it, "the regulation of the verious and interfering interests...involves the spirit of party and faction in the necessary and ordinary operations of government."[81] In this respect, Beard concludes that the primary object of government in making laws, beyond the mere repression of physical violence, is to define the specific "rules which determine property relations of members of society."[82]

It was this theory of constitutionalism, coupled with Beard's Madisonian conception of class conflict, that brought the economic basis of the U.S. constitutional struggle into such sharp relief. In *An Economic Interpretation of the Constitution*, Beard hypothesized that the constitutional struggle had lined up as a conflict between a nationalist commercial party and a localist agrarian party, i.e., capital vs. land. If this hypothesis was correct, (and Beard thought it was), then the implication of a vulgar economic determinism was clearly that the Constitution should *not* have been ratified. Indeed, Beard observed both before and after the publication of *An Economic Interpretation* that the Confederation of the critical period was a constitutional arrangement that ensconced the agrarian politics of local legislatures generally dominated by farmers.[83]

Consequently, the great puzzle for Beard was always to explain how the Federalists had wrenched political change from a seemingly insurmountable agrarian majority. The constitution's adoption was therefore an illustration of the open-ended and *political* character of class struggle and not, as Corwin charged, an attempt to prove the theory of economic determinism. Quite the contrary, Beard's goal was to demonstrate that the constitution succeeded in creating favorable political conditions for a commercial republic when the preponderance of economically determined social forces seemed to point towards the continuation of an agrarian confederation in the United States. In other words, it was not capitalism that made the constitution historically necessary, but the constitution that made capitalism historically possible.[84] The constitution was able to facilitate and nurture capitalist economic relations as against the agrarianism promoted by the Confederation.

Seligman's methodological influence is also evident in Beard's handling of the problem of economic reductionism. As early as 1906, Beard published a review of Jean Juares' *A Socialist History of France* in which he praised Juares for recognizing that although "the fundamental force in history is economic...the complex phenomena of social life...cannot be reduced to an economic formula." In his review, Beard insisted that "it would be false and futile to deny the relation of thought and emotion to the economic system and the precise forms of production," but he also conceded that it was equally "puerile to explain summarily by the evolution of economic relations the entire movement of human thought." Beard was convinced that "thus restricted, the economic interpretation of history will doubtless be accepted by most scholars who aim at objectivity."[85]

Thus, similarly in 1915, Beard responded to specific charges of economic reductionism by emphasizing that the main point of his chapter on the economic interests of the Founding Fathers was simply to establish "that members of the convention were of the capitalistic rather than of the agrarian interest, and whether they made money out of the constitution was specifically stated to be of no consequence to the main thesis."[86] Instead, Beard's main objective was to define key political actors as classes in relation to the existing economic and social structure. What he offered was a theory of structure, rather than a theory of motivation.

On the other hand, if Beard's almost exclusive focus on economic relations seemed extreme to some readers at the time, Beard enjoined the polemical context of his work as a defense much in the same way that Engels had done for Marx. Beard points out that he never claimed his book was "the only interpretation possible," nor that political culture (e.g., ideas) had played no role in the Founders' actions. Beard noted, much as Seligman had done, that the method of economic interpretation always presented "a relative rather than an absolute explanation."[87] Consequently, Beard argued that his intent was always to artificially juxtapose his own economic hypothesis against idealist and sectional interpretations for polemical purposes. Beard felt justified in this strategy because it was those interpretations that arbitrarily excluded the possibility that the ratification struggle "may have been conditioned if not determined by economic interests and activities."[88] Thus, *An Economic Interpretation* was not necessarily incompatible with other interpretations but, in Beard's view, might actually reveal that members of certain classes had an elective affinity for various ideas or that sectional interests entailed more than large states versus small states or northern versus southern states.

Notes

1.   Pope McCorkle, "The Historian as Intellectual: Charles Beard and the Constitution Reconsidered," *American Journal of Legal History* 28 (1984): 314-63.

2. Corwin, "Review of Economic Interpretation of the Constitution of the United States," p. 65. Similarly, Orin G. Libby, "Review of *Economic Interpretation of the Constitution of the United States* by Charles A. Beard," *Mississippi Valley Historical Review* 1, 1 (June 1914): 114-15, decried Beard's "partisan appeal to class prejudice" and rebuffed him "for arousing class feelings over questions that have long since passed into history."

3. Blinkoff, *The Influence of Charles A. Beard Upon American Historiography*; Hofstadter, "Charles Beard and the Constitution," in Beale, ed., *Charles A Beard*, pp. 75-80; Brown, *Charles Beard and the Constitution*, pp. 5-23.

4. Theodore Clark Smith, "The Writing of American History in America, 1884-1934," *American Historical Review* 40 (April 1935): 447.

5. Richard B. Morris, "Why the Constitution Was Adopted," *Saturday Review* (May 19, 1956): 60-61. Diggins, "Power and Authority in American History," p. 702, observes that in the 1950s: "Beardianism became almost synonymous with Marxism." Likewise, Hanley, "Christian History for America," p. 326,

6. Robert E. Brown, *Reinterpretation of the Formation of the American Constitution* (Boston: Northeastern University Press, 1963), p. 2.

7. Ernest Earnest, *The Single Vision: The Alienation of American Intellectuals, 1910-1930* (New York: New York University Press, 1970), p. 85.

8. Bloom, *Closing of the American Mind*, pp. 56, 28-29.

9. Allan L. Benson, *Our Dishonest Constitution* (New York: B. W. Huebsch, 1914), pp. 5-35.

10. Joseph Freeman, *An American Testament: A Narrative of Rebels and Romantics* (New York: Octagon Books, 1973), p. 110.

11. Theodore Draper, *American Communism and Soviet Russia* (New York: Viking Press 1960), pp. 272-75.

12. Beard, *Economic Interpretation of the Constitution*, p. viii. Beard read Marx as an undergraduate at DePauw University and he thoroughly re-read Marx at least twice in his later life (i.e., the 1930s and 1940s). See Forrest McDonald, "Charles A. Beard," in Cunliffe and Winks, eds., *Pastmasters*, p. 112. Also see, William Appleman Williams, "A Note on Charles Austin Beard's Search for a General Theory of Causation," *American Historical Review* 62 (October 1956): 59-80; Eric F. Goldman, "The Origins of Beard's *Economic Interpretation of the Constitution*," *Journal of the History of Ideas* 13 (April 1952): 234-49.

13. Beard, *Economic Interpretation of the Constitution*, p. xii.

14. Ibid., p. 15.

15. Freeman, *An American Testament*, p. 112; Nore, *Charles A. Beard*, p. 31.

16. Beard, *Economic Interpretation of the Constitution*, p. 14. Charles A. Beard, "The Economic Basis of Politics," *New Republic* (September 27, 1922): 128.

17. Beard, *Economic Basis of Politics*, p. 57.

18. Ibid., pp. 35-42,

19. Beard, "Introduction to the 1935 Edition," *Economic Interpretation of the Constitution*, pp. vi, xiii. Also, Charles A. Beard, "Democracy and Education," *Social Research* 4 (September 1937): 395: "If you will read the *Federalist*, written before Marx was born, you will find there the theory of the class struggle as the basis of political institutions, and the theory of a necessary dictatorship in times of great social crisis."

20. Max Lerner, *Ideas Are Weapons: The History and Uses of Ideas* (New York: Viking Press, 1939), p. 161.

21. White, *Social Thought in America*, pp. 120, 121.

22. Lerner, *Ideas are Weapons*, p. 165.
23. White, *Social Thought in America*, p. 124.
24. Douglass Adair, "The Tenth Federalist Revisited," *William and Mary Quarterly* 8 (January 1951): 48-67.
25. Skinner, "Motives, Intentions, and the Interpretation of Texts," pp. 393-408. McDonald, "Charles A. Beard," in Cunliffe and Winks, eds., *Pastmasters*, p. 114, "rules out the possibility that Beard was merely using a revered Founding Father as protective coloration for unpopular ideas...all Beard's writings during his great creative period as a historian, 1913 to 1933, show him to have been a consistent Madisonian, as he understood Madison."
26. Joseph Dorfman, *The Economic Mind in American Civilization*, 5 Vols. (New York: Augustus M. Kelley, 1969), Vol. 3, pp. 254-56. Seligman's academic reputation was based on his expertise in public finance and tax policy.
27. Nore, *Charles A. Beard*, pp. 30-31.
28. Wish, *The American Historian*, p. 266, is one of the few intellectual historians to acknowledge that "Charles Beard read this [i.e., Seligman's] book and apparently agreed with its main tenets."
29. E. R. A. Seligman, "Economic Interpretation of History," *Political Science Quarterly* 16 (December 1901): 612-40; *Political Science Quarterly* 17 (March 1902): 71-98; *Political Science Quarterly* 17 (June 1902): 284-312.
30. E. R. A. Seligman, *The Economic Interpretation of History* (New York, 1924), 2nd edition revised, p. 53.
31. Henri See, *The Economic Interpretation of History* (New York: Augustus M. Kelley, 1968).
32. James E. Thorold Rogers, *The Economic Interpretation of History* (New York: G. P. Putnam's Sons, 1888).
33. James E. Thorold Rogers, *A Manual of Political Economy: for school and colleges*, 3rd edition (Oxford: Oxford University Press, 1876).
34. John Bright and James E. Thorold Rogers, eds., *Speeches on Questions of Public Policy by Richard Cobden* (London: Macmillan, 1880); James E. Thorold Rogers, ed., *Speeches on Questions of Public Policy by John Bright* (London: Macmillan, 1883).
35. Eduard Bernstein, *Evolutionary Socialism* (New York: Schocken Books, 1961), pp. 39, 140-41.
36. Max Weber, *The Protestant Ethic and the Spirit of Capitalism* (New York: Charles Scribner's Sons, 1958), pp. 55, 277, fn. 84. See, Clyde W. Barrow, "Styles of Intellectualism in Weber's Historical Sociology." *Sociological Inquiry* 60 (February 1990): 47-61; Ashcraft, "German Historicism and the History of Political Theory," pp. 302-320.
37. Seligman, *Economic Interpretation of History*, p. 3. This is the passage cited by Beard, *Economic Interpretation of the Constitution*, p. 15. Likewise, in 1925, Barnes, *The New History and the Social Studies*, p. 18, one of Beard's colleagues at Columbia reiterates: "Without for a moment committing itself to the Feuerbach-Marxist determinism, the newer synthetic history recognizes that civilization has a fundamental economic basis, that the state of scientific knowledge and technological processes at any period determines the manner in which the economic struggle will be carried on, and that the nature of the economic process will to a very large extent decide the nature of the prevailing social relations and political institutions."
38. For example, Beard, *Contemporary American History, 1877-1913*, p. 32, paraphrases Seligman's general statement as his interpretive principle: "The student

of social and political evolution is concerned rather with the effect of such material changes upon the structure of society, that is, with the rearrangement of classes and the development of new groups of interests, which are brought about by altered methods of gaining a livelihood and accumulating fortunes. It is this social transformation that changes the relation of the individual to the state and brings new forces to play in the struggle for political power." In 1929, Beard was a conference panelist at a session devoted to "The Synthetic Principle in American History." In explaining his methodological position, Beard was still paraphrasing Seligman's general statement of the method of economic interpretation: "...all men, women, and children, all the time, must have food, clothing, and shelter, and that the ways in which they acquire these necessities have a profound, constant, and inescapable influence on all departments of their life, political, moral aesthetic, and religious. Economic development therefore furnishes one structure for grouping." Charles A. Beard quoted in "North Carolina Meeting of the American Historical Association," *American Historical Review* 35, 3 (April 1930): 485.

39. Jurgen Herbst, *The German Historical School in American Scholarship: A Study in the Transfer of Culture* (Port Washington, NY: Kennikat Press, 1972); Also see, Charles F. Thwing, *The American and German University: One Hundred Years of History* (New York: Macmillan, 1928); Also, see, Ashcraft, "German Historicism and the History of Political Theory."
40. Seligman, *Economic Interpretation of History*, p. 50.
41. Ibid., p. 58.
42. Beard, *Economic Interpretation of the Constitution*, p. vii; Charles A. Beard, "The Frontier in American History," *New Republic* (February 16, 1921): 349-50.
43. On the relation between geography, section, and economic divisions among German historians, see Harry Elmer Barnes, *A History of Historical Writing*, 2nd edition revised (New York: Dover Publications, Inc., 1963), pp. 249-55; Barnes, *The New History and the Social Studies*, Chap. 2.
44. Seligman, *Economic Interpretation of History*, p. 62. Cf. Bernstein, *Evolutionary Socialism*, p. 17.
45. Seligman, *Economic Interpretation of History*, pp. 92. 67, 63, 17. Cf. Beard, "Introduction to the 1935 Edition," *Economic Interpretation of the Constitution*, pp. xvi-xvii.
46. Cf. Barnes, *History of Historical Writing*, p. 382.
47. Beard, "The Economic Basis of Politics," p. 128.
48. Karl Marx, *A Contribution to the Critique of Political Economy* (New York: International Publishers, 1970), pp. 20-21.
49. Bernstein, *Evolutionary Socialism*, pp. 3, 17.
50. Goldman, "The Origins of Beard's *Economic Interpretation of the Constitution*," pp. 234-35; Williams, "A Note on Charles Austin Beard's Search," p. 61; Nore, *Charles A. Beard*, p. 46; Borning, *Political and Social Thought of Charles A. Beard*, p. 34.
51. For example, Achille Loria, *The Economic Foundations of Society* (London: Swan, 1899). Loria's work was well known to readers of the *Political Science Quarterly*. See Lee Benson, "Achille Loria's Influence on American Economic Thought: Including His Contributions to the Frontier Hypothesis," *Agricultural History* 24 (October 1950): 182-99.
52. Seligman, *Economic Interpretation of History*, p. 109.
53. Ibid., pp. 24, 108. Cf. Georg Lukacs, *History and Class Consciousness* (Cambridge: M. I. T. Press, 1971): "Let us assume for the sake of argument that recent

research had disproved once and for all every one of Marx's individual theses. Even if this were to be proved, every serious orthodox Marxist would still be able to accept all such modern findings without reservation and hence dismiss all of Marx's theses *in toto*—without having to renounce his orthodoxy for a single moment...orthodoxy refers exclusively to *method*" (p. 1).

54. Seligman, *Economic Interpretation of History*, pp. 53, 105.
55. Ibid., p. 106.
56. Ibid., p. 86.
57. Merriam, "Recent Advances in Political Methods," in Farr and Seidelman, eds., *Discipline and History*, pp. 130, 144.
58. Barnes, *A History of Historical Writing*, p. 303
59. Melvin M. Knight, "Introduction to the American Edition," See, *The Economic Interpretation of History*, pp. 17-18.
60. Eugene Genovese, "Beard's Economic Interpretation of History," in Marvin C. Swanson, *Charles A. Beard: An Observance of the Centennial of His Birth* (Greencastle, IN: DePauw University, 1974), p. 35.
61. Charles A. Beard and Mary R. Beard, *America in Mid-Passage* (New York: Macmillan, 1939), p. 915.
62. Beard, "The Economic Basis of Politics," p. 128. Italics added by author.
63. Beard and Beard, *America in Mid-Passage*, p. 881; Charles A. Beard, "Property and Democracy," *The Social Frontier: A Journal of Educational Criticism and Reconstruction* 1 (October 1934): 13-15.
64. Max Lerner, "Charles Beard's Political Theory" in Beale, ed., *Charles A. Beard*, pp. 36-37.
65. Williams, "A Note on Charles Austin Beard's Search," p. 62.
66. John R. Commons, *Institutional Economics: Its Place in Political Economy* (New York: Macmillan Co., 1934); Joseph Dorfman, *Institutional Economics: Veblen, Commons, and Mitchell Reconsidered* (Berkeley: University of California Press, 1963); Ross, *Origins of American Social Science*, Chap. 4.
67. Commons taught at Indiana University while Beard was an undergraduate at DePauw University. See Herring, "Charles A. Beard: Freelance Among the Historians," p. 642. Also, see, Marcell, *Progress and Pragmatism*, p. 261. For background, see Lafayette Harter, *John R. Commons: His Revolt Against Laissez-Faire* (Corvallis: Oregon State University Press, 1962); Roger Horne, "John R. Commons and the Progressive Context," *Midwest Quarterly* 32 (Spring 1991): 324-37; John Dennis Chasse, "John R. Commons and the Democratic State," in Marc R. Tool and Warren J. Samuels, ed., *State, Society, and Corporate Power*, 2nd Edition, Completely Revised (New Brunswick, NJ: Transaction Publishers, 1989), pp. 131-56.
68. R. H. Coase, "The Nature of the Firm," *Economica* 4 (1937): 390; Eirik G. Furubotn and Rudolf Richter, "The New Institutional Economics: An Assessment," in Eirik G. Furubotn and Rudolf Richter, eds., *The New Institutional Economics* (College Station: Texas A&M University Press, 1991), p. 9; Also, R. H. Coase, "The Problem of Social Cost," *Journal of Law and Economics* 3 (1960): 1-44; Brent McClintock, "Institutional Transaction Analysis," *Journal of Economic Issues* 21, 2 (June 1987): 673-681; Thrainn Eggertsson, "The Role of Transaction Costs and Property Rights in Economic Analysis," *European Economic Review* 34 (1990): 450-57.
69. Douglass C. North, "The New Institutional Economics," *Journal of Institutional and Theoretical Economics* 142 (1986): 230-37, observes that "the whole development of the new institutional economics must be not only a theory of property

rights and their evolution but a theory of the political process, a theory of the state, and of the way in which the institutional structure of the state and its individuals specify and enforce property rights" (p. 233). Thus, North concludes that even today a central "building block in the new institutional economics is a theory of the way in which political institutions evolve and the way in which the institutional structure modifies and defines the property rights structure and enforces that structure" (p. 233).

70. One notable exception is John R. Commons, *A Sociological View of Sovereignty* (New York: Augustus M. Kelley, 1965).

71. James Madison, *The Federalist Papers* (New York, New American Library Edition, 1961), p. 79.

72. Ibid., p. 79.

73. When Beard first met John R. Commons, he was working on a lengthy essay, entitled "A Sociological View of Sovereignty," that was later published in the *American Journal of Sociology* (1899/1900). Commons' thesis in the essay is that "the laws governing property and labor constitute the bulk of its [i.e., the state's] functions, and the legislatures, courts, and executives have been created expressly for, and are busied mainly with, the regulation of this important institution." The link between Madisonian political theory and institutional economics is evident when one recognizes the striking similarity between Commons' thesis and the Madisonian passages cited by Beard. See Commons, *A Sociological View of Sovereignty*, p. 85.

74. Charles A. Beard, "The Potency of Labor Education," *American Federationist* (July 1922): 500-02.

75. Beard, *Economic Interpretation of the Constitution*, p. 13.

76. Similarly, Commons, *A Sociological View of Sovereignty*, pp. 45, 49.

77. Beard, *Economic Basis of Politics*, p. 69.

78. Beard, *Politics*, p. 20, defines "the essence of the state" as "the exercise of sovereign authority by some person or group of persons."

79. Beard, *Economic Basis of Politics*, p. 36.

80. Charles A. Beard, *American Government and Politics*, 5th edition (New York: Macmillan, 1930), p. 126.

81. Madison, *The Federalist Papers*, p. 79. Beard, *Economic Interpretation of the Constitution*, pp. 14-15, also cites Madison on the following: "From the protection of different and unequal faculties of acquiring property, the possession of different degrees and kinds of property immediately results; and from the influence of these on the sentiments and views of the respective proprietors ensues a division of society into different interests and parties" (*The Federalist*, p. 78).

82. Beard, *Economic Interpretation of the Constitution*, pp. 12-13.

83. Charles A. Beard, *The Supreme Court and the Constitution* (New York: Macmillan, 1912), p. 81; Charles A. Beard and Mary R. Beard, *The Rise of American Civilization*, 2 Vols. (New York: Macmillan, 1927), Vol. 1, pp. 306-07.

84. Forrest McDonald, "The Constitution and Hamiltonian Capitalism," in Robert A. Goldwin and William A. Schambra, eds., *How Capitalistic Is the Constitution?* (Washington, DC: American Enterprise Institute, 1982), pp. 57-71, concurs with this interpretation. McDonald concludes that the Constitution "did not, in a stroke, terminate existing conditions and usher in the age of capitalism....the Constitution did make the transformation possible" (p. 57). McDonald agrees that "the establishment of the Constitution thus was a benchmark in the evolution of systems of political economy for it made possible — though not inevi-

table — the transformation from the old order to the new" (p. 50). In particular, McDonald identifies the creation of a single national market (i.e., internal free trade), the obligation of contract clause, the open-ended provisions on taxes and public debt as laying the political and legal foundations for capitalism. Hamilton's fiscal program and Marshall's judicial decisions applied and institutionalized these provisions to create and build a capitalist state.

85. Beard, "Review of *A Socialist History of France* by Jean Juares," pp. 111-12. After making this point repeatedly at an academic conference in 1929, Beard was cornered on the train home by a group of scholars who continued challenging his emphasis on economics in history. See William Appleman Williams, "Charles Austin Beard," in Harvey Goldberg, ed., *American Radicals: Some Problems and Personalities* (New York: Monthly Review, Inc., 1957), p. 297, and Beale, "Charles Beard: Historian," in Beale, ed., *Charles A. Beard*, p. 123, who both recount that with "his patience gone, his blue eyes sparkling like high-voltage electricity, and a scalpel's edge on his voice," Beard finally exploded: "I never said that economic motives explain everything! Of course, ideas are important. And so are ethical concepts. What I have always said and all I have said is that, among the various motives impelling men to action, the struggle for food, clothing, and shelter has been more important throughout history than any other. And that is true, isn't it? —*Isn't it?*"

86. Charles A. Beard, *Economic Origins of Jeffersonian Democracy* (New York: Macmillan, 1915), p. 106. H. Hale Bellot, *American History and American Historians: A Review of Recent Contributions to the Interpretation of the History of the United States* (London: Athlone Press, 1952), p. 88, recognized that Beard's investigation of the Founders' personal financial interests deflected the debate onto issues of "moral integrity" and "human motives," while "the historically more important corollary was forgotten. This corollary was that the Constitutional convention represented effectively only one of the two economic interests that were in conflict in the United States between 1783 and 1787...And that branch of the thesis was of fundamental importance." Unfortunately, scholars continue to misrepresent Beard's analysis of the Founder's property holdings in terms of personal and self-interest; for example, Cass R. Sunstein, "The Enduring Legacy of Republicanism," in Stephen L. Elkin and Karol Edward Soltan, eds., *A New Constitutionalism: Designing Political Institutions for a Good Society* (Chicago: University of Chicago Press, 1993), pp. 174-206, who notes matter of factly that "Charles Beard and others, of course, have attributed the content of the Constitution to self-interested motivations."

87. Seligman, *Economic Interpretation of History*, p. 158.

88. Beard, *Economic Interpretation of the Constitution*, p. x. On this point, Beard apparently presupposed a theory of elective affinity developed by Seligman, *Economic Interpretation of History*, pp. 98-133

3

Realistic Dialectics

In 1934, Charles Beard's presidential address to the American Historical Association (AHA) fanned a simmering controversy among historians and social scientists by embracing the philosophy of historical relativism.[1] Beard defined history as "contemporary thought about the past....an act of choice, conviction, and interpretation respecting values."[2] During the next few years, Beard attempted to clarify his philosophical assumptions with a rudimentary epistemology called realistic dialectics.[3] His excursion into dialectics provoked an intense philosophical debate among historians and social scientists, but in the 1930s Beard was already swimming against the intellectual tide. He was challenging historians' attachment to scientific history, the prevalence of moral and philosophical absolutism among academic philosophers, and a nascent fascination with behavioralism in the social sciences that only grew stronger after his death in 1948.[4]

Two Problems of Realistic Dialectics

Critics have focused on two problems in Beard's conception of realistic dialectics. First, philosophers and historians frequently argue that Beard's historical relativism is incompatible with his method of economic interpretation. To resolve the perceived dilemma, scholars have constructed an early Beard (1901-1933) and a later Beard (1934-1948), which claims that Beard abandoned the method of economic interpretation after 1933. Max Lerner introduced the idea of two Beards in a 1948 eulogy with his claim that Beard "managed to move from a theory of economic determinism all the way over to the easy and amorphous theory of 'multiple causation'."[5] In 1954, Whitaker T. Deininger advanced the same thesis in a highly influential essay which argues that Beard's historical relativism "represented a significant change in the scholar who had written an *Economic Interpretation of the Constitution of the United States* (1913)."[6] Shortly thereafter, Elias Berg published an engaging and detailed analysis of Beard's methodological statements and concludes "that economic explanations were less frequent in his later works" and that this change "was probably also due to his relativistic ideas."[7] Notably, Richard Hoftstadter weaves the "two Beards" thesis into the very fabric of his intellectual biography to explain Beard's AHA presidential address as the climax to "a long and leisurely retreat from the economic interpretation of history into historical eclecticism."[8] American intellectual historians now routinely accept Hofstadter's well-honed narrative that "in the early and middle 1930s Beard underwent an intellectual conversion from a firm adherence to the economic interpretation of history to a form of historical relativism that proved impossible to square with his earlier views."[9]

Second, it is also asserted that Beard's methodological writings disintegrate into an ambiguous and self-contradictory philosophical eclecticism beginning with his AHA presidential address. In the late 1930's, Beard's writings on historical relativism were challenged immediately with strident rejoinders by positivists and other advocates of epistemological absolutism. Berg argues that Beard was not a systematic or penetrating thinker and that his effort to articulate a realistic dialectics resulted only in a "fragmentary and very crudely and ambiguously expressed theory."[10] This view is again echoed by Richard Hofstadter who observes that most of the philosophers and historians who write about Beard's work on the problem of historical knowledge judge "it to be not only derivative but fragmentary, obscure, and sometimes contradictory."[11] Ellen Nore, Beard's biographer, even suggests that Beard was "in active resistance to all comprehensive theories of explanation" during the 1930s.[12] Similarly, Lloyd Sorenson claims in a highly influential essay that Beard's realistic dialectics is a "rather precariously constructed concept."[13]

In challenging these views, Cushing Strout suggests that Beard's philosophical thought did not take the form of an abstract philosophical system, because Beard was less concerned with the symmetry of axioms and absolutes than with constructing a particular interpretation of American history. Thus, while Beard's central philosophical assumptions often appear fragmentary and unsystematic in comparison to those of the "great thinkers," Strout suggests provocatively that Beard's work "has at least the living logic of a point of view struggling for expression and development" *through the act of writing history*.[14] Even Berg's acclaimed critical analysis of Beard's historiography agrees that his fragmentary comments on historical method still provide the necessary "elements in a coherent, although very vague, theory."[15]

This chapter identifies the sources of that vague and fragmentary logic in Beard's historical writings and suggests that the intelligibility of Beard's logic is often hidden in footnotes, discussions of secondary sources, and borrowed terminology that Beard referenced to avoid the diversions of abstract philosophy. It is important to recognize that in his own day Beard could assume a scholarly audience that was familiar with many figures—generally well-known at the time— who have fallen into relative obscurity since the end of World War II, including most notably George W. F. Hegel, Benedetto Croce, Max Scheler, and Karl Mannheim.[16] As should be evident to anyone familiar with this list of thinkers, these underpinnings locate Beard's thought within a Hegelian tradition of historical philosophy that culminated in the sociology of knowledge in the 1930s. It is Beard's "Hegelianism," and especially his selective appropriation of various Continental neo-Hegelians, that allows one to understand his realistic dialectics as a non-deterministic (i.e., non-positivist) conception of history. Ultimately, it is Beard's Hegelianism that provides the bridge between historical relativism and the economic interpretation of history. Thus, while Beard never appropriated an entire philosophical system, it is possible to reconstruct a reasonably coherent Beardian historiography in which the eclectic sources of his thinking are each anchored in the problems of post-Hegelian philosophy.[17]

Benedetto Croce: History as Subjectivity

Beard was awakened to the epistemological problems of historical social science by his reading of Benedetto Croce's *History: Its Theory and Practice* in the early 1920s.[18] Croce was an Italian philosopher and historian most noted for his reconstruction of the Hegelian system at the turn of the century. Croce's system of historical philosophy was

translated into English between 1909 and 1921 and was initially published in Great Britain.[19] The English-language version of Croce's
History was published in London in 1918; in the United States it was
published in 1921, as the fourth and final volume of Croce's philosophical system.[20] Croce's neo-Hegelian idealism had a limited impact in the United States, but his final volume on history immediately
captured the attention of American historians.[21]

In the early 1920s, the history clubs at Columbia University and the
New School for Social Research (which Beard directed at this time)
were meeting jointly to discuss current books on history and historiography. According to Roy F. Nichols, a graduate student who participated in these study circles, Croce's *History* was a focus of discussion
soon after its publication in English. Croce's writings were debated by
historians at the two institutions.[22] Beard was almost certainly exposed to Croce's work during these meetings and, according to Beard's
own account, Croce's *History: Its Theory and Practice* influenced his
thinking over the next two decades.[23] Croce's influence became so
fundamental to Beard's philosophical assumptions about history that
he invited Croce to attend the 1934 meeting of the American Historical Association to hear him deliver his controversial presidential address on historical relativism.[24]

Croce's reconstruction of Hegel seems to have influenced Beard on
three points that were each consistent with the new history and that in
fact provided Beard with an epistemological foundation for the new
history. In particular, Croce claimed that the three fundamental principles of historiography are "the conception of *development*, that of
end, and that of *value*."[25] Croce observes that *the practical act of
writing history* requires every historian to engage three basic assumptions: (1) that there is development (otherwise there is no *history* to
write); (2) that there are ends to history (otherwise we must write
everything); and (3) that there is value to history (otherwise there is
no reason to write anything).

Croce considered Hegel's dialectical logic to be his greatest contribution to philosophy because it made the concept of *historical development* a necessary component of philosophical analysis.[26] However,
Croce dismissed Hegel's reference to the end of history as a "cosmo-
logical romance" because it asserts the ability to grasp the totality of
history concretely.[27] Thus, in a manner similar to Marx before him,
Croce severed dialectical logic from Hegel's particular conception of

the end of history on the principle that Hegel's formulation of the dialectic contained a basic error.[28] Croce reconstructs the Hegelian dialectic as follows:

> The two abstract elements[thesis and antithesis], or the opposites taken in and by themselves, he calls *moments*...the word 'moment' is sometimes also applied to the third term, the synthesis. The relation of the first two to the third is expressed by the world 'solution' or 'overcoming' (*Aufheben*). And that, as Hegel intimates, means that the two moments in the separation are both negated, but preserved in the synthesis...[Thus] to speak accurately, in the dialectic triad we do not think *three* concepts, but *one* single concept, which is the concrete universal.[29]

Croce criticizes Hegel's version of the dialectic for confusing the logical doctrine of distincts with the doctrine of opposites. The difference is that distincts emanate from *within* a common original source (i.e., a thesis), whereas opposites *must be opposites*. Thus, Hegel's dialectical "solution" or "overcoming" of opposites must postulate an *a priori* synthesis, i.e., the postulate of a transcendent Spirit culminating in the Absolute Idea; whereas the doctrine of distincts requires no such transcendence, but only immanence. Hence, by substituting the doctrine of distincts for the doctrine of opposites, Croce was able to jettison Hegel's transcendent Spirit and replace it with the immanence of individual subjectivity (i.e., spirit with a small "s").[30] In place of a single World History determined by destiny to realize the Absolute Idea as its final synthesis, one is left with multiple histories organized around competing subjective ideas (i.e., theses). In this manner, Croce claimed to have expunged the "theological residue at the bottom of Hegel's historiography" and, hence, he dismissed any suggestion that spirit can have meaning or existence outside of *individual subjectivity* and consciousness.[31] As a result, a final transcendent and synthetic history is rendered impossible, because history always remains an open-ended, incomplete, and partial construction conceptualized in the form of competing *theses*.

However, Croce's subjectivization of spirit implies that "all the characteristics of History can be reduced to the definition and identification of History with the individual judgment."[32] History does not unfold before a contemporary observer since the ends of history are never given in the objective development of history itself. For history to exist, it must be recorded and this entails its selection, arrangement, and construction through the concepts, criteria, and values of living contemporary individuals.[33] Significantly, Croce argues on the basis of his subjectivistic perspective that there is potentially an infinite number of facts that one might select for consideration in writing history and thus he concludes that "all learned men...in fact, *select*, and all are advised to *select*."[34] It would not be possible to write history if we tried to write everything either simultaneously (Being) or chronologically (being).

From a practical perspective, the problem of "the end of history" is nothing more than the attempt to identify some criterion on which to base the selection of facts *a priori* (i.e., the individual choice of how to begin or end a history). Yet, in Croce's view, the existence of a rational selection criteria presupposes the impossible; namely, that we already know all the potential facts and are, therefore, in a position to make that selection on other than arbitrary grounds. Because the rationality of selection presupposes an impossible knowledge of totality, Croce insists that "no logical criterion can be named that shall determine what news or what documents are or are not useful and important...*The criterion is the choice itself*, conditioned...by the practical and scientific needs of a definite moment or epoch." Croce intimates that the process of selecting and ordering facts into narratives "may quite well make use of apparent logical distinctions...but in the final analysis the decision is always given from practical motives."[35] Therefore, Croce concludes that Universal History as conceptualized by Hegel is impossible in principle. When a "Universal History" is written it is merely an *interested claim* resulting from "the strange proposal of closing the infinite progression" of history. Croce was convinced that even a simple glance at any one of the universal histories would prove that they are really "'particular histories'—that is to say, they are due to a particular interest centered in a particular problem, and comprehend only those facts that form part of that interest and afford an answer to that particular problem."[36]

The meaning (end) of historical development is always defined by its relation to contemporary *values* since only "an interest in the life of the present can move one to investigate past fact."[37] A decision to conduct research and to write history is always motivated by an individual interest in some contemporary problem. Thus, the act of writing history establishes a polemical relationship to the present as an attempt to influence contemporary events by assigning the past some particular historical meaning, purpose, or direction that has value for the present and future. The value of history resides in the paradox that it can be written only by choosing to assume a knowledge of the totality (i.e., an end) that is impossible to possess in fact. Consequently, Croce points out that every historian "possesses in a more or less reflective way his theory of history, because...every historian implicitly or explicitly conducts a polemic against other historians (against other 'versions' and 'judgment' of a fact), and how could he ever conduct a polemic or criticize others if he did not himself possess a *conception* of what history is and ought to be, to which to refer, a *theory* of history?"[38]

While Croce dismisses the idea of Universal History in his critique of Hegel, he does not dismiss the idea of General History. Croce notes that the antithesis of Universal History is the positivistic or scientific emphasis on specialized or particular histories "which expose the various orders of facts one after the other as so many...compartments or little boxes, containing political history, industrial and commercial history, history of customs, religious history, history of literature and of art, and so on, under so many separate headings." According to Croce, the chief failure of a purely scientific or empirical approach to history is "presenting these [particular] histories as without relation between one another, not dialecticized, but aggregated." As a result, Croce concludes "that *history* remains to be written after the writing of those histories in this disjointed manner." Indeed, to the extent that one attempts to conceptualize the ends of history consciously, Croce argues that "*nothing exists but general history*," for "when the relation is not broken and history is thought in the concrete, it is seen that to think one aspect is to think all the others at the same time," (i.e., to think their interrelation).[39]

This critical insight led Croce to collapse the categories of philosophical speculation into the practice of history. Indeed, Croce claims that one of the most important implications of his subjective idealism is that "there is neither philosophy nor history, nor philosophy of history, but history which is philosophy and philosophy which is history."[40] Insofar as philosophy is concerned with the categories of knowledge (logic and epistemology), judgment (ethics), and being (ontology), Croce insists that history engulfs philosophy *at a practical level*, because "historiography has for content the concrete life of the spirit."[41] In writing history, we come to know (i.e., epistemology) those portions of the past (i.e., being) that are meaningful to the present (i.e., judgment). In this sense, Croce argues that philosophy "cannot of necessity be anything but the *methodological moment of historiography*: a dilucidation of the categories constitutive of historical judgments, or of the concepts that direct historical interpretation."[42] Consequently, Croce insists that philosophy "is neither beyond, nor at the beginning, nor at the end of history, nor is it achieved in a moment or in any single moments of history. It is achieved *at every moment* and is always completely united to facts and conditions and conditioned by historical knowledge."[43]

On this final point, Croce's arguments clearly anticipate the sociology of knowledge. In fact, Croce was concerned that his idealist position had so historicized the concept of spirit that he cautioned readers not to confuse his position with another approach "similar in appearance."[44] Croce identified the recent development of "social historiography" as an attempt to record "the history of the human soul [i.e., spirit] in its practical aspect; either when it produces general histories of *civilization* (always due to particular motives and limited by them), or when it presents histories *of classes, peoples, social currents, sentiments, institutions*, and so forth."[45] Croce distinguished this approach to spirit as one which assumes "that true history consists of the history of societies, institutions, and human values," rather than the subjective spirit of individuals.[46] Therefore, Croce was critical of this new approach because it assumes that "the *a priori* synthesis, which is the reality of the individual judgment...is also the reality of philosophy and history."[47] In contrast, Croce insisted on the idea of spirit as individual subjectivity and, therefore, he ultimately reduces the categories of written history to an extension of personal belief and commitment.[48]

Croce and Beard

Beard's admiration of Croce did not lead to him to accept Croce's entire philosophical system. Instead, Beard appropriated Croce's key philosophical concepts only to the extent that they were consistent with the new history.[49] Like Croce, Beard defined written history as "contemporary thought about the past."[50] However, in contrast to Croce's subjective idealism, Beard drew an ontological distinction between history-as-actuality (reality), history-as-record (knowable reality), and history-as-thought (written history). Beard postulates history-as-actuality as an objective but unknowable totality which in-cludes "all that has been felt, thought, imagined, said, and done by human beings since the beginning of mankind's operations on this planet."[51] History-as-record is equally objective with respect to its tangible existence, but it is far more limited in scope because it in-cludes only those documents, memorials, autobiographies, eye wit-ness accounts, artifacts and other forms of empirical evidence which provide a basis for written history. Written-history is always a frag-mentary narration of history-as-actuality limited in its objectivity by history-as-record and by the finite mental capacities of the individual historian.[52] Thus, Beard challenges the metaphysical historians (e.g., Hegel) and the scientific historians (e.g., Ranke) by opening a wide chasm between history-as-actuality and written history.[53]

Beard noted that Universal History in the tradition of Hegel has always sought to "array the fullness of history as actuality" into a closed system providing a final cause or meaning to human events. Beard concludes that no historian has ever achieved this goal, al-though he acknowledges that Karl Marx came closer than any other person in achieving the ideal of Universal History.[54] At the same time, Beard was aware that both the Marxist and Hegelian approach to American history had been generally rejected by professional histori-ans in favor of so-called scientific history.[55] Social scientists were abandoning historical approaches to sociology, economics, and poli-tics in favor of behavioral and positivistic approaches borrowed from the physical sciences.[56] Significantly, an important element of this transition in each discipline was the willingness to jettison the concept of historical or social totality as speculative metaphysics.[57]

However, without a concept of history-as-actuality, all that is left are the competing antinomies of empirical-positivist and subjectivist philosophy.[58] The scholar is left to assert either that reality is a mere chaos of "facts" or a mere chaos of "opinion." In contrast, Beard looked for a new ground that was neither empiricist nor subjectivist by proposing a philosophical critique of history and social science anchored in a simple or common sense realism. The starting point for this common sense realism is the proposition that every statement by a historian or social scientist "asserts facts or opinions or both."[59] Beard defined a historical fact as a statement that can be verified by historical records such as: "Columbus landed on the island of Hispanola in 1492." It is common sense to acknowledge that history-as-record is always incomplete when measured against the totality of history-as-actuality. Thus, it is impossible to fully verify any historical interpretation within the "scientific" constructs of positivism, but this does not mean that history and interpretation are reduced to subjective opinion as with Croce. History-as-record still provides a real objective basis (limited as it may be) for verifying and falsifying many important historical facts that are accumulated over time as historical knowledge.[60]

For instance, different persons might give the island of Hispanola a different name (e.g., the natives), while the Chinese and Hebrew calendars might assign a different date to the event of Columbus' discovery of the island. The objective reality of the event is not in dispute and it is the reality of the event that allows one to translate names from one language to another and translate dates from one calendar to another. The very possibility of these translations depends on the objective reference provided by the record, and even where disputes about facts exist, disagreements can often be arbitrated by an appeal to history-as-record. Hence, Beard concludes that "vast bodies of social facts are well established and systematically organized and are as 'true' for human purposes as the truths of physics."[61] Beard was confident that "facts, multitudinous and beyond calculation, are known" and they are accepted as facts by reasonable persons conversant with history-as-record.[62] However, amidst an ever-growing multitude of social and historical facts, not to mention the virtual infinity of potential facts to be discovered in history-as-actuality, Beard concedes that our knowledge, both individual and social, is always "limited to fragments—important fragments, no doubt—of the whole number of personalities and occurrences" that make up history-as-actuality.[63]

Consequently, Beard took it for granted that no one would ever really "gather the fruits of their researches into one mighty synthesis, to construct a scheme of ideas proportionately and artistically mirroring the total reality which they are seeking to describe." Yet, Beard insisted simultaneously that any scholar who would "rise above the barest [fact-collecting] routine must take thought of that responsibility."[64] The mere banality that no historian will ever succeed at writing an absolutely true Universal History does not mean that historians or social scientists can proceed intellectually without a conception of totality. Quite simply, our shared experience as historians and social scientists suggests that whenever "we consider the intrinsic nature of the various realities included under the head of social science...or their place in the unfolding of history, we are in the presence of universality far beyond our grasp." For example, any historian or social scientist who decides to conduct a specialized factual study is always aware that they "strike into a seamless web too large for any human eye." Our awareness of history-as-actuality is *in the things not studied or the facts not known*, which inevitably lead every scholar back toward "dim and fragmentary pictures of the whole."[65]

For instance, Beard notes that anyone—scholar or layman— who has ever thought about history always proceeds by arranging "events in neat little chains of causation which explain, to their satisfaction, why succeeding events happened."[66] Yet, in the practical act of arranging these facts every historian, (indeed every person), identifies certain events as more important than other events or selects specific factors as more important than other factors in constructing an explanation of events or in understanding their meaning for the present. Thus, in the practical act of conceptualizing and writing particular histories, every historian encounters phenomenologically the existence of a totality (i.e., history-as-actuality) as a limitation on what is known. In other words, until an individual historian or social scientist makes a conscious choice to stop their inquiry at some point in time, or to limit their study to a specialized topic, that individual will encounter ever receding times and circumstances that establish an insurmountable ontological barrier to their ability to succeed at Universal History or positive social science. Unable to actually grasp this ontological totality, and despite the experience and awareness of history-as-actuality, it becomes necessary to adopt some *conception* of totality in order to write history. It is this *a priori* conception of totality that provides a basis for arranging personalities, selecting events, and gathering data into a narrative and which makes any narrative meaningful (or meaningless) with respect to the present. This conception of totality also defines an author's "interest" in writing history.

Similarly, in the social sciences, Beard observes that when social scientists seek to establish some area of behavioral uniformity, i.e., a covering law to explain events or institutions: "...these so-called areas of uniformity impinge upon other areas which condition, if they do not determine, the uniformities in question." For example, political scientists often rely on economic interests to explain political behavior. Economists often make assertions about human nature and psychological motivation to explain economic behavior, while psychologists may then turn to biology or sociology to explain the origins of motivational patterns. The experience of every historian and social scientist confirms that history-as-actuality presents no sharp analytic divisions (e.g., disciplines) and no clear beginnings or endings. Quite the contrary, Beard argues that "in its total context all human affairs are enclosed in a mesh so tight that the eye can discover no broken parts or gaps" within the continuum of historical and social being. Beard claims that *"in all of this there seems to be something real,* which comports with knowledge, which is subject to verification and approval by the consensus of experience." Consequently, Beard makes the phenomenological claim that all historians and social scientists must ultimately locate their particular phenomena "in the totality of history in time unfolding."[67]

The point of encounter with totality is the preliminary assumptions and conceptual ordering of the facts that occurs *in the process of thinking and writing history.* For example, Beard suggests that historians and social scientists may agree upon many "facts" about a particular event or phenomena such as that a man named Christopher Columbus really existed, that he set sail from Spain in 1492, etc. Yet, the facts considered relevant to explaining that event, not to mention its subsequent effect or implications for the present, "do not select themselves or force themselves automatically into any fixed scheme of arrangement."[68] In conducting research or in presenting the results of that research, one fact never automatically (or causally) leads to another fact. Instead, Beard concludes it is only "by resort to the idea of relationships" that knowledge advances, because ordering relationships provide heuristic direction in the search for new facts. Furthermore, it is only by defining relationships between facts, events, and persons that those phenomena take on meaning for persons in the present. Consequently, Beard concludes that "the nature and forms of human occurrences are constantly 'explained' or given meaning in terms of these relationships" and, for that reason, "a written history of a country or an age is a statement of relationships," rather than a mere collection of facts and "its 'meaning' whatever the purpose of the writer, springs from this fact."[69]

Hence, Beard points out that all historical narratives must proceed "upon some assumption or assumptions respecting the nature of things or upon the assumption that no assumption has been made." Beard insists that "unless some things are taken for granted, assumed, and some common principles accepted, discussion cannot proceed at all."[70] However, as a historian and a realist, Beard did not see any point in pursuing such arguments *at a philosophical level*. To do so, as Beard knew from his reading of Croce, inexorably took one down the path of epistemological subjectivism. While Beard adopted many of Croce's philosophical arguments that were consistent with the new history, he was never prepared to embrace the unlimited relativism entailed by Croce's subjective idealism.[71]

Between Marx and Croce

A central theme in Croce's subjectivist critique of Hegel was that Hegel failed to escape the paradox of dualism. Although Hegel explained political development as the self-actualizing Spirit thinking itself, Hegel acknowledges that the "idea of Spirit, is something merely general and abstract...which *as such*—however true in itself—is not completely real." As a result, Hegel's system always required a *second* substance to bring the idea of Spirit into Existence (i.e., reality) and he identified this second substance as "the Will—the activity of man in the widest sense." In contrast to Hegel's *Logic* or the *Phenomenology of Spirit*, this dualism is at the core of his *Philosophy of History*. In the former works, Hegel is delucidating categories of mind from within itself and following the phenomenology of abstract Spirit thinking itself through those categories. However, in the *Philosophy of History*, Hegel acknowledges that it is only through Will that "the Idea, as well as abstract characteristics generally, are realized and actualized, for of themselves they are powerless." Indeed, in passages that sound more like Marx's *German Ideology*, Hegel claims that "the motive power that puts them [i.e. ideas] in operation, and gives them determinate existence, is the need, instinct, inclination, and passion of man" (i.e., interests). Hence, according to Hegel, ideas and interests interact as "the warp and the woof of Universal History," although Hegel identifies passions and interests as "the sole springs of action" in history. The paradox of Hegel's dualism, as both Marx and Croce understood, was that Spirit depended on the passions and material interests to give it existence, concreteness, and motion in history. Hegel was aware of this dilemma, because he attempts to resolve the paradox with his famous appeal to "the cunning of reason," i.e., that the Idea somehow "sets the passions to work for itself" behind the scenes of visible history.[72]

Marx emphasized that his materialist dialectic was the "direct opposite" of Hegel's, because it regards ideas as "nothing else than the material world reflected by the human mind, and translated into forms of thought."[73] In contrast to Croce, Beard was predisposed to resolve Hegel's dualism in favor of the material factors of history and, in fact, Beard was fond of quoting Marx's and Engels' *The Holy Family* to emphasize that "the 'idea has always made itself ridiculous in so far as it has been detached from 'interest'."[74] Thus, Beard rejected Croce's subjective idealism as a solution to Hegel's dualism and, partly for this reason, Beard reread Marx in the 1930s.[75] At the same time, however, Beard was simultaneously distancing himself from Marx*ists* by criticizing "those who still cling to mechanistic determinism, whether theological or materialistic."[76] Beard consistently rejected attempts to label his philosophical position as "Marxist" or "dialectical materialist," because materialism had mechanistic connotations that Beard associated with positivism.[77] Thus, in describing his own work as a *realistic* interpretation of history, Beard was grasping for an approach that could occupy the philosophical ground *between* dialectical materialism (i.e., Marx) and dialectical idealism (i.e., Hegel, Croce).[78] From this point of view, Beard concludes that:

> ...an ideal written history would present certain conditioning realities and forces in their long perspective. It would give the physiographic setting of the several nations—sea, river, plain, mountain and valley—rich or poor in natural resources, harsh or mild in climate. On this would be built the great framework of interests in church, state, class, regions, community, and economy, and the clashes of interest arising in the course of time. Running parallel with the movement of interests would be the movement of ideas, always within their realistic setting....To be brief, an ideal written history would portray the drama enacted by the human spirit within the conditioning, but not absolutely determining, framework of the material world.[79]

Beard argues that the dialectical element of his realist interpretation is that historical development is organized "as a stormy unfolding of ideas and interests, in conflict and tension, presenting antitheses in thought and experience, and yet enclosed in a larger unity."[80] Beard emphasizes that "under this conception [of realistic dialectics], history is viewed as an assertion of ideas and interests, antagonism to ideas and interests thus asserted, and resolution of the conflict by victory and adjustment. Hence the formula: thesis, antithesis, and synthesis."[81]

The identification of social conflict (thesis-antithesis) as the motor of historical development was merely common sense to Beard and, in a similar manner, he demystified the concepts of dialectical "transcendence" and "synthesis" by placing them on a historical foundation. Beard historicized the concepts of transcendence and synthesis by suggesting matter of factly that "the victory of a class, an interest, or a nation over another seldom, if ever, makes a *tabula rasa*," because such a victory never "completely extinguishes the ideas and interests of the vanquished." Thus, as a general rule, Beard suggests that the result of historical conflict is always that:

> ...some compromises are reached, either in fundamentals or details, even though one set of ideas and interests wears the label of triumph. A part of the past survives the defeat and is incorporated in the new. This adjustment, compromise, or merging of survivals with victories is in substance neither the one nor the other of the conflicting sets of ideas and interests. It is in some measure a reconciliation of contradictions, a synthesis embracing both.[82]

Thus, from a purely historical perspective, Beard argues for "recognizing as real the existence of identicals and opposites in relationships." Beard suggests that in writing history "we seem driven to accept 'the interpenetration of opposites'" and "to represent this interpenetration, some covering conception thus becomes necessary." This covering conception is always "a kind of synthesis of the two which treats them as things related, not as independent particulars."[83]

As a starting point for historicizing the dialectic, Beard calls attention to the passages on America in Hegel's *Philosophy of History* which he cites as a "beautiful example" of the philosopher "pretending to expound the inner secret of history."[84] To reconstruct Beard's intentions against this Hegelian background, it is necessary to remember that Hegel considered the State "the perfect embodiment of Spirit." Importantly, Hegel historicized this abstract claim by identifying "the definite *substance* that receives the form of universality" in the State with "the Spirit of the People....which erects itself into an objective world." However, because the State is an *abstraction* in Hegel's idealist system, Hegel concludes that "it is only by a Constitution that the *abstraction*—the State—attains life and reality" in historical time.[85] Constitutions concretize the idea of the State as a real historical embodiment of the spirit of the people.

Significantly, Hegel argued that America did not have a "real" state to fully embody and actualize the spirit of its people and, therefore, at the time he wrote, the United States had existed outside the dialectic of historical time. For this reason, Hegel pointed to America as "the land of the future, where, in the ages that lie before us, the burden of the World's History shall reveal itself."[86] Beard evidently took this idea seriously, as did his dissertation advisor John W. Burgess, because it implies that the adoption of the U.S. Constitution and the subsequent process of state-building in America is a continuation of the Hegelian dialectic, i.e., the Idea attaining full self-consciousness of itself as Freedom through the Spirit of the People.[87] Therefore, it was always implicit in Hegel's philosophy that the Prussian State could not be the end of history, because the construction of an American state was the continuation of World History. In this context, Beard concludes that the meaning and end of history "whatever it may be, will come out of the movement and conflict of ideas and interests in the United States."[88]

Max Scheler and the Frames of Reference

While Beard accepted Croce's argument that historians must adopt some conception of development as an organizing thesis, he did not embrace the subjectivistic claim that a potentially infinite number of interpretive frameworks are available to individuals. If Croce's radical subjectivism was *historically correct*, then the extant histories of a given period ought to manifest a bewildering chaos of interpretive frameworks, each one peculiar to the individual historian. As a matter of fact, Beard knew that there was never an unlimited number of interpretive frameworks and, therefore, philosophical subjectivism could always be challenged historically simply by identifying the possible and extant frames of reference. Thus, instead of pursuing further philosophical speculations, Beard turned to his own knowledge of history and to the German sociologists of knowledge, in particular, for a historical account of the ordering frameworks that structure historical and social scientific writing.

Beard started referring to "frames of reference" and "schemes of reference" in the early 1930s as part of an effort to identify their logical form and substantive content in contrast to Croce's endemic philosophical vagueness. Most intellectual historians attribute the source of this concept to Croce, but the idea, as such, never appears in any of Croce's writings.[89] Rather, it is Max Scheler who was the first social

scientist to specifically introduce the concept of "schemes of reference" in his *Mensch und Geschichte*; a fact suggesting that Scheler's
influence on Beard has been underestimated, if not ignored completely.[90]

Beard did not use the concept exactly as Scheler formulated it, for
as with Croce, there is no evidence that Beard was the least bit familiar with any of Scheler's work beyond this single essay. Moreover,
Beard often confused the meaning of the term by applying it freely to
different ideas derived from many different sources. Not surprisingly,
Beard's sloppiness, as well as his distaste for fully developing even
his own theoretical arguments, has led to charges that he was confused
and uncertain as to what he really meant by "frames of reference."
This criticism may be partly true, but Beard's specific usages of the
term do achieve a certain coherence with the hypothesis that he was
attempting to conceptualize concrete frames of reference as structural
matrices consisting of three hierarchically ordered layers of ideas consistent with Croce's three fundamental principles: (1) ontological assumptions about totality (i.e., development); (2) the philosophy of
history (i.e., ends); and (3) ideology (i.e., values).

First, Beard claimed that individual subjectivity was limited
ontologically to the extent that "only three broad conceptions of all
history as actuality are [logically] possible."[91] This claim is evidently
not derived from any single source and Beard seems to have relied on
his own expansive knowledge of Universal History for practical guidance in specifying the three possibilities. One possible ontological
assumption is that history as actuality is chaos and that "every attempt
to interpret it otherwise is an illusion."[92] For Beard, the chief contemporary exemplar of this ontological assumption was Leopold von Ranke,
the originator of scientific history, who accepted the empiricist claim
that reality is a swirl of discreet and isolated "facts" to be documented
objectively by reference to archival records.[93] On this assumption,
history is "anecdotally selected and episodically expounded" and, therefore, the Rankeans tended to select great events and figures (i.e., good
stories) as the focus of their histories.[94]

A second possible assumption "is that history as actuality is part of
some order of nature and revolves in cycles eternally."[95] Beard cited
numerous exemplars of cyclical history such as the biological meta-
phors of growth and decay used by Brooks Adams and Oswald
Spengler; the physics-derived action-reaction scheme of Arnold

Toynbee; or the classical Greeks who viewed history as a recurring cycle of monarchy, aristocracy, democracy, and tyranny.[96] A third possible assumption is that "history moves in a line, straight or spiral, and in some direction."[97] Needless to say, if one accepts the latter assumption, then one must answer the question: in what kind of line and in what direction? As Beard noted, this ontological assumption is usually linked to a specific idea of progress which sees history as moving from "the low level of primitive beginnings, on an upward gradient toward a more ideal order."[98] Beard cited figures as diverse as Condorcet, Adam Smith, Karl Marx, and Herbert Spencer as exemplars of progressive history.

The three logical possibilities are that history is chaotic and has no direction, that history continually repeats itself, or that history moves in some direction toward an end.[99] Beard recognized that ontological assumptions about totality are usually woven into the structure of a narrative so tightly that most historians are unaware of their existence and would even deny that they have any preconceptions. Furthermore, a particular ontological assumption does not necessarily imply a specific content (i.e., end) to the philosophy of history. It is logically conceivable that historians can articulate more than one idea of progress, or identify different types of cycles, compatible with the formal ontological assumption.

Yet, here again, in contrast to Croce's subjectivist claims, Beard argues that the *actually existing* frames of reference "have been reduced to a small number, each enclosing turns or nuances of its own."[100] In particular, Beard cites Scheler's essay, *Mensch und Geschichte* (1929), "for having ingeniously classified historical frames of reference for the ordering of 'facts' in Western history."[101] On at least two occasions, Beard engaged in lengthy discussions of Scheler's *Mensch und Geschichte* to exemplify the concrete frames of reference utilized in extant philosophies of history.[102] Scheler concluded after thorough research that he could identify only five fundamental ideas in Western civilization that are each accompanied by a special conception of history.[103] These philosophies of history each link a conception of totality (i.e., development) to a particular conception of human nature (i.e., end or purpose).[104] Scheler labeled these five schemes of reference the idea of the Superman, the idea of devolution, the Judeo-Christian idea, the idea of *homo sapiens*, and the idea of *homo faber*.

As a purely historical observation, Scheler suggests that the metaphysics of chaos has been linked exclusively to the philosophy of the "great man" in history. Where there is nothing but chaos, history assumes order and meaning (i.e., totality) solely as a consequence of great individuals who bring order out of chaos. The metaphysics of chaos suggests a history that can only be measured "by the shining figure of superman, responsible and glad to assume responsibility...the culmination of being itself." Scheler surmises that because the metaphysics of chaos denies the existence of any preexisting structure, "collective forces in history are not simply denied...they are always reduced again to *personal causality*."[105]

By the same token, the ontology of cycles has usually been linked to the idea of devolution. Scheler was well-versed in Oriental philosophies and he recognized that cyclical conceptions of history inject a sharply discordant note into modern Occidental thinking, which is largely based in one or another version of linear history. A cyclical conception of history often challenges the underlying optimism of Western philosophy, because the main assumption of most cyclical histories is "the necessary *decadence* of man...a decadence which it considers inherent in the very nature and origin of man." For the most part, Western conceptions of cycle have been "structurally identical with the normal stages of aging and death. The life force is progressively overcome by the inner law of the process which the organism has released while aging." Thus, while "different cultures may accomplish this process at different times," the term of "humanity as a whole is set in the not too distant future."[106]

In direct contrast to philosophies of history based on chaos and devolution, Scheler identified three philosophies of history that rely on a concept of linear development or progress. In Western civilization, the first and oldest philosophy of history is the Judeo-Christian scheme of reference which interprets history as a theodicy of salvation. Scheler certainly recognized that there were many variations on this theme, largely denominational in nature, but each of them shares the characteristic that the human race will achieve salvation "through the God-man with his dual nature who thus reestablished the condition of men as children of God."[107]

A second linear philosophy of history is based on the idea of *homo sapiens*. The main anthropological assumption of this scheme of reference is that human nature is stable and eternal because it is constituted by "a *specific agent*, which pertains only to it, reason." Scheler emphasized "that almost all specifically philosophical anthropology from Aristotle to Kant and Hegel...has not significantly changed" in two thousand years with respect to this assumption. When linked to the ontology of linear development, the idea of *homo sapiens* suggests that history is the self realization of man's nature as a rational being.[108]

Finally, a third philosophy of linear history is derived from the idea of *homo faber*, i.e., man as a builder or tool-making animal. This approach assumes that "man is not primarily a rational being...but a *'creature of drives'*" and therefore no more than a "highly evolved creature."[109] Scheler identified three innate human drives: hunger, which is the basis of economic activities; power, which is the basis of political activities; and sex, which is the basis of marriage and kinship.[110] Scheler identifies three philosophies of *homo faber* that "depend upon which of the three above mentioned types of drives is accorded the major role."[111] An economic interpretation of history accords priority to the "fight for feeding place...the *drive for nourishment*." While this view of history is associated with Marx, it is equally evident in the works of Adam Smith and Herbert Spencer. The political interpretation of history, illustrated by Hobbes and Machiavelli, "examines the outcome of the struggle for political (thus not economic) power, i.e., the struggle between states for supremacy and those of classes and groups within the states." The last interpretation of *homo faber*, exemplified by Schopenhauer and Gumplowicz, is derived from Scheler's claim that the sex drive manifests itself conceptually in theories of blood line and race. Thus, this racial interpretation of history "finds the significant variable of all development in the *mixing and purifying of blood*, as well as in the cycles of reproduction and procreation." [112]

Aside from the fact that Beard constantly refers back to these schemes of reference in his discussions of realistic dialectics, Scheler's allusion to "faith" in a totalizing concept of meaning and human nature is also significant to understanding Beard's historical method. Scheler points out that even though the five philosophies of historical progress unfold very different pictures of humanity's past and future, they all have one characteristic in common:

> ...the belief, more or less pronounced, that *history forms a great unity*, and the more or less pronounced faith in a meaningful evolution, an inescapable movement of history toward *one* great and noble objective. They have a common,

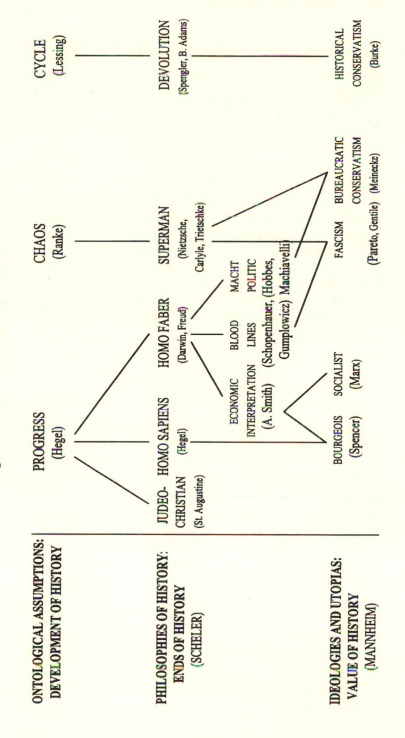

FIGURE 3.1
Logical Structure of the Frames of Reference

powerful faith in some kind of evolution of human values, of man himself, even though they emphasize different aspects and values.[113]

Croce never explicitly uses the term "faith," but Beard's single most important essay on historical relativism is entitled, "Written History as an Act of Faith." Meiland has characterized the essay as "at once the strongest, most fully developed and detailed" exposition of Beard's philosophical assumptions and yet it is also considered the "most perplexing statement of his position."[114] When Beard's essay is read in the context of Scheler's *Man and History*, Beard's fundamental claims are more intelligible. First, Beard argues that in the process of writing history, the historian "performs an act of faith, as to order and movement, for certainty as to order and movement is denied to him by knowledge of the actuality with which he is concerned."[115] Second, it is the fact that every historian must adopt a philosophical scheme of reference that gives meaning to Beard's assertion that "by taking for its data all that has been done and said on this earth since time began, history furnishes substance for philosophy and, in assuming an ordered form and progression, history becomes a philosophy."[116]

Kark Mannheim: From the Philosophy of
History to the Sociology of Knowledge

A scheme of reference also assigns *value* to historical events and persons by establishing "a more or less definite pattern of things deemed *necessary*, things deemed *possible*, and things deemed *desirable*."[117] Thus, every philosophy of history contains implications that are ideological (necessary) or utopian (desireable) in relation to specifiable historical interests. Intellectual historians have been strangely puzzled by this statement, but it is a simple fact that Beard consistently specifies the meaning of this claim by references to Karl Mannheim's *Ideology and Utopia*. Indeed, as Nash observed more than thirty years ago: "...even a casual perusal of Beard's writings on historiography will reveal the impact Mannheim's sociology of knowledge had on him."[118]

Beard recognized that the word "ideology" already had numerous usages by the 1930s, but he followed Mannheim in suggesting that its sociological usage applies to a style of thinking "more or less consciously conceived, which presents reasons for believing that a particular country, community, or class possesses inherent virtues, should be respected by other countries, communities, and classes, and should not be disturbed in its privileges, claims, and contentions."[119] An ideology represents these claims as "necessary" by virtue of God's will, Natural Law, biology, or on the basis of some other ontological assertion that confers transcendent status on these claims. Hence, ontological assumptions and a philosophy of history are integral components of any ideology.

On the other hand, the word utopia suggests a style of thinking that contrasts "the world as it appears to be...with some ideal scheme." Thus, utopias always pass judgment on what ought to be and attempt to visualize this ideal order.[120] Once again, ontological assumptions and a philosophy of history help to establish utopias as desirable, possible, or necessary. Importantly, as with the relation between ontological assumptions and philosophies of history, no philosophy of history logically implies a particular ideology or utopia. For instance, even though it is widely associated with Marxism and socialism, an economic interpretation of history also underpins the conception of historical development elaborated by Adam Smith and William Graham Sumner, i.e., ideologies that are diametrically opposed to socialism. Conversely, it is conceivable that the same ideology or utopia might rely on different ontological assumptions or philosophies of history, e.g., Christian socialism vs. Marxian socialism. Nevertheless, and again in contrast to Croce's subjectivism, Beard accepted Mannheim's assessment that contemporary European styles of thinking could be classified under five headings: (1) bureaucratic conservatism (Ranke, Meinecke); (2) historical conservatism (Burke); (3) bourgeois (Locke); (4) socialist (Marx); and (5) fascist (Pareto, Gentile). Even though these styles of thinking were not duplicated in the United States exactly, Beard was convinced that parallel "variants appear in American intellectual life and affect thinking about the 'facts' of American society."[121]

This historical encyclopedia of schemes of reference is important to Beard's historiographic method, because it establishes that Beard does not endorse the unlimited relativism advanced by Croce or indeed by contemporary postmodernists. In fact, as a response to this charge, Beard emphasizes that:

> ...the skepticism of historical relativity which some historians have drawn from the recognition of subjective operations in all historical constructions [i.e., Croce] is checked by the recognition of the fact that there are not available as

many distinct schemes of reference as there are historians. Although the number is not yet positively determined, inquiries into those actually employed in past historical writings...indicate that both the number and character of the frames of reference are knowable.[122]

Beard contributed to the confusion about his realistic dialectics by characterizing it as a "limited relativity."[123] Scheler and Mannheim would not have accepted this designation and thus it obfuscates the fact that Beard did not embrace relativism at all, but instead embraced the principle of *relationism* articulated in Karl Mannheim's *Ideology and Utopia*.[124] The relationist (as opposed to a relativist) epistemological position is that:

Even though what it means for a proposition to be true is a result of human conventions, and even though these conventions could have been otherwise than they are, and even though they contain ideological components, it does not follow that this proposition cannot be objectively true in an important sense. Thus, men decide what it means to say that 'it is raining outside', but men do not decide, *given this meaning*, whether this proposition is true, i.e., they do not decide whether it is raining—for *that* they have to look and see.[125]

On this point, Beard seems to have understood Mannheim substantively, since in describing the implications of a "limited relativity," Beard points out that "given any scheme of reference chosen, whether liberal, fascist, or Marxian, there may be scrupulous and critical use of sources and facts and, so far, a degree of scientific exactness." The factual claims of any scheme of reference, as well as their projections of the future, are "open to practical testing in the movement of history as time unfolds."[126] Unlike subjectivism and relativism, relationism does not reduce history and social science to individual opinion, myth, or metaphor.

In this respect, Maurice Mandelbaum's influential critique of historical relativism, and his critique of Beard in particular, simply misunderstands the explanatory claims of the sociology of knowledge.[127] Mandelbaum published the first systematic attack on historical relativism in large part as a reaction to Beard's presidential address to the American Historical Association. Thus, not coincidentally, Mandelbaum's rejoinder was directed specifically at Croce, Beard, Scheler, and Mannheim. However, Mandelbaum's critique depends fundamentally on his misleading tendency to impute to Beard, Scheler, and Mannheim, subjectivist positions that are attributable only to Croce. In contrast to relativism, Beard's relationism argues only that the social and political *meanings* of the schemes of reference are determined by their objective *relation* to contending groups and classes in society and history. The basic assumptions of a scheme of reference are ideological (or utopian) insofar as they derive social meaning from their relationship to particular classes in real history. However, to the extent that schemes of reference are independent of the subjective consciousness of *particular individuals*, they establish forms of meaning and validity that do not allow the reduction of "truth" to mere individual opinion.[128]

Moreover, Beard insisted with Mannheim and Scheler that not all schemes of reference will appear equally plausible given specific historical conditions or long-term patterns of development; nor will different classes and other groups have a randomly dispersed affinity for different schemes of reference. The mental and emotional structures of a particular scheme of reference must accord with the collective will—or spirit—of a specific historical group of persons. Beard defines a collective will as the "will of that number of persons in a given society united by ties of common interests and ideas, and capable of acting through a leadership which brings it to focus and transforms it to action."[129]

World-Historical Individuals, such as statesmen or intellectuals, are those individuals who most accurately represent the collective will (spirit) of a designated group through their actions or writings and, consequently, such visions often incorrectly bear the stamp of an individual's name (e.g., the Hamiltonian vision or the Jeffersonian vision).[130] Importantly, the fact that a scheme of reference explains the course of events does not mean that such conceptions identify the "real causes" of history in some ultimate metaphysical sense. Rather, schemes of reference explain history and make it meaningful to participants and thus become plausible because they seem to manifest a symmetry with the emerging actuality of historical development.[131] In this respect, schemes of reference that survive the test of real history and social conflict do so by their almost prophetic ability to discern current and long-range tendencies within society and to rationalize and project those tendencies into the near and distant future.[132] Beard concludes that a scheme of reference and its associated ideas "seem to be potent only when they fit, with some mysterious exactness, into the actuality of things in the process of development, now slowly altering great intellectual patterns by steady accumulation and now effecting fateful decisions in a time of crisis when a little push here or there appears to give a new course to human affairs."[133]

The tendency to confuse relationism with relativism is ultimately the basis for assertions that Beard's economic interpretation of history is incompatible with his so-called historical relativism. The intellectual historians who have constructed the false dichotomy between an early and a late Beard have failed to recognize that in following Mannheim Beard views the schemes of reference as conditioned by their relation to class structure which, in the final analysis, is determined by economic factors, especially the development of relations to production.[134] For Mannheim, the sole historiographic problem in defining this relation is "to show how, in the whole history of thought, certain intellectual standpoints are connected with certain forms of experience, and to trace the intimate interaction between the two in the course of social and intellectual change."[135]

By specifying these relations for modern societies, Mannheim provides the methodological bridge back to an economic interpretation of history. Quite notably, therefore, in the midst of his alleged relativist doubts, Beard was still insisting that "it has seemed to me, and does now, that in the great transformations in society...economic 'forces' are primordial or fundamental, and come nearer to 'explaining' events than any other 'forces'."[136] As Beard observed, common-sense realism requires one to acknowledge that "mankind works with material instruments within geographical settings" and thus "a material scaffolding...cannot be ignored by those would understand the past as it was and the present as it is—foreshadowing always a future eternally in the process of becoming."[137] Indeed, at the height of his alleged conversion to historical relativism, Beard reiterated that "seventeen years' experience and study have confirmed rather than traversed that [economic] thesis....and I see no reason to change the underlying conception."[138]

The End of American History as an Act of Faith

The scheme of reference that frames any general history is what Beard calls an act of faith. When faced with the totality of all times and circumstances, the historian must come to a decision about the process of history as a whole in order to give that history a meaning and a purpose in contemporary life. There are only a finite number of schemes of reference given within the structure of a particular historical society and, therefore, the historian must commit (consciously or unconsciously) to an interpretation based on the assertion that certain empirically and historically observable tendencies will play themselves out to some schematic conclusion. The act of faith not only identifies these tendencies, it commits to them, and by designating them as the dominant tendencies in historical development, it facilitates their development by providing intellectual direction to the social agents that carry these tendencies in real history. Thus, the act of faith embedded in a scheme of reference closes the hermeneutic circle of an open-ended totality by assigning an end and purpose to historical events.

Beard was certainly aware that the relationships designated as causes by scientific historians and social scientists were actually nothing more than statistical correlations as opposed to behavioral laws. Beard points out that the designated "'laws' in human affairs seem to be in the nature of correlations, averages, and coincidences, rather than absolute laws embracing every person and event in any particular set of correlations or averages."[139] Consequently, even where modern statistical methods could be employed to identify behavioral uniformities or patterns of social development, these patterns were at best *tendencies* or *trends* that depend on human institutions for their reproduction and persistence.

The importance of this distinction is that behavioral uniformities and historical tendencies do not have the same status as laws in physics or chemistry. Furthermore, assurance in their validity systematically diminishes over the long-run, because competing tendencies (i.e., contradictions or antitheses) are always at work that may undermine their continuation. Thus, Beard cautions that realistic dialectics "can describe conditions 'favorable to' this or that action taken but it cannot show that this action was 'inevitable'."[140] In fact, to the extent that such behavioral uniformities have an institutional existence, the false certainties of social science break down as society changes. At precisely those moments when large-scale historical change is occurring, (i.e., when the meaning of history or the purpose of society is at stake), social science is rendered useless, first, because its uniformities are in the process of dissolution and, second, because it cannot identify what tendency *should* be followed or which competing tendency *will* actually prevail. At best, the end and meaning of history can only be imputed by an act of faith, because every end is the result of historical conflicts and tendencies that are unfinished.

Therefore, a historian's scheme of reference, and the act of faith implied in its adoption, bridges the present and the future, as well as the present and the past.[141] The fundamental assumptions and tendencies projected by a scheme of reference make every individual who writes history a "product of his age" whose "work reflects the spirit of the times, of a nation, race, group, class, or section."[142] In adopting a scheme of reference, the historian either implicitly or explicitly declares an alliance with an existing group or class whose actions not only provide the basis of the interpretation, but the existential grounding for the scheme of reference. Hence, by writing history, the historian intervenes in history from a particular perspective and helps channel history in a specific direction by contributing to a particular ideology or utopia. For this reason, Beard suggests that every historian is "a statesman, without portfolio."[143] Beard consciously described his own act of faith as a dimly divined collectivist democracy that would be carried forward in America by the industrial working class.[144]

Notes

1. Charles A. Beard, "Written History as an Act of Faith," *American Historical Review* 39 (January 1934): 219-31. Maurice Mandelbaum, *The Problem of Historical Knowledge: An Answer to Relativism* (Freeport, NY: Liveright Publishing Corporation, 1938), p. 17, is the most prominent critic to describe Beard's philosophical assumptions as historical relativism. Beard contributed to this misnomer and it was adopted subsequently by most commentators. See, for example, Beale, "Charles A. Beard: Historian," in Beale, *Charles A. Beard*, p. 140; Lloyd R. Sorenson, "Charles A. Beard and German Historiographical Thought," *Mississippi Valley Historical Review* 42 (September 1955): 274-87; Elias Berg, *The Historical Thinking of Charles A. Beard* (Stockholm: Almqvist & Wiksell, 1957); Gerald D. Nash, "Self-Education in Historiography: The Case of Charles A. Beard," *Pacific Northwest Quarterly* 52 (1961): 108-15; Borning, *The Political and Social Thought of Charles A. Beard*, pp. 156-63; Strout, *The Pragmatic Revolt in American History*, pp. 6-9; Skotheim, *American Intellectual Histories and Historians*, p. 99; Hofstadter, *The Progressive Historians*, pp. 304-13; Jack Meiland, "The Historical Relativism of Charles A. Beard," *History and Theory* 12, 4 (1973): 405-13.
2. Beard, "Written History as an Act of Faith," pp. 219-220.
3. The term "realistic dialectics" appears at least twice in Beard's methodological works. See, Charles A. Beard, "That Promise of American Life," *New Republic* 81 (February 6, 1935): 350-52; Charles A. Beard, *The Discussion of Human Affairs* (New York: Macmillan Co., 1936), p. 116.
4. Timothy Paul Donovan, *Historical Thought in America: Postwar Patterns* (Norman: University of Oklahoma Press, 1973), p. 59.
5. Lerner, "Charles Beard's Stormy Voyage," p. 22.

6. Whitaker T. Deininger, "The Skepticism and Historical Faith of Charles A. Beard," *Journal of the History of Ideas* 15 (October 1954): 573-88.

7. Berg, *Historical Thinking of Charles A. Beard*, p. 56. Similarly, Higham, *Writing American History*, p. 137, agrees that Beard "largely abandoned interpretation in economic terms" during the 1930s.

8. Hofstadter, *The Progressive Historians*, p. 313.

9. Ibid., p. 304. Likewise, Higham, Krieger, and Gilbert, *History*, p. 126, claim that Beard "was rejecting, without openly saying so, the deterministic implications of his own earlier scholarship." Similarly, Marcell, *Progress and Pragmatism*, p. 274, argues that "Beard scarcely acknowledged the conflict. Society was organic and interrelated, yet economic activity was the principal cause of social change."

10. Berg, *Historical Thinking of Charles A. Beard*, pp. 58, 70.

11. Hofstadter, *The Progressive Historians*, p. 305; Marcell, *Progress and Pragmatism*, p. 265; Commager, *The American Mind*, p. 303.

12. Nore, *Charles A. Beard*, p. 68; Lerner, "Charles Beard's Political Theory," in Beale, ed., *Charles A. Beard*, p. 45.

13. Sorenson, "Charles A. Beard and German Historiographical Thought," p. 284.

14. Strout, *The Pragmatic Revolt*, pp. 6-7, 157.

15. Berg, *Historical Thinking*, p. 19. Cf. Marcell, *Progress and Pragmatism*, p. 266; Ellen Nore, "Charles A. Beard's Act of Faith: Context and Content," *Journal of American History* (March 1980): 850-66.

16. Barnes, *A History of Historical Writing*, p. 293, finds that "Hegelianism and nationalism, in combination, proved amply adequate to hold most historians firmly in the service of political history." Barnes observes that "the Hegelian theory of the state and the spirit of nationalism" was a "political obsession" of American historians prior to World War I. F. R. Ankersmit, *History and Tropology: The Rise and Fall of Metaphor* (Berkeley and Los Angeles: University of California Press, 1994), p. 46, concludes similarly that beginning with Mandelbaum in the 1930s "Anglo-Saxon philosophy of history had from the very beginning isolated itself from one-and-a-half centuries of profound and penetrating thinking about the writing of history."

17. I am building on Nash, "Self-Education in Historiography," p. 114, who suggests that even though "Beard's philosophy of history was clearly an eclectic, rather than an original, creation...yet it was not self-contradictory. Indeed, it possessed a coherent unity."

18. Charles A. Beard, "A Historian's Quest for Light," *Proceedings of the Association of History Teachers of the Middle States and Maryland*, 29 (1931): 12-21; Marcell, *Progress and Pragmatism*, p. 265.

19. Benedetto Croce published a four volume series entitled collectively, *Philosophy of the Spirit*. The four volumes in sequence are Benedetto Croce, *Logic as the Science of the Pure Concept* (London: Macmillan and Co., Ltd., 1917); Benedetto Croce, *Philosophy of the Practical: Economic and Ethic* (London: Macmillan and Co., Ltd., 1913); Benedetto Croce, *Aesthetic as Science of Expression Pure Linguistic* (London: Macmillan and Co., Ltd, 1909); Benedetto Croce, *The Theory and History of Historiography* (London: G. C. Harrap, 1921).

20. The 1921 United States edition of Croce's fourth volume was retitled, *History: Its Theory and Practice* (New York: Harcourt, Brace, and Co., 1921).

21. David D. Roberts, "Croce in America: Influence, Misunderstanding, and Neglect," *Humanitas*, Vol. 8, No. 2 (1995): 3-34.

22. Roy F. Nichols, *A Historian's Progress* (New York: Alfred A. Knopf, 1968), pp. 50-51. For additional background on this Hegelian milieu, see Martin Jay, *The*

Dialectical Imagination: A History of the Frankfurt School and the Institute of Social Research, 1923-1950 (Boston: Little, Brown, and Co., 1973).

23. Malcolm Cowley and Bernard Smith, eds., *Books That Changed Our Minds* (New York: Doubleday, Doran, and Co., 1940), p. 19.

24. Beard, "Written History as an Act of Faith," p. 229. Croce was unable to attend the meeting, but he sent a letter that was entered into the official records of the convention.

25. Croce, *History*, p. 83.

26. For example, G. W. F. Hegel, *The Philosophy of History*, translated by J. Sibree (Buffalo, NY: Prometheus Books, 1991), p. 11, observes that: "Even the ordinary, the 'impartial' historiographer, who believes and professes that he maintains a simply receptive attitude...brings his categories with him, and sees the phenomena presented to his mental visions, exclusively through these media."

27. Croce, *History*, pp. 53, 62. Croce goes on to lament that "the road of progress to the infinite is as wide as that to hell, and if it does not lead to hell it certainly leads to the madhouse," (p. 54).

28. Cf. Benedetto Croce, *Historical Materialism and the Economics of Karl Marx* (New Brunswick, NJ: Transaction, 1981).

29. Croce, *History*, pp. 21-22.

30. Derrida's critique of the Hegelian dialectic parallels Croce's and, not surprisingly, Derrida's "logic of the supplement" (i.e., of difference) is not substantially different from Croce's "logic of the distinct." See Jacques Derrida, *Of Grammatology* (Baltimore: Johns Hopkins University Press, 1976).

31. Croce, *History*, p. 103.

32. Croce, *Logic*, p. 279. Croce, *History*, p. 5, indicated that the fourth volume of his system should "be looked upon as a deepening and amplification of the theory of historiography" already outlined in his *Logic*.

33. Croce, *Logic*, p. 310.

34. Croce, *History*, p. 109.

35. Ibid., pp. 109-10. For this reason, Croce, ibid., p. 55, claims that "we know at every moment all the history that we need to know; and since what remains over does not matter to us, we do not possess the means of knowing it."

36. Ibid., p. 57.

37. Ibid., p. 12.

38. Ibid., pp. 172-73.

39. Ibid., p. 121.

40. Ibid., p. 83.

41. Ibid., p. 151.

42. Ibid., p. 153. Later, Croce again observes that "philosophy shows itself to be a dilucidation of the categories of historical interpretation," ibid., p. 162.

43. Croce, *Logic*, p. 324.

44. Croce, *History*, p. 106.

45. Ibid., pp. 148-49.

46. Ibid., p. 106.

47. Croce, *Logic*, p. 324.

48. Nash, "Self-Education in Historiography," p. 112. Cf. Jean Francois Lyotard, *The Postmodern Condition* (Minneapolis: University of Minnesota Press, 1984) and Jacques Derrida, *Writing and Difference* (London: Routledge and Kegan Paul, 1978) who articulate an equivalent subjectivist position in contemporary philosophy. See Ankersmit, *History and Trope*, Chap. 7, who observes that "Lyotard is far from being the first to attack metanarrative. It will be obvious to

anyone that Lyotard's metanarratives are identical to so-called speculative philosophies of history...the kind of systems that were built by Hegel, Marx, Spengler, Toynbee."

49. Nash, "Self-Education in Historiography," p. 112. The most extensive treatment of Beard's fascination with Croce is Nore, "Charles A. Beard's Act of Faith," pp. 852-56.

50. Beard, "Written History as an Act of Faith," p. 219, cites Croce, *History: Its Philosophy and Practice* as the source of this definition. Cf. Hegel, *The Philosophy of History*, p. 8, who defines the philosophy of history as "nothing but the *thoughtful consideration of it* [i.e., history]." Elsewhere, Beard, *Discussion of Human Affairs*, p. 76, defines history-as-actuality as "every phase of culture; it is the absolute totality of all personalities and occurrences, past, present, and becoming, to the end of time."

51. Charles A. Beard, "Grounds for a Reconsideration of Historiography," in Merle Curti, ed., *Theory and Practice in Historical Study: A Report of the Committee on Historiography* (New York: Social Science Research Council, 1946), p. 5, fn. 1. Elsewhere, Beard, "Written History," p. 225, observes that "the totality of history as actuality which embraces all times and all circumstances."

52. White, *Social Thought in America*, pp. 224-27, for an excellent discussion of these distinctions.

53. Donovan, *Historical Thought in America*, pp. 132-33, suggests that the historical relativists' main achievement was to clarify "the distinction between history and written history which had been constantly blurred during the heyday of the scientific school....the relativist attack on the major presupposition of the scientific school was basically successful in that the wide chasm between history and written history was again clearly demonstrated."

54. Beard, "Written History," p. 219, fn. 2, and p. 223.

55. Breisach, *American Progressive History*, Chaps. 1-2. Beard, *Economic Interpretation of the Constitution*, pp. 1-2, identifies the work of George Bancroft, *History of the Formation of the Constitution of the United States*, 2 Vols. (New York: D. Appleton and Co., 1882) as exemplary of a quasi-Hegelian approach that relies on metaphysical explanations of historical events (e.g., the constitutional convention). For background, see Barnes, *A History of Historical Writing*, pp. 232-34, 266-75, who notes that "it has long been assumed that the perfection of historical science is only a matter of securing an increasingly perfected adoption of the ideals of von Ranke and his school."

56. Beard, *Discussion of Human Affairs*, p. v, observes that "a number of mathematicians and physicists...have recently carried the methods, symbols, and conceptions of their world over into the discussion of human affairs" and that such methods have "largely monopolized the super-reflections of the Anglo-Saxon world." For an account of this process, see, Ricci, *Tragedy of Political Science*; Seidelman, *Disenchanted Realists*; Gunnell, *Descent of Political Theory*, esp. Chap. 10; Clyde W. Barrow, *Universities and the Capitalist State* (Madison: University of Wisconsin Press, 1990), Chap. 5.

57. G. G. Iggers, *The German Conception of History* (Middletown, CT: Wesleyan University Press, 1984).

58. Lukacs, *History and Class Consciousness*, pp. 110-39, remains the best analysis of the antinomies of bourgeois thought.

59. Beard, *Discussion of Human Affairs*, pp. 7-14.

60. I have found Homer Carey Hockett, *The Critical Method in Historical Research and Writing* (New York: Macmillan Co., 1955) an exceptionally valuable methodological reference in reconciling the principles of critical realism with an

appreciation of the practical limits to objective knowledge in history-as-record.

61. Charles A. Beard, *The Nature of the Social Sciences in Relation to Objectives of Instruction* (New York: Charles Scribner's Sons, 1934), pp. 33-34.

62. Beard, "Written History," p. 22.

63. Beard, *Nature of the Social Sciences*, p. 39; Charles A. Beard, "That Noble Dream," *American Historical Review* 41, 1 (October 1935): 83, elsewhere reiterates: "Since the history of any period embraces all the actualities involved, and since both documentation and research are partial, it follows that the total actuality is not factually knowable to any historian, however laborious, judicial, or faithful he may be in his procedures. History as it actually was, as distinguished, of course from particular facts of history, is not known or knowable." Similarly, Beard's friend and colleague, Barnes, *History of Historical Writing*, p. 379, argues that in working with the new history "a common-sense attitude must prevail. The relative significance of historical materials is to be determined, in part, by the nature of the period in which they fell, and in part by their bearing upon contemporary life, but in either case practically and immediately by the purpose the writer has in mind."

64. For more recent elaborations on this idea, see, H. Fain, *Between Philosophy and History* (Princeton, NJ: Princeton University Press, 1970); P. Munz, *The Shapes of Time* (Middletown, CT: Wesleyan University Press, 1977). B. T. Wilkins, *Has History Any Meaning? A Critique of Popper's Philosophy of History* (Ithaca, NY: Cornell University Press, 1978). More recently, Ankersmit, *History and Tropes*, p. 47, concludes that "it is therefore not surprising that the failure to discredit speculative systems effectively formed one of the first cracks in epistemological (i.e., scientific or positivist) philosophy of history."

65. Charles A. Beard, *A Charter for the Social Sciences in the Schools* (New York: Charles Scribner's Sons, 1932), pp. 1, 7-8.

66. Beard, "Written History," p. 223.

67. Beard, *Discussion of Human Affairs*, pp. 39, 79, 63 (italics added by author), 75.

68. Beard, "Written History," p. 220.

69. Beard, *Discussion of Human Affairs*, pp. 60-61.

70. Ibid., pp. 12-13.

71. Nash, "Self-Education in Historiography," pp. 112-13, points out that "no sooner had he [Beard] accepted this aspect of Croce's theory than he set about to find a way to circumscribe it" and to find "a way out of Croce's subjectivism." Also, Nore, "Charles A. Beard's Act of Faith," p. 856, concludes that Beard's "many references to Croce's writings did not mean that Beard accepted the solipsistic position of Croce's relativism...he was careful not to follow Croce over the abyss to solipsism. Beard took from Croce's thought only those aspects that vindicated and strengthened the relativistic stance already apparent in the New History."

72. Hegel, *Philosophy of History*, pp. 20-23, 32-33.

73. Karl Marx, *Capital*, Vol. I (New York: Modern Library, 1906), p. 25; Also, Karl Marx, *The German Ideology* (New York: International Publishers, 1970), pp. 46-47; Marx, *Contribution to the Critique of Political Economy*, pp. 20-21, where he observes that "the totality of these relations of production constitutes the economic structure of society, the real foundation, on which arises a legal and political superstructure and to which correspond definite forms of social consciousness."

74. Beard, "That Promise of American Life," p. 351. Beard contends that "ideas, whether imported or locally developed, do not alone make history. They are always associated with interests, material and substantial" (p. 350). Cf. Karl

Marx and Freidrich Engels, *The Holy Family, or Critique of Critical Criticism* (Moscow: Progress Publishers, 1975). This statement is remarkably similar to Max Scheler, *Problems of a Sociology of Knowledge* (London: Routledge and Kegan Paul, 1980), p. 54: "Where ideas do not find forces, interests, passions, drives, and their 'business' objectified in institutions, they are utterly meaningless *in real history*...There is no such thing as the 'cunning of the idea' (Hegel), enabling an idea to come upon interests and affections from the rear, as it were, to 'make use' of them."

75. Marcell, *Progress and Pragmatism*, p. 267.
76. Charles A. Beard, *The Open Door at Home: A Trial Philosophy of National Interest* (New York: Macmillan Co., 1934), p. 21.
77. Beard, "That Promise of American Life," p. 351. Marcell, *Progress and Pragmatism*, p. 314.
78. Beard, "That Promise of American Life," p. 350.
79. Beard, *Nature of the Social Sciences*, pp. 60-61.
80. Beard, "That Promise of American Life," p. 350. Beard frequently cited a short article published by Kurt Riezler in 1924 as a shorthand reference for this conception of realistic dialectics. See Kurt Riezler, "Idee und Interesse in de politischen Geschichte," [Ideas and Interest in Political History] *Dioskuren* (Munich) III (1924): 1-13. For example, Beard, *Nature of the Social Sciences*, p. 60; Charles A. Beard and Alfred Vagts, "Currents of Thought in Historiography," *American Historical Review* 42 (April 1937): 479; Beard, "Author's Preface to New [1935] Edition," *Economic Interpretation of the Constitution*, p. iii. Riezler was an instructor at the New School for Social Research during the 1920s.
81. Beard, *Discussion of Human Affairs*, p. 116.
82. Ibid., p. 116.
83. Ibid., p. 66.
84. Beard, "Written History," p. 219, fn. 2.
85. Hegel, *Philosophy of History*, pp. 17, 50, 74, 43-44.
86. Ibid., p. 86.
87. Biographers and intellectual historians have tended to downplay Beard's strong association with John W. Burgess, a leading professor of comparative constitutional law while Beard was a graduate student and a faculty member at Columbia University. John W. Burgess, *Political Science and Comparative Constitutional Law*, 2 Vols. (Boston: Ginn and Co., 1902) was a Hegelian who conceptualized comparative constitutional development, particularly in the United States, as an extension of the Hegelian (idealist) dialectic. See Barnes, *History of Historical Writing*, pp. 233-34, 259-60; Nore, *Charles A. Beard*, p. 30. Gunnell, *Descent of Political Theory*, p. 55, reminds us that during the formative decades of the political science discipline, which Burgess helped to establish, there was no one who "propagated the Teutonic theory of state and the Hegelian image of history as long and as assiduously as Burgess." Although Burgess was the foremost proponent of Teutonicism and Hegelianism in Anglo-American constitutional law, he was not alone in this endeavor. See William Stubbs, *The Constitutional History of England*, 3 vols. (Oxford: Clarendon Press, 1878); James Bryce, *The American Commonwealth*, 2 Vols. (London: Macmillan Co., 1888); Frederick J. Stimson, *The American Constitution* (New York: Charles Scribner's Sons, 1914). Beard was familiar with these works, since he either footnoted them in *An Economic Interpretation of the Constitution* and/or reviewed them in the *Political Science Quarterly*.
88. Beard, "That Promise of American Life," p. 351.

89. For instance, Nash, "Self-Education in Historiography," p. 112, suggests that Croce's "most important" influence on Beard was his "formulation of the 'frame of reference'." Nore, "Charles A. Beard's Act of Faith," p. 860 fn. 34, claims that Beard derived his "frames of reference" concept from Mannheim, but Mannheim never uses that concept specifically. Moreover, Mannheim's "styles of thinking" (i.e., ideologies and utopias) are quite different from Scheler's schemes of reference.

90. This essay was first published in German as Max Scheler, "Mensch und Geschichte," *Die neue Rundschau* (November 1926). It was republished as Max Scheler, *Mensch und Geschichte* (Zurich: Neuen Schweizer Rundschau, 1929). It is the latter version that Beard begins citing in the mid-1930s. The essay was translated into English as Max Scheler, "Man and History," in *Philosophical Perspectives* (Boston: Beacon Press, 1958), pp. 65-93. John Raphael Staude, *Max Scheler, 1874-1928: An Intellectual Portrait* (New York: Free Press, 1967) is the best English-language treatment of Scheler's work.

91. Beard, "Written History," p. 228.

92. Ibid., pp. 225, 228.

93. Leopold von Ranke, *Zur Kritik neuer Geschichtschreiber* (Leipzig: Duncker und Humblot, 1874).

94. Barnes, *History of Historical Writing*, pp. 373, 245-49.

95. Beard, "Written History," p. 226.

96. Brooks Adams, *The Law of Civilization and Decay* (New York: Macmillan and Co., 1896); Oswald Spengler, *Decline of the West* (New York: Alfred A. Knopf, 1926). Beard identified Brooks Adams's book as one of only three books that "changed the direction of his thinking," along with Benedetto Croce's, *History: Its Theory and Practice* and Mannheim's, *Ideology and Utopia*. See Cowley and Smith, *Books That Changed Our Minds*, p. 19.

97. Beard, "Written History," p. 228.

98. Ibid., p. 226.

99. Karl Lowith, *Meaning in History* (Chicago: University of Chicago Press, 1949), is an excellent, if critical, review of the major philosophies of history. Also, Frank E. Manuel, *Shapes of Philosophical History* (Stanford: Stanford University Press, 1965), reconstructs the cyclical and the progressive "shapes" of philosophical history, while arguing that "these shapes of philosophical history are today still recognizable as competing intellectual and emotional alternatives, and we are continually choosing between them" (p. 5).

100. Beard, *Discussion of Human Affairs*, p. 103.

101. Beard, *Nature of the Social Sciences*, p. 72, fn. 7, first cites Scheler's essay in 1934.

102. Ibid., pp. 72ff; Beard, *Discussion of Human Affairs*, pp. 103-10.

103. Scheler, "Man and History," p. 69. Scheler notes that his "aim is to explain only the *present* intellectual context of the problem. We shall describe a few, to be exact, *five, basic types of man's consciousness of himself,* in order to outline, as sharply as possible, the various interpretations of the nature of man, as found today in our Western civilization. We shall further show how a particular kind of *historical approach*, i.e., a basic concept of human history, specifically characterizes these ideas" (p. 68).

104. Scheler, "Man and History," p. 69, concludes that the most important reason why "so many and such different conceptions of history and sociology are in bitter struggle with each other today is that these conceptions of history are based on fundamentally different ideas of the nature, structure, and origin of

man." Thus, Scheler insisted that "whether or not the historian, sociologist, or philosopher of history is conscious and aware of it, each historical doctrine is based on a particular kind of [philosophical] anthropology."

105. Ibid., pp. 90, 93. Scheler mentions the work of Thomas Carlyle, Heinrich von Trietschke, Stefan George, and Friedrich Gundolf as examples of this philosophy of history.
106. Ibid., pp. 82, 86. Scheler mentions Oswald Spengler and Theodor Lessing as exemplars of this philosophy of history.
107. Ibid., pp. 69-70. Scheler mentions St. Augustine as an example of this philosophy of history.
108. Ibid., pp. 70-72. Scheler mentions G. W. F. Hegel as an example of this philosophy of history.
109. Ibid., p. 76ff.
110. Scheler, *Problems of a Sociology of Knowledge*, pp. 57-70.
111. Scheler, "Man and History," pp. 79-80.
112. Ibid., p. 80.
113. Ibid., pp. 81.
114. Meiland, "The Historical Relativism of Charles A. Beard," p. 405.
115. Beard, "Written History," p. 226. Beard, "That Noble Dream," p. 87, emphasizes that "the effort to grasp at the totality must and will be continued, even though the dream of bringing it to earth must be abandoned."
116. Beard, *Charter for the Social Sciences*, pp. 18-20.
117. Beard, *Nature of the Social Sciences*, p. 181; Beard, "Written History," p. 227.
118. Nash, "Self-Education in Historiography," p. 113.
119. Beard, *Nature of the Social Sciences*, p. 17, cites Mannheim's *Ideology and Utopia* as his source. Also see, Beard, *Charter for the Social Sciences*, pp. 14-15, where he describes ideologies as "defense mechanisms or rationalizations of given orders of society."
120. Beard, *Nature of the Social Sciences*, p. 18. Beard notes that the concepts of ideology and utopia can overlap to a certain extent, for example: "It was possible for the ideologue of the English landed aristocracy in the eighteenth century to imagine that its government was utopian — the best conceivable — the nearest to perfection on earth; but as a rule there is an element of futurity in utopianism."
121. Beard, *Nature of the Social Sciences*, pp. 18, 19; See, Mannheim, *Ideology and Utopia*, pp. 117-46, for his discussion of these five styles of thinking.
122. Beard and Vagts, "Currents of Thought," p. 480. Borning, *Political and Social Thought of Charles A. Beard*, p. 156.
123. Beard and Vagts, "Currents of Thought," p. 481. Marcell, *Progress and Pragmatism*, p. 295, is one of the few intellectual historians to recognize that Beard "carefully drew back from the abyss of complete historical relativity...Beard strove to find a middle way between the extremes of historical determinism and historical nihilism." For an excellent discussion of this point, see Harry J. Marks, "Ground Under Our Feet: Beard's Relativism," *Journal of the History of Ideas* 14 (October 1953): 628-33.
124. Mannheim, *Ideology and Utopia*, p. 78, identifies "two separate and distinct solutions to the problem of what constitutes reliable knowledge—the one solution may be termed *relationism*, and the other *relativism*."
125. Brian Fay, *Social Theory and Political Practice* (Boston: George Allen and Unwin, 1975), p. 41; Mannheim, *Ideology and Utopia*, pp. 79-80: "...once we recognize that all historical knowledge is relational knowledge, and can only be formulated with reference to the position of the observer, we are faced, once

more, with the task of discriminating between what is true and what is false in such knowledge." See also, Richard J. Bernstein, *Beyond Objectivism and Relativism* (Philadelphia: University of Pennsylvania Press, 1983).

126. Beard and Vagts, "Currents of Thought," pp. 481, 482; Curti, *The Growth of American Thought*, p. 709.

127. Mandelbaum, *Problem of Historical Knowledge*, p. 19, claims that "the radical novelty in historical relativism lies in the fact that it claims that the truth of the work, its meaning and validity, can only be grasped by referring its content to these conditions." In fact, the sociology of knowledge claims that *the meaning* of a work can only be understood relative to those conditions and competing *standards and criteria of truth* can be explained by those conditions, but the determination of 'truth' is objectively defined (i.e., independent of any particular individual) by those standards and criteria.

128. Mannheim, *Ideology and Utopia*, p. 210, defines his styles of thinking as "concrete, discoverable structures of mentality as they are to be found in living individual human beings. We are not thinking here of some purely arbitrarily constructed unity (like Kant's 'consciousness as such'), or a metaphysical entity which is to be posited beyond the concrete minds of individuals (as in Hegel's 'spirit').

129. Beard, *Nature of the Social Sciences*, p. 74, fn. 1. This statement closely parallels Scheler's analysis of the group-mind, *Problems of a Sociology of Knowledge*, pp. 36-47 and Mannheim's conception of the collective unconscious, *Ideology and Utopia*, pp.33-54.

130. However, Beard, *Charter for the Social Sciences*, p. 16, lamented that few historians in his own time were "bold enough to attempt to grasp destiny by the forelock and bring it down for our examination." He cited Hegel's *Philosophy of History*, Spengler's *Decline of the West*, Rousseau's *Social Contract*, and Marx's *Das Kapital* as exemplary models of historical writing for contemporary society.

131. Beard, "Grounds for a Reconsideration of Historiography," p. 12.

132. Charles A. Beard, "Review of *Political Thought in England from Locke to Bentham*, by Harold J. Laski," *New Republic* (November 17, 1920): 303, contends that "one of the tests of true greatness" for a philosopher is the ability to "discover the future in the tendencies of his living present...to see things as they really are and are becoming." Thus, Beard chastised Harold Laski — and by implication the sacred canon of political theory — for devoting one-fifth of a book on political thought in England to Burke, while giving only one paragraph to Thomas Paine. Beard opined "how much nearer to justice it would be to reduce Burke's space and to give Paine half of it. The latter, agitator that he was, divined the long future while Burke could only choke with the froth and fume of rage when he tried to consider the men who were desperately engaged in making it." Likewise, see Hans Kohn, "A Historian's Creed for Our Time," *South Atlantic Quarterly* 52 (July 1953): 341-48.

133. Beard, *Charter for the Social Sciences*, pp. 25-26.

134. Ibid., pp. 78-86 on relationism.

135. Ibid., p. 81.

136. Beard, "Introduction to the 1935 Edition," *Economic Interpretation of the Constitution*, p. xlviii.

137. Beard, *Charter for the Social Sciences*, p. 7; Beard, *Discussion of Human Affairs*, pp. 59-60. Cf. Hegel, *Philosophy of History*, pp. 79-86, for an instructive comparison.

138. Charles A. Beard, "Preface to New Edition," in Charles A. Beard, in *The Economic Basis of Politics* (New York: Alfred A. Knopf, 1934), pp. i, v. Skotheim, *American Intellectual Histories and Historians*, p. 99, concurs that Beard's "convictions on the validity of the economic interpretation did not vanish from his histories through adherence to a theoretical relativism."
139. Beard, *Discussion of Human Affairs*, p. 32.
140. Ibid., p. 118.
141. Berg, *Historical Thinking*, p. 59.
142. Beard, "Written History," p. 220.
143. Beard, *The Open Door at Home*, p. 138; Beard, "Written History," p. 226.
144. Beard, "Written History," p. 228

4

American Political Development

The Progressive Synthesis

In one of his last published works, Vernon Louis Parrington authored the introduction to a book entitled *The Growth and Decadence of Constitutional Government*, where he endorsed the book's claim that ratification of the U.S. Constitution had been accompanied by bitter class divisions.[1] Parrington described the ratification struggle as a political "clash between aristocracy and democracy" and an economic class struggle "between the greater landed and financial interests and the agrarian interests" of the new republic. He concurred with the author, James Allen Smith, that the two struggles in reality were one and that the Constitution was "a deliberate and well considered protective measure designed by able men who represented the aristocracy and wealth of America; a class instrument directed against the democracy."[2]

Parrington was convinced in retrospect that the rediscovery of the undemocratic essence of the federal constitution was "the chief contribution of the Progressive movement to American political thought." He identified a work by James Allen Smith on *The Spirit of American Government* (1907) as the culmination of a political phase in historical constitutional criticism that had begun during the Populist revolt with such leading intellectual figures as Woodrow Wilson, Frank Goodnow, Charles Merriam, Sydney George Fisher, John Bach McMaster, and Simeon Baldwin.[2] Richard Hofstadter identifies many of these scholars as an informal brain trust to the Progressive movement.[3] Parrington himself observes that collectively they wielded a

direct and stimulating influence in shaping the program of the Progressive party by providing its political leaders with a "convincing
explanation of the reasons for the failure of democracy in American
political practice." By locating these alleged failures in "the conservative temper of the Constitution," these intellectuals gave theoretical
direction to the Populist and Progressive movements in their effort to
democratize government with the direct primary, referendum, recall,
women's suffrage, direct election of U.S. Senators, etc. Parrington
traces the origins of this critique to the traditional American ideals of
Jeffersonian democracy.[4]

At the same time, Parrington credited Charles A. Beard's *Economic
Interpretation of the Constitution* (1913) with initiating an economic
phase of constitutional criticism which explained "the aristocratic spirit"
of its makers in terms of their class position.[5] Finally, Parrington
identifies James Allen Smith's last major work, *The Growth and Decadence of Constitutional Government* (1930) as the beginning of a theoretical synthesis of the political and economic phases of constitutional
criticism that fused Smith's political interpretation of the Constitution
with Beard's economic interpretation.[6] The Great Depression provided the social context in which a Smith-Beard-Parrington synthesis
was widely adopted as the basis for a liberal theory of the state,[7] and
the progressive synthesis still remains a significant undercurrent in
American political thought.[8]

A significant outcome of the polemic surrounding this synthesis is
that defending, refuting, or modifying Charles Beard became a focal
point for either defending or refuting progressive conceptions of constitutional formation and political development. Yet, paradoxically,
shortly after the emergence of the progressive synthesis, Beard sought
to extract himself from its grasp. In 1935, Beard admonished readers
that when he wrote the book in 1913 "he had in mind no thought of
forwarding the interests of the Progressive party" and was only "influenced more or less" by the critical spirit of the times.[9]

Despite the denial, contemporary scholars persistently identify Beard
as a major figure in the development of Progressive political thought
or as a leading figure in the liberal school of American historiography.[10] Most have been satisfied to dismiss his denials as a half-hearted
and dissembling effort to defend himself against widespread charges
of ideological and political partisanship. Yet, Beard did not seem
particularly impressed when he reviewed Smith's book in 1908 and

soon after the publication of his *Economic Interpretation* he privately criticized Smith's book to Senator Robert LaFollette (who was then under its spell) for its interpretive errors.[11] Moreover, Beard continually directed barbs at Populists, Progressives, and liberals for their archaic economic conception of the United States as a middle class society and, consequently, for what he called their fuzzy Jeffersonianism.[12] Not only did he indicate that he wanted more thoroughgoing reforms than most Progressives and liberals, by the late 1930s he was characterizing the New Deal as a minor gain for the American working class.[13]

In this chapter I once again document that Beard's intentional statements should be taken seriously in understanding his political thought. Beard's conception of American political development was substantially different from the Populist, Progressive, and liberal tradition that emerged during the age of reform.[14] The following analysis concludes that efforts to incorporate Charles Beard's economic interpretation of the U.S. Constitution into a progressive synthesis or a liberal consensus are, as Beard stated, fundamentally misguided from the outset. The supposed fusion of Smith's and Parrington's early political interpretation with Charles Beard's economic interpretation has resulted in a confused muddling of two very distinct political theories.[15] A careful comparative analysis reveals that in many respects Beard adopted a critical standpoint that challenged the Progressives' conceptualization of American constitutional development.

To document these differences, a liberal and Beardian paradigm of U.S. constitutional development is reconstructed around six categories of historical analysis: (1) an explanation of constitutional origins in terms of the political intentions of the Founders; (2) conceptualization of the American Revolution and the critical period (1783-1787); (3) the Constitutional convention; (4) the ratification struggle; (5) a theory of the state and political development; and (6) each theory's derivative conception of the possibilities for political change. When Beard's economic interpretation is juxtaposed to the liberal paradigm it becomes evident that Beard is a social democratic critic of the liberal tradition in American political thought.

The U.S. Constitution in Progressive Political Theory

Vernon Parrington traced the political origins of the Progressive interpretation of the U.S. Constitution directly to the Populist rebellion of the 1890s. In his description, Progressive political theory was an attempt to conceptualize the liberal revolt against the "custodianship of government by financial and industrial interests." During the 1890s and early 1900s, progressive social and economic legislation was routinely defeated in legislatures or set aside by the courts as unconstitutional. As a result, Parrington observes, the democratic majority began "to question the reason for the bonds that constrained its will."[16]

John Bach McMaster, a prominent nineteenth century social historian, reports that most people initially explained these defeats with vague references to "times like the present." In McMaster's words, social and economic reform was often thwarted because "the Boss is everywhere" and "the high places of many state and municipal governments are filled by men...greatly to be condemned."[17] This early muckraking phase of political critique, which focused on individual corruption, eventually deepened into a general distrust of the judicial exercise of sovereign powers after the Supreme Court declared the Federal Income Tax Law of 1894 unconstitutional.[18] Critics began reexamining the intentions of the Founding Fathers with reference to judicial review and they were eventually led to question the very system of government established by the Constitution.[19] How was it, critics asked, that a Constitution enacted upon democratic principles and adopted with the consent of the people could be used so effectively to thwart the will of the majority? Political thinkers began suggesting that the answer to this question was not the corruption of individual politicians, but the original spirit of American government, which was essentially undemocratic.[20]

As scholars and political activists began reexamining American constitutional development from this perspective, many of them concluded that a majority of Americans had been aware of this undemocratic spirit at least until the end of the Jacksonian movement, which Parrington describes as "a frontier uprising against the rule of eighteenth century aristocracy." However, Parrington suggests that after manhood suffrage was established during the Jacksonian revolt, the electorate was "content to leave democracy to its own devices" and became inattentive to its subsequent development. The public's inattentiveness to government had two consequences for American politics, according to Parrington. The Jacksonian Era set in motion a policy of laissez-faire economic development that would later provide the Gilded Age plutocracy with an opportunity to exploit a "lawless and unregulated individualism" to again subordinate democracy and make government "the mouthpiece and agent of property interests."[21] At the same time, the political life of the country, and with it the interpretation of the Constitution, was left to the predominant influence of lawyers.

Expanding on the latter theme, J. Allen Smith argues that the domination of constitutional interpretation by lawyers provided a tactical advantage to conservatives in American politics. Smith was convinced that lawyers are inherently inclined to adopt an abstract formalistic approach to constitutional interpretation, which substitutes the legal fiction of popular sovereignty for the aristocratic spirit of its real makers. Therefore, attorneys assumed that basic questions of democratic political principle had been settled permanently by the Constitution.[22] The result was that all political discussion in the United States increasingly took "for granted the essential soundness of the constitutional groundwork of our political society." Political disputes were "concerned almost exclusively with questions of constitutional interpretation," while "the larger aspects of social justice and political expediency were subordinated to a legal conception which practically ruled out of order all discussion" except that which pertained to "laws and policies within the field left open to legislation by existing constitutional law as authoritatively interpreted by the courts."[23]

The increasingly legalistic foundation of American politics was thus viewed as largely responsible for a decline in popular civic intelligence since the end of the Jacksonian movement. A major share of the responsibility for civic declension was also placed at the doorstep of American intellectuals. Smith claimed, for instance, that almost without exception, the "older and more conservative school of writers on political science" had assumed the "convenient political fiction" that the Constitution was based on popular sovereignty and the consent of the governed. Scholars had actively supported the aristocratic elite by popularizing this legal fiction in university classrooms and "even in elementary books on civics designed for students in the public schools."[24] Sydney George Fisher complained that the standard histories of the time were full of omissions consciously intended "to build up nationality, and to check sectionalism and rebellion," since the literary class did not "altogether like successful rebellion."[25]

The ideological effect of this political mythology on civic intelligence was to separate "current political thinking from those basic ideas that supply the standards by which not only ordinary legislation but even constitutions should be judged."[26] As a result, even popular rebellions in the United States began accepting the constitutional framework as a basis for political action—since to criticize the Constitution "was to attack the very foundation of the state itself," and that foundation according to legal fiction was the principle of democracy and popular sovereignty to which these rebellions claimed allegiance. American rebellions were therefore locked into a cyclical logic which committed them to renewing the very document which obstructed their success.

The theoretical problem this posed for Populist and later Progressive political thinkers was how to break out of the cycle of renewal and declension in a new political direction. Their solution was to juxtapose a *historical* criticism of the Constitution against the prevailing legal fiction in an effort to demonstrate that its real intent had always been to thwart the development of popular democracy. This technique enabled Populists and Progressives to pursue two closely related political objectives simultaneously. First, by using historical criticism to debunk a political mythology based on legal fiction, critics could undermine popular adherence to the mythology and, thereby, their idolatry of the Constitution. Yet, this tactic was merely a preliminary step toward the second and larger goal of raising the overall civic intelligence of the citizenry by returning debate to a period of constitutional development when the basic issues of political theory and economic justice were still present as day to day elements of political discussion[27]

John Bach McMaster's widely acclaimed *History of the People of the United States* (1883) had already introduced scholars and educated lay audiences to the idea that combining social and political history was "necessary to a correct understanding of the peculiar circumstances under which our nation was formed and grew up."[28] Under the impetus of the Populist revolt, there was soon a spate of multivolume "histories of the people," "true histories" of particular events, and analyses of "the spirit" of American government. As the contours of a Populist and, subsequently, a Progressive reinterpretation of constitutional development took shape, Parrington found "it was the struggle of 1789 over again."[29]

A major pillar in legitimizing the Populist and Progressive movements was the effort to establish them as heirs of the American Revolutionary tradition. These first revisionists asserted that the true history of the American revolution could not be found in a biography of George Washington, the actions and speeches of prominent statesmen, or in the proceedings, memos, decisions, and decrees of the Continental Congress. On the contrary, the true history of the American Revolution was the mob riots in major cities, the demonstrations by artisans and small merchants organized in the Sons of Liberty, the military preparations of the Minutemen, sabotage by common laborers, and the revolutionary grass roots seizure of power by local Committees of Safety.[30] The Revolution was portrayed as a violent sequestration of Loyalist properties on behalf of tenants and small farmers. There were concentration camps for Loyalists, tar and featherings of government officials, assassinations, vandalism and arson of public buildings, summary executions, lynchings, spying, plotting, and deceit. It was a far cry from the gentlemanly separation portrayed by conservative historians. The American Revolution was certainly much more than the mere reassertion of lawful rights seen by legal scholars. Instead, Populists and Progressives recaptured the social meaning of the Revolution *as a revolution* and placed their own constituency at its center by emphasizing the role of the people in organizing and fighting this revolution from below through their own local and state organizations.[31] For instance, Fisher argued that the American Revolution was such "an ugly and unpleasant affair," so full of "atrocities, mistakes and absurdities" that it was not the kind of decorous event in which "scholarly, refined, and conservative persons might have unhesitatingly taken part."[32]

Consonant with this picture, the Continental Congress was widely portrayed as a body of conservative aristocrats earnestly seeking accommodation with an oppressive and unpopular British autocracy. It was pointed out that the people had been constructing a network of local revolutionary organizations and preparing militarily for years prior to the meetings of the Continental Congress. Only after the people initiated a revolution independently did the Continental Congress step forward and take charge of the citizen army outside Boston. Even then it was mainly because they feared the consequences of an armed rabble engaged in revolution under the guidance of their own leadership. Thus, Congress determined to make the best of a bad

situation by usurping national leadership of the Revolutionary movement in hope of limiting its objectives to simple political independence. From this time forward, the political gap between populist
radicals and aristocratic conservatives came to define the contours of
a two party American politics.[33]

For Smith, the distinguishing trait of the radical populist revolution
was its distrust of governmental authority and its attempt to protect
individuals "against unwarranted interference at the hands of the
state."[34] This aim received its clearest philosophical formulation in
the Declaration of Independence written by Thomas Jefferson. The
Declaration of Independence ensconced four political principles in the
American Revolution which, according to Populists and Progressives,
defined the spirit of democracy. These four principles consisted of popular sovereignty or government by consent of the people, the inviolability
of certain universal and inalienable individual rights, the ultimate and
irrevocable right of the people to rebel and/or overthrow their government, and the opposition to large, professional standing armies in time of
peace.[35] This democratic political doctrine was institutionalized during
the Revolution in a new set of written state constitutions.

Populists and Progressives identified the early state constitutions
with an ideal-typical model of radical populist democracy.[36] A chief
characteristic of populist democracy was a constitutional bill of rights
absolutely safeguarding the inalienable individual liberties such as
freedom of speech, assembly, press, religion, trial by jury, and the
right to bear arms. The most radical democracies even extended formal recognition to the right of revolution in their bill of rights. In
addition, the radical democracies all established some form of elective
representative government with an institutional arrangement based on
legislative supremacy.[37] This arrangement ideally included a unicam-
eral legislature with representatives serving short elective terms during short sessions that were governed in all matters by simple majority rule.[38] This structure was reinforced by weak governorships (sometimes elected by the legislature), which possessed no veto power.
Judges were elective and did not exercise any power of judicial review. Taxes were also low because of small governments, low official
salaries, and especially because of the absence of large peacetime
standing armies.[39]

The Articles of Confederation were also defended as an integral
component of this governmental structure. While the Articles did noth-

ing to abridge the internal sovereignty of the radical state governments, they did institutionalize the revolutionary pattern of voluntary
inter-state cooperation on a unified foreign policy and national defense. Yet, lacking any independent power of taxation, or the ability to
maintain a standing army, the central government could not become a
centralized vehicle of oppression or tyranny.[40]

These radical state governments were glorified for adopting a number of democratic policy advances during the Revolutionary and
Confederal period. A majority of the states erected constitutional guarantees of religious liberty, while the Congregational and Episcopalian
churches were disestablished in many states where they had once been
an official state religion supported by taxation.[41] Primogeniture and
entail were abolished to obstruct the intergenerational accumulation of
large hereditary estates and to promote a wider diffusion of land ownership. Debt-ridden farmers, tenants, and artisans were assisted by
new issues of paper money, collection moratoriums, stay laws, and the
abolition of debtors' prisons. There was a general movement toward
the promotion of public education. In some instances, slavery and the
slave trade were abolished or restricted. In addition, a new policy for
the disposition of western lands (i.e., the Northwest Ordinance) foreshadowed the westward expansion of this agrarian democratic society.[42] Parrington lauded the period as one in which agrarian majorities were continuously enacting legislation favorable to the poorer
classes.[43]

Writers in this school of thought were willing to concede that these
actions adversely affected the political power, social status, and vested
economic interests of an aristocratic minority of wealthy merchants,
creditor/financiers, planters, lawyers, and churchmen. Hence, they argued, an aristocratic party organized in each state against the radicals
"in response to the demands of financial and landed interests."[44] The
series of bitter clashes that emerged in each state between radical-
populist and conservative-aristocratic parties placed "the vital issue...of
majority or minority control of the new venture in republicanism" at
the center of political debate.[45] As Populists and Progressives interpreted these events, the radical party was winning in most states until
1787-1788.

This does not mean that they painted an entirely idyllic picture of
the period. The polemical context in which Populists wrote made it
almost impossible not to acknowledge certain problems. Nineteenth

century conservatives writing in the midst of their own agrarian upheavals unanimously condemned the critical period. They described it
as an era of gradually increasing ineptitude on the part of state governments. They denounced the early state governments for repeatedly
thwarting a national vision and represented the Confederation as a
central government which could less and less function, while the country drifted toward anarchy.[46] The critical period (1783-1789) was
berated by conservative historians as one dominated by economic
stagnation, ruinous inflation, unemployment, agricultural and commercial bankruptcy, and the collapse of credit. The state governments
were portrayed as lawless, demagogic legislative tyrannies that were
violating the natural rights of (propertied) minorities. The Confederation was held up as a financially bankrupt government that could not
support its on-going operations or pay the interest on foreign and
domestic loans. The Confederation was perceived as so weak that it
could not enforce its own treaties against the states and was thus an
object of international derision with emissaries humiliated in foreign
courts. With virtually no navy, and leagues of unsecured border lands,
both Spain and England were threatening to invade American territory. Meanwhile, rivalries between the states were leading to civil war
and a break-up of the Confederation.

The peoples' historians agreed that economic conditions were far
from perfect, but they suggested that conditions during the critical
period were no worse than one might expect in a small country recov-
ering from a protracted revolution. Given the often desperate economic circumstances following the Revolution, these historians argued that the states' resort to paper money was a responsible public
policy which brought relief to a majority of the population. Furthermore, they argued that most states were fairly cautious in their use of
paper money and not subject to the mania portrayed by the Founding
Fathers. By 1786-1787, they pointed to indicators which supported
claims that state monetary policies had actually achieved their objectives. These historians observed a gradual upswing in trade, manufacturing, farm prices, and commerce. Debtor relief was largely successful and, because states were major debtors themselves, state finances
were also improving by 1787. As a consequence, modern defenders of
the radicals' achievements argued that states were already backing
away from paper money issues by 1787 or correcting any excesses
made necessary by desperate times.[47]

Similarly, the new liberal historians acknowledged that frictions between the states presented the Confederation with some difficult political problems. However, these again were viewed as no worse than those confronting any new nation and certainly not as strong as the forces of inter-state cooperation. Disputes over trade and commerce were being resolved with various compacts (e.g., Annapolis) between the affected states. The Confederation was steadily removing territorial disputes through negotiation and mediation. Finally, the Ordinance of 1787 successfully resolved the western lands dispute, opened them to settlement, and provided a new source of income to the Confederation.[48] By 1787, Populists and Progressives tended to see a strong, prosperous, and expanding democracy. Any problems remaining with the political organization of the Confederation would have been solved with a few simple amendments to the Articles. It was exactly for this reason, and with explicit instructions to this effect, that the Philadelphia convention was convened in 1787.

However, like others in the Progressive school, Parrington found that "business interests had taken alarm at the prospect of a future government more friendly to poverty than to wealth." Consequently, Parrington argues that wealthy aristocrats had been "quietly casting about for ways and means of taking control out of the hands of the agrarian democracy."[49] The aristocratic group saw the movement to amend the Articles as a perfect opportunity to initiate a conservative counterrevolution under the cloak of popular consent.[50] Woodrow Wilson agreed that the Constitutional convention had "been originated and organized upon the initiation and primarily in the interest of the mercantile and wealthy classes."[51]

When the convention finally assembled in the summer of 1787, individual Populist and Progressive descriptions of its membership differ little from one another. It was composed of "typical representatives of the conservative upper class," gentlemen of financial and social standing who were worried "that the lower classes would eventually secure control of all the state governments."[52] Smith and Parrington noted that members of the convention all possessed wealth and culture and represented the aristocracy of America.[53] One clever wag who wrote an essay on "the Funding Fathers" called the convention a conspiracy of financial trickery orchestrated by the swindlers of a propertied aristocracy.[54] Parrington identifies this propertied aristocracy as a coalition of the older gentry, the professional classes, ambitious Revolutionary officers, and Southern planters led by a powerful money group, which had greatly increased its wealth by financing the war and through currency and land speculation. The net result was a "close working alliance of property and culture for the purpose of erecting a centralized state."[55]

The new liberal critiques were in sharp contrast to the conservative interpretations in vogue among scholars and publicists at the time. For instance, Bancroft argued that studying the formation and adoption of the Constitution would enable students to find moral truth.[56] George Ticknor Curtis claimed that the Founding period conveyed eternal verities because the U.S. Constitution was based on the "law of the moral government of the Universe" as manifested through the "mental, moral, and physical constitution of the Founders." He was convinced that no amount of intellectual power and ingenuity would have been sufficient to write the Constitution without the special moral completeness which made the convention "a body of great and disinterested men."[57] Oscar Straus contributed to this deification by tracing the origins of the convention to "ecclesiastical causes which operated from the time the Pilgrims set foot upon our continent."[58]

Progressive critics, on the contrary, usually portrayed members of the Constitutional convention as motivated by contempt for the people whom they "looked upon as a revolutionary body."[59] The Founders were derided as men who feared democracy and this explained why the Convention met in secrecy; namely, to erect an "adequate protection against democratic control with its populistic measures."[60] Smith asserts that "the chief concern of the framers of the Constitution was to guard against the development of popular sovereignty in the sense of untrammeled majority control."[61] The document which finally emerged from the secrecy of the convention was therefore "in plan and structure...meant to check the sweep and power of popular majorities."[62] In other words, the Constitution was endowed with an inherently conservative temper, because it institutionalized the aristocratic spirit that motivated the Founders.[63]

The concept of an aristocratic spirit of American government was at the core of an essentially structuralist theory of the state. Populists and Progressives identified four characteristics of the new Constitution which violated the original spirit of democracy and were, therefore, further evidence of its anti-democratic intent. The first was that the proposed constitution originally lacked a bill of rights safeguarding individuals against the arbitrary exercise of federal authority. This violation was compounded by conferring sweeping powers upon the central government over commerce, trade, currency regulation, foreign policy, and national defense. In addition, the Constitution violated the principle of popular sovereignty and majority rule through an otherwise unnecessary system of checks and balances. These included long terms and indirect election of the Senate (designed especially to make it an aristocratic check on government); a quasi-monarchical chief executive selected by indirect election, possessing a veto on legislative decisions, and commanding a standing army; and finally appointive judges with life tenure who were nominated by the President and approved by the Senate. Similarly, the amending process was so difficult that a small intransigent minority could more easily obstruct change than a large majority could effect change.[64]

The central government's new power to raise and maintain a standing army and to suppress domestic insurrections was considered a direct assault on the local militias. It was a power which therefore undermined the very foundation of popular sovereignty. The new Constitution thus rejected the right of revolution, which only the militias could guarantee. By strengthening the federal government with a new Constitution, it could subsequently act as "an effective check, both on the more democratic state governments and on the people of the country as a whole."[65] Consequently, the new constitution was considered a "reactionary document" inherently opposed to democracy.[66]

According to Smith, this view of the Constitution enabled one to understand the subsequent development of American political institutions. By subordinating democracy to the aristocratic spirit, the Constitution set in motion and sustained a pattern of institutional hegemony which rendered democracy more feeble as the system developed.[67] This theory of the state provided the first principle for a populist philosophy of American history, which traced the growth and decadence of constitutional government. The period from 1776 to 1789 was interpreted as a brief era of triumph for the growth of democratic constitutionalism. The entire course of American history since that time had been a degenerative phase of constitutional decadence, punctuated by cyclical periods of populist rebellion.[68]

The historical agency which fueled this growth and decadence was the recurring conflict between radical democrats and wealthy aristocrats. The struggle for ratification of the Constitution was merely a continuation of this great American conflict. For example, Woodrow Wilson wrote that the Constitution was "urged to adoption...under the concerted and aggressive leadership of able men representing a ruling class" who possessed a "conscious solidarity of material interest."[69] Smith was equally convinced that partisans of the Constitution were "conservative by inheritance, education, and interest."[70] Parrington refers to the struggle as a contest of large landed and financial interests against smaller agrarian interests.[71]

What marked the ratification struggle as a turning point in American politics, however, was that the aristocratic class finally revealed its true "political depravity" in its panic for counterrevolution. Smith accused them of using a "familiar conservative artifice" by falsely blaming "the excesses of democracy" and the Confederation's limited government "for the evils which followed the Revolutionary War."[72] Parrington summarized Federalist propaganda in the following way:

> The widespread depression was attributed to populist policies, and all the evils from which the country was suffering were laid at the doors of agrarian legislatures...Astute politicians like Hamilton seized the opportunity and crystallized the discontent by the ingenious argument that the trouble was too much agrarianism, that agrarianism resulted from too much democracy, and that the inevitable end of too much democracy was universal anarchy.[73]

Thus, through skillful propaganda by the Federalists, "the ideal of popular democratic rule received a sharp set back."[74] Yet, they also insisted that far more than misleading propaganda was involved in the Federalist victory. McMaster alleges that the Founding Fathers "were always our equals, and often our masters" in filibustering, gerrymandering, "stealing governorships and legislatures...using force at the polls," distributing patronage, and using other "frauds and tricks."[75] McMaster concludes that the Constitution was ratified (and then by a narrow margin) only because its supporters used dishonest parliamentary tactics (e.g., Pennsylvania), bribed state convention delegates (alleged in New York), paid for votes in the delegate elections, disrupted the polls through violence, gerrymandered electoral districts to favor eastern mercantile and tidewater constituencies, bribed newspaper editors or purchased opposing newspapers outright. In other words, the margin of victory in the ratification struggle was the Federalists' political depravity.

In this scenario, the new government was "set over against the people as a check on their power" once the Constitution was ratified.

The minority of influential groups in the United States had ever since been able to wage a continuing struggle against popular authority with great success. At the same time, the persistence of the struggle to "return" government to the people resulted in a cyclical history of political declension symbolized by recurring popular revolts: the Jeffersonian rebellion, the Jacksonian revolution, a Civil War, Greenbackers, Populists, Progressives, and New Freedom liberals.[76] Out of this conflict emerged the paradoxical result that each revolt foreshadowed and made inevitable a further movement toward governmental absolutism in order to check the growing turbulence of popular discontent.[77] The constitutional system did yield to the pressures of democracy with each cycle of revolt, but only insofar as concessions were necessary from time to time to keep the entire framework of checks and restrictions from breaking down. Even though the aristocratic spirit was predominant in the new Constitution, the framers were not able to eradicate the democratic spirit completely. They had to reserve certain powers to the more democratic states, establish a popular branch in the House of Representatives, and ultimately accept a Bill of Rights as a condition for overcoming resistance to ratification of the Constitution. These concessions always remained as platforms from which radicals could launch constitutional democratic revolts. In certain respects, this platform had been strengthened by the universal male suffrage won during the Jacksonian revolution, and the three amendments (13th, 14th, 15th) extracted at the expense of a Civil War.

Nevertheless, the predominance of an inherently aristocratic spirit in the Constitution "hampered and retarded democracy at every juncture."[78] Smith complained that universal suffrage gave people the appearance of political power without much of the substance. Even though property qualifications had been removed from the franchise, the influence of the dominant class and *de facto* disfranchisement of the people had been perpetuated with numerous other obstacles: residence requirements, educational and literacy tests, viva voce voting, vestiges of the property requirement for voting on property taxes and bond issues, discriminatory apportionment, and the perpetuation of low civic intelligence.[79]

On those occasions when the people did manage to circumvent these obstacles, the system of checks and balances came into play to thwart the majority will. The most frustrating of these checks for

Populists and Progressives was the exercise of judicial review by that branch of government which was the most insulated from the people and the most aristocratic in spirit. It was universally agreed by thinkers of this persuasion that judicial review had "been used with telling effect for the purpose of defeating democratic reforms."[80] What is more, when they examined the Constitution and its history, they concluded there was no ground for believing that judicial review was accepted "by the convention as a whole...by any influential class of that time" or by the general public.[81] Quite the contrary, judicial review was yet another unprincipled usurpation of power by the Federalists and their political heirs. Indeed, it had become the chief vehicle for conservatives to further centralize authority in the Supreme Court where it was "subject to no effective political limitation."[82]

Smith's development of this thesis returns to the idea that it was mainly conservative lawyers who first proposed vesting the interpretation and guardianship of the Constitution in the federal courts. They were supported by conservative Federalists who did not consider the Constitution, as originally adopted, sufficient protection against the dangers of democracy. Consequently, in Smith's rendition, lawyers and the more conservative Federalists sought to graft the idea of judicial supremacy onto the system of checks and balances to further subordinate the democratic element in government, i.e., the House of Representatives and state governments.[83] Since it was assumed that the professional classes usually take the side of government in a revolution, it was believed that giving sovereignty to the courts would put government safely beyond the reach of public opinion.[84]

Smith even suggests that lawyers and conservative Federalists undertook "a carefully directed educational campaign" to prepare the public for the introduction of judicial review. They were careful not to support it as a conservative safeguard, but deceitfully appealed to popular hostility towards government by popularizing it as a check on government authority.[85] It was during this campaign that the legal fiction of the Constitution as a fundamental law imposed by the people was widely diffused.[86] Once this view was established in the popular mind, conservatives began advancing the "notion of the Supreme Court as an impersonal organ of the Constitution, uninfluenced by prejudice, passion, or interest."[87] The logical conclusion to this simple syllogism was that in exercising judicial review the courts were merely defending against violations of the Constitution and, thereby, upholding the original will of the people.

Because the subterfuge "was gradually and adroitly insinuated into the public mind," conservatives were further able to centralize political authority in the Supreme Court. This finally made the Constitution an adequate bulwark of conservatism, which yielded only to ruling class sentiment through the power of final interpretation.[88] Smith and Parrington were convinced that anyone who read the early decisions invoking judicial review would readily perceive that "judicial hostility to popular control" of government guided these decisions.[89] Hence, the widely accepted legal fiction which supported the conservative political mythology provided democratic legitimation to "a doctrine of governmental absolutism." This had finally left the ruling class free to pursue its own ends unchecked by popular power.[90]

Smith and Parrington further argue that the centralization of power in the federal government afforded special protections to organized wealth that enabled a small capitalistic group to overcome the natural competitive and state governmental restraints that otherwise would have inhibited the accumulation of monopolistic wealth. Only through the special protection of a national government had bankers, land speculators, railroads, stock jobbers, and other robber barons successfully accumulated vast fortunes. The wealthy willingly shared these ill-gotten fortunes with political bosses and party officials (through bribes and campaign contributions) as the price for continued protection. Moreover, this protection was increasingly necessary since the monopolistic economy relied "less upon efficiency in the production of wealth than upon the power to decrease wages and increase prices" to enlarge profits.[91]

The political effect of this historical alliance was that society was structured more and more as a struggle between economic classes, rather than through competition between equal individuals. Importantly, the sharpening of this class struggle following the Civil War had ushered in the final stage of American constitutional decadence in the construction of a large scale, professional, permanent military force. A standing army had become "necessary to insure adequate protection for capital in time of economic turmoil" both at home and abroad.[92]

What then were the prospects for a renewal of political democracy in America? One strategy for Populists and Progressives was to rely on the more democratic States and States' Rights as a countervailing power to federal authority. In cities and towns one could draw on the sovereignty of state government to establish municipal home rule in the form of autonomous city charters. Hence, state constitutional and municipal reform became vehicles for organizing localized concurrent majorities.[93] With enough time and enough success, they could gradually restructure the American state and neutralize federal authority from the bottom up. For radicals like Smith, however, such activity was of "little importance except in the strictly subordinate field of state legislation." Moreover, he noted that such efforts were "much criticized by conservatives" and could always be restrained or reversed by the use of judicial review.[94] In the final analysis, the standing army could always intervene against the states to enforce decisions of the federal government.

The only other constitutional method of circumventing these obstructions was the amendment process. Yet, as early as 1898, Simeon Baldwin had already convinced many Populists that this goal was virtually impossible.[95] He pointed out that since the Bill of Rights had been extracted as the price for ratification, only three amendments of significance (13th, 14th, 15th) had been adopted. These amendments had been won only at the expense of civil war. Even then, like the original Constitution, they had been forced through with questionable legality. In 1930, J. Allen Smith still argues that little had changed since Baldwin's earlier observation. In his view, the 16th (Income Tax) amendment had been the only successful effort to correct "judicial misinterpretation" in more than half a century.[96]

This left only one plausible option. Nothing short of a revolutionary public sentiment would ever likely produce any fundamental change in the spirit of American government.[97] When Smith and Parrington wrote their final volume on *The Growth and Decadence of Constitutional Government*, however, this possibility seemed equally remote. The people still lacked "an active and intelligent interest in the political and economic problems with which the government has to deal."[98] Traditional agrarianism had suffered its final defeat. Meanwhile, they observed, academic political scientists and economists had again joined the Swiss guards of American political mythology.[99] American politics had come full circle, but there were no more Sons of Liberty.[100]

The Political Theory of Economic Interpretation

It was the background of agrarian defeat which impressed Charles Beard when he returned to the United States in 1902 after attending graduate school at Oxford University (1898 - 1902) and spending a summer traveling in Germany (1900).[101] However, Beard approached the agrarian defeat from an altogether different theoretical perspective. In Europe, Beard had complemented his extensive knowledge of Marx with studies in recent Marxist political economy, French socialism, Fabianism, and comparative economic statistics. He was particularly influenced by the rise of German Social Democracy and by Eduard Bernstein's classic on *Evolutionary Socialism*.[102] He had been an early activist in the Labour Party and was so popular among British workers that Ramsay Macdonald considered him a potential Cabinet minister for a Labour government. A significant aspect of Beard's early political activity was his part in founding Ruskin College, Oxford (1899) which was devoted to the political education of the English working class.[103] These experiences convinced Beard that *politically* the United States was lagging behind other industrial nations.[104]

Beard identified the continuing attachment to fuzzy Jeffersonianism as a key to understanding this political underdevelopment.[105] One component of Jeffersonian political philosophy was its advocacy of the democratic idea. Beard explicitly defined this concept as a belief in "government resting on a popular base and controlled directly or indirectly by all adults without distinction of property." In this sense, he argued, *political democracy* had been achieved in the United States practically, if not completely, by 1835.[106] Moreover, since that time, a succession of continuing electoral reforms had made the principle more and more an effective reality. These reforms included the party convention, the Australian ballot, direct primaries, civil service reform, initiative, referendum, and recall, direct popular election of U.S. Senators, de facto modification of the electoral college by the party system, and African-American and women's suffrage.[107]

However, Beard observed that the rise of the democratic idea in America had to be understood relative to its peculiar historical origins in this country. It was significant for Beard that the "movement for democracy in America had received its impetus from mechanics, industrial workers, and farmers" at a time when farmers and independent artisans were still the bulwark of the democratic parties.[108] As a result, the meaning of the democratic idea in America has always been interpreted within the larger framework of Jeffersonian political economy and Jacksonian social theory.[109] This framework infused the democratic idea with a myth of rugged American individualism which presupposed a laissez-faire, egalitarian, social economy composed predominantly of small farmers, entrepreneurs, shopkeepers, and independent workmen.[110]

As a consequence, Beard argued, the central problem of American democracy had never been the Constitution, but the distribution of wealth and opportunity. Yet, when confronted by the ever widening gulf of economic inequality in the United States, radical Jeffersonian democrats were always constrained by their *own* political mythology.[111] The only democratic solution available to this radicalism was a restoration of American life to its original pristine strength and freedom.[112] This always entailed a retreat to the States' Rights or localist participatory democracy of the critical period and a return to Jeffersonian political economy. Consequently, where Populists and Progressives were successful at the state and local level, they always adopted policies which "favored the development of the class of small property owners." They attempted "to check the absorbing power of great corporations" and "maintain the individualistic system of competition" by encouraging "widespread diffusion of farming lands" and by assisting "the class of small traders, merchants, and manufacturers."[113] At the national level, Jeffersonian radicals pursued the break up of trusts, legislation against unfair and monopolistic business practices, and a definition of "the rules of the business game in such a way that small men with small capital can play it." In this respect, the chief preoccupation of contemporary Jeffersonian democrats was really "the battle between great capitalists and the middle class." Populism and Progressivism were to this degree ideologies of the middle classes engaged in a contest with corporate capital.[114]

Beard claimed that "whatever merits the creed may have had in the days of primitive agriculture and industry," it was "not applicable in an age of technology, science, and rationalized economy."[115] The agrarian democracy pursued by Populists, as well as the middle-class and small business democracies envisioned by Theodore Roosevelt and Woodrow Wilson, respectively, were equally unreal and unattainable.[116] For Beard, Jeffersonian political economy was a "type of economic society such as had never before appeared in the history of the world and can never exist again" in the United States.[117] Instead, the inexorable course of economic development in both industry and agriculture was towards concentration, rationalization, and socialization. This was why "efforts at the restoration of competition among primitive units of enterprise had failed" and would inevitably continue to fail. Populist and Progressive policies were not in line with this inexorable course of economic development.[118] Rather, "their mouths were worked by ancient memories" of an eighteenth century society.[119]

Furthermore, Beard was concerned that a Jeffersonian concept which appealed mainly to the middle classes was no longer sufficient to sustain the democratic idea within this course of economic development. He emphasized that as a consequence of the concentration and socialization of production, the United States was now "mainly a nation of industrial workers, white collar employees, debt-burdened farmers, tenants, share croppers, and casual laborers."[120] Hence, the mass social base of American democracy was shifting away from a lower middle class of small property owners and farmers to the growing army of industrial workers.[121] Yet, Populism and Progressivism were only aware of the existence of a working class to the extent that its members were prevented from becoming small and self-respecting businessmen.[122] Their social and labor policies therefore never went beyond an amalgam of Protestant morality, public education, and Americanization designed to deny the existence of a working class by trying to make them good middle-class citizens.[123]

On both counts, Beard was convinced that Jeffersonian political economy had to be expunged from the American democratic idea. Since the inexorable reality of the twentieth century was a national economy in the process of concentration, rationalization, and socialization, this trend constituted the new political economic context to which democracy would have to be adapted. In this new economic context, Beard was certain that industry (and therefore the working class) could avoid disaster only by planning. However, this new economic framework of political debate would first have to be acknowledged as a permanent feature of American society before democrats could directly confront the problems of "how much planning is necessary, by whom it can best be done, and what limitations must be imposed."[124]

From this perspective, the problems of democracy in the United States were not so much strictly political as economic and ideological. In other words, the political democracy which Beard saw as an ongoing, but basically accomplished fact had to be understood as substantively contingent on the achievement of social and industrial democracy within the parameters of the new political economy. This new concept of social and industrial democracy was advanced in terms of three principles. The first was the principle of political democracy or "the idea that the power of the state belonged to the majority of the people." This was the most valuable legacy of the Jeffersonian movements (i.e., Jacksonian democracy, Civil War, Populism, Progressivism, Wilsonian liberalism). The various electoral, party, and institutional reforms achieved by these movements had laid the basis for advancing towards social democracy.[125]

The pursuit of social democracy, however, was organized around two additional principles. One of these was the principle of public ownership wherever private profit was inherently opposed to public needs. At a bare minimum, this principle required the retention and public management of the vast U.S. government properties. Instead of land grants, leases, and sales of valuable and productive public assets, Beard demanded that all government properties be held in permanent social ownership, administered for the benefit of society, and not plundered for private gain at firesale prices. The second principle of social democracy was that state power "could be avowedly employed to control, *within uncertain limits*, the distribution of wealth."[126]

Beard argued there would be no social force "more potent than the increasing organization of industrial workers" as a carrier of social democracy.[127] Consequently, he believed that labor was about to play a historical role throughout the industrialized world "comparable to that played in the past by the military caste, the landed aristocracy, and the capitalist class."[128] However, Beard was wary that once the "organization of mass production workers by the millions got under way," it would crystallize a growing consciousness of identical interests among the middle classes as well (e.g., Progressivism, New Freedom). This would "effect a growing solidarity within their own ranks." While opposed to big business, the middle classes were also still committed to private property and individualism. As a result, they were also frequently threatened by the emerging social democratic demands of the proletariat. They would no doubt utilize all the resources at their command—the law, the press, schools and universities, civil service, and party organizations—to restrain the development of social democracy by encircling the working class with the dead weight of Progressive politics and populist ideology.[129]

Thus, from the moment Beard returned to the United States, the thrust of his political activities were aimed at educating the American working class (and future public servants) into the principles of social democracy.[130] He helped establish a branch of Oxford's Ruskin Labor College at Trenton, Missouri, in 1900.[131] When this experiment failed, he took an active part in organizing the Socialist Party's Rand School of Social Science (1906), where he briefly taught American government. He campaigned and lectured on behalf of Socialist Party candidates during this time as well. When the Socialist Party collapsed after World War I, Beard continued his activities at the New School for Social Research and helped found a national Workers' Education Bureau. For three years, he even lectured on American politics and history (1927-1929) at the New York Workers' School of the Workers' (Communist) Party.[132]

Throughout his life, Beard was committed to continuing education for adult workers, because he considered it a necessary precondition to the successful organization of an independent American labor party.[133] When examined relative to these intentions, Beard's economic interpretation of the Constitution emerges as a work motivated simultaneously by the "critical spirit of the times" and yet, exactly as he insisted, one *not* intended to further the aims of the Progressive party or mainstream liberal politics. It is more properly regarded as one component of an on-going and developing social democratic critique of the Populist, Progressive, and liberal tradition by Beard.

Beard shared polemical intentions similar to those of Populists and Progressives in only two respects. He agreed that a realist critique of theological and formal-legal interpretations of the Constitution was necessary to advance a radical tradition in American political thought, since these interpretations had been designed to inculcate a facile spirit of reverence for the document.[134] He also accepted the critical premise that an empirical-historical investigation of constitutional origins (i.e., its spirit or intent) would reveal whether or not there were any inherent structural obstacles to radical reform built into the framework of American government.

By the time Beard published *An Economic Interpretation* in 1913, Congress had already once passed an income tax (1894), adopted antitrust legislation, and set up the Interstate Commerce Commission. State legislatures were regulating child and women's labor, factory conditions, minimum wages, workmen's compensation, and unemployment insurance. In Beard's view, American politics was clearly democratic enough to allow such measures to pass. The problem was that courts were interpreting many of these measures as unconstitutional, while using anti-trust legislation to issue injunctions against strikes, break unions, and jail labor leaders. Thus, for Beard, the specific question is not whether the Constitution was anti-democratic in a formal political sense, but whether it was *anti-social-democratic*. For Beard, the real question was: did the Constitution pose a structural obstacle to the advance of *industrial* democracy in America?[135] Hence, his emphasis on an *economic* interpretation.

Constitutions for Beard are primarily tenets of fundamental law which provide a legal and political framework for the legislation, administration, and interpretation of statutory law. It was Beard's observation, however, that as a matter of historical fact most of the law is concerned with property relations. This is particularly true of commercial societies where "mere defense against violence (a very considerable proportion of which originates in forcible attempts to change the ownership of property) becomes relatively less important; and property relations increase in complexity and subtlety." As a result, the primary object of government in making laws, beyond the mere repression of physical violence, is defining the specific "rules which determine the property relations of members of society."

The classes whose rights "are thus to be determined must perforce obtain from the government such rules as are consonant with the larger interests necessary" to the "economic processes" that sustain their position as owners of a particular *kind* of property. These interests can either be safeguarded by a structure of fundamental law which preserves them as *rights*, or else the members of an interested class "must themselves control the organs of government."[136] This dilemma is always the problem of prime importance under any system of government where political power is shared by any significant proportion of the population. Particular propertied interests cannot be assured of maintaining instrumental control of the state. Nevertheless, insofar as this problem is resolved in favor of specific propertied interests by a constitution, we can refer to such groups as the politically dominant classes by virtue of the special constitutional protections they enjoy within that framework of government.

From this perspective, Beard agreed that "populism had a free hand" under the Articles of Confederation, "for majorities in the state legislatures were omnipotent."[137] Since populism meant simple majority rule, the critical period was inevitably characterized by the agrarian politics of "local legislatures generally dominated by farmers."[138] In a society where a majority of the population was engaged in agriculture, a populist constitutional structure essentially installed the agricultural interest as a dominant party with political hegemony.

Beard identified this dominant agricultural interest as a political coalition of three economic groups: small farmers (living back from the coast along a line from New Hampshire to Georgia), manorial lords (e.g., Hudson patroons, Pennsylvania and New England gentlemen, Rhode Island plantation owners), and Southern planters. These groups all shared an obvious concern with advancing the prosperity of agriculture, as well as general conditions that would safeguard and promote the ownership of land, the social prestige of land ownership, and political structures in which it could generally expect to enjoy a privileged position. The ownership of landed property established the economic basis for a realty interest or party in each state.[139]

The mass electoral base of this party was the large number of small freeholders. Nevertheless, Beard argued that small farmers generally rallied around the local agricultural class "which had the cultural equipment for dominant direction."[140] Consequently, party leaders and public office-holders of this "Jeffersonian" party were frequently much wealthier than their constituents. Beard clearly did *not* conceptualize the realty or populist party as a party of the lower class, the poor, or the propertyless as has often been claimed. Rather, the radical parties were a political coalition of landed property owners which also cut across the simple east-west geographic contours defined by the Populists and Progressives.

This party generally carried forward long-standing colonial agrarian traditions while exercising political hegemony. Taxes were shifted off land. An emphasis on political and economic localism was preserved in state constitutions and the Articles. Paper money was issued to inflate commodity prices and devalue debt. Inheritance laws were changed to promote a wider diffusion of land ownership. Western lands were opened to settlement. State religions were disestablished.[141] Thus, while Populists and Progressives emphasized the democratic character of these measures, Beard focused on their economic relation to class interests.

An important caveat in this regard is that while such measures clearly appealed to small farmers, Beard argued they were equally beneficial to wealthy members of the realty party. Localism conserved the political and economic position of wealthy landed elites at least as often as it brought yeomen to the state legislatures. Abolishing primogeniture and entail did more to benefit the second sons of large landholders and therefore to widen that class than it ever did to promote a diffusion of the yeomanry. In the South, Episcopalianism became so identified with Loyalism during the Revolution that many planters had already converted to Presbyterianism. Thus, disestablishment was also in their interest. Opening the Western lands would do as much to promote the expansion of slavery as of yeomanry. Similarly, Beard argued, the debtor class largely overlapped this general realty interest and was not just confined to small farmers or artisans. Planters and patroons were frequently heavily in debt. They benefited substantially from paper money emissions and the inflation of farm commodity prices (as in New York).[142] Consequently, large landed interests associated with the realty party could easily and honestly speak the language of radical populism.

Moreover, it is important to remember in this context that political "radicalism" in America had been defined polemically during the Revolutionary opposition to monarchical authoritarianism and parliamentary taxation. Radicalism was equated simply with safeguarding the individual "against all federal interference," preserving "to the states a large sphere a local autonomy," legislative supremacy, hostility to the presence of a standing army, and low taxes.[143] From this standpoint, a wealthy Southern slaveowner could be just as radical as any small farmer. As Beard indicated, much of the confusion surrounding this term has come from reading contemporary conceptions of radicalism back into the critical period where they simply were not relevant or even meaningful.

Beard is very clear that the working class (as a propertyless proletariat) had not yet developed a distinct class consciousness in the United States; nor had it established any trade unions or independent parties. The special problems of a working class were therefore "outside the realm of politics" at that time.[144] It was a mistake to identify contemporary concepts of working class or social-democratic radicalism with Jeffersonian populism. From a *contemporary* radical standpoint, populism was an economically reactionary ideology that obstructed the introduction and discussion of modern social-democratic concepts in American politics. Indeed, the emergence of an American proletariat and, therefore, ultimately social democracy historically pre-supposes the triumph of "Economic Federalism" (i.e., industrial capi-talism) as a condition of its own existence.

Thus, it was important to Beard's own critique to recognize that even if the realty party was satisfied with its populistic measures, the rest of the American economy was in a "state of depression."[145] Beard even cites Fiske quite favorably in describing the "disordered state of American commerce." Beard argued that the American monetary sys-tem "was in even worse confusion" as a result of the paper money emissions and defaulting public credit.[146] Likewise, Beard had noth-ing favorable to say about the central government established by the Articles of Confederation. He considered its most obvious defect the "inability to pay even the interest on the public debt." He character-ized its powers as a mere shadow that were insufficient to enforce laws and compacts "against states that insisted on following their own devices." The Congress was impotent to enforce measures of taxation. It could not uphold "commercial treaties against recalcitrant states."[147] If most state legislatures were unwilling to address the commercial crisis in a sympathetic manner, Beard made it clear that the Confed-eration government was unable to pursue an effective policy of any kind.

Furthermore, Beard observed that the great European powers still held possessions in the New World—Great Britain in Canada and the West Indies; Spain west of the Mississippi and to the south; and France in the West Indies. American commerce was heavily depen-dent on the markets in New Orleans and West India. Commercial farming on the frontier depended upon the Mississippi as an outlet for the export of agricultural commodities. Yet, defaults on foreign debts and the violation of treaties by individuals or States provided an on-going excuse for the unfavorable treatment of American merchants, ships, and goods. It also provided a pretext for provoking diplomatic difficulties and perhaps war with those countries.[148] Beard summa-rized the economic problems of the critical period in the following way:

> The holders of the securities of the Confederate government did not receive the interest on their loans. Those who owned western lands or looked with longing eyes upon the rich opportunities for speculation there chaffed at the weakness of the government and its delays in establishing order on the frontiers. Traders and commercial men found their plans for commerce impeded by local interfer-

ence with interstate commerce. The currency of the states and the nation was
hopelessly muddled. Creditors everywhere were angry about the depreciated
paper money which the agrarians had made and were attempting to force upon
those from whom they had borrowed specie.[149]

In Beard's analysis, the accumulating difficulties led to widespread
dissatisfaction among several groups. Holders of continental and State
securities became "dissatisfied with the drift of things." Army officers
and former soldiers asked for back pay and the execution of land
warrants. Some of the officers were even hatching plots "to overthrow
Congress and set up some form of military dictatorship." Meanwhile,
"merchants, manufacturers and shippers demanded a Congress at least
strong enough to regulate foreign and interstate commerce."[150] According to Beard, these politically "conservative capitalistic groups"
were finally "made desperate by the imbecilities of the Confederation
and harried by state legislatures" into organizing the other of the two
great parties which competed during the critical period.[151]

Beard called this second party coalition the personalty interest. It
was based on five economic groups structured around the ownership
of personal property. [152] These were a moneyed interest, holders of
public securities, manufacturing and shipping, speculators in western
lands, and the professional associates of these groups (i.e., the "learned
professions"). The moneyed interest included anyone with money at
interest or persons with liquid capital seeking investment. As Beard
describes it, this was not a separate class of bankers or financiers in
the modern sense, but *one component* of a vaguely defined class of
creditors which drew support from several groups within the personalty interest. Although spearheaded by wealthy Northeastern merchants,
Beard suggests that it also included some tidewater planters.[153] This
same creditor class of wealthy merchants and planter-capitalists was
also the heaviest speculator in western lands.[154]

On the other hand, holders of public securities were so widely
dispersed throughout the population that Beard found it difficult to
define a clear relationship between this interest and specific economic
groups. He found concentrations among Northeastern merchants, among
planter-capitalists, and even relatively large holdings among men of
modest means. This included small merchants, prosperous tradesmen,
shopkeepers, and even large numbers of comfortable yeoman farmers.

Beard found that farmers who lived near towns or along river val-
leys with fertile soil and easy transportation were consistently able to

produce an agricultural surplus for sale in urban markets or foreign export. Many of these were even located on the western frontier— i.e., the Connecticut River Valley in Massachusetts and New Hampshire, the Shenandoah in Virginia, etc. Their ability to generate profits through exchange and export meant they shared a general interest in urban prosperity, interstate and foreign trade, and a stable national currency. In addition, many of them had accepted public securities as payment for food during the Revolutionary War. While much of this debt had been sold off to securities speculators, many small commercial farmers still held devalued securities. Beard notes that it may have been a small proportion of the public debt relative to the total value of outstanding securities, but it was a large proportion of the total individual net savings of these small agricultural capitalists. To that degree, they too were members of the creditor class.[155]

Nevertheless, Beard concludes that the greatest holders of public securities were members of the Order of Cincinnati. Its members were a geographically dispersed middle-class "of some means" who as former officers in the Revolutionary War had been paid in land warrants or public debt.[156] Their inclusion in the class of creditors, along with some members of an urban and rural petit-bourgeoisie, meant that Beard describes a political coalition which was both geographically and socially widely diffused. By no means was it confined to wealthy coastal merchants and tidewater planters as claimed by Populists and Progressives.

Beard was even more careful to emphasize that the manufacturing and shipping interest was not exclusively a class of wealthy merchants, master mariners, or shipowners. Most domestic manufacturing was still organized in crafts, artisanry, and independent trades. It was still largely a petit-bourgeois, entrepreneurial pursuit which usually provided a quite modest standard of living.[157] Contrary to assertions by Populists and Progressives, Beard suggests that this so-called working class actually shared a community of interest with merchants, shippers, and traders—both in defending the rights of personalty (which they usually owned) and in promoting general commercial prosperity. If commerce, trade, or merchandising languished, so did the livelihood of artisans, craftsmen, tradesmen, mechanics, and seamen.

Moreover, small frontier farmers often supplemented a subsistence existence with cash income by household manufacturing, fur trapping and trading, or skilled artisanry during the winter months. Thus, one could find significant pockets of small manufacturing, village enterprise, and commerce scattered throughout the Western frontier. There were also large commercial centers in the South, such as Baltimore, Chesapeake Bay, Charleston, and Savannah. As a result, the "manufacturing and shipping interest" was neither aristocratic, nor exclusively Northeastern.[158]

From Beard's perspective, these personalty interests collectively suffered "special pressures" and "attacks from all sides" as a consequence of the realty party's political hegemony.[159] Moneyed interests suffered from the lack of uniform currency. Stay laws impaired existing contracts, while depreciated paper money was in effect an expropriation of personalty by realty debtors. Investments in western lands were insecure because State courts lacked uniformity on judicial decisions and the Confederation was weak militarily. Domestic manufacturing and shipping was disadvantaged by legal disabilities in foreign ports, but lacked domestic protections. As a result, commerce was languishing and American manufacturing was perishing. State and continental securities were in technical default and had fallen to 5 percent to 20 percent of par value—in effect, yet another expropriation of personalty from persons who had financed or fought the Revolution in good faith. Thus, in Beard's words, the American party battle emerged as "a war between business and populism."[160]

Despite their desperation, Beard observes that the capitalist coalition at first pursued the more moderate proposition of amending the Articles of Confederation. The Congress "proposed amendments to the Articles granting it the right to lay and collect certain taxes" several times when facing bankruptcy. Yet, "the Congress was completely baffled in these efforts at reform" by minorities as small as the single state of Rhode Island. When the Annapolis Convention was called to resolve commercial disputes between the states, only five states bothered to send delegates.[161] Finally, even when more favorable economic policies were secured with the existing constitutional framework, as in Massachusetts, the result was armed agrarian rebellion. Only after repeated frustrations did the capitalistic interest eventually draw together:

> in a mighty effort to establish a government that would be strong enough to pay the national debt, regulate interstate and foreign commerce, prevent fluctuations in the currency created by paper emissions, and control the propensities of legislative majorities to attack private rights.[162]

In Beard's opinion, it was one thing "to lay more stress upon personal liberty than upon social control" in "stirring up the revolt against Great Britain and in keeping the fighting temper of the Revolutionists at the proper heat." However, once "independence had been gained, the practical work to be done was the maintenance of social order, the payment of the public debt, the provision of a sound financial system, and the establishment of conditions favorable to the development of the economic resources of the new country." On the other hand, Beard agreed, the populists "had set up a system too weak to accomplish the accepted objects of government" as a result of "their anxiety to defend the individual against all federal interference and to preserve to the states a large sphere of local autonomy."[163]

Personalty interests took the lead in the movement for a new constitution precisely because they were most subject to the special pressures of these weaknesses. Most importantly, they were "bent upon establishing firm guarantees for the rights of property."[164] Thus, when Beard examined the constitutional convention as a preliminary empirical test of this hypothesis, he asked: "Were the leaders in the movement which led to the adoption of the Constitution representatives of the interests so affected?"[165]

Beard conceded that his own analysis was merely "a superficial commentary" designed to illustrate the kind of research necessary to answer this question.[166] What evidence he did offer, however, suggested that leaders of the movement for the Philadelphia convention in both the Congress and the state legislatures were representatives of the personalty interest.[167] Fully one-quarter of the *Economic Interpretation* is devoted to documenting that Convention delegates were members of those groups "whose economic interests they understood and felt in concrete, definite form through their own personal experience."[168]

Beard was quite clear in his indication that this chapter was not intended (as with the Populists and Progressives) to argue that the Founders were self-seeking swindlers looking for personal benefits from a new Constitution. If he left any doubt about this matter in his original work, he answered misinterpreters two years later in the *Economic Origins of Jeffersonian Democracy*. The main point of this chapter was simply to establish: "that the members of the convention were of the capitalistic rather than the agrarian interest, and whether they made money out of the constitution was specifically stated to be of no consequence to the main thesis."[169]

Instead, it was merely his point to establish an empirical (economic) basis for his next inference. This inference was that convention delegates shared a "conscious solidarity of material interest" and, therefore, were likely to perceive the problems of the existing constitution from a similar standpoint. Drawing on Farrand's summary of the convention debates (a work he held in high regard), Beard concludes they actually did share an implicit class consciousness which *The Federalist Papers* later elaborated "with a high degree of precision."[170] This is not meant to prove that delegates were exclusively motivated by a sense of raw economic interest, but to suggest the way in which their conceptions of justice, rights, good government, natural law, authority, and obligation revealed an elective affinity with the delegates' class position. Consequently, while they no doubt often conceived themselves to be acting out of the highest motives of justice, natural law, and national interest, those same conceptions placed certain interests (e.g., personalty) in an especially privileged position. That after all is exactly what defines the ideological component of a political theory.[171] Beard modestly points to this relationship between ideas and interests to argue that convention delegates were not "working *merely* under the guidance of abstract principles of political science."[172]

Quite interesting in this respect was Beard's "profoundly significant conclusion" that the Founding Fathers were able to place the new Constitution upon a stable foundation primarily *because* they were practical men with personal experience in economic affairs. It was his comparative reading of modern European history that constitutions written by doctrinaire theorists and intellectuals with abstract ideas as their main orientation were likely to fail miserably.[173] Yet, he wrote of the Philadelphia convention that:

> never in the history of assemblies had there been a convention of men richer in political experience and in practical knowledge, or endowed with a profounder insight into the springs of human action and the intimate essence of government.[174]

This insight into the "intimate essence of government" was their understanding of the relationship between property rights and the state in a political democracy. Consequently, Beard maintains, the convention delegates were anxious above everything else to safeguard the rights of private property (and particularly those of personalty) within the restrictions of constitutional government.[175] It is crucial at this point in Beard's argument to recognize his distinction between democracy as a general category of government and populism as a particular species of democracy characterized by limited, local government and simple majority rule.

Beard acknowledges in the context of this distinction "that members of the assembly were not seeking to realize any fine notions about democracy and equality." He even concedes that "many of the members held popular government in slight esteem."[176] Yet, it had to be remembered that just as the Founders presupposed property rights as a central feature of government, they also presupposed democracy as the existing context in which this aim had to be pursued. In a society where the majority of citizens were property owners, they had no reason to believe that any antagonism existed between property and democracy. Instead, their objections to democracy were aimed primarily at the *populist* concept of direct popular government which at that time structured the debate between radicals and conservatives.[177] These objections were usually formulated with *specific reference* to "their experience with popular assemblies during the immediately preceding years" and not in terms of an aristocratic principle of government. Beard observes that:

> With many of the plain lessons of history before them they naturally feared that the rights and privileges of the minority [i.e., personalty] would be insecure if the principle of majority rule was definitely adopted and provisions made for its exercise.[178]

Consequently, the delegates were in agreement that the "essential element" of any constitutional revisions would be "the doctrine that the popular branch of government cannot be allowed full sway, and least of all in the enactment of laws touching the rights of property." At the same time, they never rejected the basic principles of democracy such as popular sovereignty, limited and representative government, federalism, and individual rights. What the Founders did reject was populism. This meant the Founders faced a peculiar dilemma in constructing a stable and efficient government that would subserve their permanent interests. They had to safeguard "on the one hand against the possibilities of despotism" by a minority and "on the other against the onslaught of majorities."[179]

The first question faced by delegates in approaching this problem was whether or not a few amendments to the Articles would be sufficient to achieve the various aims of the Convention. Delegates were virtually unanimous on the question that amending the Articles as designated by their instructions was a waste of time. These instructions were cast aside in favor of the "extraordinary measure" of writing an entirely new document. Beard does observe that such an act might conceivably be called a *coup d'etat*; yet, contemporary scholars always ignore that he felt it was "fortunate" for the cause of national union that "the delegates threw off the restrictions placed upon them by their instructions."[180]

Beard repeatedly indicates throughout his works that the scheme of government constructed by the Convention was:

> designed to effect, along with a more adequate national defense, several commercial and financial reforms...and at the same time afford an efficient check upon state legislatures that had shown themselves prone to assault acquired property rights, particularly of personality, by means of paper money and other agrarian measures.[181]

However, the peculiar feature of American politics was that a property qualification on the suffrage was not a suitable vehicle for protecting property rights in the specific sense that they preoccupied the Founders. Inasmuch as "the convention was especially eager to safeguard the rights of personal property, a freehold qualification did not seem to offer an adequate remedy." It was the realty interest that was responsible for the assaults on personality. On the other hand, "a large personality qualification on voters would have meant the defeat of the Constitution by the farmers who were, of necessity, called upon to ratify it." This exceptional complication forced delegates to shift away from the usual direct economic qualifications prevalent in Europe to an indirect system of checks and balances to secure the rights of property—particularly personal property.[182] The system of checks and balances was therefore not an anti-democratic feature of the Constitution, but a means of safeguarding personality interests *within* a politically democratic framework where realty interests were predominant.[183] Indeed, in 1941, when asked by graduate students at Johns Hopkins whether he was still satisfied with his *Economic Interpretation*, Beard replied that he probably should have emphasized "not so much that the framers were not democrats as that they *were* republicans in a world where republicanism was forward-looking."[184]

Once this "remarkable instrument" was written, however, Beard notes that its supporters still faced the task of securing adoption from states torn with popular dissensions.[185] Beard argues that the Founders were afraid state legislatures would oppose the new document because it reduced their powers. It was also feared that a direct popular vote would lead to its defeat by an agrarian majority. Hence, they chose ratification by state conventions as a way to mediate its consideration by the best citizens of each state.

Beard analyzed the political economy of delegate selection as a measure of the degree to which the constitutional struggle fell along a personalty-realty division of parties. Since he concluded that the Constitution was written by representatives of the personalty party "to subserve their permanent interests," he inferred that as an economic document, it would appeal "directly and unerringly to identical interests in the country at large." Beard's data indicated that Antifederalist delegates "almost uniformly came from the agricultural regions, and from the areas in which debtors had been formulating paper money and other depreciatory schemes."[186] Federalists found greater support in urban commercial centers where personalty was concentrated. Nevertheless, they also drew support from a substantial portion of agricultural capitalists.[187]

Beard's expository analysis of writings and statements by leading thinkers of the time is also used to demonstrate that participants in the ratification struggle were empirically conscious of the conflict in exactly these terms. Beard elaborates their understanding of "a deep-seated conflict between a popular party based on paper money and agrarian interests and a conservative party centered in the towns and resting on financial, mercantile, and personal property interests generally." Yet, contrary to Progressives, Beard is also quite explicit in his statement that "a war between 'aristocracy' and 'democracy' was observed only by partisans whose views were distorted by the heat of battle." He claims it was generally understood at the time that "one class of property interests was in conflict with another."[188]

The Populist and Progressive analyses of constitutional origins indicated that the Constitution should have been defeated by a large margin of farmers and mechanics in any honest and truly democratic election. However, Beard's more complex analysis led him to conclude that the margin of victory either way would invariably have been very close. As a consequence, he puts forward a number of possibilities which on balance seemed to account for the Federalist victory.

By meeting in secret, Federalists seized the political initiative by springing a new Constitution on their opponents who were clearly unprepared for this turn of events. It was obvious to Beard that proponents of ratification had disregarded the existing process of amending the Articles and had resorted to an extra-legal plebiscite. This and some other irregularities caught the radicals unprepared. Populist and Progressive critics placed a great emphasis on this fraud, deception, and illegality as the explanation for ratification. However, Beard explicitly surveys those accusations and concludes that nothing beyond ordinary political maneuvering, including some irregular and unethical conduct, ever took place. If there was real fraud or bribery, it was isolated and not sufficient to explain the outcome. Indeed, Beard is even bold enough to suggest that Federalists were probably more honest than they had to be at the time and were certainly at least acting well within the political standards of the day.

Likewise, Beard observes that 20 to 33 percent of all adult white males were disenfranchised by widespread property qualifications.[189] This primarily excluded propertyless mechanics, day laborers, seamen, and tenants. Yet again, contemporary commentators ignore the obverse implication of Beard's analysis which is that two-thirds to four-fifths of all white males were enfranchised; a figure that is consistent with examinations that claim to debunk Beard by citing such figures as if they were a new discovery. Indeed, Beard's critics have persistently neglected the fact that Beard points out explicitly that universal white male suffrage would have made no difference to the outcome. Insofar as a propertyless proletariat did exist (and in some places had the vote), Beard finds "they voted with the major interests of the cities in favor of the Constitution as against the agrarians."[190] An extension of their vote would have made for more lopsided victories in districts where Federalists were already the strongest.

Beard did agree that the apportionment of delegates overrepresented the urban personalty districts and thus may have given the minority party parity at the State conventions. Ultimately, however, the real explanation for the Federalist victory was *political mobilization*. Beard's figures indicated that only 2 to 20 percent of the eligible electorate turned out to vote. He argues that voter turnout in the cities was higher than in rural areas because of better political organization, the ease of voting, and the greater influence of press and public information. Federalists had a greater incentive to vote because of their circumstances. Finally, more of their leaders possessed *the kind* of talent, professional abilities, and liquid wealth necessary to wage modern pamphlet campaigns, newspapers wars, speaking tours, etc.[191]

Antifederalists, on the contrary, "suffered from the difficulties connected with getting a backwoods vote out to the town or county elections." There were "long journeys in bad weather."[192] News traveled slower and through fewer sources. Furthermore, because the Antifederalists' rural mass base was poor and uninfluential, there was often no money to carry on their campaign in areas where the Antifederalists were expected to do well. By contrast, the Federalists' urban mass base of artisans, craftsmen, and shopkeepers were easily accessible and could usually afford a few pennies for a newspaper or pamphlet.

In the context of these observations, the worst Beard could say about the Federalists' tactics at the state conventions is that they won "the victory in eloquence, logic, and pure argumentation."[193] They successfully mobilized their own urban constituency, forged alliances with related interests (e.g., commercial farmers and entrepreneurial planters), and persuaded enough delegates in crucial states at the crucial time to carry a small margin of victory. The margin of victory or defeat was the historically contingent result of unrelenting political vigor on the part of the Federalists.[194]

This conception of political action was also at the center of Beard's analysis of the economic spirit of the Constitution. Unlike the Populists and Progressives, Beard did not believe this spirit entailed a *structuralist* theory of the capitalist state. Indeed, Beard quickly cautioned his readers that it was "a wholly false notion to regard the Constitution-making process as completed with the ratification of the instrument." Quite the contrary, the Constitution was simply "a proposition for the conduct of public affairs." There was "no magic in the language of the instrument of government" that could guarantee the political domination of personalty interests or the complete exclusion of agrarian politics.[195]

The Constitution provided a framework of rules, offices, powers, and obstacles *which if used properly* would more readily *facilitate* the building of a capitalist state than would the Articles (and vice versa). Nevertheless, the specificity of this state still had to be constructed through a variety of additional mechanisms. According to Beard, the "real character" of the new American state would be "determined by the measures of law and administration established under it." The "general language of the Constitution needed to be filled with concrete meaning in the form of definite statutes." Its clauses had to be interpreted favorably "by men rightly affected toward the new instrument." Ultimately, this "depended upon the character of the men who filled the offices and determined the policies and measures of the new government."[196] Political mobilization and the relative balance of active social forces remained a key factor in the larger determination of the economic character of the state. Consequently, there was no doubt in Beard's mind that the Constitution was periodically "transformed in the hands of those who from generation to generation had exercised political power."[197]

Beard understood these transformations as the outcome of a continuing historical conflict between agriculture and capitalism (or populist vs. liberal democracy) and not as a struggle between democracy and aristocracy. For Beard, the persistence of this conflict was at the heart of the American party battle and, therefore, it determined the meaning of attendant struggles over the interpretation of the Constitution.[198] As opposed to the structuralism of Progressive theory, Beard argued that it was political parties which organized the personnel, statutory agenda, administration, and interpretation of the Constitution. This meant that the actual process of government could only be "set in motion and kept going by the political parties" and could not exist independently of them.[199]

This was particularly true of the American state which, according to Beard's analysis, incorporated the spirit of capitalism *alongside* the spirit of democracy.[200] Each of the two parties (Federalists-Republicans) formed during the struggle for ratification emphasized one of these spirits over the other as the basic principle of its political agenda and in its interpretation of the Constitution. Hence, depending upon which party wielded instrumental control of the state, its spirit would alternately shift in one direction or another. It was the antinomy of Hamiltonian capitalism vs. Jeffersonian democracy that defined the contours of Beard's fundamentally Hegelian philosophy of American political development.

Beard conceptualized the period of 1787-1801 as a turning point in the economic development of the United States primarily because it set a capitalist state in the heart of an agricultural civilization. The Federalists not only won a constitutional framework more advantageous to the task of promoting capitalist development, but they were able to extend that initiative for another twelve years with national electoral victories. Their instrumental control of national government was crucial to building a capitalist state and to setting in motion the forces of capitalist development (i.e., a historical thesis).[201] Although the party of business (Federalist-Whig-National Republican-Republican) periodically suffered setbacks or encountered obstacles in the form of agrarian and populist rebellion, opponents of the Hamiltonian system could never fully roll back the previous achievements of capitalism, nor dislodge its privileged position within the state. Each time the capitalist party returned to power, it started from a position more advanced than the last time. Consequently, it could push its economic interests that much further ahead—a sort of two steps forward, one step back.[202]

In the course of this advance, Beard identifies the Civil war and the Populist rebellion as the next most crucial developments in the economic defeat of a radical populist or realty/agrarian interest. The Civil War destroyed the Southern planter wing of agrarian opposition. It also yielded the 14th amendment, higher tariffs, railroad land grants, and internal improvements which unleashed a second wave of industrial expansion.[203] The final economic triumph of capitalism was marked by the decline and failure of the Populist rebellion (1890s).

On an economic plane, Beard derided Populism as an anachronistic middle-class revolt against the industrialization of agriculture at the turn of the century. By this time, Beard argued that agriculture was already a capitalistic business enterprise in which the major participants were either agribusinessmen or landless proletarians, tenants, and sharecroppers.[204] Hence, the economic thesis of American history was a narrative of the triumph of the spirit of capitalism.

Yet, American history moved simultaneously along another track of antithetical *political* development. In their efforts to stave off the triumph of an industrial capitalist economy, the periodic agrarian rebellions did achieve real political victories. The ratification struggle yielded the Bill of Rights. Jacksonian democrats won universal white male suffrage and open party conventions. The Civil War at least produced a formal emancipation and enfranchisement of African-Americans. Greenbackers and their successors produced the Australian ballot; Populists the direct primary; Progressives the direct election of U.S. Senators and women's suffrage; New Freedom liberals the federal income tax amendment.

From this perspective, American history had been the outcome of a dialectical contest between two competing principles—Hamiltonianism and Jeffersonianism. In the course of this contest, each idea canceled that element in its opposite that was not in conformity with the larger spirit of American civilization.[205] What Beard called "political federalism" (e.g., Hamilton and John Adams) had from the outset been forced to concede the basic principle of popular sovereignty. Any pretensions to political elitism practically disappeared by 1828 when even the Whig party was forced to adopt the language of Jacksonian democracy. By his own time, Beard could accurately argue that it "has now become the fashion of conservative leaders to celebrate the principles of Thomas Jefferson."[206] American capitalism had embraced the democratic idea.

On the other hand, Jeffersonian economics was steadily pushed aside by the victory of a Hamiltonian political economy. As the spirit of capitalism unfolded over the course of American history, its inexorable movement was towards economic concentration and generalized inequality while, in contrast, the spirit of democracy was inexorably moving towards the generalization of equality. Hence, even while capitalism embraced the democratic *idea*, each subsequent clash between capitalism and democracy placed the two principles in a more profound antagonism with one another, particularly since the economic advance of capitalism was generating a new political antithesis in the form of a propertyless democratic majority: i.e., the proletariat.[207] In this historical context, Beard envisioned social and industrial democracy as the *aufheben* of American history. It was the absolute idea of American civilization which suspended and transcended those antinomies through a fusion of economic federalism with Jeffersonian democracy. Only through social and industrial democracy would the spirit of American civilization fully emerge in its absolute and final form.

Significantly, there was only one economic group whose historical advance was *necessarily* dependent on the triumph of *both* principles and this was the industrial working class. Prior to the Civil War, the American proletariat supported ratification of the Constitution *and* Jacksonian democracy. Subsequently, Beard identified the various third party movements in which labor was a participant with the gradual emergence of the social democratic idea. The Labor Reformers (1872), Greenback-Labor Party (1876-1884), United Laborites (1888), Populists (1892-1896), and Socialists (1901-1920) had, each in their turn, contributed something to the clarification of a social democratic alternative. Each of these parties arose from the regular cycles of temporary economic distress engendered by the capitalist economy. In Beard's opinion, however, all of these parties had been "inadequate to the demands of party warfare."[208]

Beard offered two inter-related explanations for their inadequacy as political vehicles of social democracy. The labor movement (especially the A. F. of L.) had not yet fully abandoned the Jeffersonian economics of its artisanal predecessors. To a large degree, the American working class had never shed the Jacksonian conception of itself as an independent, lower-middle class of artisans and craftsmen. Consequently, it continued to follow the lead of middle-class Populists, Progressives, and liberals. This was partly a problem of political education (i.e., ideology), but it was mainly one of economic organization.[209] By the 1920s, Beard argued that an economic basis for the social democratic vision was being laid in the growing organization of industrial unions. These unions fully accepted industrial concentration and proletarian status as the framework in which to redefine the meaning of contemporary democracy. Nevertheless, Beard suspected that the American working class was peculiarly impervious to Marxian socialism because of its long tradition of constitutional democracy.[210] Therefore, he placed his hope in the possibility of a British style independent labor party based on the industrial unions.

In the meantime, many of labor's first rudimentary steps toward industrial democracy were being struck down by federal courts. Did this mean that the Constitution was an inherent obstruction to industrial democracy? Beard concluded it was not; under ordinary circumstances the constitutional system of checks and balances clearly dissolved the energy of popular majorities, but it had never been capable of withstanding concerted assaults during periods of mass political mobilization. During such times, the parties had succumbed to democratic pressures and, subsequently, these became instruments for securing other structural changes in the state.[211] These changes had gradually laid the groundwork for social democratic legislative victories in which the balance of economic burdens was partially shifted from labor to business.[212]

The one persistent obstacle to further movement towards social democracy was the U.S. Supreme Court. Beard characterized it as "the great defender of private property."[213] Yet, even this barrier could not pose a permanent obstacle in Beard's opinion. He suggested that amendment and judicial reinterpretation were feasible methods of constitutional change.

Beard was unquestionably aware of the Populist and Progressive positions in this controversy. In his textbook on *American Government and Politics*, Beard notes: "there arose at the opening of this century an extensive criticism of the amending process...In short it seemed impossible to amend the Constitution in the regular course of things."[214] However, Beard claims that "this spell was broken by the adoption of the income tax amendment in 1913, followed shortly by amendments establishing the popular election of Senators, prohibition, and woman suffrage."[215] Beard was equally anti-populist in his own position on judicial review. As early as 1912, Beard devoted a journal article and a book to a direct refutation of the Progressive claim that judicial review was a Federalist usurpation of authority. Judicial review was defended as a sound, inherent, and originally intended element of the checks and balances system.

Instead, the key elements that enabled the Supreme Court to defend personalty against social democratic assaults were specific concepts and assumptions of judicial reasoning introduced as precedents by Federalist judges. One of these obstacles was the legal meaning of free contract and the obligation of contract. Beard observed that "all thinking persons for many a generation" agreed that government was obligated to enforce contracts entered into freely. However, government was also responsible for defending persons against contracts (e.g., wage contracts) in which inequality between the parties turned contracts into a coercive instrument of disguised oppression.[216] For Beard, this was already well established legal precedent.

The contemporary problem with applications of the precedent was the underlying myth of individualism which still guided its interpretation and enforcement. This was a historical cultural barrier introduced into legal reasoning that was shared by both Federalists and Jeffersonians.[217] Whether consciously or not, American judicial precedent had also presupposed the sociology of petit-bourgeois production as the reference from which free contract derived its meaning. Strongly guided by precedent, American jurists ignored the fact that "vast masses of property are becoming socialized" in new forms of corporate and collective ownership. Hence, judges effectively denied "the existence of classes in the United States and based their judicial reasoning on the false premises of universal equality and liberty."[218] The meaning of judicial doctrine was therefore being interpreted with reference to specific political philosophies (Hamilton and Jefferson) that were both archaic in their sociological assumptions.[219]

The most significant concept linking constitutional reasoning with these archaic assumptions was the *persona ficta* which regarded corporations as persons under the 5th and 14th amendments. Beard complained that in a legal system where corporate persons enjoy all the rights and protections of natural individuals "the dice of fortune are loaded" on the side of the corporations. No one could "deny the disparity between individual natural persons and individual corporate persons in wealth, economic power, and political influence."[220]

Consequently, the real question of original intention for Beard was not whether judicial review was an intended part of the Constitution, but whether personhood and constitutional rights were intended to apply to corporations in the same way as they are applied to natural persons. His analysis of historical evidence on the origins of the 5th amendment made it:

> fairly certain that the first ten Amendments to the Constitution refer, at least primarily, to the rights of natural persons—human beings, and not to the rights of corporations—fictitious persons. When the origin of the amendments is reviewed, and the character of their supporters examined, it seems impossible to believe that the mass of people who demanded, sponsored and ratified the amendments had corporations in mind.[221]

In fact, it was not until the various decisions of the Marshall Court that the obligation of contract clause was used in conjunction with the *persona ficta* to protect corporations against the populist assaults of state legislatures. This protection was consciously extended in the 14th amendment by some promoters, but was not generally understood by ratifiers. The thrust of Beard's argument was that *only through judicial interpretation* had rights accorded to natural and mortal persons been protected against Congress, state constitutional conventions, state legislatures, city councils, and other governmental agencies. For the same reason, however, judicial reinterpretation was sufficient to remove or alter those protections.[222]

What was the practical likelihood that this could or would happen? Beard argued that the Supreme Court had actually thrown itself resolutely across currents of powerful interests and ideas only four times in American history: the Dred Scott case, the efforts to block federal policy during and just after the Civil War, nullification of the 1894 Income Tax Law, and nullification of the National Industrial Recovery Act. Every one of these efforts failed. Dred Scott was reversed by Civil War and by the 13th, 14th, and 15th amendments. The meddling in Civil War policy initiatives was stopped by curtailing the Court's appellate jurisdiction and by adding two judges to pack the Court. The income tax was later established by constitutional amendment. By 1937, labor unrest, a new effort to pack the Court, and threats to amend the Constitution were sufficient for the Court to reverse itself a fourth time.[223]

Whether or not courts could block social and economic change, therefore, largely depended on the gravity of the crisis itself. Courts had blocked social and economic change only where the underlying historical forces were transitory. In those instances where social forces were advancing deep seated changes, the courts had always adapted themselves or been forced to adapt by the changing balance of social and political power. Thus, as the Great Depression brought corporate interests and the public interest into sharper antagonism, Beard predicted that the "dual system of equal rights for natural persons and for corporate persons" would become increasingly untenable in the context of modern political democracy.[224] The contest between corporations and democracy placed the "rights of property of a few hundred artificial persons...over against the rights and property of 120,000,000 natural persons." Under these circumstances, Beard predicted a domestic economic crisis or the international decline of American might would finally activate popular power to "break in upon the rights of property held in mortmain by deathless corporations." In the midst of the Great Depression, Beard speculated that "if corporations cannot provide employment for the millions of the American proletariat— for such we have, in spite of all claptrap to the contrary—can corporate persons expect to protect themselves forever, through constitutional and judicial processes?" He concluded that "it seems reasonable to expect a negative answer to this fateful question."[225]

Notes

1.   Vernon Louis Parrington, "Introduction," in James Allen Smith, *The Growth and Decadence of Constitutional Government* (New York: Holt, Rinehart, and Winston, 1930), p. x.

2. Ibid., pp. xi-xii. Vernon Louis Parrington, *Main Currents in American Thought*, 3 Vols. (New York: Harcourt, Brace, and World, Inc., 1930), Vol. 3, p. xxv.

3. Richard Hofstadter, *The Age of Reform* (New York: Alfred A. Knopf, 1955), p. 154.

4. There are several works which analyze both the political influence and the Jeffersonian origins of this style of thought. On Smith, see Eric F. Goldman, "J. Allen Smith: The Reformer and his Dilemma," *Pacific Northwest Quarterly* (July 1944): 195-212; Howard E. Dean, "J. Allen Smith: Jeffersonian Critic of the Federalist State," *American Political Science Review* (December 1956): 1093-1104; Thomas C. McClintock, "J. Allen Smith: A Pacific Northwest Progressive," *Pacific Northwest Quarterly* (April 1962): 49-59. On Parrington, see William T. Utter, "Vernon Louis Parrington," in *The Marcus W. Jernegan Essays in American Historiography* (Chicago: University of Chicago Press, 1937); Granville Hicks, "The Critical Principles of V. L. Parrington," *Science and Society* (Fall 1939): 443-60; Richard Hofstadter, "Parrington and the Jeffersonian Tradition," *Journal of the History of Ideas* (October 1941): 391-400; James L. Colwell, "The Populist Image of Vernon Louis Parrington," *Mississippi Valley Historical Review* (June 1962): 52-66; Skotheim, *American Intellectual Histories and Historians*, pp. 124-48; Hofstadter, *The Progressive Historians*, pp. 349-436. On McMaster, see Eric F. Goldman, *John Bach McMaster; American Historian* (Philadelphia: University of Pennsylvania Press, 1943).

5. Parrington, "Introduction," *Growth and Decadence*, p. x. Likewise, Parrington, *Main Currents in American Thought*, Vol. 3, pp. 408-09. In fact, books by two American Socialist Party organizers antedated Beard's book in initiating this economic phase. See A. M. Simons, *Class Struggles in America* (Chicago: Charles H. Kerr and Co., 1903) and *Social Forces in American History* (New York: Macmillan Co., 1911), pp. 6-31; James Oneal, *The Workers in American History* (Terre Haute, in 1910). These books were successful with popular audiences, Goldman, "The Origins of Beard's *Economic Interpretation of the Constitution*," p. 244, but they were dismissed by academic scholars for being avowedly Marxist. Lerner, *Ideas are Weapons*, p. 157, affirms this point. Other Marxist treatments of the constitutional struggle were Gustavus Myers, *History of the Supreme Court of the United States* (Chicago: Charles H. Kerr and Co., 1912); Arthur W. Calhoun, *The Worker Looks at Government* (Katonah, NY: Brookwood Labor College, 1927); Anton Bimba, *History of the American Working Class* (New York: International Publishers, 1936), pp. v-60.

6. See Benjamin E. Lippincott, "The Bias of American Political Science," *Journal of Politics* 12 (1940): 125-39. The earliest effort to fuse Smith and Beard was published by a New York Socialist Party state legislator. See Benson, *Our Dishonest Constitution*. A lesser known effort was Robert Livingston Schuyler, *The Constitution of the United States* (New York: Macmillan Co., 1923).

7. Hofstadter, "Charles Beard and the Constitution," in Beale, ed., *Charles A. Beard*, pp. 81-88. Matthew A. Fitzsimons, Alfred G. Pundt, and Charles E. Nowell, eds., *The Development of Historiography* (Port Washington, NY: Kennikat Press, 1967), p. 424. For example, Jacob Mark Jacobsen, *The Development of American Political Thought* (New York: The Century Co., 1932); John McConaughy, *Who Rules America? A Century of Invisible Government* (New York: Longman, Green and Co., 1934); John D. Hicks, *The Federal Union: History of the United States to 1865* (Boston: Houghton-Mifflin Co., 1937); Robert A. East, *Business Enterprise in the American Revolutionary Era* (New York: Columbia University Press, 1938); Louis M. Hacker, *The Triumph of American Capitalism* (New

York: Simon and Schuster, 1940). The most influential contemporary version of this synthesis is Merrill Jensen, *The Articles of Confederation: An Interpretation of the Socio-Constitutional History of the American Revolution, 1774-1781* (Madison: University of Wisconsin Press, 1948); Merrill Jensen, *The New Nation: A History of the United States during the Confederation 1781-1789* (Boston: Northeastern University Press, 1981); Merrill Jensen, *The Making of the American Constitution* (Princeton, NJ: D. Van Nostrand and Co., 1964).

8. Even contemporary critics acknowledge that the Beardian "influence on American thought has not greatly diminished" despite a resurgent wave of counter-Progressive criticism. Paul Eidelberg, *The Philosophy of the American Constitution: A Reinterpretation of the Intentions of the Founding Fathers* (New York: Free Press, 1968); Paul Eidelberg, *A Discourse on Statesmanship: The Design and Transformation of the American Polity* (Urbana: University of Illinois Press, 1974); Catherine Drinker Bowen, *Miracle at Philadelphia: The Story of the Constitutional Convention May to September 1787* (Boston: Little, Brown, and Co., 1966); Herbert J. Storing, *What the Antifederalists Were For* (Chicago: University of Chicago Press, 1981).

9. Beard, *Economic Interpretation of the Constitution*, pp. vi, xiii.

10. Goldman, "The Origins of Beard's *Economic Interpretation*," pp. 236-46; Lerner, "Charles Beard's Political Theory," in Beale, ed., *Charles Beard*, pp. 25-45; Strout, *The Pragmatic Revolt*, p. 115; Hofstadter, *The Progressive Historians*, pp. 75-80; Dennis L. Thompson, "Introduction to the 1972 Edition," in Smith, *Growth and Decadence*, p. xviii; Skotheim, *American Intellectual Histories*, pp. 87-109.

11. Charles A. Beard, "Review of *The Spirit of American Government* by J. Allen Smith," *Political Science Quarterly* (March 1908): 136-37; Letter to Robert LaFollette quoted in Nore, *Charles A. Beard*, p. 55.

12. Charles A. Beard, "Review of *The New Freedom: A Call for the Emancipation of the Generous Energies of a People*, by Woodrow Wilson," *Political Science Quarterly* 29 (September 1914): 506-507; Charles A. Beard, "Jefferson and the New Freedom," *New Republic* (November 14, 1914), p. 18; Charles A. Beard, "Review of *Property and Contract in their Relation to the Distribution of Wealth* by Robert T. Ely," *Political Science Quarterly* (September 1915), p. 511; Charles A. Beard, "The Myth of Rugged American Individualism," *Harper's Monthly Magazine* (December 1931), pp. 19-22; Charles A. Beard, *Jefferson, Corporations, and the Constitution* (Washington, DC: National Home Library Foundation, 1936), pp. 26-32. For extensive criticisms of Woodrow Wilson and Theodore Roosevelt, see Beard, *Contemporary American History, 1877-1913*, pp. 254-377, passim.

13. Beard and Beard, *America in Mid-Passage*, p. 673; Goldman, "Charles Beard," in Beale, ed., *Charles A. Beard*, p. 2.

14. Hofstadter, *Age of Reform*, p. 133, argues that the intellectual roots of Progressive political theory are found in the Populism of the 1890s. This continuity was sustained on a political level because after 1900 Populism and Progressivism merge: "a working coalition was forged between the old Bryan country and the new reform movement in the cities." Nevertheless, he still identifies two strains of thought among Progressives after 1900. One strain was influenced chiefly by the Populist inheritance. The other, while Populist in character, was "mainly a product of urban life" concerned with "labor and social welfare, municipal reform, the interest of the consumer" (p. 133). Herbert Croly, *Progressive Democracy* (New York: Macmillan Co., 1915), pp. 11-20, notes that during the 1912

Presidential campaign, the latter strain split into two divergent economic interpretations of American politics: Progressivism and social or industrial democracy. Depending upon their attitudes towards Roosevelt, the social democrats chose either to anchor the left-wing of the Progressive Party (e.g., Croly) or the right-wing of the socialist movement (e.g., Beard).

15. Robert E. Thomas, "A Reappraisal of Charles A. Beard's *An Economic Interpretation of the Constitution of the United States*," *American Historical Review* 5 (January 1952): 370-75.

16. Parrington, "Introduction," in Smith, *Growth and Decadence*, p. x.

17. John Bach McMaster, *With the Fathers: Studies in the History of the United States* (New York: D. Appleton and Co., 1897), pp. 107-9. Likewise, Croly, *Progressive Democracy*, p. 5, comments in retrospect that "the time was not ripe either for a searching diagnosis or for effective remedial measures. Its dominant characteristic was that of resentment against individuals."

18. Parrington, "Introduction," in *Growth and Decadence*, p. ix. For example, Dean William Trickett, "Judicial Dispensation from Congressional Statutes," *American Law Review* (January 1907): 65-91; Louis B. Boudin, "Government by Judiciary," *Political Science Quarterly* (June 1911): 238-70; Gilbert Roe, "Our Judicial Oligarchy," *LaFollette's Weekly Magazine* (June 24, 1911): 7-9; Gilbert Roe, "Why the People Distrust the Courts," *LaFollette's Weekly Magazine* (July 1, 1911): 7-9; Walter Clark, "Some Defects in the Constitution of the United States," *Congressional Record* (July 31, 1911): 3374-77; Frank J. Goodnow, *Social Reform and the Constitution* (New York: Macmillan, 1911); Myers, *History of the Supreme Court of the United States*; William L. Ransom, *Majority Rule and the Judiciary* (New York: Charles Scriber's Sons, 1912); Louis B. Boudin, *Government by Judiciary*, 2 Volumes (New York: William Goodwin, Inc., 1932). For background, see Owen M. Fiss, *Troubled Beginnings of the Modern State, 1888-1910* (New York: Macmillan Publishing Co., 1993), esp. Chaps. 1-2.

19. Parrington, "Introduction," in Smith, *Growth and Decadence*, pp. ix-x; Croly, *Progressive Democracy*, p. 12.

20. Parrington, *Main Currents*, Volume III, p. xxv.

21. Parrington, "Introduction," in Smith, *Growth and Decadence*, p. ix.

22. Smith, *Growth and Decadence*, p. 59; Parrington, *Main Currents*, Vol. 3, p. xxv; Frank J. Goodnow, *Politics and Administration: A Study in Government* (New York: Macmillan Co., 1900), pp. 1-2.

23. Smith, *Growth and Decadence*, pp. 57-58.

24. Ibid., pp. 59-60; Goodnow, *Politics and Administration*, p. 1.

25. Sydney George Fisher, *True History of the American Revolution* (Philadelphia: J. B. Lippincott Co., 1902), p. 8. Similarly, Barnes, *The New History and the Social Studies*, p. 5, observes that "the most important historians of the nineteenth century still conceived and executed their works according to the belief that the chief purpose of history was to glorify the national past rather than to recount in a faithful manner the real facts and forces connected with national cultural development." For example, Bancroft, *History of the Formation of the Constitution of the United States*; Bryce, *The American Commonwealth*; George Ticknor Curtis, *Constitutional History of the United States from the Declaration of Independence to the Close of the Civil War*, 2 Volumes (New York: Harper and Brothers, 1889-1896); Judson S. Landon, *The Constitutional History and Government of the United States*, (Boston: Houghton-Mifflin Co., 1889); T. M. Cooley, *Constitutional History of the United States* (New York: G. P. Putnam's

Sons, 1889); Albert Bushnell Hart, *Formation of the Union, 1750-1829* (London: Longman, Green and Co., 1892); John Fiske, *The Critical Period of American History, 1783-1789* (Boston: Houghton-Mifflin Co., 1893); C. Ellis Stevens, *Sources of the Constitution of the United States* (New York: Macmillan and Co., 1894); James Bradley Thayer, *Legal Essays* (Boston: Boston Book Co., 1908).

26. Smith, *Growth and Decadence*, p. 60.

27. Barnes, *History of Historical Writing*, p. 385, observes that "by tracing back to their beginnings our own culture and institutions, we can not only better understand our own age but can also destroy that reverential and credulous attitude toward the past which is the chief obstacle to social and intellectual progress and the most dangerous menace to society." Lawrence Goodwyn, "Organizing Democracy: The Limits of Theory and Practice," *Democracy* 1, 1 (January 1981): 41-60, offers an identical critique of how the founding is still "obscured by layers of mystifying historical literature that blurred the identities of the specific historical actors" engaged in the revolutionary and constitutional struggles (p. 44).

28. John Bach McMaster, *History of the People of the United States* (New York: D. Appleton and Co., 1883), Volume I, p. 2. Barnes, *History of Historical Writing*, p. 262, credits McMaster with making "social history popular in this country." Fitzsimons, Pundt, and Nowell, eds., *The Development of Historiography*, p. 417. Importantly, Paul K. Conkin, "Intellectual History," in William H. Cartwright and Richard L. Watson, Jr., eds., *The Reinterpretation of American History and Culture* (Washington, DC: National Council for the Social Studies, 1973), p. 240: "A social historian accepts the challenge of writing about whole populations, or at least about large groupings of people...Even the earliest self-denominated social historians reflected an interest in the life of the common people, of the masses, of the laboring class."

29. Parrington, "Introduction," in *Growth and Decadence*, p. xi. Likewise Charles Warren, *The Making of the Constitution* (Boston: Little, Brown, and Co., 1929), pp. 747-48.

30. Cf. Contemporary revisionist scholarship along the same line includes, Elisha P. Douglas, *Rebels and Democrats* (Chapel Hill: University of North Carolina Press, 1955); Philip S. Foner, *Labor and the American Revolution* (Westport, CT: Greenwood Press, 1976); Gary B. Nash, *The Urban Crucible: Social Changes, Political Consciousness, and the Origin of the American Revolution* (Cambridge: Cambridge University Press, 1979); R. S. Longley, "Mob Activities in Revolutionary Massachusetts," *New England Quarterly* (March 1933): 98-130; Herbert M. Morais, "Artisan Democracy and the American Revolution," *Science and Society* (Summer 1942): 227-249; Staughton Lynd, "The Mechanics in New York Politics, 1774-1778," *Labor History* (Fall 1964): 224-246; Jesse Lemisch, "Jack Tar in the Streets: Merchant Seamen in the Politics of Revolutionary America," *William and Mary Quarterly* (July 1968): 371-407; Pauline Maier, "The Charleston Mob and the Evolution of Popular Politics in Revolutionary South Carolina, 1765-1784," *Perspective in American History* 4 (1970): 173-98; Charles S. Olton, "Philadelphia Mechanics in the First Decade of the American Revolution, 1765-1775," *Journal of American History* (September 1972): 311-26.

31. The people were defined primarily as small farmers (both yeomanry and tenants), but also included small merchants, artisans, craftsmen, and tradesmen. Marxists such as Simons and Oneal added a Jacksonian twist to this concept by including laborers and seamen. Conceptually, these groups were all consolidated

into a Revolutionary working class.

32. Fisher, *True History*, p. 9.

33. Allan Nevins, *The American States During and After the Revolution, 1775-1789* (New York: Macmillan Co., 1924), pp. 15-74. Cf. J. A. Woodburn, *The Causes of the American Revolution* (Baltimore: John Hopkins University Press, 1892). Arthur M. Schlesinger, *The Colonial Merchants and the Revolution* (New York: Columbia University Press, 1918).

34. Smith, *Growth and Decadence*, p. 15. This goal included the desire of small merchants to break government protected monopolies on trade, shipping, and commerce; of artisans to break protected manufacturing monopolies; and of small farmers to reopen western lands to settlement. See Woodburn and Schlesinger cited in fn. 33. More recent treatments of these questions are Thomas P. Abernathy, *Western Lands and the American Revolution* (New York: D. Appleton-Century Co., 1937); George Olien Virtue, *British Land Policy and the American Revolution* (Lincoln: University of Nebraska Press, 1953); Oliver Morton Dickerson, *The Navigation Acts and the American Revolution* (Philadelphia: University of Pennsylvania Press, 1951); Jack M. Sosin, *Agents and Merchants: British Colonial Policy and the Origins of the American Revolution, 1763-1775* (Lincoln: University of Nebraska Press, 1965); Joseph A. Ernst, *Money and Politics in America, 1755-1775; a study in the Currency Act of 1764 and the political economy of the Revolution* (Chapel Hill: University of North Carolina Press, 1973).

35. The intellectual origins of this doctrine were always identified with John Locke's political philosophy. See Nevins, *The American States*, pp. 120-22; Parrington, *Main Currents*, Volume 1, pp. 271-76; Smith, *Growth and Decadence*, p. 14; Croly, *Progressive Democracy*, pp. 50-57; Charles Edward Merriam, *A History of American Political Theories* (New York: Macmillan Co., 1903), pp. 38-95. Recent analyses of its historical social origins among the English political radicals of this era are Neal Wood, *John Locke and Agrarian Capitalism* (Berkeley: University of California Press, 1984) and Richard Ashcraft, *Revolutionary Politics and Locke's Two Treatises of Government* (Princeton, NJ: Princeton University Press, 1986).

36. Nevins, *The American States*, pp. 126-64. It was recognized that individual States did not equally conform to this model in all its details. Since there was an active contest between radical and conservative factions in the states, the degree of constitutional radicalism was contingent upon the strength and organization of radical forces in each particular state. North Carolina and Pennsylvania were usually identified as the two states most closely approximating this model. Maryland and New York were at least initially regarded as the two most conservative constitutions. See Cecelia M. Kenyon, "Constitutionalism in Revolutionary America," in J. Roland Pennock and John W. Chapman, eds., *Constitutionalism* (New York: New York University Press, 1979), pp. 84-121, whose analysis is surprisingly consistent with this earlier position; Willi Paul Adams, *The First American Constitutions: Republican Ideology and the Making of the State Constitutions in the Revolutionary Era* (Chapel Hill: University of North Carolina Press, 1980).

37. Smith, *Growth and Decadence*, p. 21, observes that in the revolutionary context of these radical democracies, popular sovereignty or "the consent of the governed meant more than the consent of the qualified voters." Even when excluded from the franchise, "the majority were recognized as having rights which they could defend and enforce" *directly* "even against the state itself." The operative

guarantee of popular sovereignty was in the final analysis not the franchise, but *the local militia*. Since the people retained direct control of military force (and the states had no standing army), the people were always in a position to revoke their consent at will by overthrowing the government (Shay's rebellion, for example). Therefore, elections were little more than a technical procedure for selecting government officials. They were *not* a measure of consent or legitimacy. Thus, most of the state constitutions would not qualify as democratic (much less radical) when judged by classical concepts of direct participatory democracy or liberal republicanism. See Carole Pateman, *Participation and Democratic Theory* (Cambridge: Cambridge University Press, 1970), pp. 1-44; C. B. MacPherson, *The Life and Times of Liberal Democracy* (Oxford: Oxford University Press, 1977). However, the Populists especially were talking in terms of a *populist* democracy based on simple absolute majority rule in which elections were not the most important component. See Parrington, *Main Currents*, Volume 1, pp. 278-79; Elaine Spitz, *Majority Rule* (Chatham: Chatham House Publishers, Inc., 1984), pp. 101-33 on the distinction between liberal and populist democracy.

38. Short sessions were supposed to facilitate office-holding by ordinary farmers. They could travel the short distance to a State capital, sit in a legislature from January to March after harvesting crops in the fall, but before sowing new ones in the spring. Short terms were supposed to keep legislators close to the people and facilitate the circulation of office-holders, thereby preventing the development of an entrenched political class.

39. J. Allen Smith, *The Spirit of American Government* (New York: Macmillan Co., 1907), pp. 18-21; Smith, *Growth and Decadence*, pp. 16-26: Nevins, *The American States*, pp. 117-70.

40. Smith, *Spirit*, p. 22-25.

41. Religious liberty and disestablishment were often integral aspects of the alleged aristocratic/democratic conflict because of a widely perceived relationship between social position and religious domination. Episcopalian, orthodox (Old Side) Presbyterianism, and orthodox Congregationalism were perceived as formal, staid, hierarchical religions, with an elective affinity for gentlemen, planters, wealthy merchants, and educated professionals. Evangelical denominations such as Baptists, Methodists, New Light/Separate Congregationalists, and the New Side Presbyterians were perceived as more democratic in their organization, their offering of universal salvation and, therefore, in their elective affinity for the common and/or uneducated person. See Helmut Richard Neibuhr, *The Social Sources of Denominationalism* (New York: Henry Holt and Co., 1929); Richard Hofstadter, *Anti-Intellectualism in American Life* (New York: Vintage Books, 1962), pp. 56-90; E. Digby Baltzell, "Religion and the Class Structure," in Seymour Martin Lipset and Richard Hofstadter, eds., *Sociology and History: Methods* (New York: Basic Books, 1968).

42. Nevins, *The American States*, pp. 420-69.

43. Parrington, "Introduction," to Smith, *Growth and Decadence*, p. xi.

44. Ibid., p. xi; Nevins, *The American States*, pp. 206-419. Students of Frederick Jackson Turner perceived closely related sectional or geographic divisions within the states. They suggested that local geographic conditions often led to sectional concentrations of economic groups or classes because of the limitations or advantages these conditions provided for specific kinds of economic activities (e.g., fishing, farming, etc.). Hence, in the South, electoral returns suggested a split between tidewater planters and inland savannah farmers; in New Jersey

between northeastern Hudson patroons and southwestern small farmers; in Massachusetts and Pennsylvania between eastern urban merchant/financiers and western frontier farmer/debtors. See Orin Grant Libby, *The Geographical Distribution of the Vote of the Thirteen States on the Federal Constitution, 1787-1789* (Madison: University of Wisconsin Press, 1894); William A. Schaper, "Sectionalism and Representation in South Carolina," *Annual Report of the American Historical Association* (Washington, DC: Government Printing Office, 1901); Charles H. Ambler, *Sectionalism in Virginia* (Chicago: University of Chicago Press, 1910).

45. Parrington, "Introduction," to Smith, *Growth and Decadence*, p. xi.

46. Andrew C. McLaughlin, *A Constitutional History of the United States* (New York: D. Appleton-Century Co., 1935), p. 137; Andrew C. McLaughlin, *The Confederation and the Constitution, 1783-1789* (New York: Harper and Brothers Publishers, 1905); Fiske, *The Critical Period*, pp. 134-86.

47. Nevins, *The American States*, pp. 541-43. Cf. Elmer James Ferguson, *The Power of the Purse: A History of American Public Finance, 1776-1790* (Chapel Hill: University of North Carolina Press, 1961).

48. Nevins, *The American States*, pp. 544-605.

49. Parrington, "Introduction," to Smith, *Growth and Decadence*, p. xi.

50. Smith, ibid., p. 79; Merriam, *History of American Political Theories*, pp. 96-142.

51. Woodrow Wilson, *Division and Reunion, 1829-1889* (New York: Longman, Green, and Co., 1898), p. 12.

52. Hicks, *The Federal Union*, p. 197.

53. Smith, *Spirit*, p. 27; Parrington, "Introduction," to Smith, *Growth and Decadence*, p. xii.

54. McConaughy, *Who Rules America?* pp. 14-19.

55. Parrington, *Main Currents*, Volume 1, p. 278.

56. Bancroft, *History of the Formation of the Constitution*, Volume 1, pp. 6-7.

57. George Ticknor Curtis, *History of the Origin, Formation and Adoption of the Constitution of the United States, With Notices of Its Principal Framers*, 2 Vols. (New York: Harper & Bros., 1854-1858), Volume 1, pp. 371-90; David Jayne Hill, "A Defense of the Constitution," *North American Review* (March 1917): 389-97.

58. Oscar S. Straus, *The Origin of the Republican Form of Government in the United States of America* (New York: G. P. Putnam's Sons, 1885), p. viii. The vision of manifest destiny was often accompanied by racial disquisitions about God's conferral of special political genius on the Anglo-American race. See Bryce, *American Commonwealth*, Volume 1, p. 25; Stimson, *The American Constitution*. The classic work on the Teutonic origins of the U.S. Constitution is Burgess, *Political Science and Comparative Constitutional Law*. The theophany underpinning these views has been resurrected recently by Bowen, *Miracle at Philadelphia*, who calls the Constitution a miracle. Bowen celebrates the writing of the Constitution with an "outmoded romanticism" laden with "Bancroftian notions," (pp. ix-x). Likewise, see Eidelberg, *Philosophy of the American Constitution* and Allan Bloom, ed., *Confronting the Constitution* (Washington, DC: The AEI Press, 1990) for Straussian interpretations.

59. McMaster, *With the Fathers*, p. 108.

60. Parrington, "Introduction," in Smith, *Growth and Decadence*, p. xi; Hicks, *The Federal Union*, p. 198.

61. Smith, *Growth and Decadence*, p. 79.

62. Wilson, *Division and Reunion*, p. 12.

63. Parrington, "Introduction," in Smith, *Growth and Decadence*, pp. xii, x; Parrington, *Main Currents*, Volume I, pp. 283-326. Warren, *The Trumpeters of the Constitution*, pp. 10-12, criticized efforts to "minimize their greatness and to emphasize their commonness." According to Warren, in American political culture, the proper role of constitutional history was to highlight those traits that made the Founders "superior to the ordinary man" and, thereby, to "show how the life of a great man may serve as a model and incentive to us."

64. Smith, *Spirit*, pp. 40-185; Smith, *Growth and Decadence*, p. 79; Simeon E. Baldwin, *Modern Political Institutions* (Boston: Little, Brown, and Co., 1898). Goodnow, *Politics and Administration* derived a further anti-democratic implication from the separation of powers. He argued this separation made it impossible for politics (i.e., the legislated will of the people) to directly control administration (i.e., the execution of the will of the people). Therefore, parties were an inherent extra-legal component of the Constitution that were structurally *necessary* to coordinate the two branches of government. Since political parties are private associations under the law, they became a vehicle for private interests, especially party bosses and the wealthy, to discipline the popular will under the disguise of formally democratic elections.

65. Smith, *Growth and Decadence*, p. 79.

66. Smith, *Spirit*, pp. vii, 27-39.

67. Ibid., pp. 186-87.

68. There were exceptions. Woodrow Wilson, *Division and Reunion*, and Woodrow Wilson, *A History of the American People* (New York: Harper and Brothers, 1901) interpreted the Jacksonian upheaval as a second "beginning of democracy" in the United States. While he accepted the populist interpretation of the Constitution and the continuing hegemony of the aristocratic spirit in American politics, Wilson argued that each cyclical revolt did erode some of that hegemony. Wilson's New Freedom was supposed to finally return power to the people. Cf. Woodrow Wilson , *The New Freedom* (New York: Doubleday, Page and Co., 1913). Also, John Bach McMaster, *The Acquisition of Political, Social, and Industrial Rights of Man in America* (Cleveland, OH: Imperial Press, 1903).

69. Wilson, *Division and Reunion*, pp. 12-13; Wilson, *History of the American People*, Volume V, pp. 79-83.

70. Smith, *Growth and Decadence*, p. 80.

71. Parrington, "Introduction," Smith, *Growth and Decadence*, pp. xii-xvi; Parrington, *Main Currents*, Volume 1, pp. 278-279. While Wilson and Libby accepted this analytic framework as a working hypothesis, they also identified several cross-cutting cleavages—both economic and regional—which influenced Beard's critique of the Progressive interpretation.

72. McMaster, *With the Fathers*, p. 71; Smith, *Growth and Decadence*, p. 80.

73. Parrington, *Main Currents*, Volume 1, p. 279.

74. Ibid., p. 279. See, Vernon Louis Parrington, Jr., ed., "Vernon Parrington's Views: Economics and Criticism," *Pacific Northwest Quarterly* (July 1953), p. 105, where Parrington insists that "the mercantile aristocracy has rarely triumphed openly...It has had to reach its ends by devious paths"

75. McMaster, *With the Fathers*, p. 71.

76. Ibid., pp. 74-75; Smith, *Growth and Decadence*, p. 114.

77. Smith, *Growth and Decadence*, p. 85. Smith claimed that "the relatively small class controlling the means of production under present day capitalism realize that they need the protection of a large government friendly to their interests...Capitalism being a form of class control, could not survive without

government support...A permanent military force, therefore, is necessary to insure adequate protection for capital in time of economic turmoil" (pp. 215-16).

78. Smith, *Spirit*, pp. 331-32.
79. Ibid., pp. 51-58.
80. Smith, *Spirit*, p. 300.
81. Smith, *Growth and Decadence*, pp. 86-98.
82. Smith, *Spirit*, pp. 65-124; Smith, *Growth and Decadence*, p. 102.
83. Smith, *Growth and Decadence*, p. 97-102.
84. Ibid., p. 102; Fisher, *True History*, p. 8.
85. Smith, *Growth and Decadence*, p. 97.
86. Ibid., pp. 97-114. Smith juxtaposed historical claims against this legal fiction to demonstrate that there was "no justification for the claim that it [the Constitution] was an expression of the popular will...the facts concerning the framing, adoption, amendment, interpretation, and enforcement of this instrument furnish no substantial basis for this belief."
87. Ibid., p. 100. Croly, *Progressive Democracy*, pp. 46-57, indicates that social democrats were extremely critical of Smith's argument, especially on this point. Looking at the conflict from an *economic* perspective, Croly contends that only in certain respects were "the interests of the farmers opposed to those of the capitalists; but in still more fundamental respects they were capable of adjustment. Both parties were seeking the satisfaction of individual economic purposes." To this degree the interests of the two classes did not coalesce, but "they ran along parallel lines." Thus, "American democrats at the end of the eighteenth century soon found that they had no imperative reason to be dissatisfied with the Constitution" even though "they would have preferred a weaker government."
88. Smith, *Growth and Decadence*, pp. 100-101.
89. Ibid., pp. 109-10; Smith, *Spirit*, p. 300.
90. Smith, *Growth and Decadence*, pp. 162-85.
91. Ibid., pp. 202-16; Goodnow, *Politics and Administration*, pp. 252-53; Wilson, *The New Freedom*, pp. 87-115.
92. Smith, *Growth and Decadence*, p. 202-16.
93. Frank J. Goodnow, *Municipal Home Rule* (New York: Macmillan Co., 1895); Herbert Croly, *The Promise of American Life* (Boston: Northeastern University Press, 1989. Reprint of 1909 Edition), Chap. XI.
94. Smith, *Growth and Decadence*, pp. 111-61.
95. Baldwin, *Modern Political Institutions*, p. 328.
96. Smith, *Growth and Decadence*, pp. 111-12; Smith, *Spirit*, p. 40-64.
97. Smith, *Spirit*, p. 338. Croly, *Progressive Democracy*, pp. 6-13, charges Baldwin and Smith with "hopeless superficiality and utter ignorance of the recorded history of government and human society." He argued that Populism failed because it was always led by local malcontents with superficial economic grievances. It was therefore "unintelligently planned, insufficiently informed and inadequately organized." According to Croly, the real problem was that American citizens consistently failed "to live up to the high intellectual and moral responsibilities imposed upon them" by the Constitution. Thus, the solution lay in a vigorous social education of the citizenry.
98. Smith, *Growth and Decadence*, p. 52; Goodnow, *Politics and Administration*, pp. 204-5.
99. Parrington, *Main Currents*, Volume 3, p. xxvii.
100. Gene Wise, *American Historical Explanations: A Strategy for Grounded Inquiry* (Min-

neapolis: University of Minnesota Press, 1980), surveys this recurring contest between progressive and counter-progressive approaches to American historiography.

101. Beard grew up on a successful and comfortable farm in Indiana. He was attending DePauw University during the heyday of the Populist Party. He received an extensive introduction to the works of Karl Marx while attending DePauw. See Nore, *Charles A. Beard*, Chap. 1; Philips, "The Indiana Education of Charles A. Beard," pp. 1-15.

102. Goldman, "The Origins of Beard's *Economic Interpretation*," pp. 234-36; Williams, "A Note on Charles Austin Beard's Search for a General Theory of Causation," pp. 61-62; Borning, *The Political and Social Thought of Charles A. Beard*, p. 46.

103. Ruskin College defined its mission as taking "men who have been merely condemning our social institutions and teaching them instead how to transform those institutions," Eden Paul and Cedar Paul, *Proletcult* (London: Leonard Parsons, 1921), p. 54; Phillips, "Charles Beard, Walter Vrooman, and the Founding of Ruskin Hall," pp. 186-91; Wilkins, "Charles A. Beard on the Founding of Ruskin Hall," pp. 277-84.

104. Goldman, "The Origins of Beard's *Economic Interpretation*," pp. 234-36.

105. Beard, "Jefferson and the New Freedom," p. 18.

106. Charles A. Beard, "The Rise of the Democratic Idea in the United States," *Survey Graphic* (April 1937): 201-02.

107. On this point, Beard acknowledges the influence of his Columbia mentor Frank Goodnow, *Politics and Administration*. He accepts Goodnow's argument that parties, state electoral laws, federal statutes organizing the judiciary and bureaucracy, and tradition must all be regarded as informal, but equally important parts of the U.S. Constitution. Thus, Beard argues that *most* of the important democratic modifications to American constitutional structure have occurred at this informal level. Hence, looking only at formal amendments is a misleading measure of actual change. See Beard, *American Government and Politics*, 5th edition, pp. 81-126.

108. Beard, "Rise of the Democratic Idea in the United States," pp. 201-2; Charles A. Beard, *Public Policy and the General Welfare* (New York: Farrar and Rinehart, 1941), p. 52.

109. Cf. John S. Pancake, ed., *Thomas Jefferson: Revolutionary Philosopher, A Selection of Writings* (Woodbury: Barron's Educational Series, Inc., 1976), pp. 111-40; Joseph L. Blau, ed., *Social Theories of Jacksonian Democracy* (New York: Liberal Arts Press, Inc., 1954).

110. Beard, "Myth of Rugged American Individualism," pp. 13-22; Beard, *Public Policy and the General Welfare*, p. 52, suggests that "the rise of democracy represented a movement of humane forces deeper than capitalism, deeper than the accumulation of profits. Yet the idea of democracy has never been entirely dissociated from the forms and distribution of wealth." Cf. Dorfman, *The Economic Mind in American Civilization*, Volume I, pp. 348-49.

111. A direct challenge to this mythology is Frank Bourgin, *The Great Challenge: The Myth of Laissez-Faire in the Early Republic* (New York: George Braziller, 1989).

112. Beard, "Review of *The New Freedom*," pp. 506-507.

113. Beard and Beard, *America in Mid-Passage*, p. 673. As an example, see Charles A. Beard, "The Constitution of Oklahoma," *Political Science Quarterly* (March 1909): 95-114.

114. Beard, "Review of *The New Freedom*," p. 507.

115. Beard, "Myth of Rugged American Individualism," p. 22.

116. Beard, "Jefferson and the New Freedom," p. 18.

117. Beard and Beard, *The Rise of American Civilization*, Volume 1, p. 132; Beard, *Jefferson, Corporations and the Constitution*, pp. 24-26.

118. Beard, "Myth of Rugged American Individualism," pp. 19-22; Charles A. Beard, "Social Change v. the Constitution," *Current History* (July 1935), p. 346; Beard, *Contemporary American History*, pp. 234-37.

119. Beard, "Myth of Rugged American Individualism," p. 19.

120. Beard, *Jefferson, Corporations, and the Constitution*, p. 26.

121. Beard and Beard, *The Rise of American Civilization*, Vol. 1, p. 538; Beard and Beard, *America in Mid-Passage*, pp. 515-35.

122. Beard, "Review of *The New Freedom*," p. 507.

123. Croly, *Progressive Democracy*, pp. 15-17, shares Beard's critique of Populism and the Wilsonian New Freedom. He comments favorably upon Beard's *Economic Interpretation of the Constitution*, while criticizing Smith's *Spirit of American Government*. However, unlike Beard, Croly argues that Theodore Roosevelt and the Progressive party of 1912 are agencies of social democracy (pp. 378-407). On the other hand, Beard considered TR "the idol of the American middle-class" because "Mr. Roosevelt, in all of his recommendations, took the ground that the prevailing system of production was essentially sound." See Beard, *Contemporary American History*, pp. 254-61.

124. Beard, "Myth of Rugged American Individualism," p. 22.

125. Beard and Beard, *Rise of American Civilization*, Vol. 2, pp. 543-65.

126. Ibid., p. 577. Italics mine, C. W. B.

127. Ibid., p. 538.

128. Beard, "Potency of Labor Education," pp. 500-2.

129. Beard and Beard, *America in Mid-Passage*, pp. 557-72.

130. Nore, *Charles A. Beard*, pp. 28-29, 51.

131. Forrest W. Beers, "A New Labor College," *American Federationist* (January 1901): 14.

132. Nore, *Charles A. Beard*, pp. 28-52; Bertram D. Wolfe, *A Life in Two Centuries: An Autobiography* (New York: Stein and Day, 1981), p. 395; "Classes Open at Workers' School," *Daily Worker*, October 16, 1928, p. 2:2; Barrow, "Counter-Movement Within the Labor Movement," pp. 395-417.

133. Nore, *Charles A. Beard*, p. 94.

134. Beard, *Economic Interpretation of the Constitution*, pp. 1-11; Charles A. Beard, "Review of *The American Constitution* by Frederic J. Stimson," *Political Science Quarterly* (June 1908): 340-43; Charles A. Beard, "Review of *The Constitution of the United States* by David K. Watson," *Political Science Quarterly* (September 1911): 549-51.

135. Beard's first two systematic discussions of the Constitution in 1912 were explicit polemical attacks on the Progressive interpretation. He rejected their defense of the critical period and the Confederation, but more importantly, he rejected the claim that judicial review was a belated usurpation of authority. Beard defended judicial review as an intended and vital component of the constitutional system. See Charles A. Beard, "The Supreme Court — Usurper of Grantee?" *Political Science Quarterly* (March 1912): 1-35; Beard, *The Supreme Court and the Constitution*.

136. Beard, *Economic Interpretation of the Constitution*, p. 13. Contemporary debates on the theory of the state resurfaced as a contest between these structural and instrumental standpoints. See Nicos Poulantzas, *Political Power and Social Classes*

(London: New Left Books, 1973); Ralph Miliband, *The State in Capitalist Society* (New York: Basic Books, Inc., 1969).

137. Beard, *Supreme Court and the Constitution*, p. 81.

138. Beard and Beard, *Rise of American Civilization*, Volume 1, pp. 306-7; Charles A. Beard, "Minority Rule in America," *American Mercury* 37 (February 1936): 190-96.

139. Beard, *Economic Interpretation of the Constitution*, pp. 26-30.

140. Beard, *The Economic Origins of Jeffersonian Democracy*, pp. 399, 429, 467.

141. For a neo-Beardian account of this period, see Jackson Turner Main, *Political Parties Before the Constitution* (New York: W. W. Norton, Inc., 1973).

142. Beard, *Economic Interpretation of the Constitution*, pp. 26-30.

143. Beard, *Supreme Court and the Constitution*, pp. 77-78.

144. Beard, *Economic Interpretation of the Constitution*, p. 25. Cf. Robert Eldon Brown, *Middle-Class Democracy and the Revolution in Massachusetts, 1691-1780* (Ithaca, NY: Cornell University Press, 1955), pp. 366-67; Jensen, *Articles of Confederation*, pp. viii-xii, 240, who notes appropriately that contemporary leftists seem oblivious to "the fact that this class consciousness derived not from an industrial but from an agrarian-mercantile economy. The vast majority of revolutionary leaders and followers were property-owners or property-minded."

145. Beard and Beard, *Rise of American Civilization*, Volume 1, pp. 301-4.

146. Beard, *American Government and Politics*, 5th edition, pp. 64-65.

147. Ibid., pp. 62-66; Charles A. Beard, *The Enduring Federalist* (Garden City, NY: Doubleday and Co., Inc., 1948), p. 28.

148. Ibid., pp. 28-29.

149. Beard, *Supreme Court and the Constitution*, pp. 80-81.

150. Beard, *The Enduring Federalist*, pp. 28-29. Morris, "Why the Constitution Was Adopted," p. 33, argues that his own work on the critical period undermines Beard's analysis in *Economic Interpretation* because it documents that "the people did not have to be persuaded that conditions were bad." In this vein, and like many other historians, Morris suggests that Beard reversed his stand on the critical period later in his career. However, this claim ignores Beard's unfavorable comments on the critical period made at the beginning of his career in *The Supreme Court and the Constitution* (1912) and that appear in every major book dealing the subject thereafter, including *The Rise of American Civilization*, Vol. 1 (1927), *American Government and Politics*, 5th Edition (1930), and *The Enduring Federalist* (1948).

151. Beard, *Supreme Court and the Constitution*, pp. 76-77. Political conservatism in this historical context simply meant support for a greater concentration of government authority in the national government, stronger national defense, wider powers of taxation, restriction of the sphere of State powers/sovereignty, greater checks and balances (e.g., judicial review and an independent executive), and the ability of the national government to enforce its laws directly against citizens. It emphasized a national as opposed to local politics.

152. For example, see McDonald, "The Constitution and Hamiltonian Capitalism," in Goldwin and Schambra, eds., *How Capitalistic Is the Constitution?* pp. 49-74, who documents specifically that cultural values and property law "were biased against capitalism in two crucial ways. One was that personal property in most of its forms was treated as inferior to real property—that is, land...The other bias was that land law itself was tilted against development" (p. 52). Similarly, in his seminal work, Morton J. Horowitz, *The Transformation of American Law, 1790-1860* (Cambridge, MA: Harvard University Press, 1977) cites numerous ex-

amples of how the common law, as interpreted by American courts in the eighteenth century, discouraged, prevented, or punished efforts by landowners to develop their property or put it to non-agricultural uses.

153. Beard, *Economic Interpretation of the Constitution*, p. 31. Cf. Aubrey C. Land, "Economic Base and Social Structure: The Northern Chesapeake in the Eighteenth Century," *Journal of Economic History* (December 1965):639-54.

154. Beard, *Economic Interpretation of the Constitution*, p. 49.

155. Ibid., p. 39; Beard, *Economic Origins of Jeffersonian Democracy*, p. 391. Cf. East, *Business Enterprise*, p. 279; Jackson Turner Main, *The Antifederalists: Critics of the Constitution, 1787-1788* (Chapel Hill: University of North Carolina Press, 1961), pp. 2-8; Robert Allen Rutland, *The Ordeal of the Constitution: The Antifederalists and the Ratification Struggle of 1787-1788* (Norman: University of Oklahoma Press, 1965), pp. 68-69.

156. Beard, *Economic Interpretation of the Constitution*, p. 39.

157. Ibid., pp. 38-50.

158. Libby, *Geographical Distribution*; Wilson, *Division and Reunion*, pp. 12-14; Wilson, *History of the People*, Volume 5, pp. 79-80.

159. Beard, *Economic Interpretation of the Constitution*, p. 50.

160. Beard, *Supreme Court and the Constitution*, p. 81.

161. Beard, *The Enduring Federalist*, p. 29; Beard, *American Government and Politics*, 5th edition, pp. 67-69; Beard, *Supreme Court and the Constitution*, p. 81-85.

162. Beard, *Supreme Court and the Constitution*, p. 76.

163. Ibid., pp. 78-79.

164. Ibid., p. 81.

165. Beard, *Economic Interpretation of the Constitution*, p. 52.

166. Ibid., p. 54. Despite the impressive advance of recent empirical criticisms by Robert E. Thomas, Robert E. Brown, and Forrest McDonald, a careful reading of Beard and his critics would indicate that still "not even the elementary data necessary to test Beard's main hypothesis have been systematically collected," that on balance it still retains its plausibility as a beginning hypothesis, and that it is premature to set Beard aside. See Lee Benson, *Turner and Beard: American Historical Writing Reconsidered* (Glencoe: Free Press, 1960); Jackson T. Main, "Sections and Politics in Virginia, 1781-1787," *William and Mary Quarterly* (January, 1955): 96-112; Main, *The Antifederalists*; Jackson T. Main, "Charles A. Beard and the Constitution: A Critical Review of Forrest McDonald's *We the People*," *William and Mary Quarterly* (January, 1960): 86-102.

167. Beard, *Economic Interpretation of the Constitution*, pp. 55-72.

168. Ibid., pp. 73-151; Beard, *Supreme Court and the Constitution*, p. 75.

169. Beard, *Economic Origins of Jeffersonian Democracy*, p. 106.

170. Beard, *Economic Interpretation of the Constitution*, p. 216. Charles A. Beard, "Review of *The Records of the Federal Convention of 1787* by Max Farrand," *Political Science Quarterly* (September 1911): 551-53, refers to Farrand's summary as an "admirable work" that "has completely superseded all other publications." Furthermore, George S. Counts, a friend and colleague of Beard's for many years, observes that Beard "never tired of comparing the *Federalist* favorably with the best social and political thought of Europe." See "Charles Beard, the Public Man," Beale, ed., *Charles A. Beard*, p. 247.

171. Karl Marx, "The German Ideology," in Robert C. Tucker, ed., *The Marx-Engels Reader*, 2nd Edition (New York: W. W. Norton Co., Inc., 1978), pp. 172-74. Consistent with this conception of ideology, see Beard, *Politics*, p. 12, in which

he argues as early as 1908 that "the older philosophers naively gave expression to the opinions which logically fitted their respective environments and then apparently unconsciously assigned universal validity to their cogitations."

172. Beard, *Economic Interpretation of the Constitution*, pp. xvi, 73. Italics added by author.

173. Ibid., p. 151.

174. Beard, *American Government and Politics*, 5th edition, p. 69.

175. Ibid., p. 71; Beard, *Supreme Court and the Constitution*, p. 90.

176. Beard, *Supreme Court and the Constitution*, p. 89-90.

177. Robert W. Shoemaker, "'Democracy' and 'Republic' as Understood in Late Eighteenth-Century America," *American Speech* 41 (1966): 83-95.

178. Beard, *Supreme Court and the Constitution*, p. 89.

179. Ibid., pp. 95, 90, 80; Beard, *American Government and Politics*, 5th edition, pp. 70-71.

180. Beard, *American Government and Politics*, 5th edition, p. 73-74.

181. Beard, *Economic Origins of Jeffersonian Democracy*, p. 3.

182. Beard, *Economic Basis of Politics*, p. 55.

183. Beard, *Supreme Court and the Constitution*, pp. 94-97; Beard, *American Government and Politics*, 5th Edition, p. 73.

184. As told by Counts, "Charles Beard, the Public Man," p. 250. Elsewhere, Counts tells a similar story in which he asked Beard, "If you were writing your economic interpretation today would it be different." Beard replied: "Yes, it would be very different. I wrote as if the constitution's convention had been held in the 20th century, when it was held as a matter of fact at the end of the 18th century, but since I was writing it as if it had occurred in the 20th century, I made it appear to be a very conservative document. Well, as a matter of fact, since it was written in the 18th century, it was a very radical document. As so if I were writing it today, I would stress that point—a very radical document," Counts quoted in Dennis, *George S. Counts and Charles A. Beard*, pp. 19-20. Cf. Dorfman, *The Economic Mind in America*, Vol. 3, pp. 348-49, who is one of the only previous commentators to recognize that "Beard granted that the Constitution had been formulated and carried through by the large propertied interests, but he claimed that these interests represented the forces of progress...it was the radical 'populist' philosophy of Jefferson and his distrust of government that had led to the establishment of that weak and inefficient instrument of government, the Articles of Confederation."

185. Beard, *Supreme Court and the Constitution*, p. 97.

186. Beard, *Economic Interpretation of the Constitution*, pp. 188, 291.

187. Beard, *Economic Origins of Jeffersonian Democracy*, p. 195. Identifying the economic *constituency* of the delegates was often more important to Beard than the economic interests of individual delegates. In a similar test, two years later, Beard analyzed Congressional voting behavior on Hamilton's economic proposals. He examined their votes with reference to the geographic distribution of public securities in their districts and with reference to their own personal holdings of public securities. Beard concludes that nearly all members of Congress "represented the dominant economic interests of their respective constituencies rather than personal interests" when and *if* the two were in conflict.

188. Beard, *Economic Interpretation of the Constitution*, pp. 292, 294-96.

189. Ibid., pp. 240-42. This claim is consistent with recent findings. See Chilton Williamson, *American Suffrage; From Property to Democracy, 1760 to 1860* (Princeton, NJ: Princeton University Press, 1960).

190. Beard, *Economic Interpretation of the Constitution*, p. 25.
191. Morris, "Why the Constitution Was Adopted," p. 33, is incorrect in asserting that "Beard completely ignores the probability that the people were persuaded by the sheer weight of superior argument."S
192. Beard, *Economic Interpretation of the Constitution*, p. 252.
193. Ibid., p. 227.
194. Cf. Orin G. Libby, "Review of *Economic Origins of Jeffersonian Democracy* by Charles A. Beard," *Mississippi Valley Historical Review* 3, 1 (June 1916): 99-102.
195. Beard, *Economic Origins of Jeffersonian Democracy*, pp. 85, 106.
196. Ibid., pp. 86-87. Beard and Beard, *Rise of American Civilization*, Vol. 1, p. 81.
197. Beard, *American Government and Politics*, 5th edition, p. 101.
198. Charles A. Beard, *The American Party Battle* (New York: Macmillan Co., 1928), pp. 141-42.
199. Beard, *American Government and Politics*, 5th edition, p. 126.
200. McDonald, "The Constitution and Hamiltonian Capitalism," p. 57, agrees that the Constitution failed to establish a pure capitalist state, because it retained vestiges of the old republican legal structure; although on balance, he contends, its mandates "leaned toward the capitalistic world that was aborning."
201. Beard and Beard, *Rise of American Civilization*, Volume 1, pp. 336-51.
202. Ibid., Volume 1, pp. 349-627.
203. Ibid., Volume 2, pp. 13-207.
204. Charles A. Beard, "The Contest Between Rural and Urban Economy," *Bulletin of the University of Georgia: Institute of Public Affairs and International Relations* 30, 2, Serial No. 466 (November 1929): 70-78.
205. Charles A. Beard and Mary R. Beard, *The American Spirit: A Study of the Idea of Civilization in the United States* (New York: Macmillan, 1942).
206. Charles A. Beard, "Jefferson in America Now," *Yale Review* (December 1935): 241-57.
207. Beard, "The Rise of the Democratic Idea," pp. 201-3.
208. Beard and Beard, *Rise of American Civilization*, Vol. 2, pp. 321-24.
209. For his stinging criticisms of the AFL, see, Beard, *Contemporary American History*, pp. 249-52.
210. Beard and Beard, *Rise of American Civilization*, Vol. 2, pp. 248-52.
211. Beard, *American Government and Politics*, 5th edition, p. 101; Charles A. Beard, "Review of *Political Parties: A Sociological Study of the Oligarchical Tendencies of Modern Democracy* by Robert Michels," *Political Science Quarterly* (March 1917): 153-55.
212. Beard and Beard, *Rise of American Civilization*, Vol. 2, pp. 576-663.
213. Beard, *American Government and Politics*, 5th edition, p. 117.
214. Ibid., p. 83.
215. Ibid., p. 83.
216. Beard, "Review of *Property and Contract*," p. 511.
217. Beard, *Jefferson, Corporations, and the Constitution*, pp. 24-26. Cf. Croly, *Progressive Democracy*, pp. 51-56.
218. Charles A. Beard, "Review of *Popular Government* by William A. Taft," *Political Science Quarterly* (December 1918): 594-96.
219. For similar critiques, see Roscoe Pound, "Liberty of Contract," *Yale Law Journal* (May, 1909): 454-87; Felix Frankfurter, "Hours of Labor and Realism in Constitutional Law," *Harvard Law Review* (February, 1916): 353-73.
220. Beard, *Jefferson, Corporations, and the Constitution*, p. 27.

221. Ibid., pp. 15-16.
222. Ibid., pp. 16-24; Charles A. Beard, "Political Science in the Crucible," *New Republic* 13 (November 17, 1917): 3, observes that "when powerful economic groups in the country have sought to block progressive and humane legislation and logic has failed in the forum, the mysteries of constitutional law have been invoked with firm assurance. Pollock v. the Farmers' Loan and Trust Company and Lochner v. New York—there they stand, not forever, but until political and social forces (not forgetting the grim reaper, Death), change the courts."
223. Beard, "Social Change v. the Constitution," pp. 345-52.
224. Beard, *Jefferson, Corporations, and the Constitution*, pp. 24-26.
225. Ibid., p. 32, 27.

5

The Workers' Republic

It has never been easy to interpret the work of Charles A. Beard using traditional ideological categories from either American or European political thought. Political theorists and intellectual historians have identified Beard as both a Jeffersonian and a Hamiltonian. Others have described him as a Progressive, a liberal, a corporate-liberal, a Tory-radical, and a Marxian socialist.[1] Notably, with the exception of those few scholars misguided enough to view Beard as a Jeffersonian, most students of Beard's political thought have defended their claims by pointing to Beard's growing enthusiasm for a planned economy during the 1930s. However, as George Soule noted early in the controversies over Beard's work, the concept of planning was an omnibus word during the 1930s that was given "a different content by any number of its advocates, practitioners, and opponents." In a political sense, the concept was attractive during the decade because it vaguely denoted one's opposition to laissez-faire capitalism without "involving the proponent in endless arguments about specific panaceas" for the Great Depression.[2] In substance, therefore, discussions of economic planning during this period included everything from Wilsonian liberalism to communism and fascism. Thus, it is no surprise that previous efforts to locate and evaluate Beard's work on the basis of this concept have never proven wholly satisfactory. Furthermore, Beard made little effort to clarify this ambiguity in most instances, since he frequently referred to his conception of a planned economy as industrial democracy or collectivist democracy.

Thus, in lieu of any clear statement to the contrary, political theorists and intellectual historians have largely accepted Harold Laski's early assessment of Beard's political thought. In a collection of essays that provided the first systematic attempt to evaluate Beard's legacy to American political thought and historiography, Laski claimed that Beard "has never drawn conclusions of a Marxist, or, in any decisive way, even a socialist character....Beard is a collectivist, but not a socialist."[3] Bernard Borning followed this lead in the first and only book devoted entirely to a reconstruction of Beard's political and social thought, by observing that Beard was inclined only toward "a modified form of 'capitalist democracy'."[4] More recently, Raymond Seidelman has echoed these earlier claims with his conclusion that Beard merely "wanted to extend the scope and range of collectivist-style reforms" adopted during the New Deal, but Seidelman agrees that Beard's ideas were "hardly socialist."[5] Indeed, since his death in 1948, most analyses of Beard's political and historical thought have located his ideas somewhere within the vague progressive spectrum of an emerging New Deal liberalism.[6]

By contrast, Ellen Nore is perhaps the only contemporary scholar to challenge the dominant interpretation of Beard's political thinking with her suggestion that Beard's programmatic proposals for economic and constitutional reform were actually far left of the New Deal. Nore argues that in contrast to the New Deal liberals: "Beard did not want to save capitalism, but rather to go beyond it to a new system" and, in this respect, she insists that "Beard was very sympathetic to socialism."[7] Indeed, when *Forum* magazine asked several prominent scholars to describe their vision for America in 1934, Beard offered a simple answer: "It is a workers' republic."[8] In fact, as I argue below, if one examines the details of Beard's blueprint for economic and constitutional reform during the 1930s, it is one of the most radical proposals put forward during the Great Depression. Beard authored several provocative books and articles from 1931 to 1934 in which he outlined a plan for economic and political restructuring that went far beyond the boundaries of welfare liberalism and New Deal economic policy.

In elaborating his conception of a post-capitalist workers' republic, Beard offers insights that break through the stale categories of American liberalism and conservatism, particularly those anchored in the dichotomies between public and private property, state intervention vs. market incentives, welfare provision vs. individual initiative. Beard simultaneously elaborates a critique of laissez-faire capitalism anchored in historical and institutional economics and a left-critique of the liberal welfare state anchored by a Madisonian conception of republican government. Importantly, even to the extent that Beard articulates a socialist vision for the future, it is a uniquely hybrid socialism that extends republicanism (not radical democracy) into the economic sphere through a constitutional restructuring of property rights.[9]

Tendencies of Capitalist Development

Beginning with the publication of his first book in 1901, Beard concluded that two developmental tendencies were incrementally establishing the economic basis for a transition from capitalism to some type of post-capitalist society. First, Beard explicitly accepted "the socialist conception (set forth by Marx and Engels in 1848) that competition destroyed itself and that the whole movement of industry was inevitably toward consolidation."[10] Second, Beard was convinced not only that "all Western civilization is founded on technology," but that the "inner necessity of technology is rational and planful."[11] Consequently, he argued consistently throughout his life that the competitive system of laissez-faire capitalism would gradually self-destruct and be replaced inexorably with a consolidated system of finance and industry requiring institutionalized mechanisms for the rational planning of production and distribution.

Despite the fact that most political economists were still wedded to a laissez-faire model of capitalism, Beard argued that historical analysis revealed "three main forces driving directly towards combination" in finance and industry. In the first instance, as competition intensifies between units of production in a market economy, Beard observed that "the margin of profit becomes smaller and smaller, and to make up for the fall in prices, an increased output is necessitated." However, because all the units in a given industry cannot expand their output, the result is that stronger units extend their operations, and the weaker ones perish. Thus, marginal producers are eventually driven out of the market, while more efficient producers gain market share. A second force promoting industrial concentration was that "almost every branch of industry is over-capitalized, and the running of all the plants connected with any given trade soon creates overproduction, stagnation, and ruination." Consequently, to protect themselves against the negative effects of over-capitalization, businessmen willingly combine through mergers and thereby "adjust their output to the ascertained demand, and thus secure regularity and safety" in their returns on capital. Finally, Beard argued that businessmen were learning from practical experience that ruthless competition was simply a wasteful and "unproductive warfare against each other," and that it made more sense "to save this waste, and thereby increase their profits" by uniting together in trusts, corporations, and industrial associations. As Beard noted wryly against the rising tide of neo-classical economics: "capitalists are not in business to demonstrate any abstract principles, or to substantiate the logic of their early apologists, but to make money. If they can do it under competition well enough; but if combination pays better, they combine."[12]

Beard began documenting these claims in *Contemporary American History* (1914), where he noted accurately that "an increasing proportion of the business of the country has passed steadily into corporate, as contrasted with individual, ownership." For a political historian, Beard broke new ground methodologically by drawing on the 1909 Census of Business to support his earlier theoretical claims. He found that only 25.9 percent of all business enterprises in America were incorporated, but that these corporate establishments employed 75.6 percent of all wage earners in the United States by 1909. Similarly, they accounted for 79.0 percent of the total value of all production by American businesses. Perhaps more dramatically, Beard calculated that only 3,061 (1.14 percent) of the 268,491 business establishments reported in 1909 employed 30.5 percent of all wage earners and accounted for 43.8 percent of the total value of all production in the country. Beard concluded that "it is, in fact, this absorption of business by a small number of concerns which marks the great concentration of modern industry."[13]

By the onset of the Great Depression, Beard could draw on a wealth of sources, including studies by economists Harry Laidler and Gardiner Means, to document that business corporations "are now so well organized and concentrated that about two hundred of them control from thirty-five to forty-five percent of the business wealth of the country."[14] Relying on Laidler's study, *The Concentration of Control in American Industry* (1931), Beard argued that operational monopolies, duopolies, and oligopolies controlled key sectors of the American economy by the 1930s: banking, insurance, electrical power generation, mineral extraction, telecommunications, selected fields of manufacturing (i.e., automobiles, aircraft, shoes, railroad cars, sewing ma-

chines, agricultural machinery, chemicals, matches, rubber), and selected areas of agriculture (sugar, meat packing, bread).[15]

In addition, Beard accepted the idea early on that the increasingly
concentrated system of production was being further centralized into
integrated financial groups anchored in the J. P Morgan and the Chase
National Bank (Rockefeller). These financial groups could each be
identified through an intimate network of cross investments and interlocking directorates that connected the largest financial and industrial
corporations into discreet systems of mutual interest.[16] While other
and smaller financial groups had been identified by scholars, in Beard's
view, the evidence indicated that "two mammoth groups [i.e., Morgan
and Rockefeller] constitute the heart of the business and commercial
life of the nation."[17]

The net result, as Beard observed dialectically, is "that the free
competitive regime which obtained at the beginning of this century
wore itself out, and another order based on entirely different principles has been developed" from the very process of competition.[18]
Historically, the fundamental trend of the American economy was
clearly "away from scattered, local, individual ownership and management toward corporate ownership and management" operating on
a national scale. Quite significantly, Beard emphasized, that "despite
constant efforts on the part of the state and federal governments to
prevent this consolidation of industries [i.e., anti-trust legislation], the
movement went on as if inexorably."[19]

At the same time, Beard regarded technology as a second major
force that was altering the economic basis of American civilization.
Beard defined technology as consisting of both "laboratories, machines, and physical equipment" and the "vast body of exact knowledge respecting the forces and material of nature."[20] Again, Beard
noted that the productive force of technology was creating fundamental antitheses between the requirements of modern industry and the
philosophy of agriculture inherited from the previous two centuries.[21]
Importantly, anticipating a later generation of critical theorists, Beard
argues that technology is inherently centripetal, rational, and efficient
"in its inner logic and practical applications."[22]

First, Beard observes that wherever technology becomes a central
feature of industry and transportation, it contributes powerfully "to the
concentration of productive activities—to the integration of small
plants—thus running counter to the individualistic and free-will meth-

ods prevailing in the days of handicrafts." Beard observed that the adoption of modern technology by industry required a constant and enormous capital investment. This meant that entry into more and more industries would be closed to the small entrepreneur. In addition, securing a return on such enormous investments would require technology-based industries to pursue the economies of mass production and to pursue organizational forms that promote a constant and full utilization of the industrial capacities that were growing exponentially. In this respect, technology was reinforcing, if not determining, the historical trend toward industrial concentration and financial centralization. Indeed, Beard concludes that "horizontal and vertical trusts and interlocking directorates are the inevitable outcome of technical rationality functioning under its law of efficiency."[23]

Second, technology also reinforced the drive to rationalize industrial organization because rapid advances in productivity made it necessary to plan production, investment, consumption, employment, wages, and prices on a national scale. Beard noted as early as 1914, that within the limits of their operations individual corporations already proceed according to plans.[24] Corporations routinely projected sales targets, invested in advertising to guarantee appropriate levels of consumption, and planned output levels accordingly. Similarly, big business was increasingly receptive to the notion of collective bargaining because it buffered employment, production, and wages against market volatility and labor strife.[25]

In addition, Beard pointed to the growth of trade and industrial associations as further evidence that industry was moving inexorably toward self-collectivization and rational planning. By the mid-1930s, Beard could point out accurately that "all important branches of manufacturing and selling are now organized" into special associations based on trade or industry—railway, iron and steel, oil, electrical, retailing, exporting, etc. In turn, these associations were federated into city, state, and national chambers of commerce. While these organizations existed partly for political, civic, and propaganda purposes, Beard also called attention to the fact that "among the separate or particular industries, periodical conferences are held and efforts are made to establish and apply 'fair trade practices' and to substitute collective rules for 'cut-throat competition'." In more and more cases, Beard found that rules standardizing industrial production and business competition were being formulated by business associations working under the auspices of the Department of Commerce, the Bureau of Standards, and other scientific or economic bureaus of the federal government.[26] Given this trend, Beard speculated that "had the anti-trust laws not intervened, the tendency of business concerns to organize and adopt constitutions for their own government would doubtless have been accelerated."[27]

Finally, Beard argued that current trends in business organization and technological development were guided by the principle of efficiency. Beard defined the efficiency principle as "the performance of the largest amount of work with the least expenditure of energy" and, like Thorstein Veblen, he considered scientists, engineers, technicians, and production managers to be the chief carriers of the principle.[28] It was these professional employees, and not capitalists, who had solved the problem of production and, thereby, "brought the abolition of undeserved poverty and misery within the range of the practicable for the first time in human history."[29] The central issue in modern societies for Beard was no longer the problem of producing enough for everyone, but a problem of distributing what was produced to everyone.

Indeed, at the critical juncture of the Great Depression, when distributive problems were all too evident, Beard assembled and edited a collection of essays by prominent scientists and engineers who viewed the Depression as a failure of planning and engineering. Beard's theoretical objective was to demonstrate that members of the new professional managerial class "do not identify with historic capitalism in its crude form, indifferent to wages, hours, and conditions of employment" and that such individuals were deeply concerned about the distribution of wealth and income.[30] However, the emergent technocracy was constrained in its ability to address the distributive side of the efficiency equation by their role as employees of capitalist enterprises and, to this degree, Beard attributed the failure to solve distributive problems to the "intellectual unpreparedness of the citizens rather than the desires of the technicians."[31]

Thus, while the promise of widely distributed abundance was latent in corporate organization and technology, the actualization of this ideal was dependent on the ability of workers to organize a historical movement toward industrial and social democracy. The trend toward concentration and centralization of industry had to be countered by an equal and antithetical movement demanding the socialization of private corporations and the distributive process. In fact, Beard was certain that the increasing organization of industrial workers, particularly in the new social and industrial unions, would act as a powerful catalyst toward a post-capitalist collectivist democracy.[32] In an article published by the AFL's official journal, Beard predicts that labor was about to play a historic role throughout the industrialized world "comparable to that played in the past by the military caste, the landed aristocracy, and the capitalist class."[33]

By the early 1920s, Beard could actually point to socialist and labor governments in Germany, Austria, and Great Britain as historical evidence for this claim. In Germany, Beard observed that capitalists were driving relentlessly toward the consolidation and centralization of industry "with the support of a semi-socialist government."[34] At the same time, a Social Democratic government was expanding the German welfare state, while the Weimar constitution extended unprecedented protective and participatory economic rights to German workers.[35] Great Britain was also "swinging steadily in the direction of state capitalism with its usual concessions to labor in the form of pensions, unemployment insurance, and similar measures."[36] Importantly, for Beard, the tangible outcome was essentially the same regardless of whether workers forced concessions on capitalists from below through powerful trade unions or imposed mandates on capitalists from above through socialist governments. The institutional result was a decisive abandonment of laissez-faire capitalism for a new form of corporate-centered state capitalism.

Despite weak trade unions and the absence of a viable labor or socialist party, Beard suggests as early as 1914 that even the United States was making halting and sporadic movement in the same direction. Beard had already begun to document the tendency of American capitalists to organize industrial and trade associations for the purpose of standardizing production and business practices. Beard could also document, however tentatively, that as elsewhere the centralization of capital in the United States was being "accompanied by a consolidation of the laboring classes and the evolution of a more definite political program for labor." Despite the American Federation of Labor's official anti-socialism, Beard pointed out that its political program favored municipal and government ownership of natural monopolies and an extensive array of labor legislation including the minimum wage, workmen's compensation, sanitary laws for factories, federally-mandated reductions in work hours, the prohibition of child labor, government pensions for sickness, old-age, and disability, free universal public education, and anti-injunction legislation. In other words, Beard noted with irony, that if one stripped away the political rhetoric of prominent AFL bureaucrats and looked at the union's proposed policies, one would have to conclude that the AFL's legislative program "leaned decidedly toward 'state socialism'" and was not substantially different from the platform of the American Socialist Party.[37] This bifurcation of rhetoric and reality persuaded Beard even more strongly that collectivist tendencies were driven forward by underlying economic forces existing independent of the conscious will or motives of individuals.

Consequently, Beard was convinced that the parallel movements toward organized capitalism and social democracy would also converge in the United States in some form of state capitalism. As this transition occurred in the coming decades, Beard anticipated that the central focus of economic debate would shift away from the simple issue of planning or no planning to the more subtle problem of "how much planning, by whom, under whose auspices, and to what ends?"[38] In this context, the lines demarcating capitalism from socialism would be increasingly eroded by new institutions designed to solve the practical problems of macro-economic management, industrial planning, and redistribution.

The Great Depression: Between Marx and Keynes

As early as 1901, while still in graduate school, Beard had embraced the principle that the "recurring maladjustments" between production and consumption in capitalist economies (i.e., depressions) were the effect of a contradiction between "the 'social form of production and the individual form of appropriation and exchange'."[39] However, despite his early extensive training in political economy, socialism, and statistics, it was not until the 1930s that Beard systematically returned to this thesis in an effort to explain the Great Depression.[40] Beard offered his most extensive treatment of this subject in *The Open Door at Home* (1934) where he challenged the prevailing pre-Keynesian theory that the Great Depression had been caused by overproduction and by surplus industrial and agricultural capacity.[41] The overproduction thesis was widely accepted by business people, many historical and neo-classical economists, and by federal policy-makers with two major implications for early New Deal policy. First, it was the theoretical basis of the policies initiated by the National Industrial Recovery Act (1933) and by the Agricultural Adjustment Act (1933).[42] These policies sought to stem price declines and restore profits by stabilizing production and by eliminating surplus capacity through industry-wide planning. Second, the overproduction thesis was also linked to claims that surplus production could be absorbed by the aggressive penetration of foreign export markets. Thus, it emphasized an expansionist foreign policy to secure larger export markets on the assumption that domestic markets were saturated.

Beard was favorably inclined toward NIRA and the AAA mainly because they at last recognized what Beard considered "the inexorable trend in business consolidation, accelerated it, and made use of it in a great national emergency."[43] Furthermore, NIRA and the AAA explicitly abandoned the policy of laissez-faire for one that involved the government directly in "planning, co-ordinating, and controlling industry and agriculture with a view to escaping the ruinous effects of periodical business panics."[44] While these policies represented a definite advance over laissez-faire, Beard also argued that policies based on the overproduction thesis were severely limited by the assumption that domestic markets were saturated and were therefore unable to absorb surplus production. Beard suggested that in principle "the amount [of goods and services] that the American people *can* use or consume is a variable...difficult to disclose by any methods of research." Nevertheless, in the midst of mass unemployment and growing poverty, Beard doubted that Americans had "all the food they need...all the shoes they need, all the furniture they can utilize, the kind of homes required for comfort and decency."[45] In other words, hidden within the overproduction thesis is the assumption that surpluses exist because they cannot be disposed of *at a profit* to the owners of land and capital, rather than because of fully sated public and private needs. In this respect, it was only because government allowed "free reign to the profit-making motive, without regard to consequences," that "society permits the extremes of expansion and contraction."[46]

Beard further challenged the overproduction thesis with the hypothesis that domestic commodity surpluses were in fact created socially by the growing inequalities of wealth and income that accompanied the consolidation and centralization of land and capital. Beard noted that all claims regarding the existence of surplus production assumed "the private ownership and manipulation of the means of production and, consequently, the distribution of wealth, or buying and consuming power, associated with a high degree of concentration in the ownership and management of the means of production." In his view, "this is an assumption of the first magnitude," because the distribution of wealth "is not determined for all time by a force, like that of gravity, outside the control of human will and policy." Quite the contrary, Beard maintained that "within some limits of necessity, which cannot be exactly determined, the distribution of wealth has, is being, and can be, altered by collective action." Thus, further innovations could be adopted to effect "changes in the using and consuming power of the people of the United States" and, according to Beard, such changes should be effected by public and collective action.[47]

For these reasons, Beard concluded that the cause of the Great Depression, and of the business cycle in general, was not overproduction, as such, but a structural "unbalance between plant or productive capacity on the one side and consumer buying-power on the other." Importantly, Beard frequently reiterated his view that "the disproportionate allocation of wealth to plant extension is owing in the main to the concentration of ownership which places too large a share of annual wealth produced in the hands of a small number of people who simply cannot spend it on consumption goods but must pour it into the already overcrowded capital, or plant extension, market." Thus, in the short- to intermediate-term, Beard favored income redistribution policies that would minimize this structural imbalance by increasing consumer demand at the expense of idle capital. The chief mechanisms identified by Beard are progressive income taxation linked to redistributive public expenditures for social goods and to "the endless struggle of capital and labor over wages, hours, and working conditions."[48]

However, Beard quickly moved beyond this Keynesian solution to the Great Depression, mainly because he had long regarded income (i.e., consumer demand) as a derivative function of property ownership (i.e., wealth). Individuals derive interest, rents, profits, and dividends from the ownership of land or capital. Other individuals derive wages and salaries from the possession of labor or skills. Importantly, it is property rights (i.e., law) that establish any claim to the proceeds (i.e., income) attached to the productive use of property.[49] Thus, the comparative distribution of income in society will in large part depend, first, on the distribution of wealth among individuals and, second, on the comparative legal rights attached to various forms of property by the state which is responsible for enforcing these claims.[50]

Significantly, therefore, Beard was attuned to the theoretical claim that the fundamental problem of economic crisis and underconsumption was not solely a problem of income distribution, but of *wealth distribution*. Beard's analysis led to the conclusion that a permanent solution to the problem of income distribution would require "an efficient distribution of wealth," rather than a permanent reliance on government-sponsored income transfers.[51] Given the corporate organization of modern economies, and the impossibility of a return to a small producer economy, Beard's analysis implied that it was necessary to redistribute wealth through a variety of collectivist mechanisms such as state ownership, cooperative or employee ownership, the democratization of corporate stock ownership, profit-sharing, and lesser measures such as corporate income taxation and state regulation.[52]

Equally important, since Beard regarded income as the product of the legal and political rights attached to certain forms of property, Beard called for a constitutional readjustment of the comparative property rights attached to land, capital, and labor. The most important readjustments necessary to the creation of a workers' republic would be to define the concept of public property and to recognize "labor" as a form of property entitled to special protections under the Constitution. With regard to the first point, Beard pointed out that during previous periods of economic transition, rights to things once recognized as private property were either altogether abolished (e.g., slaves) or transferred politically from one legal claimant to another (e.g., women's wages once belonged to their husbands). In a movement analogous to the abolition of slavery, Beard suggested that "we are coming to believe that many kinds of property shall not belong to any private person or corporation" (e.g., wilderness, natural resources, technical monopolies).[53] Thus, for Beard, a central problem of constitutional readjustment would be "what kinds of property that are now privately owned shall be turned into public property?"[54] On this matter, Beard had been convinced since the turn of the century that "the tendency is obviously toward public control of the means of life."[55]

The related problem of constitutional readjustment was to accord legal, and even constitutional, status to trade unions "for protecting and increasing property rights in labor." In Beard's schema, the contest between capitalists and workers over the sale of labor was "a contest over the very essence of property, that is, income, and the attitude of the government toward the matter is of the utmost importance" to the outcome of the contest.[56] In both instances, the key theoretical distinction between Beard and Marx is that Beard saw the transition to a workers' republic as based in a wider extension of property rights to groups and individuals, rather than in the mere abolition of private property.

Technocracy and Syndicalism

Furthermore, Beard frequently criticized Marx for failing to give "any specifications for the operation of a socialist society" and for being "even less specific in matters of trade and exchange among societies founded on socialist principles."[57] Beard also chastised contemporary Marxian theorists for being preoccupied with debates on how to seize political power. Beard was unimpressed with the endless dispute over vanguard vs. mass parties and revolution vs. evolution. Instead, he suggested that socialists of all persuasions would do better to spend more time on policy analysis and public administration than on grand-scale political theory and the Machiavellian intrigues of state power.[58] In the long-run, the ability to represent the interests of workers effectively would not depend exclusively on winning elections (or on assassinating Czars), but on the ability of socialist policy-makers to formulate workable blueprints for a planned economy and on the ability of their public administrators to implement those policies effectively.[59] Thus, in 1931, "Beard risked a concrete suggestion which, whatever its defects, showed that in his mind the prime necessity was to set up administrative machinery that might make control of the whole economy possible" in the United States.[60]

As Beard had predicted, when the bottom fell out of the economy in the early 1930s debates on economic policy were no longer centered on whether national planning would supplant laissez-faire, but shifted to the technical details of how much planning was necessary, who should do the planning, and what limitations should be imposed on planning?[61] Between 1931 and 1934, Beard was joined in proposing some form of national economic planning by virtually every major interest group in the country. The early years of the Great Depression produced a spate of national economic blueprints, including Beard's Forum Plan; the Swope Plan by Gerard Swope of General Electric; the U.S. Chamber of Commerce Plan; the New York Plan by Governor Franklin D. Roosevelt; the Hoover Plan by President Herbert Hoover;[62] the LaFollette Plan by Governor Philip LaFollette of Wisconsin; the Ten Year Plan by economist Stuart Chase; an endorsement of planning by the American Federation of Labor; and many less ambitious proposals for specific relief policies or industries.[63]

Beard republished his own Forum Plan in 1932 as part of an edited collection that included copies of most of the major plans in circulation at the time. The plans ranged from Herbert Hoover's voluntary associationism,[64] to full-blown state-capitalism (Swope), to a heavily socialized mix economy with deep command structures (Beard, Chase). In a final effort to influence New Deal policy, Beard further elaborated upon his original blueprint with his publication of *The Open Door at Home* (1934). In his writings on economic planning, Beard never strayed from his early belief that capitalism had "perverted and distorted the whole end and aim of our industrial organisation, by establishing false standards of value." Consequently, a fundamental premise of post-capitalist economic planning in his view was "to distinguish between value in relation to price on the markets, and value in relation to human needs."[65]

Thus, in contrast to most plans which established industrial or agricultural price stabilization (i.e., profits) as their prime directive, Beard argued that the underlying principle of national economic planning should be the public interest. Beard acknowledged that concepts of the public interest can be a shadowy realm but, for this reason, he insisted it was necessary to define the concept explicitly and "to fix positive benchmarks for future guidance."[66] In *The Open Door at Home*, Beard defined "the supreme interest of the United States" as "the creation and maintenance of a high standard of life for all its people and ways of industry conducive to the promotion of individual and social virtues within the frame of national security."[67]

Beard's definition of the public interest made it clear that merely restimulating economic growth did not qualify as a successful economic policy. Because the public interest requires a high standard of living for all citizens, Beard emphasized that increases in national wealth and income must entail its wide and equitable distribution. Thus, the first step toward implementing a national economic plan would be the development and adoption of a national standard-of-life budget. The standard-of-life budget was to disclose in detail "the physical requirements of a high standard of life in terms of food, clothing, shelter, comforts, and conveniences."[68] It should be emphasized that Beard's proposed standard-of-life budget is quite different from the measurements of poverty eventually developed by the Social Security Administration, the Bureau of Labor Statistics, and the Census Bureau. The latter budgets designate a standard of poverty and the idea is that no one should fall below the poverty level. Beard's objective was to designate a minimum standard of *living* that included comforts and conveniences and, therefore, he set a far more ambitious middle-class standard for redistribution than most New Deal liberals.[69]

Moreover, under Beard's plan, there would not only be a system of national income accounts, but a system of national macro-budgeting. The centerpiece of this system would be a composite standard-of-life budget which calculated the total goods and services necessary to maintain the official standard-of-life for all families and individuals in the United States. The national macro-budget could then be translated into total production targets for various sectors of industry, agriculture, and foreign trade. The final element of the planning structure would be "the adoption of means and policies calculated to keep the productive mechanism of the United States running at a high and even tempo."[70] As already noted, Beard accepted the Keynesian premise that the key problem was to stimulate "a large increase in the buying and consuming power of the American people" and he was willing to accept arguments that "a great deal of wealth can be transferred by taxation and other devices from unnecessary capital outlays to consumers eager for goods."[71]

In this regard, however, it is important to note that Beard was very suspicious of the liberal welfare state. First, a mere system of doles and transfer payments failed to meet Beard's criteria of public interest which demanded not only a high standard of living for all Americans, but its achievement through "ways of industry conducive to the promotion of individual and social virtues." From a purely economic perspective, Beard was willing to acknowledge that "doles, pensions, allotments, and outright gifts may for the time being, create an enlarged purchasing power," but he was deeply concerned that "a long continuance of such methods, however, justified as temporary expedients, will doubtless create ways of life ruinous to productive industry and make millions of men and women wholly unemployable." In the classical republican tradition, Beard warned architects of the welfare state that "Rome once kept a large portion of her urban proletariat satisfied with bread and circuses, but as a long-run operation the experiment was disastrous."[72]

Beard viewed economic planning and constitutional adjustment as a way to avoid the European system of doles and allowances. Indeed, without economic planning Beard envisioned an ever-increasing underclass that would be impoverished and dependent on the dole. As work skills and the attachment to labor deteriorated over the long-run, such a class would become economically and morally unfit to participate *as workers* in a workers' republic. Unlike most liberals and leftists, therefore, Beard did not see the only threat to republican government in the unchecked power of corporate capitalists. Potentially, an equal threat was posed to the republic, and especially to a workers' republic, by the slow evisceration of the working class through technological displacement and dependency on the dole.[73] A policy aimed at securing industrial stabilization and profits at the expense of republican virtues would in the end lead the American republic down a path of dissolution, rot, and decay from below by the very proletariat that was the harbinger of its future. As Beard observed, "labor is not a curse. It is ill-requited and despised labor in degrading conditions that is a curse."[74] In contrast, the maintenance of civic virtues central to the republican ideal of worker-citizenship would require a *working* class that is independent and self-sufficient.[75]

A second objection to welfare liberalism emerged from Beard's view that income is a derivative function of property ownership and property rights. For this reason, Beard considered progressive taxation and income redistribution insufficient mechanisms for addressing the root source of inequality. For example, Beard wrote favorably of Graham Laing's book, *Toward Technocracy* (1933), for its ability to "illuminate the issues raised in the popular discussion" of planning.[76] One of the central themes of this book was that "schemes of unemployment insurance...old-age pensions, and the like...have proved of immense value wherever they have been adopted, but they do not affect the basic conditions which produce poverty and misery."[77] A real solution to the inefficient distribution of wealth required an economic program far more radical than liberals' emerging fascination with Keynesian demand management.

Importantly, Beard often compared the early years of the Great Depression (1931-1934) to the critical period (1783-1787) of American history.[78] Thus, in a move analogous to 1786, Beard proposed that Congress authorize the creation of a National Economic Council (NEC) that would write an economic program to be submitted to the country for approval, including "any changes in the Constitution and laws deemed necessary for the realization of planned economy."[79] Presidential appointments to the NEC were to be based on functional, as opposed to geographic, representation with at least equal weight granted to representatives of business and labor.[80] Once approved by constitutional amendment or judicial decree, Beard suggested that all highly concentrated industries be placed under the jurisdiction of the NEC by declaring them national public service enterprises affected with public interest. In this manner, the NEC would extend the application of a principle already well-established in constitutional law "to cover all enterprises fundamental to a high standard of American life."[81] All industries under NEC jurisdiction were to be operated and regulated as public utilities and "controlled in accordance with fundamental rules already in force in this field: prudent investment, standard services, equitable charges, and a fair return on capital."[82]

Technical advice to the NEC would be provided by a Board of Strategy and Planning (BOSAP) and a new Bureau of Standards (BOS) created by the consolidation of all industrial research agencies within the federal government. The Bureau of Standards was to extend its current activities to include the standardization of all commodities produced under the jurisdiction of the National Economic Council. In addition, it was to assume responsibility for all government-sponsored research, federal laboratories, and agricultural experiment stations, and to allocate research funds and projects in accordance with national planning, investment, and development priorities.

The BOSAP was modeled after the War Industries Board with several industrial and economic divisions each headed by a production engineer. BOSAP's responsibility was "to make a survey of the resources and productive facilities of the country" in order to support the development of a national economic plan.[83] Consistent with Beard's emphasis on employment as the basis of a high standard of living, Beard argued that the central concern of BOSAP's planning should be to promote "the maximum output of goods in each division" (i.e., full employment), while raising wages and reducing prices. By imposing a rule of prudent investment and fair return, excess profits would become available for *direct reallocation at the point of production* in the form of higher wages to employees and in the form of lower prices to consumers. These reallocations would help stimulate a virtuous circle of rising consumer demand, increased output, rising employment, etc.

Beard always emphasized that regulation, control, and planning would be more effective to the degree that industry was allowed to consolidate and centralize of its own accord. Consequently, Beard often recommended repeal of the Sherman and Clayton Anti-Trust Acts, preferring to rely on economic planning and state controls than on trust-busting, small business development, and artificially maintained competition still advocated by the small business liberals (e.g., Senator Borah).[84] Significantly, for Beard, repeal of the anti-trust laws was merely a formal preliminary to the syndication of those industries under NEC jurisdiction. Beard proposed that all corporations in each industry under NEC jurisdiction be encouraged to affiliate into national holding companies or industrial syndicates. Member companies of each syndicate would have to meet minimum wage and price standards, workplace safety rules, minimum production standards, fair business practices, and output quotas established for each syndicate. In turn, corporate members of the syndicates would receive access to a low-interest (or no-interest) Capital Reserve Account and employees would be covered by a Social Insurance Account. Similarly, as with all regulated utilities, investors would be guaranteed a fair return (i.e., three percent) on their investment (See Figure 5.1).

Beard recognized that surplus profits over the designated fair return might arise due to unexpected efficiency, and indeed he proposed an incentive structure designed to promote increased output and productivity among employees. Beard's plan called for all surplus profits to be divided among two national accounts. A share of all surplus profits would be distributed directly to employees in the form of graduated bonuses. This meant that employees would receive a gradually larger percentage of surplus profits, the more such profits exceeded the designated fair return; thus, creating an incentive to exceed production quotas, implement efficiencies and technological innovations, maintain quality standards, and promote sales of their products. The remaining share of surplus profits would be divided between a Capital

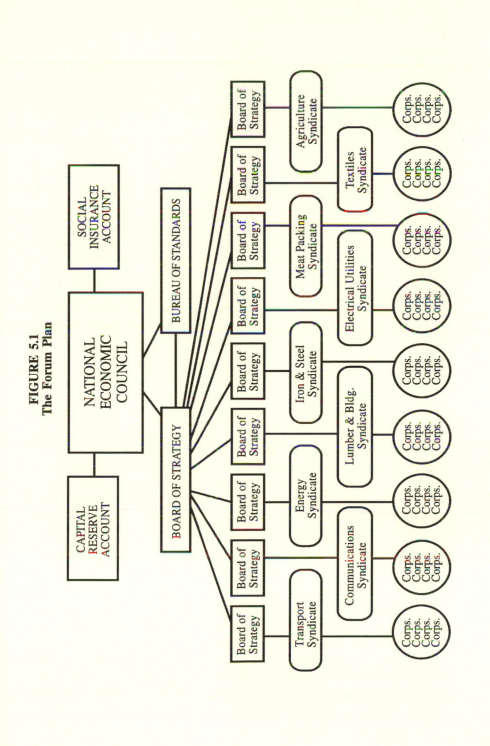

FIGURE 5.1
The Forum Plan

FIGURE 5.1 (cont.)

NATIONAL ECONOMIC COUNCIL: Functional representation based on each syndicate's relative economic importance to the overal economy.

CAPITAL RESERVE ACCOUNT: Financed by 25% of all surplus profits + earmarked graduated inheritance tax.

SOCIAL INSURANCE ACCOUNT: Financed by 25% of all surplus profits.

BOARDS OF STRATEGY AND PLANNING: Syndicate BOSAP'S consist of the chief production engineer from each affiliated corporation The central BOSAP consists of the chief production engineers from each syndicate.

SYNDICATES: Holding companies with government equity positions in most large corporations affiliated with the syndicate. Syndicates develop a plan for the industry and establish production standards, production quotas, investement levels, research and development strategy, employment targets, fair profit standards, and labor policies for affiliated corporations.

CORPORATIONS: Primarily joint government/employee owned ventures. Government equity acquired by purchasing outstanding stock with Freedom Bonds of equal principal value and paying 3% interest. Remaining large equity positions may be purchased by the CRA or taxed off by graduated inheritance tax. May also include private corporations that adhere to the production standards, production quotas, fair profit standards, and labor policies established by the relevant syndicate. Boards of Directors elected by shareholders.

Reserve Account (CRA) and a Social Insurance Account (SIA). The CRA proposed by Beard is similar to the Swedish Investment Reserve Account in that it would make low-interest or no-interest loans available to the corporate members of each syndicate for capital investment and for research and development.[85] Beard also suggested that the proceeds from inheritance and income surtaxes be deposited into the CRA for amortization purposes or new construction. The SIA was to defray the costs of unemployment insurance, workmen's compensation, plant shutdown for changes in machinery, crop failures, job retraining, etc.[86]

The syndicated structure proposed by Beard was widely discussed during the 1930s and has continued to receive occasional attention from historians. However, most scholars have interpreted Beard's proposal incorrectly as one based exclusively on the principles of public utility regulation.[87] Marxists have often debunked Beard's plan as "the ideal administrative state based on private property."[88] In this regard, William Appleman Williams links Beard to the corporate-liberal wing of the Progressive coalition (i.e., corporate liberalism) and concludes that his five-year plan "represented the triumph and fulfillment of one of the major themes of Progressive thinking as it developed prior to World War I."[89]

A more stinging criticism still lingering over Beard's proposal is George Soule's observation that Beard's blueprint was not unlike the design of the corporate state introduced by the Italian Fascists.[90] Extending this theme, John P. Diggins has documented that corporate-liberals in America were often attracted to fascism's corporatist ideology even while such individuals were repulsed by its dictatorial political and military institutions.[91] In fact, in this context, Beard once suggested that: "it would be a mistake to allow feelings aroused by contemplating the harsh deeds and extravagant assertions that have accompanied the Fascist process (as all other immense historical changes) to obscure the potentialities and the lessons of the adventure....in reconciling individualism and socialism, politics and technology."[92] At the same time, it is impossible to accept the charge that Beard had any serious affinity for fascism, because he later described it "as the actual domination of high capitalism over the working classes through the agency of dictatorship, resting on military force and financed in considerable measure by large industrial interests."[93] In fairness to Beard, Soule himself recognizes that Beard "did not expect that the essence of American democracy would be altered" by the adoption of his blueprint for planning and syndicated industry.

Claims that Beard was a proponent of corporate-liberalism, state-capitalism, or even corporate-fascism are all equally misguided to the extent that they fail, for whatever reason, to recognize those elements in Beard's blueprint that drew heavily on Lenin's New Economic Policy. In the early years of the Great Depression, Beard not only reread Marx, he was reading newly translated pamphlets by Lenin and Trotsky, whom he considered "profound and systematic students of history and the social sciences." Beard was singularly impressed with Lenin's pre-Revolutionary pamphlet, "The Threatening Catastrophe" (September 1917), which described "the utter breakdown of the Russian economy under headway—the collapsing transport facilities, industries, agriculture, with famine, unemployment, and misery everywhere."[94] In that pamphlet, Lenin proposed a new economic system based on nationalization of the banks, compulsory syndicalization of industry and agriculture, partial nationalization of the syndicates (i.e., state ownership positions), and the administration of syndicates by joint councils of employees, engineers, and directors (i.e., private and state shareholders).[95]

Nevertheless, William Appleman Williams argues that Beard cannot be considered a socialist because his five-year plan rejected the "radical confiscation of private property."[96] Williams' claim is technically correct only if one takes the term radical confiscation to mean confiscation by force and without compensation. However, in his five-year plan, Beard did suggest a process by which "the private stockholder, who ordinarily does nothing for industry but sign proxies and grumble when dividends are reduced, would be eliminated in the end."[97] Beard's concern was to devise a process of socialization that was orderly, non-violent, and constitutional. Furthermore, in response to similar criticisms in his own day, Beard again pointed to Lenin's early proposals for economic restructuring:

> These measures of consolidation and organization in economy, under workers' control, supplemented by heavy income and inheritance taxes, Lenin offered to Russia, as her social system seemed to be falling to pieces in the autumn of 1917. He did not propose a confiscation of property except where owners resisted the nationalizing process. He proposed nationalization, rationalization, universal labor duty, modifications in the distribution of income and workers' control in the State. He did not favor immediate socialization and the transfer of administrative responsibilities to workers' and peasants' soviets.[98]

However, in devising a system of orderly transition, Beard drew upon the experience of municipalities that had socialized various industries such as railway transit, gas and electrical utilities. Based on his extensive involvement in municipal consulting during the 1910s and 1920s, Beard had concluded that public ownership of natural monopolies was more efficient and more effective than government regulation.[99] In fact, while director of the New York Bureau of Municipal Research, Beard authored a report (1919) which recommended municipalizing the New York City transit system and detailed the procedure for accomplishing that goal using the City's bonding authority and the power of eminent domain.[100]

Beard drew on his earlier study of the New York City transit system to recommend a similar process for socializing major industries under the jurisdiction of the National Economic Council. Beard proposed that the United States Government finance extensive nationalizations with Freedom Bonds that would pay 3 percent interest to bondholders. Outstanding stocks of corporations affiliated with the Syndicates would be purchased through an exchange of stocks for bonds of equal fair market value. Beard evidently grasped the principle of the leveraged buy-out long before Michael Milken introduced junk bonds to the United States, since the bonds' interest was to be paid out of the profits of the newly socialized firms acquired in the debt for equity exchange. Thus, Beard wrote with his usual sardonic wit: "no confiscation of property is contemplated here." Indeed, he argued that federal bonding authority and the power of eminent domain would enable the NEC to socialize the Syndicates and Corporations "without violating a single American economic tradition."[101]

Interestingly, not a single commentator on Beard's blueprint has ever recognized that he introduced a uniquely syndicalist element into his version of democratic socialism by proposing that a large percentage of the new government-owned stocks be distributed among the directors, managers, and employees of the several Corporations. These stocks were to pay graduated dividends based on efficiency in operation and production as yet a further incentive for employees to increase efficiency and productivity. The final result of this government-sponsored leveraged buyout is that vested interests in the economy would be "turned over to engineers and workers, leaving the bondholder with his three percent and liable to a stiffer inheritance tax than is now imposed."[102]

In agriculture, Beard concluded that small farmers—the mythic carriers of republican virtue in America—had been a declining class since the end of the nineteenth century. As with proletarian doles, Beard rejected the standard call for price subsidies and grants to farmers as a failure to address the real crisis in agricultural economy. As deeply as it stung the American psyche, Beard was convinced that "efficiency calls for a concentration in certain branches of agriculture as in manufacturing and transporting." Consequently, he insisted that for policy-makers "to proceed on the assumption that wheat can be profitably raised on small farms...in competition with gigantic enterprises...is to pursue a delusion bound to be ruinous in the end, no matter how much money the Farm Board pours into the wheat pit."[103]

Instead, Beard predicted that the future of agriculture lay in crop specialization coupled with large-scale, capital-intensive farming. He forecast that "capitalism will take over large agricultural areas — specializing them, introducing more capital and machinery, increasing production, controlling and adjusting prices with respect to the price levels of other commodities, working the two systems of economy (i.e., capitalism and agrarianism) into one, so that traditional agriculture will utterly disappear" in the United States.[104] Moreover, as with industry and commerce, Beard observed that already: "powerful associations in cotton growing, wheat raising, dairying, fruit culture, and other branches are operating today in connection with the Federal Farm Board and Department of Agriculture. Standardization, the introduction of scientific methods, and cooperative marketing are in rapid process of development."[105]

In his Five-Year Plan, Beard proposed to accelerate this process through an Agricultural Syndicate operating under the National Economic Council. The first step in agricultural planning would be a survey of all agricultural lands in each state with lands classified according to fertility and agricultural uses. Upon completion of the survey, the Agricultural Syndicate would create a public farm corporation in each state. These corporations would use the power of eminent domain to acquire large tracts of marginal farm lands which could not be tilled profitably by traditional methods, but which could be tilled profitably using modern capital-intensive agricultural methods over large areas. Like other syndicated industries, the farm corporations would be managed and operated as state-owned public utilities. However, Beard suggested that individual farmers be allowed to cede their lands to the state Agricultural Corporation, or its local subsidiary, in exchange for an equivalent equity interest in the Corporation. In addition, individual farmers or agribusinesses could agree to have their lands cultivated as part of a syndicated tract, without surrendering direct ownership of the land, so long as they agreed to abide by specific conditions established by the Corporations or Syndicate regarding output, crops, wages, and working conditions.

Constitution for a Commonwealth

The creation of a workers' republic required a broad application of eminent domain under the constitutional principle of "businesses affected with a public interest." However, Beard's blueprint was developed in the early years of the New Deal (1931-1934) when federal courts were still not prepared to accept a radical break with laissez-faire policies. Beard was acutely aware of the fact that judicial interpretations can change but, for this same reason, he also emphasized that "whatever the courts might say with respect to such a principle, it would be supreme if established by constitutional mandate."[106] Thus, he preferred a constitutional amendment explicitly authorizing economic planning.

Furthermore, based on his experience with municipalizations, Beard had long been aware that state-ownership did not necessarily constitute "a gain for socialism in any sense, for it does not mean necessarily any increase in the power of the working class in government."[107] Beard sought to address this problem partly through a mix of worker-ownership, profit-sharing, and shareholder democracy, but he also harbored no illusions that the socialization of industry or the redistribution of wealth and income would result in a classless society. Rather, socialist policies would create new classes, new interests, and new sources of division that would still require the constitutional protection of worker rights and the protection of the new forms of property from unruly factions.[108]

Beard pointed out that any modern economy, including a socialist economy, includes "miners, machinists, electricians, engineers, accountants, transport workers, draftsmen, managers, and a hundred other kinds of specialists." While these economic groups might be "temporarily welded together in a conflict with their capitalist employers," Beard predicted that "they will be divided over the distribution of wealth among themselves after the capitalists have been disposed of." Hence, the problem of balancing fundamental property rights among competing groups and classes would still be of central concern to a workers' republic. Rephrasing Madison's *Tenth Federalist* in modern terms Beard suggested that:

> ...a landed interest, a transport interest, a railway interest, a shipping interest, an engineering interest, a manufacturing interest, a public-official interest, with many lesser interests, grow up of necessity in all great societies and divide them into different classes actuated by different sentiments and views. The regulation of these various and interfering interests, whatever may be the formula of ownership of property, constitutes the principal task of modern statesmen and involves the spirit of party in the necessary and ordinary operations of government.[109]

As already noted, Beard considered the early years of the New Deal analogous to the critical period that culminated in the Constitution of 1789 so his modernization of Madison's *Tenth Federalist* ought to be taken seriously. In the same way that the critical period had resulted in a shift from an agrarian to a commercial republic, Beard anticipated an equally momentous shift from a commercial to a workers' republic. Deeply impressed by the rise of Social-Democratic and Labor governments following World War I, Beard was keenly attuned to developments in those countries where changes of government had also been accompanied by new constitutions. Consistent with his economic interpretation of history, Beard speculated that since "economic conditions are rapidly becoming the same all over the world with similar legal results, then we may, with proper warrant, expect very soon a new and lively examination of constitutional principles to break in upon us."[110]

In summarizing the general thrust of postwar constitutional change in Europe, Beard concluded that "under the pressure of many influences, most of them socialistic, the constitutions created during the revolutions of our day have introduced a new concept of the relation of the citizen to the state." Notably for Beard, the new constitutions emerging from the reconstruction of Europe "showed marked traces of the socialist concept of society."[111] In this context, Beard singled out "the well-framed proclamations of the Weimar Constitution" as the most promising model for a workers' republic.[112] He described the Weimar Constitution as "a prophecy of the future" because it so explicitly provided for the socialization of industry and fundamentally realigned the constitutional balance of rights and privileges in favor of workers as opposed to capitalists and landholders.[113]

In fact, Beard was so enthusiastic about the Weimar Constitution that he interceded personally with Alfred A. Knopf to secure the translation and publication of Rene Brunet's, *The New German Constitution* (1928). In his foreword to the book, Beard could scarcely conceal his adoration for a constitution that "vibrates with the tramp of the proletariat." In the Weimar Constitution, Beard found that Germans had synthesized "the strength of Hamilton's government with the democratic control so vaunted by Jefferson" and, consequently, Germans embarked on "an experiment that ought to stir our deepest interest." Significantly, Beard found that the Weimar's "provisions for social, not to say socialistic, enterprise...offer noteworthy contrasts to our own fundamental law."[114]

Beard identified ten provisions of the Weimar Constitution that fundamentally redefined the relationship between individual property rights and the public interest. This goal was achieved, first, by explicitly subordinating economic liberty and property rights to positive law and, second, by making explicit provisions for the public ownership of industry, land, and natural resources. What might be called "The Economic Bill of Rights for a Commonwealth" (Section V) included the following provisions:[115]

(1) The economic liberty of the individual is expressly protected, but only within the limits of the equally express and superordinate principle that "economic life must conform to the principles of justice, with the object of assuring humane conditions for all" (Article 151).

(2) The freedom of contract is expressly protected, so long as it is "in accordance with the laws" (Article 152).

(3) The right of private property is expressly guaranteed by the Constitution, but "its nature and limits are defined by law" (Article 153).

(4) The right of private property "implies property-duties" so that the "exercise thereof shall at the same time serve the general welfare" (Article 153).

(5) The expropriation of private property may occur "for the benefit of the community and by due process of law," but there shall be "just compensation" (Article 153).

(6) The right of inheritance is expressly guaranteed, but only "in accordance with the civil law" (Article 154).

(7) The distribution and use of land is supervised by the state and land may be expropriated to improve agriculture. All increments in land values "arising without the application of labor or capital to the property inures to the benefit of the community as a whole" (Article 155).

(8) "All mineral resources and all economically useful forces of nature are subject to the control of the state. Private royalties may be transferred to the state, as may be provided by law" (Article 155).

(9) "The Commonwealth may by law, without impairment of the right to Compensation, and with a proper application of the regulations relating to expropriation, transfer to public ownership private business enterprises adapted for socialization" (Article 156).

(10) "Labor is under the special protection of the Commonwealth. The Commonwealth will adopt a uniform labor law" (Article 157).

Finally, in his Five-Year Plan, Beard refers to the German experience with economic councils and functional representation as a model for the National Economic Council that was to oversee syndicated industries in the United States. Under the Weimar system, Article 165 of the Constitution guaranteed the right of workers and salaried employees "to co-operate on equal terms with employers in the regulation of wages and working conditions, as well as in the entire economic development of the productive forces." To facilitate this process, Article 165 mandated the creation of workers' councils and economic councils at the factory, local, district, and national level. The workers' councils were to represent wage-workers and salaried employees. The economic councils were to represent employers (whether state or private) and other interested classes of people (e.g., consumers, stockholders, bondholders, creditors). The district and national councils were required to meet together periodically for the purposes of carrying out "joint economic tasks and co-operating in the execution of the laws of socialization." The joint National Economic Council was required to include representatives of all substantial vocational groups according to their economic and social importance.

Importantly, a key difference between the Weimar system and the soviet system as conceived by European council communists (and even by Lenin) is that the National Economic Council was only authorized to submit economic legislation to the Parliament, but it was not empowered to adopt or implement statutory acts without approval from the political branches of government.[116] Sovereignty remained in the government and was not transferred to the workers' or economic councils as in a pure soviet system. Like democratic socialists in Germany, Beard argued that the continuing supremacy of political governments was necessary because a council system excluded large segments of the population from representation and thus violated the principle of democracy.

Notes

1. Borning, *The Political and Social Thought of Charles A. Beard*, p. 33.
2. George Soule, "Beard and the Concept of Planning," in Beale, ed., *Charles A. Beard*, p. 64-65. Likewise, Otis L. Graham, Jr., "The Planning Ideal and American Reality: The 1930s," in Stanley Elkins and Eric McKitrick, eds., *The Hofstadter Aegis: A Memorial* (New York: Alfred A. Knopf, 1974), p. 260, observes that during the 1930s "people in and out of government called for 'planning', but differed widely in their definition of the term, or in the depth of their commitment to the departures from tradition which might be required." The evolution of the planning idea is discussed in James B. Gilbert, *Designing the Industrial State: The Intellectual Pursuit of Collectivism in America, 1880-1940* (Chicago: Quadrangle Books, 1972) and William E. Akin, *Technocracy and the*

American Dream: The Technocratic Movement, 1900-1941 (Berkeley and Los Angeles: University of California Press, 1977). For significant treatments of how economic planning was implemented during the 1920s and 1930s, respectively, see Guy Alchon, *The Invisible Hand of Planning: Capitalism, Social Science, and the State in the 1920s* (Princeton, NJ: Princeton University Press, 1985); Otis L. Graham, Jr., *Toward a Planned Society: From Roosevelt to Nixon* (New York: Oxford University Press, 1976).

3. Laski, "Charles Beard," in Beale, ed., *Charles A. Beard*, pp. 15, 19.
4. Borning, *The Political and Social Thought of Charles A. Beard*, p. 87.
5. Seidelman, *Disenchanted Realists*, p. 251, fn. 3.
6. Strout, *Pragmatic Revolt in American History*, p. 6; Hofstadter, *The Progressive Historians*, pp. 185-86.
7. Nore, *Charles A. Beard*, pp. 46, 69, 153. Beard, "Political Science in the Crucible," p. 4.
8. Beard, "The World As I Want It," p. 333.
9. In some ways, Beard anticipates the concept of new property advanced by contemporary legal scholars as a way to legitimate a vast array of judicially created rights. See Charles Reich, "The New Property," *Yale Law Journal* 73, 5 (April 1964): 733-87; C.B. MacPherson, *Property: Mainstream and Critical Positions* (Toronto: University of Toronto Press, 1978), Chaps. 1, 12; Martin Shapiro, "The Constitution and Economic Rights," in M. Judd Harmon, ed., *Essays in the Constitution of the U.S.* (Port Washington, NY: Kennikat Press, 1978), pp. 74-98; Frank Michelman, "Property as a Constitutional Right," *Washington and Lee Law Review* 38 (Fall 1982): 1101-109. The concept of new property seeks to ensconce liberal welfare and redistributive policies within the umbrella of constitutional protections by sanctioning numerous entitlement and public interest claims to income and property as rights. By comparison, Beard's concept of new property is more republican than Great Society liberal. Thus, in Beard's view, new property rights may supplement the direct ownership of land, labor, and capital by citizens, but it cannot substitute for direct ownership. See Michael W. McCann, "Resurrection and Reform: Perspectives on Property in the American Constitutional Tradition," *Politics and Society* 13, 2 (1984): 143-76, who surveys the new property literature critically and questions its actual historical capacity to transcend the limits of liberal capitalism.
10. Beard, *Contemporary American History*, p. 237. Marx, *Capital*, Vol. 1, p. 685, formalized this claim as the General Law of Accumulation: "With the increasing mass of wealth which functions as capital, accumulation increases the concentration of wealth in the hands of individual capitalists."
11. Charles A. Beard, "A 'Five-Year Plan' for America," *Forum* (July 1931): 1; also reprinted in Charles A. Beard, ed., *America Faces the Future* (Boston: Houghton Mifflin Co., 1932), pp. 117-40.
12. Beard, *Industrial Revolution*, pp. 49-50. See Glenn Porter, *The Rise of Big Business, 1860-1910* (New York: Thomas Y. Crowell Co., 1973) for historical background.
13. Beard, *Contemporary American History*, pp. 36, 233-34.
14. Charles A. Beard, "The Rationality of Planned Economy," in Beard, ed., *America Faces the Future*, p. 404. See Gardiner C. Means, *The Structure of the American Economy* (Washington, DC: Government Printing Office, 1939); Gardiner C. Means, "Business Concentration in the American Economy," in Richard C. Edwards, Michael Reich, and Thomas Weisskopf, eds., *The Capitalist System*, (Englewood Cliffs, NJ: Prentice-Hall, 1972), pp. 145-56.

15. Beard, "The Rationality of Planned Economy," in Beard, ed., *America Faces the Future*, p. 404. See Harry Laidler, *The Concentration of Control in American Industry* (New York: Thomas Y. Crowell Co., 1931). For economic and historical background, see Ralph Nelson, *Merger Movements in American Industry: 1895-1956* (Princeton, NJ: Princeton University Press, 1956).

16. Paul A. Baran and Paul M. Sweezy, *Monopoly Capital* (New York: Monthly Review Press, 1966), p. 17, define a financial group as a "number of corporations under common control, the locus of power being normally an investment or commercial bank or a great family fortune." For a summary of the contemporary literature on this topic, see Barrow, *Critical Theories of the State*, pp. 18-21.

17. Beard, *Contemporary American History*, p. 233. Beard based his analysis primarily on John Moody, *The Truth About the Trusts: A Description and Analysis of the American Trust Movement* (New York: Moody Publishing Co., 1904). The idea of integrated financial groups was pioneered in the late nineteenth century by the German Social Democratic theorist Franz Hilferding, *Finance Capital* (Boston: Routledge and Kegan Paul, 1981). In 1912, the idea gained wider credibility in the United States as a result of Congressional hearings. See *Report of the Committee Appointed Pursuant to H.R. 429 and 574 to Investigate the Concentration of Money and Credit by the U.S. House Banking and Currency Committee*. 62nd Congress, 2nd Session. 1913.

18. Beard, *Industrial Revolution*, p. 53.

19. Beard, *Nature of the Social Sciences*, pp. 125-26; Charles A. Beard, "The Anti-Trust Racket," *New Republic* (September 21, 1938): 182-84.

20. Beard, *Nature of the Social Sciences*, pp. 101-102.

21. Charles A. Beard, "The Contest Between Rural and Urban Economy," *Bulletin of the University of Georgia: Institute of Public Affairs and International Relations* 30, 2, Serial No. 466 (November 1929): 70-78. For a similar analysis, see Croly, *The Promise of American Life*, pp. 16-26.

22. Beard, *The Nature of the Social Sciences*, p. 123.

23. Beard, "Five-Year Plan for America," p. 1.

24. Beard, *Contemporary American History*, p. 404.

25. Cf. James Weinstein, *The Corporate Ideal in the Liberal State: 1900-1918* (Boston: Beacon Press, 1968). Likewise, see John Kenneth Galbraith, *The New Industrial State* (Boston: Houghton-Mifflin Co., 1978), Chaps. 1-4, 15-20, for a recent argument of the same type.

26. Cf. A. Hunter Dupree, *Science in the Federal Government: A History of Policies and Activities to 1940* (Cambridge, MA.: Harvard University Press, 1957).

27. Beard, *The Nature of the Social Sciences*, p. 128; William Z. Ripley, *Trusts, Pools, and Corporations* (New York: Ginn and Co., 1905) was one of the first to point out that the new forms of big business were designed primarily to overcome the difficulty of regulating production levels and prices within industries in order to assure steady profits.

28. Beard, *The Nature of the Social Sciences*, p. 102. Cf. Thorstein Veblen, *The Engineers and the Price System* (New York: Augustus M. Kelley, 1965. Reprint of 1921 edition); Thorstein Veblen, *Absentee Ownership and Business Enterprise in Recent Times* (New York: B. W. Huebsch, 1923).

29. Charles A. Beard, "Summary—Planning of Civilization," in Charles A. Beard, ed., *Toward Civilization* (London: Longman, Green, and Co., 1930), p. 304. David W. Noble, *The Progressive Mind, 1890-1917* (Minneapolis: University of Minnesota Press, 1980), p. 28.

30. Beard, "Summary—Planning of Civilization," p. 304. Cf. Barbara Ehrenreich and John Ehrenreich, "The Professional Managerial Class," *Radical America* 11 (March-April 1977): 7-31.
31. Beard, "Introduction," in Beard, ed., *Toward Civilization*, p. 18.
32. Cf. Andre Tridon, *The New Unionism* (New York: B. W. Huebsch, 1912); Jacob M. Budish, *The New Unionism in the Clothing Industry* (New York: Harcourt Brace, 1920); James O. Morris, *Conflict within the AFL: A Study of Craft vs. Industrial Unionism* (Ithaca, NY: Cornell University Press, 1958).
33. Beard, "The Potency of Labor Education," pp. 500-02.
34. Charles A. Beard, *Cross Currents in Europe Today* (Boston: Marshall Jones Co., 1922), p. 131.
35. Rene Brunet, *The New German Constitution* (New York: Alfred A. Knopf, 1928), Chaps. 3, 6.
36. Beard, *Cross Currents in Europe Today*, p. 131.
37. Beard, *Contemporary American History*, pp. 249, 250-52.
38. Beard, "The Rationality of Planned Economy," in Beard, ed., *America Faces the Future*, p. 403.
39. Beard, *The Industrial Revolution*, p. xvii. In the same work, Beard quotes John Stuart Mill to the effect that: "the deepest root of the evils and iniquities which fill the industrial world is not competition, but the subjection of labour to capital, and the enormous share which the possessors of the instruments of industry are able to take from the produce" (p. xvii).
40. For instance, Charles A. Beard, "The Rationality of Planned Economy," in Beard, ed., *America Faces the Future*, p. 400.
41. Carl Parrini and Martin J. Sklar, "New Thinking about the Market, 1896-1904: Some American Economists on Investment and the Theory of Surplus Capital," *Journal of Economic History* 43, 3 (September 1983): 559-78; Mary O. Furner, "The Republican Tradition and the New Liberalism: Social Investigation, State Building, and Social Learning in the Gilded Age," in Michael J. Lacey and Mary O. Furner, eds., *The State and Social Investigation in Britain and the United States* (New York: Woodrow Wilson Center Press and Cambridge University Press, 1993), pp. 171-241.
42. Robert F. Himmelberg, *The Origins of the National Recovery Administration: Business, Government, and the Trade Association Issue, 1921-1933* (New York: Fordham University Press, 1976); Van L. Perkins, *Crisis in Agriculture: The Agricultural Adjustment Administration and the New Deal* (Berkeley and Los Angeles: University of California Press, 1969).
43. Beard, *The Nature of the Social Sciences*, p. 128. Elsewhere, Charles A. Beard and George H. Smith, *The Future Comes: A Study of the New Deal* (New York: Macmillan Co., 1933), p. viii, observed that the New Deal "accepts the inexorable collectivism of American economy in fact, and seeks to work out a policy based on recognition of the main course of our economic history."
44. Beard, *The Nature of the Social Sciences*, pp. 149-50. William J. Barber, "The Divergent Fates of Two Strands of 'Institutionalist' Doctrine During the New Deal Years," *History of Political Economy* 26, 4 (1994): 569-87; Frederic S. Lee, "From Multi-Industry Planning to Keynesian Planning: Gardiner C. Means, the American Keynesians, and National Economic Planning at the National Resources Committee." *Journal of Policy History* 2, 2 (1990): 186-212.
45. Beard, *The Open Door at Home*, p. 49.
46. Beard, "The Rationality of Planned Economy," in Beard, ed., *America Faces the Future*, p. 402.

47. Beard, *The Open Door at Home*, pp. 48, 72. See John Commons, *The Distribution of Wealth* (New York: Macmillan Co., 1893), esp. Chaps. 4-5, for the institutionalist theory that supports this claim. In contrast to neo-classical economists who argued that economic rents were the product of natural advantages (whether location, fertility, managerial talent), Commons argues that privileged comparative advantages are socially derived monopoly advantages conferred by law and legal title (e.g., corporate charters, patents, franchises, protective tariffs, tax subsidies, etc.).

48. Beard, *The Open Door at Home*, pp. 224, 48.

49. Charles A. Beard and Mary R. Beard, *American Citizenship* (New York: Macmillan Co., 1914), p. 54, observe that "a property right is a *human* right to use and enjoy material things necessary to life...Property rights also have to do with ways of securing food, clothing, and shelter." Based on his own review of the book, it is certain that Beard had read Richard T. Ely, *Property and Contract in Their Relation to the Distribution of Wealth*, 2 Vols., (New York: Macmillan Co., 1914), which is considered the institutionalist classic on this topic. See also, John R. Commons, *The Legal Foundations of Capitalism* (New York: Macmillan Co., 1924). For contemporary extensions of this idea, see, R. A. Gonce, "The New Property Rights Approach and Commons' Legal Foundations of Capitalism," *Journal of Economic Issues* 10 (December 1976): 765-97; R. Larry Reynolds, "Institutionally Determined Property Claims," in Marc R. Tool and Warren J. Samuels, ed., *State, Society, and Corporate Power*, pp. 237-45. Furubotn and Richter, "The New Institutional Economics," in Furubotn and Richter, eds., *The New Institutional Economics*, pp. 1-32, observe that the new institutional economics "seeks to extend the range of applicability of neo-classical theory by considering how property-rights structure and transaction costs affect incentives and economic behavior" (p. 1). See also, De Alessi, "Development of the Property Rights Approach," in Furobotn and Richter, eds., *The New Institutional Economics*, pp. 45-53.

50. The idea that property does not inhere in its thingness but exists as a bundle-of-rights between people appeared as early 1913. See, Wesley Hohfeld, "Some Fundamental Legal Conceptions as Applied in Judicial Reasoning," *Yale Law Journal* 23 (1913): 16-59. For surveys of this conception, see Charles Donahue, Jr., "The Future of the Concept of Property Predicted From Its Past," in J. Roland Pennock and John W. Chapman, *Property: NOMOS XXII* (New York: New York University Press, 1980), pp. 28-68; Thomas C. Grey, "The Disintegration of Property," in idem, pp. 69-85. Grey finds that after Hohfeld's pathbreaking article, the "bundle-of-rights" concept of property "became part of the stock-in-trade of the legal realist movement" (p. 85). Grey notes that "acceptance of the bundle-of-rights conception breaks the main institutions of capitalist private law free from the metaphor of ownership as control over things by individuals. Mature capitalist property must be seen as a web of state-enforced relations of entitlement and duty *between persons*, some assumed voluntarily and some not."

51. Beard, *The Open Door at Home*, p. 224. Likewise, Beard argues that "an efficient distribution of wealth within the United States would largely eliminate the unbalance between capital extension and consumption, provide domestic use for a considerable part of the so-called surplus, and reduce the pressures of the outward thrusts—thrusts which engender rivalries abroad" (p. 225).

52. Charles A. Beard, "Monopoly in Fact and Fiction," *Events* 4 (November 1938): 383-87.

53. Charles A. Beard, "The Blessed Profit System," *New Republic* (December 26, 1934): 188-90. For example, see McCann, "Resurrection and Reform," pp. 143-76, who documents that "the actual legal prerogatives of property owners have undergone vast changes throughout our nation's history."

54. Beard and Beard, *American Citizenship*, pp. 57-59. As early as 1908, Beard, *Politics*, p. 12, called attention to the fact "that men's ideas have differed fundamentally as to what particular things should constitute private property...For example, man himself was once regarded as the proper subject of ownership; the feudal privileges and the tithes swept away by the French Revolution were forms of property no less real than industrial stocks; the rotten boroughs abolished by the Reform Bill of 1832 were marketable holdings; vast areas of the open seas were once claimed by Spain; and high roads were formerly private possessions. Thus some forms of property have disappeared altogether; the public has laid hold of domains once reserved to the individual; and private rights are becoming more and more penetrated with notions of public welfare. The great question of any age, therefore, is not shall private property as such be abolished, for the nature of man demonstrates that it cannot be, but what forms of property shall be permitted, and to what public uses shall they be subjected."

55. Beard, *Industrial Revolution*, p. 80. Similarly, Beard and Beard, *American Citizenship*, p. 62, claim "the tendency now is toward increasing the amount of property which is publicly owned, toward restricting the use of private property for the convenience of the public and the welfare of the working people, and toward the prevention of all kinds of money-making schemes by which clever persons rob the industrious."

56. Beard, *American Citizenship*, p. 61.

57. Beard, *The Open Door at Home*, pp. 104-11.

58. Beard, *Public Policy and the General Welfare*, p. 5, complains that "despite brave pamphlets and bold speech emanating from splinters and fragments, Marxists are utterly bewildered in the presence of practical issues."

59. Beard, "Methods of Training for Public Service," p. 904: "An industrial democracy can not long endure without a sound and efficient public service." Similarly, in discussing the problems of municipal socialism, Beard, *American City Government*, p. 102, argued that "the branch of municipal government which maintains the most intimate contact with life and property is the group of administrative officers...These subordinate officers afford little of the spectacular in the regular discharge of their duties, but upon them really depends the excellence of a city's government." Charles A. Beard, "A Constitution Before the Fact," *The Nation* 111 (December 8, 1920): 666, notes that complex administrative technique "is to be the very foundation of the great society – if it is to endure at all."

60. Soule, "Beard and the Concept of Planning," in Beale, ed., *Charles A. Beard*, p. 65.

61. Beard, "Myth of Rugged American Individualism," p. 22.

62. President's Research Committee on Social Trends, *Recent Social Trends in the United States* (New York: Whittlesey House, 1934).

63. Soule, "Beard and the Concept of Planning," in Beale, ed., *Charles A. Beard*, p. 66. For a historical account of this movement, see Graham, Jr., "The Planning Ideal and American Reality," in Elkins and McKitrick, eds., *The Hofstadter Aegis*, pp. 257-99. Many of these blueprints are reproduced in Beard, *America Faces the Future*, Part II.

64. Ellis J. Hawley, "Herbert Hoover, the Commerce Secretariat, and the Vision of an 'Associative State', 1921-1928," *Journal of American History* 61 (1974): 116-40.

65. Beard, *Industrial Revolution*, pp. 100-101.

66. Beard, "The Rationality of Planned Economy," in Beard, ed., *America Faces the Future*, p. 406.

67. Beard, *The Open Door at Home*, p. 210.

68. Ibid., p. 217.

69. Beard preferred that experts define the Standard-of-Life Budget. Thus, it is instructive that Stuart Chase, a progressive economist, proposed "A Ten Year Plan for America" quite similar to Beard's Forum Plan. Chase proposed a minimum standard of living for all families of at least $5,000 annually, an amount equal to the average annual salary of a full professor at the time. Also see, Graham A. Laing, *Towards Technocracy* (Los Angeles: Angelus Press, 1933), Chap. 18. Such proposals were also fairly common among British socialists. See R. Palme Dutt, *Socialism and the Living Wage* (London: Independent Labour Party, 1926). Also, Noel Thompson, "Hobson and the Fabians: Two Roads to Socialism in the 1920s," *History of Political Economy* 26, 2 (1994): 203-20 for how the living wage debate played out in Great Britain's Labour Party.

70. Beard, *The Open Door at Home*, p. 224.

71. Ibid., p. 227; Beard, "The Rationality of Planning," in Beard, ed., *America Faces the Future*, pp. 408-409.

72. Beard, *The Open Door at Home*, p. 227.

73. Paradoxically, Beard anticipated much of the contemporary neo-conservative critique of welfare liberalism. Cf. Charles Murray, *Losing Ground* (New York: Basic Books, 1984).

74. Beard, *The Open Door at Home*, p. 227; Beard, "The Rationality of Planned Economy," in Beard, ed., *America Faces the Future*, pp. 408-09.

75. According to Beard, *American City Government*, p. 318: "intelligence and skill are the very basis of social democracy," and these were not characteristics he ascribed to the Roman proletariat in contrast to the Marxian proletariat.

76. Charles A. Beard, "Introduction," in Laing, *Towards Technocracy*, p. 5.

77. Laing, *Towards Technocracy*, p. 62.

78. Beard, "Introduction," in Ibid., p. 8; Beard, "The Rationality of Planned Economy," in Beard, ed., *America Faces the Future*, pp. 409-10.

79. A watered-down version of Beard's proposal was filed as a bill by Senator Robert LaFollette. A copy of the bill is included in Beard, ed., *America Faces the Future*, pp. 413-16. The jurisdiction of the NEC would include transportation (railways), communications (telegraph and telephone), fuel (oil, gas, coal), iron and steel, lumber and building materials, electrical utilities, textiles, meatpacking, agriculture, wholesaling, and retailing. In 1939, Charles A. Beard, "By Charles A. Beard," *The Christian Science Monitor* (July 22, 1939), p. 5, again proposed that the President "call into conference representatives of Congress, business enterprise, labor, and agriculture and ask them, in the light of the brutal facts before us, to formulate positive measures designed to put into full motion our economic resources....From the President's conference might emerge a statement of controlling principles, to be discussed by the nation...Then the necessary legislation and administrative machinery could be provided by Congress."

80. Beard, "Five-Year Plan for America," p. 5, observes that "the exact weight to be assigned to each element will be a matter of great delicacy, but criteria can be evolved and in the process the experience of Germany with economic councils may be studied with profit." See Brunet, *The New German Constitution*, pp. 77-91, 236-68. Also, Cf. John R. Commons, *Proportional Representation* (New

York: T. Y. Crowell, 1896), who proposed replacing geographic representation in Congress with functional representation based on economic groups.

81. Beard, "Five-Year Plan for America," p. 5.

82. Beard, "The Rationality of Planned Economy," in Beard, ed., *America Faces the Future*, p. 406.

83. A less ambitious version of the proposed agency was created during the 1930s in the National Resources Council (later the National Resources Planning Board). See Charles E. Merriam, "The National Resources Planning Board: A Chapter in American Planning Experience," *American Political Science Review* 38 (December 1944): 1075-88; John D. Millett, *The Process and Organization of Government Planning* (New York: Columbia University Press, 1947); Marion Clawson, *New Deal Planning: The National Resources Planning Board* (Baltimore, MD: Johns Hopkins University Press, 1981).

84. David A. Horowitz, "Senator Borah's Crusade to Save Small Business From the New Deal," *The Historian* 55 (1993): 693-708.

85. Martin Schnitzer, *The Swedish Investment Reserve: A Device for Economic Stabilization?* (Washington, DC: American Enterprise Institute, 1967).

86. Beard, "Five-Year Plan for America," p. 7.

87. For example, Carter Goodrich, "The Climate for Planning: Review of *America Faces the Future*, edited by Charles A. Beard," *New Republic* (March 9, 1932): 105; Soule, "Beard and the Concept of Planning," in Beale, ed., *Charles A. Beard*, p. 66.

88. Freeman, *An American Testament*, p. 106.

89. William Appleman Williams, *Americans in a Changing World: A History of the United States in the Twentieth Century* (New York: Harper and Row, 1978), pp. 235-36.

90. Soule, "Beard and the Concept of Planning," in Beale, ed., *Charles A. Beard*, p. 67.

91. John P. Diggins, *Mussolini and Fascism: The View From America* (Princeton, NJ: Princeton University Press, 1972).

92. Charles A. Beard, "Review of *Making the Fascist State* by Herbert W. Schneider," *New Republic* (January 23, 1929): 277-78.

93. Beard, *The Open Door at Home*, p. 105. The same thesis is central to Marxist critiques of fascism, Cf. Daniel Guerin, *Fascism and Big Business* (New York: Monad Press, 1973, 2nd American edition); R. Palme Dutt, *Fascism and Social Revolution* (Chicago: Proletarian Publishers, 1974. Reprint of the 1934, 2nd edition).

94. Charles A. Beard, "Lenin and Economic Revolution," *New Republic* 75 (May 17, 1933): 22. Beard draws an obvious analogy between the collapse of imperial Russia and America during the Great Depression. Thus, Harry Gideonse, "Nationalist Collectivism and Charles A. Beard," *Journal of Political Economy* 43 (December 1935): 778-99, criticizes Beard's Forum Plan on the mistaken assumption that Beard had embraced Soviet style state socialism.

95. In response to critics who dismissed such plans as mere state capitalism, Beard cites Lenin approvingly to the effect that: "Socialism is nothing but the next step forward from state-capitalist monopoly. In other words, Socialism is nothing but state-capitalist monopoly *made to benefit the whole people*; by this token it ceases to be capitalist monopoly." Lenin quoted in Beard, "Lenin and Revolution," pp. 22-23.

96. Williams, *Americans in a Changing World*, p. 236.

97. Beard, "Five-Year Plan for America," p. 7. Elsewhere, Beard, *Contemporary American History*, p. 236, observes: "it remains a fact that the buying public and

the working class are paying millions in annual tribute to the holders of paper which represents no economic service whatever."

98. Beard, "Lenin and Economic Revolution," p. 23.

99. Beard, *American City Government*, pp. 218-23.

100. Nore, *Charles A. Beard*, p. 92. The theory of socialization by eminent domain was developed as a constitutional strategy for the American Socialist Party by John Spargo, *Applied Socialism: A Study of the Application of Socialistic Principles to the State* (New York: B. W. Huebsch, 1912). Beard had an early association with Spargo while teaching at the Socialist Party's Rand School of Social Science in 1906. See Recchiuti, "The Rand School of Social Science During the Progressive Era," pp. 149-61, passim.

101. Beard, "Five-Year Plan for America," pp. 7, 11.

102. Ibid., p. 7.

103. Ibid., pp. 8, 9.

104. Beard, "The Contest Between Rural and Urban Economy," p. 77. Elsewhere, Beard, *The Nature of the Social Sciences*, p. 129.

105. Beard, "Five-Year Plan for America," p. 8. Also, Beard, *The Nature of the Social Sciences*, p. 130, suggests that farmers are being "driven into co-operative or collective enterprises....as specialization increases in agriculture, farmers tend to draw together in organizations and to employ collective methods in protecting and promoting their interests."

106. Beard, "Five-Year Plan for America," p. 5.

107. Beard, *American City Government*, p. 228.

108. Beard, *Economic Basis of Politics*, pp. 72-82. Similarly, Beard, *Public Policy and the General Welfare*, pp. 157ff., argues that economic conflicts and acquisitive instincts would generate political conflict and power struggles as fully under one economic order as under another.

109. Beard, *Economic Basis of Politics*, p. 82.

110. Beard, "Foreword," in Brunet, *The New German Constitution*, p. vii.

111. Beard, *Cross Currents in Europe Today*, pp. 144-45.

112. Charles A. Beard, "Freedom in Political Thought," in Ruth Nanda Anshen, ed., *Freedom: Its Meaning* (New York: Harcourt, Brace and Co., 1940), p. 290. Beard continued to uphold the virtues of the Weimar Constitution, despite the rise of Hitler and Naziism, but concluded that "something more is needed to preserve freedom than verbal proclamations" (p. 290). The full text of the Weimar Constitution is available in Brunet, *The New German Constitution*, pp. 297-339. It was symbolically important to Beard that the Weimar Constitution is formally titled "The Constitution of the German Commonwealth."

113. Beard, "Foreword," in Brunet, *The New German Constitution*, p. vii.

114. Ibid., p. vii.

115. Beard, *Cross Currents in Europe Today*, pp. 145-46. Quotations are from the Weimar Constitution of 1919.

116. Charles A. Beard, "National Guilds," *New Republic* 25 (December 8, 1920): 50-51. On council communism, see Anton Pannekoek, *Workers' Councils* (Somerville, MA.: Root and Branch, 1970. Reprint of 1945 edition); V. I. Lenin, *The State and Revolution* (New York: International Publishers, 1974), esp. Chap. 3; Brunet, *The New German Constitution*, pp. 77-90.

6

Imperialism and Diversion

Between Internationalism and Isolationism

In 1916, Charles A. Beard was denouncing Germany as a danger to civilization and calling for American participation in World War I on the side of the Entente Allies.[1] Like John Dewey and other social-democrats, Beard saw the Great War as an opportunity to advance the interests of the European working class by breaking "the union of the Hohenzollern military caste and the German masses whose radical leaders are Social Democrats."[2] Even after the Versailles Treaty, Beard continued to embrace the Wilsonian theme that the Great War had been fought to make the world safe for democracy.[3] However, by the mid-1930s, he was staunchly opposed to war with Germany and Japan, had come to embrace the revisionist history of World War I, and even testified before Congress against the Lend-Lease Act. Thus, intellectual historians agree that somewhere between the end of World War I and the 1930s, Beard shifted from internationalism to isolationism and, indeed, a few critics have referred to him as a pacifist in his later years. Within the umbrella of this consensus, debates among biographers, intellectual and diplomatic historians, have come to center largely on identifying the timing and the reasons for Beard's "conversion" to isolationism.[4] Not coincidentally, during the 1960s and 1970s, Beard's writings on foreign policy and diplomatic history enjoyed a resurgence among many on the New Left who were constructing their own revisionist history critical of America's political and military involvement in various Third World countries.[5] Today, Beard's views are still cited in international relations and history textbooks as an example of isolationist theory in American foreign policy.[6]

Paradoxically, Beard steadfastly rejected claims that he was an isolationist and, by the 1930s, he referred to his own position as "continentalism" in contrast to both internationalism and isolationism. Nevertheless, both liberal internationalists and advocates of American imperial expansion debunked the concept of continentalism as a smokescreen for isolationism.[7] Likewise, a congressional bloc of progressive western isolationists embraced Beard as their intellectual spokesperson during the 1930s.[8] Beard did oppose America's entry into World War II and was therefore allied politically with an isolationist bloc in Congress *on this particular issue*.[9] Yet, a major result of this single-issue alliance was that Beard's intellectual differences with the progressive isolationists (e.g., Senators Nye, Borah, LaFollette) were lost in a highly charged polemical context that defined all possible theoretical positions according to one's support for or opposition to American participation in World War II.[10] Thus, from the outset, Beard's conception of continentalism was submerged in the crossfire of a bitter polemic between internationalists and isolationists, who effectively denied Beard's ability to articulate a third principle of American foreign policy.

As Beard understood, advocates of internationalism have consistently conceptualized the world order in terms of two antinomies. At a political level, global politics has been viewed as an on-going struggle between autocracy and democracy, totalitarianism and democracy, or dictatorship and freedom. It has made little difference whether the perceived enemy is the German Kaiser, the Italian duce, the Japanese Emperor, the General Secretary of the Communist Party, or a petty Third World dictator. The expansionist and destabilizing objectives of dictatorships are used to justify periodic warfare in the name of peace and to explain the need for police actions in remote corners of the world. At an economic level, internationalists and expansionists have claimed that continued American prosperity depends on exports and the penetration of international markets, and both have pursued wide-ranging trade agreements to guarantee fair trade and open markets for American goods and security for American capital. However, even as the antinomies of the "old world order" are allegedly disintegrating, American military forces remain engaged in an unprecedented number of police actions and arguably not one of them has achieved their alleged political or humanitarian objective. Likewise, there is a prevailing consensus among economists and economic policy-makers that the interests of the United States are inextricably woven into a new global economy and that a renewal of domestic prosperity depends on global competitiveness and the capture of export markets.[11]

In contrast to the prevailing view, both past and present, Beard's continentalism rests on the competing hypothesis that foreign policy and international relations are, for the most part, an extension of *domestic* economic policy and, in particular, a result of the *failures* of domestic economic policy. Consequently, Beard regarded the pursuit of free trade and open markets, as well as the accompanying pattern of escalating United States interventionism, as a political diversion from the unfinished tasks of domestic economic and social reform. In Beard's grand conception of American history, a dialectic of economic class interests propelled American political development forward, but at each crucial juncture concerted efforts at domestic reform were diverted into international conflicts as popular leaders backed down from the enormous political struggle entailed by a head-to-head confrontation with the capitalist class. Thus, as business assaults on the New Deal escalated in the mid- to late-1930s, Beard was increasingly concerned that Franklin D. Roosevelt would abandon the New Deal and divert national energies into a war with Japan just as Woodrow Wilson had abandoned the New Freedom for war in Europe.[12] Moreover, Beard was convinced that even if the United States was to win a second world war, the outward thrust of imperialism would eviscerate the social-democratic promise of the early twentieth century by entangling the United States in an endless series of military and political diversions that would siphon off economic resources and political energy into a permanent war economy.[13] The overarching goal of Beard's continentalism was to reduce America's involvement in international trade rivalries and warfare through *domestic economic restructuring*, rather than a realignment of global trade relations, international diplomacy, or military confrontation.

The Economic Basis of National Interest

As early as 1904, in his first year as an assistant professor at Columbia University, Beard taught a course on "The History of American Expansion." In that course, he sought to establish two basic theses for understanding American foreign policy: (1) the economic basis of expansion and (2) the diversionary thesis. In his syllabus, Beard suggested that American involvement in world affairs "has always extended as far as American interests" and he assigned John A. Hobson's, *Imperialism: A Study*, as a book that would make "short work of many current fallacies" on the topic.[14] Not surprisingly, Hobson's influence is evident in many of Beard's early textbooks. In his *Introduction to the English Historians* (1906), Beard argued that "the international politics of Europe for the last three centuries can be understood solely in the light of the economic interests engendered in the race for markets and territorial dominion...they are without doubt the great impelling forces in what is called 'imperialism'."[15] Similarly, in the first edition of *American Government and Politics* (1910), Beard reiterated that the United States has always "been a world power, as far as has been necessary, from the beginning of our history....the protection of our government has steadily advanced with the extension of our material interests."[16] Indeed, by 1914, in his *Contemporary American History*, Beard observed "signs that the United States was prepared economically to accept that type of imperialism that had long been dominant in British politics and had sprung into prominence in Germany, France, and Italy."[17] Much later in his career, Beard continued to acknowledge that the central economic thesis of continentalism "came from the writings of the British economist, John A. Hobson."[18]

As a second thesis in his 1904 syllabus, Beard also speculated that American expansion was having an unfavorable impact on the course of American social and political development. America's continuous involvement in warfare, literally since the time of early settlement, had produced a war spirit among the American people that only seemed to grow stronger as it was woven into the historical fabric of American political culture. Indeed, on the eve of World War I, Beard lectured student pacifists that "it was an illusion to think of Americans as a pacific people; they are and always have been one of the most violent peoples in history."[19] Similarly, on the eve of the Second World War, Beard reiterated his claim that war has "always been popular in the United States."[20] Unfortunately, he informed his students, the warlike and expansionist thrust of American political culture made it easy for the capitalist class "to divert the nation's attention from 'problems of national life'."[21] As a recent example, Beard suggested that "it was fortunate for the conservative interest that the quarrel with Spain came shortly after McKinley's election, and they were able to employ that ancient political device, 'a vigorous foreign policy', to divert the public mind from domestic difficulties."[22]

While most of Beard's work on diplomatic history and foreign policy appeared during the 1930s and 1940s, early in his academic career Beard had already established the two fundamental axioms which later structured his work on foreign policy. Subsequently, as Thomas C. Kennedy observes, Beard broached the idea of continentalism in a detailed study of the controversy over Jay's Treaty (1793) in his *Economic Origins of Jeffersonian Democracy* (1915). Later, in *The Rise of American Civilization* (1927), Beard developed the idea more extensively as part of the Hamiltonian-Jeffersonian dialectic that underlay his conception of American political development. However, it was not until the first half of the 1930s that Beard made the effort to systematically formulate a theory of foreign policy that was anchored in his economic interpretation of American history. The results of this effort were *The Idea of National Interest: An Analytical Study in American Foreign Policy* (1934) and *The Open Door at Home: A Trial Philosophy of National Interest* (1934). As Kennedy observes, "taken together these two works constitute Beard's magnum opus on the theoretical and practical aspects of American diplomatic history."[23] Although both works were historical in their approach to foreign policy, *The Idea of National Interest* was designed as a theoretical critique of the dominant ideas on foreign policy, while the *The Open Door at Home* was conceived as a programmatic work in radical political economy.[24]

Many critics consider *The Idea of National Interest* to be "the dullest book Beard ever wrote"[25] because it reads like an encyclopedia of quotations with one example after another of how leading thinkers and statesmen have used the term "national interest" over the course of American history. A more generous description of *The Idea* is that it provides "an intensive analysis of the American usages of the concept from the Founding Fathers to FDR."[26] Beard concluded that as an abstract idea the term national interest had been used by statesmen in ambiguous and contradictory ways. As a result, he argued that one could not discern any coherent analytic meaning to the idea of national interest as a logical concept. On the other hand, when American statesmen applied the concept to concrete issues of domestic and foreign policy, he concluded that the actual policies associated with national interest were identical historically to the economic and political interests of the dominant party and to the openly avowed interests of the economic groups represented by that party. Consequently, in *The Open Door at Home*, Beard sought to provide a synthetic, but historically anchored definition of the national interest materially conceived, and he defined the national interest as "a gain in wealth as measured by the prevailing economic standards — a gain in land, houses, material capital, money, credits, and exchangeable commodities." This definition implied that "the supreme interest of the United States is the creation and maintenance of a high standard of life for all its people...within the frame of national security."[27]

Importantly, however, Beard was aware that any concept of interest "involves mental attention...a state of consciousness, a wish, a purpose, more or less deliberate and rational, a determination to realize an increase in goods or wealth." To the extent that objective interests must be conceptualized in the formulation of any policy, there are "no interests without ideas."[28] These visions of the national interest typically outline "a broad program of action to be followed by the Government in conducting relations with other powers and their nationals." As Beard sought to demonstrate in *The Open Door at Home*, a foreign policy ultimately "consists of maxims, axioms, or principles to be accepted as official and applied in practice to concrete cases as they arise from day to day or circumstance to circumstance. Taken collectively these general rules are supposed to form a consistent whole, logical in its parts, devoid of mutually destructive contradictions." Moreover, when a vision captures the popular imagination, it is because it offers a meaningful "interpretation of all history, out of which all nations, provinces, and empires have emerged" and provides the people of a country with a sense of national mission or national faith.[29]

In this context, Beard frequently debunked the neoclassical and utilitarian idea of rational action as "fallacious and preposterous" because "the fact that a class possesses landed property does not automatically give that class intelligence enough to preserve and protect that property."[30] He observes that objective material interests may not be realized because "the wrong means may be chosen, or unforeseen circumstances may defeat realization."[31] Nevertheless, Beard was convinced that many potential failures and "unforeseen" circumstances can be discerned by subjecting the basic assumptions of a vision to empirical tests and by analyzing the internal logical consistency of the vision. Either type of analysis may reveal contradictions in a vision that require a systematic reevaluation of the ideas and policies associated with it. The two major works on diplomatic history and American foreign policy exemplify this analytic strategy.

The Jeffersonian Vision of American Foreign Policy

The core of Beard's economic interpretation of foreign policy was an extension of his dialectical theory of American political development. Beard concluded that, when applied to concrete policies, there had always been two competing ideas of national interest associated with the Jeffersonian and the Hamiltonian visions.[32] Both visions were fundamentally expansionist in their objectives. Going back to the earliest days of the American Republic, the Jeffersonian political constituency and its economic concerns were essentially agrarian, their expansionist aims oriented toward the acquisition of land and territory within the continental domain of North America for the purpose of enlarging a self-sufficient independent agrarian civilization. In fact, drawing on his interpretation in *The Rise of American Civilization*, Beard argued that when the Republicans came to power in 1801, its leaders embarked on a massive program of territorial expansion and agricultural imperialism. The central objective of agricultural imperialism was to satisfy the land hunger of agrarian constituents and to thereby strengthen their agrarian social base and promote the agrarian/landed social structure which Jeffersonians envisioned as the future of the American republic. The concrete results of this foreign policy were the Louisiana Purchase (1803), the War of 1812, the Florida Purchase (1819), the annexation of Texas (1845), the Mexican War (1846-1848) and the annexation of the California and New Mexico Territories, settlement of the Northwest Boundary Dispute (1846), and, finally, the Gadsden Purchase (1854).[33] Beard concludes that after the closing of the frontier in 1893, agricultural imperialism, as such, came to an end—i.e., the policy of physical conquest, occupation, and settlement of new lands by Americans was exhausted. Nevertheless, many of the broader assumptions of the Jeffersonian policy continued to hold sway among conservative politicians. Beard suggested that the Jeffersonian idea of national interest remained tied to agriculture and found a strong base of support in the agricultural lobby. Once the frontier was exhausted, the westward thrust of Jeffersonian policy turned from the acquisition of new lands to the export of agricultural surpluses.

In *The Open Door at Home*, Beard suggests that the contemporary legacy of agricultural imperialism was to be found in a view of foreign policy that he now labeled the agrarian thesis. William Appleman Williams points out that Beard's critique of the agrarian thesis was designed as a polemic against New Deal Secretary of Agriculture Henry A. Wallace "who had reasserted the [agrarian] expansionist view in his own book announcing that *America Must Choose* (1934)."[34] At the trough of the Great Depression, Wallace insisted that the United States would slip toward fascism unless it maintained and increased its overseas economic activity and, most importantly, its export of agricultural surpluses.[35] Since the strength of demand for manufactured goods was still heavily dependent on demand generated by the agricultural and rural sectors of the economy, Wallace claimed that the key to economic recovery lay in reciprocal trade agreements that would allow American farmers to export their surpluses to foreign countries. As Beard observed, Wallace's claim was firmly situated in a Jeffersonian tradition that placed agriculture and free trade at the core of U.S. international economic interests.[36]

Beard summarized the contemporary assumptions of the agrarian or Jeffersonian foreign policy as follows:

1. There are surpluses of manufactures, agricultural produce, and capital which cannot be used at home.
2. These surpluses can be disposed of abroad if tariff barriers made by special interests are lowered, other impediments to the free flow of trade are removed, either directly or through reciprocity arrangements, and international cooperation is substituted for the policy of government pressure.
3. Other nations are moving in the direction of free trade or at least can be induced to lower their tariffs and to modify their systems of licensing, quotas, bounties, and subsidies, which operate against the free and easy flow of goods.
4. Q.E.D. The problem of the surpluses is solved, prosperity is recovered or restored, the crisis is dissipated, and the national interest is secured through free trade.[37]

Beard argued that the Jeffersonian policy of free trade, fair trade, and reciprocity agreements would fail in a globalizing economy as a result of its own internal contradictions. Beard identified capital mobility as the central contradiction of the agrarian thesis. He was ahead of his time in grasping the domestic implications of global capital mobility, particularly under international free trade arrangements. Beard predicted that insofar as Jeffersonian free-traders were successful in realizing their objectives: "...it is likely that industries would gravitate as rapidly as possible to the regions where lowest cost production is available—accessibility of raw materials, cheapness of labor, long hours, and low or negligible standards of social legislation and insurance." In drawing this conclusion, he was merely extrapolating from the experience of the New England textiles industry which had been virtually destroyed by southward migration. Beard observed that even within the United States industrial regions such as New England "have been blighted by the wholesale migration of capital to sections of cheapest production—the lowest standards of life, unorganized labor easily regimented by employers, absence of labor legislation, exploitation of children, long hours, and social squalor in general." Furthermore, instead of bringing prosperity to these regions, "the transported industries immediately introduced...the social and economic degradation that accompanied the rise of the factory system a hundred years ago—the degradation that had been mitigated [previously] only by the heroic efforts of reformers."[38]

It was Beard's conclusion that international free trade would fail to bring prosperity to the United States for one simple reason: it would fail to provide the prophesied export markets in underdeveloped countries because capital would be exported, but labor standards and social legislation would not be exported with capital. The export of American capital would not substantially raise the standard of living in less developed countries, at least not in the near to immediate term but, on the other hand, it would cause a deterioration of the standard of living for U.S. workers; thus exacerbating the problem of domestic underconsumption and *pari passu, ad infinitum*. In this way, free trade would eventually undercut the drive toward social and industrial democracy that had been the hallmark of the twentieth century.

The Hamiltonian Vision of American Foreign Policy

In contrast to the Jeffersonian agrarians, Hamilton's followers and their economic interests were fundamentally commercial in nature. Consequently, Hamiltonians had always sought access to the overseas carrying trade, to foreign markets as an outlet for manufactured goods, and, eventually, to opportunities for direct foreign investment of American capital. However, it was not until after the Civil War that the United States again pursued an aggressive policy to promote full-scale industrialization. By the end of the nineteenth century, the United States had become a predominantly industrial nation and, according to Beard, this shift in the national economic base brought with it a change in the dominant foreign policy. In Beard's view, the rise of "industrial imperialism" in the late nineteenth and early twentieth centuries was promoted by an alliance of manufacturers, traders, shipowners, financiers, and naval officers.[39] Although the historical foundations of industrial imperialism could be traced back to the Hamiltonian system of protectionism and a strong navy, it achieved dominance as a foreign policy only during the 1890s. As a late entrant onto the world stage of industrial imperialism, the United States encountered a world that had been conquered already and divided among the European powers, and a consequence, it was forced to abandon the policy of overt territorial acquisition for a policy of exceptional imperialism.

For Beard, the exceptional features of America commercial imperialism were defined by three characteristics. First, it was based on controlling sea lanes, rather than territories. Beard traced the historical origins of this strategy to Commodore Perry, the first naval officer to publicly advocate a policy of imperialism and to act on it independently by opening Japan to American trading vessels (1854). Almost two decades later, Admiral Meade, again acting on his own authority, seized Tutuila (Samoa) and negotiated a treaty for a naval base that gave the U.S. navy an advance position in the South Pacific. However, Beard considered Alfred Thayer Mahan, also a naval officer, as the individual who did most to sell the idea of sea power and empire to the President and Congress. Beard regards Mahan as "the most successful propagandist ever produced in the United States" and the one who returned American foreign policy to the "pattern of *Machpolitik* outlined in the *Federalist*."[40] Most importantly, acting under the spell of the Mahan thesis, the United States asserted its strategic control of important sea lanes in the Spanish-American War (1898), particularly in the Pacific Ocean and the Caribbean Basin, by taking control of Hawaii, the Philippines, Guam, Cuba, and Puerto Rico. The two American lakes were then joined strategically by taking over and completing the Panama Canal project (1904).[41]

The open door policy was a second characteristic of America's exceptional imperialism. Rather than seeking to monopolize access to colonial markets, America's late entry onto the world stage placed it in the position of seeking to open foreign markets to free and fair competition. Beard often claimed that this exceptional strategy accounted also for the exceptionally moralistic overtones of American imperialism, because it allowed U.S. leaders to play the role of world liberator, i.e., freeing colonies from European masters (e.g., Cuba, Philippines) and domestic dictators (e.g., Panama). This allowed American statesmen and corporate elites to conceal their economic and political aims behind populist rhetoric ("making the world safe for democracy"), while the domination of foreign economies through direct investment and foreign loans could be presented under the ideological rubric of development aid and assistance.[42]

Third, the opening of markets to non-colonial masters paradoxically provided the entree for America's version of neocolonialism, i.e., dollar diplomacy, or the export of surplus capital through direct foreign investment and foreign loans. By relying on capital investment rather than military occupation as a strategy of territorial penetration, Beard emphasized that American "imperialism does not rest primarily upon a desire for more territory, but rather upon the necessity for markets in which to sell manufactured goods and for opportunities to invest surplus accumulations of capital." Hence, the chief prerequisite of the American form of imperialism "is not the annexation of colonies, but 'free trade' and security of direct foreign investments, and the ability to repatriate profits."[43] At the same time, this three-pronged imperialist strategy enabled U.S. foreign policy-makers to position the United States as a "leader of the free world" by protecting and policing sea lanes from control and domination by expansionist powers; to claim that it was liberating subjected peoples from control by European or other despotic powers; and to insist that it was investing in the economic future of less developed countries, rather than exploiting them or rendering them dependent on U.S. economic, financial, and military power. To this extent, U.S. imperialism was a two-faced Janus that appeared one way to its victims and competitors and quite the opposite to the American public.

In *The Open Door at Home*, Beard identifies the underlying assumptions of industrial imperialism to construct a second analytic view of American foreign policy that he labeled the industrialist thesis. He summarizes the industrialist thesis as follows:

> American industry, under the regime of technology, is producing more commodities than the American people can use or consume, and the 'surplus' must be exported. The accumulations of capital in private hands in the United States are larger than can be employed advantageously at home, that is, profitably, so that there is a 'surplus' for exportation. American agriculture likewise is producing more than the American people can use or consume and the 'surplus' must be sold in foreign markets. Outlets for these increasing 'surpluses' of goods and capital must and can be found abroad, through channels of commerce; otherwise the development of American industry and agriculture, with corresponding opportunities for gains and profits, will be slowed down, and brought, perhaps, to an impasse or deadlock which cannot be broken. It is, therefore, a question of commercial expansion or stagnation and decay.[44]

Once again, Beard argued that the industrialist thesis contained internal contradictions that lead either to its economic self-destruction or into warfare with competitor nations. First, while American proponents of the industrialist thesis insisted that the *export* of goods and capital be free from government restraint, they typically favored tariffs and quotas on the *import* of manufactured and agricultural commodities. The central paradox of a high tariff policy was that as domestic industries expanded under tariff protection, "ever more outlets for 'surpluses' of goods and capital must be found by private and public enterprise."[45] Thus, a key policy implication of the industrialist thesis is that American government and industry must become ever more aggressive in seeking foreign outlets for American goods and capital in concert with economic expansion.

The aggressive overseas expansion of American industry leads to a second contradiction in the industrialist thesis. As practiced in the United States, the policy of export-driven industrial growth assumes that all exports of surplus goods and capital redound to the national interest. Beard observes astutely: "no discrimination is made among the goods exported and the uses to which exported capital may be put." Beard extrapolated another lesson from the migration of the New England textile industry in his observation that an indiscriminate policy of free exports assumes that "the manufacturer who sells cotton goods abroad serves the national interest," and equally so, "the manufacturer who exports the latest textile machinery which, in China or

Japan for instance, cuts down the Oriental markets of American cotton-goods manufacturers."[46] Without capital export restrictions, Beard predicted that "capital exported to build branch factories and expand competing industries in foreign lands" would undercut domestic industry and employment mainly to the benefit of international finance capitalists and the emerging multinational firms, but at the expense of American workers.

Finally, a third contradiction of the industrialist thesis was its promotion of "trade opportunities, concessions, and privileges *in posse*, which may be won, gained, and held in all parts of the world by American citizens." To the degree that capital exports and the penetration of foreign markets are promoted by the state, government officials establish an implicit contract to protect the property rights of American citizens in foreign countries. In this manner, the interests of the United States are carried by business corporations into places where the possibility of actually defending such rights is remote, or where doing so inevitably requires the use of military force and persistent police actions throughout the world. Thus, Beard notes that "...besides promoting the extension of interests and activities abroad which drain off domestic 'surpluses'...the Government of the United States, according to the industrialist thesis, must defend these interests and activities against the adverse pressures and discriminations of foreign persons, corporations, and governments, and, if need be, against disorders, threats of force, and open violence abroad." Indeed, capital exports and the penetration of foreign markets had effectively extended the Fifth Amendment and the obligation of contract clause "to ships upon the high seas; commodities in warehouses and shops abroad; capital invested; mines, factories, and other plants owned in part or wholly by American citizens or corporations; concessions already won and in process of winning; lands, forests, houses, and other property owned in foreign places by American citizens and corporations; overseas possessions, protectorates, and spheres of influence and penetration against foreign governments; and similar rights, titles, and privileges *in esse* or *in posse*." Significantly, Beard found that "in promoting and defending the national interest so conceived" interested parties expect the American state to "employ all the engines of State" to protect their interests and "despite various verbal concessions to peace, the final sanction of American activities abroad is the Navy."[47]

Roosevelt and the New World Order

In *The Idea of National Interest*, Beard was again implicitly joust-ing with Franklin Roosevelt's Secretary of Agriculture, Henry A. Wallace, and also with Cordell Hull, Roosevelt's Secretary of State. Beard evidently regarded both statesmen as world-historical figures who embodied the thesis and the antithesis of American foreign policy. However, as Bernard Borning observes, Beard also seemed to imply that a new idea of national interest was evolving out of older Jeffersonian and Hamiltonian conceptions.[48] In the early years of the Roosevelt administration, the United States was sinking deeper into the Great Depression and foreign outlets for surplus commodities seemed to vanish once the economic catastrophe reached global pro-portions. Consequently, Beard was enthusiastic that early New Deal policies, such as the Agricultural Adjustment Act and the National Industrial Recovery Act, were oriented toward stimulating the domes-tic economy through domestic economic planning. Despite a new eco-nomic policy that seemed to abandon the previous emphasis on for-eign trade, Beard was concerned that no corresponding change had occured in thinking about American foreign policy. Wallace and Hull continued to emphasize the importance of exporting agricultural and industrial surpluses, while enormous funds were funneled into a naval buildup. Beard suggested that in this world-historical moment "a new conception of national interest awaited 'formulation at the hands of a statesman as competent and powerful as Hamilton and Jefferson'."[49]

Beard was convinced that through a process of fusion and dissolu-tion the two existing visions of American foreign policy would give rise to a new synthesis.[50] This *aufhebung* merely awaited a World-Historical Individual capable of giving this tendency intellectual ex-pression and political reality. Throughout his career, Beard had al-ways viewed the industrial proletariat as the economic repository of this political and intellectual *aufhebung*. However, by the 1930s, Beard was lamenting that the labor movement "counts for little" in the United States because "it has given slight attention to exigencies of large policy, domestic or foreign." The United States had nothing that "Marx could call a class-conscious proletariat, at all events on any consider-able scale."[51] Indeed, Beard had grown cynical by this time and noted that "while generally critical of 'imperialism', it [the American prole-tariat] has shared in the fruits of the system and has at times more or less dimly recognized that the benefits it has enjoyed have come from an industrial economy based extensively on the commerce of imperialism."[52] Consequently, Beard concluded in this moment of crisis that he was left with only one political strategy—a Prince who would deploy state power vigorously toward achieving this new vision of the national interest.

Beard followed Roosevelt's speeches and public appearances through the newspaper and radio from his dairy farm in Connecticut, as well as through summers spent in Washington, D.C., consulting with members of Congress. Beard was convinced initially that "the Roosevelt administration repudiates the long-dominant conception that the so-called surpluses of American industry and agriculture are inexorable surpluses for which export outlets must be found." Having abandoned this central theoretical underpinning of both the agrarian and industrial thesis, Beard claimed that "a third conception of policy, outlined by President Franklin D. Roosevelt in 1933, is now in process of formulation," but he noted that this nascent Rooseveltian vision was still "too fragmentary to be characterized by a single word or phrase." At the same, Beard was concerned that while "President Roosevelt has more or less clearly envisaged the issues involved in creating a 'sound internal economic system' for the United States, he has not yet brought the foreign policy of the United States entirely into line with his domestic theory."[53]

Despite Beard's early enthusiasm for FDR's domestic policies,[54] Beard identified contradictions in Roosevelt's thinking that he feared might jeopardize the New Deal *aufhebung*. Beard recognized that despite Roosevelt's declarations at the 1933 London Economic Conference, he nevertheless depreciated the currency by cutting the gold content of the dollar to raise domestic prices and build foreign trade. The following year, he persuaded Congress to pass the Reciprocal Trade Agreement Act in an effort to increase exports. Lurking behind the reciprocal trade program was Cordell Hull's conviction that America's long-range prosperity depended on the revival of world trade.[55] In addition, Roosevelt promoted the Export-Import Bank, increased merchant marine subsidies, and supported increased naval expenditures.[56]

In this regard, Beard concluded that the two foreign policies (i.e., Jeffersonian and Hamiltonian) had merged under Roosevelt who was pursuing economic nationalism *and* a naval buildup simultaneously. However, Beard called for a new third vision of American foreign policy that would transcend, rather than merely unite *contradictory* ambitions. Against this backdrop, he sought to play Machiavelli to Roosevelt the Prince by articulating "a conception of national interest free from gross contradictions and unattainable ambitions...an ideal conception of national interest."[57] Historians have established that *The Idea of National Interest* and *The Open Door at Home* were aimed directly at FDR and, indeed, Beard apparently pinned all his hopes for economic restructuring and for a realignment of American foreign policy on the President as Prince. Thomas Kennedy described these works as Beard's last act of faith premised on the belief that a lucid and simple critique of "the controlling assumptions of American foreign policy would encourage the Roosevelt administration to formulate policies along the lines he proposed."[58] Beard was convinced that policies framed with a view to establishing a collectivist democracy or a workers' republic were both possible and desirable as a political-economic system for the United States.

Imperialism and Capitalist Development

As Beard argued in these two works, mainstream currents of thought about international trade were dominated by the concern with exporting agricultural, industrial, and financial surpluses. Direct foreign investment and the development of export markets were believed to be the only possible solution to a structural overproduction crisis which, in turn, was the cause of the domestic business cycle.[59] Hence, the solution to domestic economic crises was to be sought in the expansion of overseas markets and the development of international trade. For this reason, Beard found that imperialist expansion was widely represented as an inexorable outcome of capitalist development and, to this extent:

> Marxian socialists and many American politicians agreed...The former contended that the very life of capitalism depended upon ever enlarging opportunities for the advantageous investment of the profits arising from industrial operations—investments in new undertakings, at home or abroad. According to this Marxian thesis, imperialism was merely the next inevitable stage of capitalist development....With the general proposition respecting the necessity for expanding trade and investments, numerous American politicians were in accord but they put the case in different language.[60]

Whether one called it imperialism, the open door policy, or dollar diplomacy was of little consequence to Beard. The theoretical key to the problem of overproduction was that all thinkers—conservative, liberal, and socialist—viewed capital exports and the development of international trade as *necessary* to the prosperity and growth of late capitalist economies. However, Beard rejected this key assumption in both its neo-classical and Marxian variant by developing an alternative analysis of: (1) the historical origins of imperialism; (2) the empirical structure of international exchange relations; and (3) the social creation of commodity surpluses.

Beard's rejection of Lenin's claim that imperialism was the highest stage of the capitalism was based largely on arguments drawn from Norman Angell's *The Great Illusion* (1910) and Joseph Schumpeter's *Imperialism and Social Classes.*[61] Angell's book was one of the first and most influential works to challenge both Mahan's big navy theory and claims by economists regarding the importance of colonies and international trade. Angell argued that the idea of imperialism was a linguistic survival of economic relations that no longer exist in the modern world of international and finance capitalism. Angell claimed that imperialism had an economic value in traditional, land-based societies, because territorial conquest produced a tangible advantage to the conqueror who could extract mineral wealth such as gold and silver, gems such as diamonds and rubies, who could promote direct settlement of the conquered territory, and reduce native inhabitants to slavery or peonage. Angell found that traditional views of imperialism continued into the period of mercantile capitalism because the preemption of newly discovered "territory by one particular nation secured an advantage for the citizens of that nation in that its overflowing population found homes."[62] Schumpeter articulated a complementary theme in suggesting that imperialism and war were cultural survivals of the feudal aristocracy's warrior ethic, rather than products of capitalist class interests.[63]

Beard drew on both thinkers to argue that traditional imperialism, in both Europe and the United States, was predominantly a political characteristic of landed classes rather than the capitalist class, particularly when it involved the thirst for land, physical conquest, occupation and settlement. Indeed, throughout the 1920s, and in direct contrast to Marxian theorists and American revisionist historians, Beard continued to place the predominant blame for World War I on the feudal landowning classes of Germany, Russia, and Austria.[64] In Europe, Beard identified the remnants of the feudal aristocracy as the main social repositories of a warrior spirit; consequently, he was persuaded by Schumpeter that there is "a powerful element of feudalism in what is called capitalist imperialism."[65] Interestingly, Beard extended this same analysis to the United States, in a modified form, where he saw the imperialist strategy originating in military (i.e., naval) and political interests, rather than in business demands.[66]

Beard ascribed considerable importance to Mahan's *The Influence of Sea Power Upon History* (1890) which sought to demonstrate that a nation's economic prosperity was dependent upon international trade and, therefore, upon the national security assured by naval supremacy.[67] Mahan's thesis won the early and enthusiastic support of Theodore Roosevelt (Assistant Secretary of the Navy) and Henry Cabot Lodge (Senate Foreign Relations Committee); fortuitously, Beard observes, historical "circumstances favored the designs of Mahan, Roosevelt, and Lodge" when "the American economy plunged into another devastating panic" only three years after the book's publication. Mahan's thesis took hold among leading Republican politicians and, as Beard suggests, it ran "like a powerful motif through state papers from the inauguration of President McKinley to the retirement of President Hoover, with variants and modifications."[68] Thus, by the close of the nineteenth century, Beard concludes, American foreign policy was little more than an aggregation of the "instrumentalities and implications of dollar diplomacy" for "the promotion of economic interests abroad." In practice, this policy included "naval bases, territorial acquisitions for commercial support, an enlarged consular and diplomatic service, an increased navy and merchant marine, and occasional wars."[69] As Kennedy suggests: "the Hamiltonian, or Federalist-Whig-Republican, application of national interest...led to increasingly greater international commitments and naval expansion, both of which heightened rivalries with other nations in the competition for markets and territories."[70]

Equally important, Beard argues that during the political and industrial conflicts of the 1890s, American "politicians were not slow to see the strategic advantages of a 'strong foreign policy' as a means of steering American minds away from domestic ills...conservative Democrats, no less than conservative Republicans, were aware of its historic utility."[71] In fact, Beard observes caustically that "the device of diverting attention from domestic troubles by engaging in foreign quarrels was old and it may be taken for granted that all politicians above the kindergarten grade, having read their Shakespeare, were familiar with it."[72] As domestic turbulence increased, foreign policy (and especially foreign wars) provided politicians with a way to deflect class struggle into international conflict and offered a way to solve the problems of "overproduction" without the kind of redistribution or economic restructuring being demanded by a restive working class. On this point, Beard insists that "loyalty to the facts of historical record must ascribe the idea of imperialist expansion mainly to naval officers and politicians rather than to businessmen."[73] Imperialism was not the inevitable consequence of capitalist development, but the result of a political alliance between conservative politicians and ambitious naval officers. In fact, Beard claimed that the global expansion of American interests was a policy that not only lacked a wide popular base, but *any substantial economic foundation in national interest.*

Following Angell, Beard argued that Mahan's "contentions were not proved; they were asserted as axioms, apparently regarded as so obvious as to call for no demonstration."[74] On the other hand, Beard was convinced that Angell's *The Great Illusion* "had conclusively demonstrated the economic wastefulness of imperialism, armaments, and war."[75] As he grew more and more concerned with foreign policy issues during the 1930s, Beard emulated Angell's earlier example by employing a balance sheet technique that "involved the calculation of the American stake in foreign trade and investment, as measured against the risk of political and military involvement that often accompanied these 'outward thrusts of power'."[76] Despite the perceived advantages of imperialism, colonies, and their ancillary armaments rivalries, Beard argued that such policies exemplified the cunning of history when analyzed from the standpoint of national economic interests alone.

The empirical thrust of Angell's assault on Mahan and the imperialists was that the alleged commercial and social advantages of imperialism and a big navy were a pure optical illusion.[77] For in contrast to traditional land-based economies, the vast proportion of wealth in mature capitalist economies exists as intangible capital: paper money, government and corporate bonds, stocks and shares, lines of credit, patents and copyrights, technical expertise, and scientific knowledge. Angell argued there was simply no way to seize these assets and no way to compel their creation in the same way that one could take slaves, seize lands for colonization, or extract gold from the ground, because intangible forms of financial and human capital retain their value only where there is security of contract, investor confidence, secure property rights, and on-going investment in science and technology. Consequently, on the eve of World War I, Angell concluded that imperial wars of conquest between advanced capitalist nations were irrational from an economic standpoint, because "if these [intangible forms of property] are tampered with in an attempt at confiscation by a conqueror, the credit-dependent wealth...vanishes, thus giving the conqueror nothing for his conquest....The value of the stocks and shares would collapse, and the credit of all those persons and institutions interested in such property would also be shaken or shattered, and the whole credit system, being thus at the mercy of alien governors only concerned to exact tribute, would collapse like a house of cards." [78]

On the other hand, Angell observes that "material property in the form of that booty which used to constitute the spoils of victory in ancient times, the gold and silver goblets, etc. would be quite inconsiderable" in relation to the intangible wealth that had been destroyed. Capital can be destroyed by war, but it cannot be conquered through war. Consequently, nations might conceivably expend huge sums on armaments to conquer essentially nothing; yet, equally important, any advantages obtained would give "to the conqueror no material advantage which he could not have had without conquest" and at much lesser expense. Angell observed early in the century that "if the British manufacturer can make cloth, or cutlery, or machinery, or pottery, or ships cheaper or better than his rivals he will obtain the trade; if he cannot, if his goods are inferior, or dearer, or appeal less to his customers, his rivals will secure the trade, and the possession of 'Dreadnoughts' will make not a whit of difference." Angell posed a direct challenge to the Mahan thesis by pointing out that "the factors which really constitute prosperity have not the remotest connection with military or naval power." [79]

Angell was among the first to point out that most international exchange and direct foreign investment occurred *between* the advanced capitalist countries. [80] Thus, even if the strategic objective was to damage a major rival in order to seize their colonies and colonial markets, no nation could afford to "permanently or for any considerable period destroy or greatly damage the trade of another, since...he would destroy his own market, actual or potential, which would be commercially suicidal." Angell observed that over the previous thirty years

(1880-1910), international finance had become independent of nationality and interwoven with global trade and industry to the point where the intangibility of an enemy's property extended to the trade and property of one's own citizens. Multinational corporations, investment banks, and central banks hold foreign currencies; financial institutions and citizens own stocks of foreign issue; domestic banks extend loans and credits to foreign nations and hold the bonds of foreign governments and corporations. Thus, insofar as these credits and intangibles are "held in various forms—as collateral and otherwise—by many important banking concerns, insurance companies," any sudden collapse of their value shatters the solvency of financial institutions and companies elsewhere. In other words, because of the delicate interdependence of international credit and finance, "the confiscation by an invader of private property, whether stocks, shares, ships, mines, or anything more valuable than jewelry or furniture—anything, in short, which is bound up with the economic life of the people—would so react upon the finance of the invader's country as to make the damage to the invader resulting from the confiscation exceed in value the property confiscated." For this reason, regardless of who might win a war between the advanced capitalist nations, the conqueror would find immediately that the "conquered" property had disappeared through devaluation, disinvestment, the collapse of credit, and capital flight and, consequently, the conqueror would soon be required "to put an end to the chaos...by putting an end to the condition which had produced it."[81]

Beard was acutely aware of this paradox following World War I. In a series of lectures delivered at Dartmouth College in 1922, he was perplexed that "the most important branch of trade of all European countries was not with the backward races of the earth which they were so eagerly struggling to conquer and hold, but with their powerful and enlightened neighbors." He noted that only a year before the outbreak of the Great War, England's business with Germany, counting exports and imports, was equal to more than one-third her entire business with all her colonies, dominions, and dependencies; in other words, "on the eve of the war, Great Britain's business with Germany —her bitterest rival—was a vital part of her economic life."[82]   As Beard's interests turned more toward foreign policy in the late 1920s, he again echoed Angell's thesis that "owing to the close interrelation of world economics, the prospects of a swift conquest and a quick getaway with the loot have been dashed."[83]

Beard's view of direct foreign investment in underdeveloped countries and its relative unimportance to capitalist economies was deeply influenced by Angell's early work on the subject. Angell insisted that "in all this talk of the open door in the undeveloped territories we seem to lose all our sense of proportion. England's trade is in relative importance first with the great nations—the United States, France, Germany, Argentina, South America generally; after that with the White Colonies; after that with the organized East; and last of all, and to a very small extent, with the countries concerned in this squabble for the open door—territories in which the trade really is so small as hardly to pay for the making and upkeep of a dozen battleships." Indeed, given the relatively minuscule trade that took place between developed nations and their undeveloped colonies, Angell concluded that they "are no source of tribute or economic profit...Economically, England would gain by their formal separation, since she would be relieved of the cost of their defence." In a direct challenge not only to Mahan, but to Hobson and Lenin as well, Angell concluded that colonies and foreign development strategies had failed to yield any discernible profit to the imperial powers, but had instead embroiled them in a senseless arms race and entangled them in the "work of police and administration which the natives cannot do for themselves."[84]

As an example, Angell cited the fiscal benefits of Russia's defeat in the Russo-Japanese War which brought a halt to Russia's "economically sterile policy of military and territorial aggrandisement." Following Russia's defeat in 1905, a corresponding decline in military appropriations allowed the Russian budget to generate a surplus for the first time in twenty years. Similarly, Angell pointed out that "ten years after the Franco-Prussian War, France was in a better financial position than Germany" with a higher per capita income and "a greater reserve of savings." Moreover, "the social and industrial renaissance of modern Spain dates from the day that she was defeated and lost her colonies [1898], and it is since her defeat that Spanish securities have just doubled in value," while Great Britain, on the other hand, had seen the value of British Consols decline twenty points since winning the Boer War (1899) and "adding the goldfields of the world to her possessions." Indeed, on a more general and even prophetic note, Angell claimed that "this recovery of the defeated nation after wars is becoming one of the commonplaces of modern history." [85]

With this argument, Angell established a key principle in Beard's critique of international trade and imperialism. On the one hand, colonies and protectorates cost more to defend and police than they returned to the national treasury in profits, employment, and tax revenues. At best, and even this was questionable in Beard's view, imperialism was profitable only for small groups within the capitalist class, who pay less in taxes to support the national security establishment than they receive back in profits, mainly because defense is largely paid for by the working and middle classes and by national capital with no direct foreign interests. From the standpoint of national interest, protectorates and the transaction costs of international trade constitute a net disinvestment from the national domestic economy into unproductive military and police activities. Beard was fundamentally convinced that commercial empires always cost more to maintain than they return in profit and this paradox explained the inevitable rise and fall of modern imperialist nations.

Again following Angell, Beard reflected on the costs of the Great War by noting that it "cost Great Britain about ten billion pounds and that the *annual interest* and other charges on her debt in 1921 amounted to three hundred fifty million pounds." Beard argued that when these costs were balanced against the small increments in international trade from the annexation of former German colonies, "we may be permitted to raise a question as to whether commercial warfare by arms 'pays' in any sense of the word."[86] In this respect, Beard again departs sharply from the Marxian conception of imperialism by noting that the United States had also incurred an unfavorable balance of trade with its Pacific protectorates since 1906 (i.e., the Philippines, Hawaii, Guam, Samoa, and Alaska), while the combined value of this colonial trade was minor in comparison to the total American stake in foreign trade. From an economic perspective, Beard argued that the United States Gross National Product would actually improve statistically by getting rid of its overseas colonies, territories, and protectorates.[87] In other words, Beard concluded that overt imperialism was *not* a rational economic solution to the problem of capital or commodity surpluses.

Nevertheless, Beard's Angellian critique of the imperialist strategy did not necessarily answer liberal internationalists or Jeffersonian free traders who argued that international trade arrangements could be devised and enforced peacefully, eliminating the military costs of foreign occupation and naval competition. Beard's chief nemesis in this camp was FDR's Secretary of State Cordell Hull who orchestrated the Good Neighbor Policy in the early years of the New Deal. Hull claimed that U.S. productive capacity was "twenty-five percent in excess of our ability to consume" and that "these glaring facts soon will compel America to recognize that these every increasing surpluses are her key economic problems, and that our neglect to develop foreign markets for surpluses is the one outstanding cause of unemployment."[88] Partly in response to such claims, the United States had only recently begun keeping better statistics on foreign trade and Beard was among the first scholars to make use of these new statistics in sparring with Hull over the direction of New Deal policy.[89] Beard found that exports had never accounted for more than ten percent of gross national product, regardless of the trade policy pursued by government.[90] In other words, Beard found that 90 percent of all commodities were produced and consumed in domestic markets; foreign trade "does not represent the margin between mere existence and prosperity, but it illustrates the importance of the domestic market and shows how little we are dependent upon foreign countries."[91] Trade statistics documented that the solution to economic crisis and the key to widespread prosperity hinged on increases in *domestic demand* and not in international competitiveness or the increased demand for exports.

On this point, Beard observed that the agrarian thesis and the industrialist thesis rested on the common assumption that economic crises and unemployment were the result of overproduction that could never be absorbed by demand generated in the domestic economy. Beard challenged FDR's Secretary of Agriculture and his Secretary of State by pointing out that neither of the dominant theories was willing to consider the "hypothesis that the surpluses, and the economic jam produced by them" can be disposed of "in the main or in large part, by alterations in the distribution of wealth in the United States — that is, by changes in the using and consuming power of the people of the United States." Beard proposed the alternative thesis that so-called "surpluses" were really a social creation of late capitalist relations to production, arguing that the very concept of a surplus presupposes "the private ownership and manipulation of the means of production and, consequently, the distribution of wealth, or buying and consuming power, associated with a high degree of concentration in the ownership and management of the means of production." In contrast to those who sought to end unemployment through increased international trade, Beard argued that a more "efficient distribution of wealth within the United States would largely eliminate the unbalance between capital extension and consumption, provide domestic use for a considerable part of the so-called surplus, and reduce the pressures of the outward thrusts—thrusts which engender rivalries abroad, extend the interests of the country beyond the reaches of adequate defense, and lead to armament rivalries and their inevitable outcome—war."[92]

As a result, Beard concluded that domestic economic restructuring—including a massive redistribution of wealth and income—was the solution to the business cycle and unemployment, since it would transform idle capital and unearned income into domestic demand. At the same time, a strategy of domestic reform would avoid the problem of international trade rivalries and its attendant arms race. For to the extent that surpluses were a side-effect of the growing inequalities of wealth and income, "the primary force in the rivalry of nations for market outlets...is the inefficient distribution of wealth at home—in other words, in the enormous accumulations of capital that cannot find high profits in domestic expansion and must go abroad or burst."[93] As Beard puts it:

> It is this unbalanced accumulation of capital—overextension of plant capacity and the inefficiency of domestic buying power—which periodically slows down production to a ruinous pace, turns fiercer acquisitive energies into the quest for foreign outlets, sets armament industries in swifter motion, extends the American stake abroad, shifts the center of the nation's gravity from its geographical center toward the borders of the world markets, and makes the economy of the country depend upon the madness of world commercial operations utterly beyond any control on the part of the United States Government.[94]

On this point alone, Beard found himself in accord with the Marxists who maintained, in theory at least, that "there was an alternative to imperialist expansion, namely, the socialization of industry and the distribution of expanding profits to domestic buyers in the form of higher and higher wages."[95] With such a policy, Beard claimed that "a high standard of national well-being is possible with a minimum reliance upon foreign trade and is desirable besides," because it reduces the likelihood of military entanglements and global police actions. Beard called his strategy of domestic economic restructuring the open door at home policy, because an immense domestic market would be opened by the proposed combination of national economic planning, the socialization of key industrial and financial sectors, a full employment policy, and income support programs. As the domestic market recovered and offered new opportunities for investment and sales, Beard speculated that market forces would reduce "the feverish and irrational methods of unloading and dumping goods on foreign countries." Moreover, as competition for foreign markets was reduced, domestic policy would have eliminated "the most fruitful source of international rivalries and wars—the source of most burdens for diplomacy."[96]

Continentalism: A Managed Trade Policy

On many occasions, therefore, Beard argues that "foreign policy is a phase of domestic policy, an inseparable phase."[97] Beard referred to the foreign policy component of the open door at home as continentalism. The fundamental assumption of continentalism is that "the principle avenue of escape from economic crisis lies, not in adjustments made at international conferences, not in outward thrusts of commercial power, but in the collaboration of domestic interests with a view to establishing the security which may come from integrated economic activities and a more efficient distribution of wealth or buying power."[98] A corollary of this assumption is that "the degree of probability that the United States will become involved in any war arising anywhere in Europe or Asia bears a direct relation to the extent of the economic interests possessed by American nationals in the affected area, and in the fortunes of the respective belligerents."[99] Hence, a crucial element of the continentalist strategy was to regulate these interests through a managed trade policy governed by the requirements of the National Standard-of-Life Budget (see Chapter 5).

Once the annual standard-of-life budget was adopted by Congress, Beard said that "engineering rationality will proceed to an analysis of the material resources of the United States and the powers of its technical arts, for the purpose of determining the extent to which American industry and agriculture can supply the stipulated requirements." At that point, Beard suggests, "it would be possible to determine with some exactness the requirements of the United States in the form of imports for the pre-established standard of life for the American nation." Thus, the chief objective of foreign trade would be the acquisition of imports deemed requisite to the defined standard of life, rather than the expansion and promotion of exports. Clearly, Beard understood that "this proposition means a reversal of the conception which lays emphasis on the export of goods immediately profitable to the private interests." Beard recommended the consolidation of international trade activities under the jurisdiction of a Federal Trade Corporation or an Export-Import Syndicate (EIS). This syndicate would be a public corporation, with appropriate commodity subdivisions, supported by technical bureaus that would study the export offerings and import needs of other nations and with "full power to control exports and imports into the United States directly and through licenses, with checks on performance provided by customs offices and shipping manifests."[100]

It was crucial to Beard's managed trade strategy that strict export prohibitions be placed on any items that endangered U.S. national security (e.g., weapons) and on capital or technology exports that undermined identified comparative advantages. Furthermore, Beard recommended the nationalization of major investment banks, mainly to control high-risk foreign lending, but also to divert capital investment back toward domestic enterprises. As a minimum fallback strategy, Beard proposed to withdraw loan guarantees and military protections to foreign loans in order to increase the risk of direct foreign investments and thus induce U.S. investment banks to accept lower domestic returns in exchange for greater security of capital. Beard speculated that such policies "will stop the reckless habits of financiers in making loans to irresponsible governments to be wasted in unproductive enterprises—a custom ruinous to American investors and of course to the peoples of the borrowing countries."[101]

Another main function of the EIS would be to prepare a list of U.S. import needs, based on the National Economic Council's Standard-of-Life Budget, and to prepare a list of goods which the United States could best afford to exchange for imports based on an NEC survey of industrial and agricultural production, i.e., a list of real surpluses determined by the standard-of-life budget. Finally, the EIS was to prepare a list of potential trading partners based on a survey of world production and natural resources. The actual process of international exchange would occur on the basis of limited trade agreements in which "selected nations will be asked to permit the entry into their territories, for fixed periods of time, specified quantities of American goods, on a free trade, a revenue, or a predetermined tariff level. In return the United States will agree to receive specified quantities of foreign goods on determinate conditions of entry."[102]

Beard was emphatic that the U.S. do business with any nation that offered the best and most favorable basis of exchange by requiring the EIS to use its needed imports list as a basis for soliciting bids from other nations or producers. Similarly, the U.S. would use its allowed exports list as the basis for soliciting bids from domestic producers. Beard envisioned a system in which the bids offering the largest desired quantity at the lowest domestic price would be accepted by the EIS. Domestic producers would be paid in domestic currency or equivalent purchasing power [e.g., trade credits, government bonds, tax abatements], less transaction costs. In the adjustment, the domestic price of all imports was to be fixed on the basis of what it would cost in the United States to produce the same values delivered abroad in exchange.[103] To avoid the disturbances of foreign currency fluctuations and price imbalances created by different national cost structures, Beard's exchange controls were designed to detach foreign trade from "the fetich of the price system." Instead, foreign exchange between the United States and other nations would be established on a value exchange system, rather than a price system. As Beard described it:

> ...the United States, having decided upon policy, would be equipped for exchange by a *knowledge* of the values of its commodities in terms of labor time, capital outlay, material cost, and standard of living. If those nations should organize their economies on similar principles, this knowledge would become extensive and common property ...thus the task of bringing exchange values into adjustment would not be an insuperable, even a difficult, performance.[104]

The primary goal of a continentalist trade strategy was clearly to attain the "least possible dependence on foreign imports." Consequently, Beard proposed that federal investment in research and development be partially linked to the import-needs list. A basic goal of science and technology policy would be to discover and invent commodities "calculated to increase the independence and security of the United States." Beard certainly understood that complete economic autonomy was impossible based on his reading of the German economist Alfred Ruhl. Ruhl's work on international trade documented that in 1927, approximately 89 percent of all U.S. imports supplemented domestic production. This classification included items that were impossible to produce in the United States, that were not currently produced in the United States, or that were produced in insufficient quantity or quality in the United States.[105] Moreover, in direct contrast to critics who labeled his plan a blueprint for autarky, Beard suggested that the total volume of foreign trade would probably increase "under a regime of economic security and efficient industry," since "the full use of the American endowment would create a national buying power of enormous proportions and a corresponding demand for foreign commodities of peculiar distinction." However, Beard was convinced that future increases in demand for imports "would be, in the main, luxuries and objects of appreciation and enjoyment not indispensable to the security and basic standard of life of the American people."[106] Therefore, he was prepared to allow free trade in articles of luxury, skill, and culture, and goods and services considered pure surplus with the knowledge that in either case the volume of these imports would be a small proportion to U.S. Gross Domestic Product.[107]

Continentalism: A National Security Policy

An open door at home policy would have direct repercussions on national security policy and military planning, just as export-driven theories of prosperity had done since the 1890s, if not earlier. Beard noted that since the 1890s, American military strategists had been obligated to plan U.S. force structures on the dictum that the United States must be prepared to protect American citizens and American property anywhere in the world at any time. As he put it, the armed forces "must be big enough to protect any American citizen who wants to make ten per cent on the bonds of Weissnichtwo or sell corn flakes, shoe horns, and collar buttons to the inhabitants of the world willy-nilly."[108] To the extent that government promoted the export of American interests throughout the world, it virtually guaranteed that the United States would be required to maintain a global military presence, particularly a naval presence. By identifying American economic interests with exports, direct foreign investments, and foreign loans, the concept of national security acquired a meaning that virtually obligated the United States to engage routinely in police actions throughout the world, ostensibly to protect American interests (i.e., citizens and property). At the same time, a global military presence increased the likelihood that the United States would be drawn into regional conflagrations in remote parts of the world through happenstance, rather than because any real security interests were at stake.

In contrast to what Beard called the Coolidge theorem, a continentalist national security policy is based on the principle of *"security of life for the American people in their present geographical home*. The size of the Army and Navy should be determined with reference to the vindication of that policy and not with reference to any other criteria."[109] Within a continentalist framework, "national defense means defense of our continental heritage, not defense of every American dollar in every part of the world against any and all powers, no matter what the issue."[110] Beard emphasized that a core assumption of continentalist policy was "the conviction that American democracy should not...assume that it had the capacity, even with the best of good will, to settle the difficult problems" of other nations.[111] Rather, as Thomas C. Kennedy observes, continentalist military planning "would necessitate the defense only of the continental homeland, Hawaii, and the Canal Zone, with small but adequate military and naval establishments."[112]   A goal of this policy would be to restrain and minimize indefensible commitments in remote parts of the world by withdrawing guarantees for private investment bankers placing loans abroad, ceasing annexations of additional territory elsewhere in the world (e.g., Philippines, Samoa, Guam), and an invitation to all Latin American nations to participate in a cooperative system for settling disputes, and the creation of a hemispheric trade zone—an idea that is again current among many international economists and diplomats.[113] Quite simply, continentalism was premised on a costs-benefits calculation: "...three or four billions of foreign commerce were relatively small as compared with the twenty or thirty billions annually wasted in idle plants, idle labor, and idle resources at home; that the frontiers for the expansion of American enterprise were within this continent, not in the fabled Indies or on the Rhine, the Danube, or the Vistula; that all about us, right here, lay the materials for a magnificent civilization."[114]

Beard understood that political institutions and institutional arrangements systematically structure policy outcomes. Consequently, a continentalist foreign policy would have to be *institutionalized* and not just adopted as a matter of ideological outlook. In this regard, Beard proposed that the separate Departments of Navy and War be consolidated under a civilian *Division* of National Defense that itself would be demoted to sub-Cabinet level directly under the supervision and control of the Department of State. Given Beard's historical analysis of the origins of American imperialism, this new arrangement was designed, first, to subordinate military interests and ambitions to civilian diplomacy, and, second, to thereby eliminate the Cabinet-level competition between diplomatic and military options, particularly since military options nearly always prevailed over diplomatic ones. Moreover, since Beard proposed that the Export-Import Syndicate be located within the Department of State, the proposed arrangement would bring all divisions of foreign policy—diplomatic, military, and commercial—under a single jurisdiction and, hopefully, be unified in a single coherent policy. In Beard's view, the proposed organization would eliminate the existing system of "divided and distracted government, which is no government, but a collection of competing agencies, bureaucracies, and politicians."[115]

In addition, Beard suggested that the conduct of foreign policy be further streamlined by a Constitutional amendment authorizing the fast-track ratification of treaties by a simple majority of both houses of Congress. This reasoning was based largely on the Senate's rejection of the Versailles Treaty and the refusal of the United States to participate in the League of Nations. Beard argued that the existing system, in which treaties could be defeated by a vote of one-third of the Senators, "surrenders the control of treaty relations to partisan and factional groups."[116] This constitutional provision was an important foundation to Beard's continentalist strategy, partly because presidents were themselves structurally diverted into military options when it was impossible to secure Senate approval of even the simplest diplomatic arrangements. At the same time, Beard's continentalist strategy depended heavily on diplomacy and on flexible, temporary, international agreements.

Beard was frequently at pains to emphasize that continentalism is not a blind isolationism. Continentalism does not reject "all collaboration with foreign powers," but instead provides a "positive program for choosing peace or war, for making *temporary arrangements* with other governments, all *in the interest of our destiny and continental security*, not in the interest of any European combination or balance of power." Beard certainly did not deny the fact that wars in Europe or elsewhere might concern the United States or affect its national interest. However, he was among the first to emphasize that regardless of its military strength, the United States would always be limited in its ability "to relieve, restore, and maintain life beyond its own sphere of interest and control—a recognition of the hard fact that the United States, either alone or in any coalition, did not possess the power to force peace on Europe and Asia, to assure the establishment of democratic and pacific governments there, or to provide the social and economic underwriting necessary to the perdurance of such governments." Beard emphasized that "continentalists did not deny the existence of responsibilities to other nations and peoples. On the contrary they favored discharging such responsibilities, always with due regard for the physical, economic, and political limits on the powers of the United States and for the solemn obligation of protecting the Republic against misadventures headed in the direction of disaster."[117]

Importantly, Beard pointed out that continentalism was anchored in a conception of American economic interests and not in pacifist philosophy. Therefore, continentalism "is not pacifism proposing peace at any price." Instead, continentalism:

> ...arranges its commitments and responsibilities in such a fashion that they may be actually defended with a maximum possibility of victory in case of war. It does not make world-wide claims and then withhold from its soldiers and sailors the power necessary to defend them in fact. It is cautious but not cowardly; circumspect, but not supine. It is pacific not pacifist.[118]

Indeed, Beard was quite explicit that continentalism implies "a possible intervention in wars actually waged within the American zone of interests." On the other hand, he was equally explicit that a continentalist policy would be "deliberately calculated to strengthen the defensive security of the United States, not to right the wrongs of Europe, force the adoption of American institutions abroad, or effect a permanent pacification of the world by cooperation with any group of powers."[119] The key to continentalism was that "with such restraints on the operations of private interests clearly defined and firmly established in advance, the Government of the United States could then decide, on the merits of the issue as public interest, whether to enter or stay out of the war."[120] In this regard, Cohen concludes correctly that "Beard's concern over American intervention, in the last war or the next, had, then, nothing to do with whether the war was 'just' or not. The problem as he described it was one of entering or staying out 'on grounds of policy conceived in the national interest as here defined'."[121]

The Grand Diversion

Unfortunately, for Beard and like Machiavelli before him, Beard was sorely disappointed and eventually embittered when the Prince set aside his books for other diversions. As Ellen Nore points out, many of Roosevelt's closest advisors such as Henry A. Wallace, Cordell Hull, and Raymond L. Buell, president of the Foreign Policy Association, were critical of Beard's continentalism because they "linked it with unacceptable changes in the capitalist system."[122] Moreover, Beard ignored the fact that during the 1920s FDR had shared Wallace's view that weak agricultural prices could be overcome by exporting farm surpluses and that by the 1930s Roosevelt was extending the same idea to industry.[123] Finally, even if Roosevelt had shared Beard's vision of a workers' republic, Beard's conception of continentalism found only limited and ambivalent support among some of the CIO's industrial unions.[124] Not surprisingly to Beard, as NIRA began collapsing, the Depression sank to new lows, and labor militancy increased, Roosevelt turned his attention to international trade and to foreign policy.

As early as 1934, Beard expressed his concern that Roosevelt's "little games" with Great Britain and Japan might result "in a grand diversion—a diversion that might not be unwelcome, should the domestic recovery program fall far short of its aims."[125] This was a likely scenario by 1935; by 1938 Beard considered the New Deal an abject failure largely because Roosevelt had been too timid to move aggressively toward centralized economic planning and outright nationalizations of industry and finance. What most concerned him was that he knew that Roosevelt also knew that the New Deal was a failure.[126] Thus, in one last effort to warn Roosevelt of the impending disaster, Beard published an article that *Scribner's Magazine* publicized as one of the most important papers he ever wrote.[127]

In an essay entitled, "National Politics and War," Beard claimed that "the present Democratic upheaval is the third statistical triumph of the kind, not the first" and Roosevelt would do well to learn from the failures of the previous two upheavals. Beard argued that "twice before in American history the party of wealth and talents has been overwhelmed at the polls." The first occurrence was marked by the election of Thomas Jefferson in 1800 and the same events were repeated again "on a scale more vast and with deeper stirrings at the bottom under Andrew Jackson in 1828."[128] Beard observed that shortly after the revolution of 1800, the Jeffersonian Republicans began an "attack on the apparatus set up by the party of wealth and talents." This assault included the removal of Federalists from national offices "which stripped them of their fees and emoluments" and an attack on the United States Bank which the Jeffersonians "assailed as the stronghold of wealth." In this manner, the Jeffersonians deprived wealth of many of its advantages in commerce which they enjoyed under discriminatory laws. Beard speculates that "what might have happened had events taken a 'normal' course, no one knows," because a war with Great Britain intervened in 1812, an expensive war which called for money and supplies that only business enterprise could furnish to the government. Consequently, an unintended result of the war was that the Hamiltonian economic system was strengthened by the Jeffersonians as businessmen and manufacturers grew wealthier by selling goods to the national government, as American manufacturing expanded due to the embargo of British goods, and "an immense national debt had been accumulated in the hands of bankers and business men."[129] Thus, a paradox of the Jeffersonian regime was that it could only sustain itself and its policies by strengthening the Hamiltonian economic system.

When Andrew Jackson was elected in 1828, it appeared to contemporaries that democracy had won an even more radical "permanent revolution." Indeed, Beard comments, "when Jackson was re-elected in 1832 the permanent revolution seemed doubly permanent—copper-riveted, in fact." Beard speculates that the party of wealth and talents "might have remained prostrate if two things had not intervened again, the same two things—the movement of business enterprise and war." He notes that in spite of their troubles:

> businessmen made headway...They built more and more factories. They opened mines. They constructed railways and telegraph lines—with bounties even from Democrats, who wanted their 'deestricts favored'. They reached out into the West and drew produce to the East by providing canals and railways and furnishing credit to farmers and warehousemen....By the middle of the nineteenth century an economic revolution had taken place despite the political upheaval. At the turn of the mid-century business enterprise overtopped agriculture in the amount of capital employed in mines, factories, railways, and urban property.[130]

Against this backdrop, Beard argues the Civil War was fought to protect the interests of the leadership wing of the agricultural/democratic party (i.e., planters), but the results were again the opposite of those intended. As a result of the Civil War:

> ...business enterprise emerged with more and better things. The national debt in the hands of bondholders had jumped into the billions. Great fortunes had multiplied. A third United States Bank, with modifications, had come into being. The tariff had been raised again and again. War profiteers had heaped up accumulated capital. The center of economic gravity had shifted nearer to the center of business enterprise. The 'permanent' revolution of 1828 had been completely undone.[131]

As Jeffersonians had been diverted by the War of 1812, Jacksonians were diverted by the Civil War because leadership of the Democratic party had been left in the hands of southern planters who would rather risk war than relinquish control of the party. Similarly, in other essays, Beard often suggested that the Populist revolt had been diverted by the Spanish-American War, while Woodrow Wilson's New Freedom had been diverted by World War I. In this historical account, Richard Hofstadter contends, Beard set down "the basic historical assumption upon which his critiques of American foreign policy were to proceed: *the United States goes to war not in response, whether right or wrong, to anything other nations do; it goes to war as a part of its own cycle of domestic politics*, because statesmen who prefer strong foreign policy to strong domestic policy seek war, or at least seek the conditions under which they can stumble into war." Certainly, one of Hofstadter's profoundest insights into Beard's thinking is his recognition that Beard's later writings on foreign policy, whatever the event or topic, "come back repeatedly to a single theme: the United States never goes to war because of anything that is happening outside its borders, but because politicians want to evade a domestic crisis or bankers and munitions makers want outlets for their capital and products."[132]

From within the framework of this historical account, Beard posed the crucial question to Roosevelt: "Is this the permanent revolution at last—the utter and final discomfiture of the party of wealth and talents?" Beard answered his own question, concluding that "judging by the past, we may be sure that the 'permanent' is not permanent." [133] Quite the contrary, there had not been any "great shift in the economic base since 1933," because "the party of wealth and talents *as an economic order* has not been decimated." Beard surmised that:

> Banks have not been nationalized, nor the railways taken over by the Government. Not a single instrumentality of economic power has been wrested from

this party. The public debt has been increased, and its members hold bonds representing that debt...This operation has strengthened, not weakened, the party of wealth and talents; in the place of defaulted and decaying farm mortgages, it holds bonds guaranteed by the Federal Government...At the end of the depression, if it ever ends, the concentration of wealth in the United States will doubtless mark a new high point in the evolution of the American economy. The party of wealth and talents survived the Jeffersonian revolution, and the Jacksonian revolution. If it has not lost its talents, it will survive the Roosevelt revolution.[134]

As the conclusion to "National Politics and War," Beard offered a dim vision of the future course of events, predicting that one of two scenarios was inevitable. The preferred course of action for Beard was a "resort to strong measures" designed to deprive capital of its economic power such as the nationalization of banks, utilities, and natural resources.[135] However, friends, such as George Soule, recount that long before Pearl Harbor, Beard was predicting "that just as Wilson had abandoned the New Freedom to embrace war in Europe, Roosevelt would desert the New Deal for war in Asia."[136] As time wore on, Beard understood that neither FDR nor the New Deal Democrats had the stomach to "advance further radical measures, such as the nationalization of the banks." Instead, both historical cycles and recent experience suggested that a "wider spread of economic calamity will culminate in a foreign war, rather than in a drastic reorganization of domestic economy."[137] Beard was increasingly strident in his criticism of Roosevelt's policies, warning that "Roosevelt has adopted the biggest navy program in the history of the country in peace time," and that "Roosevelt has not given any indication whatever that he intends to relax the competition of the United States with Great Britain and Japan for prestige and 'sea power'. Judging by the past and by his actions, war will be his choice." As early as 1935, Beard prophesied that "the Pacific war awaits" just as "the Jeffersonian party gave the nation the War of 1812, the Mexican War, and its participation in the World War." Importantly, Beard did not mean to suggest that President Roosevelt would "deliberately plunge the country into a Pacific war in his efforts to escape the economic crisis." Instead, as always, there would "be an 'incident', a 'provocation'. Incidents and provocations are of almost daily occurrence. Any government can quickly magnify one of them into a 'just cause for war'."[138] Cushing Strout concludes dramatically that Beard must have "trembled when he reflected that Jefferson, Jackson, and Wilson had all suffered their reform programs to be blighted by war" and now "the course of history threatened grimly to repeat itself."[139]

Roosevelt's quarantine speech (October 5, 1937) and the Navy Bill (January 1938) were milestones in the development of Beard's increasing hostility toward Roosevelt.[140] Stourzh emphasizes that Beard's escalating crusade against FDR should be intepreted in the light of his many warnings, issued as early as 1935, regarding the historic choices that confronted Roosevelt. In Beard's view, FDR lacked the essential heroism demanded by a world-historical moment and, consequently, the emerging vision of a social-democratic America had been lost and perhaps lost forever in the eternal rise and fall of empires. In this context, as it became clear to Beard that Roosevelt did not share his conception of national interest, a sense of personal betrayal began to infuse his publications even before FDR's re-election in 1936.[141] At the same time, Beard's condemnation of Roosevelt also emerged from elements deeply rooted in his thinking about American political development, which led him to conclude that his faith was misplaced because the promise of American life remained blocked by an unbroken cycle of diversions.[142]

Beard interpreted the events leading up to World War II through the lens of World War I and hence he certainly misread the perils of fascism and Nazism. Beard had supported the Great War on Wilsonian terms as a war to make the world safe for democracy. He was then persuaded by the revisionist history of the 1920s that it was really a war to make the world safe for capitalism. Beard continually applied this analogy to World War II with the intent of not being deceived and misled a second time, but it was precisely for this reason that he misled himself. It is impossible to know what his views would have been had he lived a few years longer, but notwithstanding such an egregious factual mistake, his predictions about the post-war world and American power proved remarkably prescient.

Beard was increasingly concerned, based partly on his World War I experiences and the first Red Scare (1919-1921), that the American Republic might fail to survive a protracted world war—that democracy and patriotism would become smokescreens for the construction of a bureaucratic-military fascism.[143] This may have been an exaggerated fear, but it contained an essential truth that was not lost on those who observed the hearings of the House Un-American Affairs Committee and the emergence of the military-industrial complex. Beard's

Sybillene warnings about the rise of Caesarism, the power of official propaganda, and the dangers of a national security state are now conventional wisdom.[144]

Furthermore, Beard predicted that the objective prospects for social democratic reform and a fundamental reconstruction of the American economic and political systems had been dashed as a direct side-effect of World War II. Although not intentional, Beard predicted that one effect of an Allied victory would be a relative strengthening of the Soviet Union. The new totalitarianism would merely provide the pretext, if not the requirement, for the United States to persist in its ongoing effort to make the world safe for democracy. As a dominant power, the United States would be more committed than ever to spending money, personnel, and materiel on a massive permanent military force that would divert resources and energy away from domestic economic reform. Once again, the hope for a new reform party — whether laborite, social democratic, socialist, or progressive — would disappear amid the hysteria of pro-Americanism, just as the Socialist party had been crushed under the weight of patriotism during World War I.

In this regard, Hofstadter finds that Beard's writings on diplomatic history are littered with "pertinent warnings against the global Messianism which has come to be the curse of American foreign policy." Hofstadter concludes that the essence of Beard's realism was his understanding that regardless of their good will "Americans do not have the duty, the capacity, or the need to patrol or moralize or democratize the rest of the world, and he was trying to state the dangers in their overreaching themselves."[145] Nore echoes this view by pointing out that a key component of Beard's continentalist theory was his recognition that "the United States had limited power, that a permanent peace could not be constructed and forced upon other nations."[146]

In the aftermath of Pearl Harbor, and later in the euphoria of winning a just war, the idea that government officials might manufacture a provocation for war had a hollow ring to New Deal liberals and even to Marxian socialists. Yet, before very long, an undeclared war would be fought in Korea (1948), the United States would intervene in Lebanon (1952), President Eisenhower would warn of the military-industrial complex, and the Gulf of Tonkin incident would give new credence to Beard's writings on foreign policy. An almost endless list of conflicts and incidents, and the discovery of a lawless underground government, seemed to confirm Beard's final warning that in matters of war and peace:

> Our fate...is no longer in the hands of the people or of Congress, despite the provision in the Constitution that vests in Congress the power to declare war. In fact wars are no longer declared. Situations exist or are created. Actions are taken by authorities in a position to act.[147]

On this and many other points, Beard's work on foreign policy was rediscovered during the era of the Cuban Missile Crisis, Vietnam, Watergate, and the Church Committee's revelations on the CIA.[148] These events and revelations gave renewed credibility to Beard's vision of the *post*-war world even though he was wrong about the events leading up to World War II.[149] Thus, when the competing demands of domestic reform and foreign war resurfaced in the 1960s, Beardian historiography provided the general framework for a revisionist New Left history.[150]

Notes

1. Freeman, *An American Testament*, p. 107; Borning, *The Political and Social Thought of Charles A. Beard*, p. 106; Nore, *Charles A. Beard*, pp. 72-74. For example, Charles A. Beard, "A Call Upon Every Citizen," *Harper's Magazine* 137 (October 19, 1918): 655-56, for an appeal to buy Liberty Bonds.
2. Charles A. Beard, "The Perils of Diplomacy," *New Republic* (June 2, 1917): 136-38; Charles A. Beard, "German Annexations and Indemnities," *New Republic* (July 14, 1917): 309-10. Most social democratic intellectuals embraced a pro-war, pro-Allied position, most notably John Dewey and Carl Becker, although Gruber, *Mars and Minerva*, p. 94, notes that Beard and Becker, despite formal declarations to the contrary, always "had considerably less faith than some of their fellow professors that the new world was already in the making." For a similar view, see Nore, *Charles A. Beard*, pp. 73-75.
3. Frederick Ogg and Charles A. Beard, *National Governments and the World War* (New York: Macmillan Co., 1919), p. v, observe that "the late conflict...was, at bottom, a struggle between two great schemes of human government—autocracy and democracy." In the same work (pp. 556-71), Beard explicitly accepts Woodrow Wilson's Fourteen Points as the explanation of America's war aims.
4. Strout, *The Pragmatic Revolt in American History*, pp. 135-38, argues that Beard was slow in becoming disillusioned with United States participation in World War I. This view is shared by Perry Miller, "Charles A. Beard," *Nation* 167 (September 25, 1948): 345, who claims that Beard did not embrace the revisionist thesis until about 1930. Likewise, see Selig Adler, "The War-Guilt Question and American Disillusionment," *Journal of Modern History* 23 (March 1951): 1-28; George Stourzh, "Charles A. Beard's Interpretations of American Foreign Policy," *World Affairs Quarterly* 28 (July 1957): 111-48; Kennedy, *Charles A. Beard and American Foreign Policy*, pp. 28-56. In contrast, Borning, *The Politi-*

cal and Social Thought of Charles A. Beard, p. 106, argues "that Beard's isolationist views were in full process of formation from the early 1920s." Higham, *Writing American History*, p. 136, argues that during the 1930s, Beard "became the principal intellectual spokesman of isolationism." Manfred Jonas, *Isolationism in America, 1935-1941* (Ithaca, NY: Cornell University Press, 1966), pp. 72-77, argues that Beard "personified, in significant ways, the academic and intellectual element in isolationism." Finally, Warren Ira Cohen, "Revisionism Between World Wars: A Study in American Diplomatic History," (Ph.D. Thesis, University of Washington, 1962), p. 144, is one of the few scholars to recognize that it has been a mistake to equate Beard's World War I revisionism with isolationism.

5. In a prescient essay, John E. Pixton, Jr., "The Ghost of Charles Beard," *The Christian Century* (October 1, 1952): 1120-22, argues that "it is in Asia that American policy is most clearly failing to limit the commitment of power to issues where it can be decisive...Whether the power of the West can be decisive in Indo-China is a matter still very much in doubt. If this is even partly true, then Beard's so-called 'isolationism' is relevant to our current attempts to formulate and implement workable policies serving an enlightened national interest." William Appleman Williams, *The Contours of American History* (New York: New Viewpoints, 1973); William Appleman Williams, *The Tragedy of American Diplomacy* (New York: Dell Publishing Co., 1962); Ronald Radosh, "Charles A. Beard and American Foreign Policy," *Prophets on the Right* (New York: Simon and Schuster, 1975), pp. 17-37; Ronald Radosh, "Charles A. Beard: World War II Revisionist," *Prophets on the Right*, pp. 39-65.

6. Stanley J. Michalak, Jr., *Competing Conceptions of American Foreign Policy: Worldviews in Conflict* (New York: Harper Collins, 1992), p. 142.

7. For instance, Henry A. Wallace, "Beard: The Planner," *New Republic* 81 (January 2, 1935): 225-27, observes that in 1934 it was common to hear Washington, D.C.'s inner circle complain that Beard "has gone isolationist," although the Secretary of Agriculture understood that Beard's theoretical position was "decidedly bigger than such simple classification as 'isolationist' or 'internationalist'." However, in 1940, Ralph Thompson, "Books of the Times," *New York Times*, May 15, 1940, p. 23, laments that Beard "has reached the ultimate isolationist stand" with his views on "continentalism (i.e., isolationism)." By 1948, John M. Mathews, "Review of *American Foreign Policy in the Making, 1932-1940; A Study in Responsibilities*, by Charles A. Beard," *American Political Science Review* (December 1948): 1190, observes confidently that "it is well known that Professor Beard is inclined toward the so-called isolationist school of thought with reference to American foreign policy." Only a few years later, Pixton, Jr., "The Ghost of Charles Beard," p. 1120, noted that Beard's works on foreign policy are "now largely ignored as mere 'isolationism'."

8. For example, Kennedy, *Charles A. Beard and American Foreign Policy*, p. 43, fn. 92, notes that Gerald P. Nye, a western progressive isolationist, asked to have one of Beard's articles reprinted in the *Congressional Record* (1940), 76th Congress, 1st Session, vol. 84, pt. 11, pp. 259-60 (the article was entitled "Neutrality: Shall We have Revision?") in support of his own position. In addition, during the late 1930s and early 1940s (before Pearl Harbor), "a number of Congressmen affiliated with the isolationist bloc often made a similar request, or in the midst of debate cited Beard as an authority in support of their argument." Stourzh, "Charles A. Beard's Interpretations of American Foreign Policy," p. 119, is typical of most scholars in referring to "the isolationist theory of continentalism."

9. Robert A. Divine, *The Illusion of Neutrality* (Chicago: University of Chicago Press, 1962); Jonas, *Isolationism in America, 1935-1941*; Wayne S. Cole, *Roosevelt and the Isolationists, 1932-1945* (Lincoln: University of Nebraska Press, 1983).

10. For example, in a headline story, the *New York Times*, November 12, 1939, p. 8E, charged Beard with recommending a policy of isolation. Jonas, *Isolationism in America*, p. 32, points out that "during the period before America's entry into the Second World War, the isolationists neither held to a homogeneous ideology nor were members of an organized movement."

11. Michael E. Porter, *The Competitive Advantage of Nations* (New York: Free Press, 1990); Robert B. Reich, *The Work of Nations: Preparing Ourselves for 21st Century Capitalism* (New York: Alfred A. Knopf, 1991); Lester Thurow, *Head to Head: The Coming Economic Battle Among Japan, Europe, and America* (New York: William Morrow and Co., 1992).

12. Charles A. Beard, "National Politics and War," *Scribner's Magazine* 97 (February 1935): 65-70; Charles A. Beard, "Industry's Attack on the New Deal," *Current History and Modern Culture* 43 (February 1936): 399-406; Soule, "Beard and the Concept of Planning," in Beale, ed., *Charles A. Beard*, pp. 69-70.

13. Counts, "Charles Beard, the Public Man," in Beale, ed., *Charles A. Beard*, p. 235, observes that Beard "was convinced that if America participated in the war, even allied victory would leave his country in a worse condition after than before the war...the passing years reveal evidence supporting his prophetic vision of the nature of the postwar world."

14. Beard quoted in Kennedy, *Charles A. Beard and American Foreign Policy*, p. 17.

15. Beard, *An Introduction to the English Historians*, pp. 423, 623.

16. Charles A. Beard, *American Government and Politics*, 1st edition (New York: Macmillan, 1910), p. 331.

17. Beard, *Contemporary American History*, p. 202.

18. Beard and Beard, *America in Mid-Passage*, p. 453.

19. Quoted in Freeman, *An American Testament*, p. 107. Kennedy, *Charles A. Beard and American Foreign Policy*, p. 7, fn. 19, observes correctly that "Beard was not a pacifist in a philosophical or religious sense." More than four months before his death in 1948, for example, Kennedy notes that "Beard expressed annoyance over a remark in *Newsweek* magazine that 'sets me down as an old-time pacifist. I have been many things but never a pacifist.'"

20. Charles A. Beard, *A Foreign Policy for America* (New York: Macmillan, 1940), p. 73. Elsewhere, Beard, *The Open Door at Home*, p. 169.

21. Kennedy, *Charles A. Beard and American Foreign Policy*, p. 17.

22. Beard, *Contemporary American History*, p. 199. Beard argues that the earliest intellectual origins of the economic interpretation of history can be traced back to Aristotle's *Politics*, especially Book V. See Beard, *Economic Basis of Politics*, pp. 27-28. In referring to "that ancient political device," Beard may have been drawing on Aristotle's observation that "when danger is imminent, men are alarmed, and they therefore keep a firmer grip on their constitution. All who are concerned for the constitution should therefore foster alarms, which will put men on their guard...They must, in a word, make the remote come near." See *The Politics of Aristotle*, translated by Ernest Barker (Oxford: Oxford University Press, 1974), p. 226. Aristotle's comments are proffered as a remedy to the causes of revolution.

23. Kennedy, *Charles A. Beard and American Foreign Policy*, pp. 66, 59. Stourzh, "Charles A. Beard's Interpretations of American Foreign Policy," p. 120, agrees

that "these two volumes present the most substantial part of Beard's writings on foreign policy."

24. Nore, *Charles A. Beard*, p. 144.
25. Cohen, "Revisionism Between World Wars," p. 148.
26. Kennedy, *Charles A. Beard and American Foreign Policy*, p. 66.
27. Beard, *The Open Door at Home*, pp. 155, 210.
28. Ibid. pp. 157-58.
29. Beard, *A Foreign Policy for America*, pp. 4, 5.
30. Beard, "Economic Basis of Politics," p. 128.
31. Beard, *The Open Door at Home*, p. 156.
32. Higham, *Writing American History*, p. 135; Stourzh, "Charles A. Beard's Interpretations of American Foreign Policy," pp. 122, 133, agrees that "Beard's economic interpretation of American foreign policy is but an application of his general scheme of Western history" that "emphatically upheld the accepted dualism of the American tradition in foreign affairs: Jeffersonians vs. Hamiltonians." See, Beard, *The Open Door at Home*, pp. v, 36-39, reiterates this dialectic as the foundation of his analysis.
33. Beard and Beard, *Rise of American Civilization*, Vol. 1, pp. 393-432. Beard argues (Vol. 1, pp. 410-11) that the War of 1812 was provoked by the United States as part of an unsuccessful effort to acquire Canada and the fur trade and to force the British to stop assisting Indians on the frontier who were obstructing the settlement of the Louisiana Territory. Beard suggests that the Florida Purchase was really a conquest initiated by Andrew Jackson (p. 432), just as the Gadsden Purchase was a sidebar to the Mexican War. Beard, *The Open Door At Home*, p. 71, fn. 1, reiterates that: "During the dominance of the planters in the Democratic party the acquisition of land at the expense of neighbors was, of course, a feature of agrarian strategy." Despite achieving most of its objectives, two strategic goals went unmet: the conquest of Canada during the War of 1812 and the Southern planters' dream of Caribbean conquests (especially Cuba and other islands with plantation-based economies).
34. Williams, *The Contours of American History*, p. 454.
35. Henry A. Wallace, *America Must Choose* (New York: Foreign Policy Association, 1934).
36. Edward L. Schapsmeier and Frederick H. Shapsmeier, *Henry A. Wallace of Iowa: The Agrarian Years, 1919-1940* (Ames: Iowa State University Press, 1968).
37. Beard, *The Open Door At Home*, pp. 71-72. In broader terms, Beard describes the implications of a Jeffersonian foreign policy as: "intra-nationalist, and anti-imperialist: it favors the annexation of contiguous unoccupied territory which can be defended without a large naval establishment and can be exploited by self-governing American farmers and planters. It opposes a large naval establishment as a danger to democracy, a menacing burden on finances, and a fomenter of international rivalries and war. In economics, it advocates free trade, tariff for revenue, or moderate tariffs, in order that surpluses of agricultural produce may be exchanged in the best market for manufactures through the medium of the lowest-cost carriers on the seas. It assails bonuses, ship subsidies, discriminations, and other bounties to manufacturers and carriers as levies on planters and farmers, imposed by government at the behest of special interests. In its view, government is primarily an agency — not too energetic — to defend the territorial heritage and keep order at home; not an agency of powerful outward thrusts to force outlets abroad for domestic surpluses" (ibid., p. 70).
38. Ibid., pp. 78-79.

39. Fred Harvey Harrington, "Beard's Idea of National Interest and New Interpretations," *American Perspective* 4 (1950): 336.

40. Beard, *A Foreign Policy for America*, pp. 38-39; Beard, *The Idea of National
Interest*, p. 101. Beard ascribes enormous influence to Alfred T. Mahan's, *The
Influence of Sea Power Upon History, 1660-1783* (Boston: Little, Brown, and
Co., 1890) and, correspondingly, he devotes a lengthy section of *A Foreign
Policy for America* to rebutting its central thesis (pp. 40-47, 74-86). Similarly,
Barnes, *History of Historical Writing*, pp. 232-33, contends that "few books
have been more influential in stimulating the disastrous growth of modern naval
armaments."

41. Beard described the post-1897 period of American diplomacy as the intensifica-
tion of an earlier Hamiltonian conception of foreign policy, but he did not
consider it a radical departure from the past. Many diplomatic historians of the
period claimed that the closing years of the 19th century marked a "new era" in
American foreign policy. However, Beard insisted that dollar diplomacy "re-
sembled in many respects the philosophy of policy expounded by leaders in the
establishment of the American Republic." See Beard, *The Idea of National Interest*, p. 111; Noble, *The Progressive Mind, 1890-1917*, p. 21, offers a similar
interpretation.

42. Martin J. Sklar, *The United States as a Developing Country: Studies in U.S.
History in the Progressive Era and the 1920s* (New York: Cambridge University
Press, 1992), Chap. 3.

43. Beard, *Contemporary American History*, pp. 202, 224.

44. Beard, *The Open Door at Home*, pp. 37-38. Cf. Ray Ginger, *The Age of Excess:
The United States From 1877 to 1914* (New York: Macmillan Co., 1965), Chaps.
8-9, who locates Progressive Era politics in a phase of capitalist development
dominated by the problems of distributing an industrial surplus. Also, Walter
LaFeber, *The New Empire: An Intepretation of American Expansion, 1860-1898*
(Ithaca, NY: Cornell University Press, 1987).

45. Beard, *The Open Door at Home*, p. 44.

46. Ibid., p. 39.

47. Ibid., pp. 40-43. Elsewhere, Beard, *Cross Currents in Europe Today*, p. 245,
notes with respect to international financiers making loans to Third World countries that "in accordance with a custom, consecrated by time, the bondholders,
whenever disturbance is threatened or a default is at hand, look eagerly to the
government at Washington to support their interests diplomatically if not more
vigorously."

48. Borning, *Political and Social Thought of Charles A. Beard*, p. 194.

49. Beard quoted in ibid., pp. 194-95; Harrington, "Beard's Idea of National Interest
and New Interpretations," p. 337

50. William MacDonald, "American Interests in Foreign Affairs," *The Saturday Review of Literature* 10 (February 24, 1934): 1, 505-6.

51. Beard, *The Open Door at Home*, p. 151, 196-97. As early as 1928, Beard wrote
to William E. Dodd, a professor of history at the University of Chicago: "Can
farmers and workingmen do anything in the presence of the steel helmeted giant
of modern business? I have my doubts, alas!," quoted in Paul W. Glad,
"Progressives and the Business Culture of the 1920s," *Journal of American
History* 53 (1966): 86, fn. 39. By 1931, Beard was so disillusioned with the
working class he remarked that: "My friend, John Dewey...believes that we need
a new party. Some thirty years ago I believed that myself. Now I believe that we
need ideas and more thinking, and then parties will take care of themselves," in

Charles A. Beard, "Address of Dr. Charles Beard," *Proceedings of a Conference of Progressives*, held at Washington, D.C., March 11-12, 1931, p. 70.

52. Beard, The Open Door at Home, p. 151. Beard (p. 169) complains: "It is also a fact that the masses may be stirred to titanic and concerted effort in war, whatever its ends alleged or real, while the same masses cannot be stirred to a similar action for some purpose of domestic and civilian economy."

53. Ibid., pp. 235, 36, 316.

54. Beard, *The Idea of National Interest*, pp. 543, 545, praises FDR's performance at the conference, noting that "it furnished the occasion on which President Roosevelt disclosed...a new conception of national interest in foreign commerce...a conception that a high standard of national well-being is possible with a minimum reliance on foreign trade and is desirable besides."

55. Harrington, "Beard's Idea of National Interest and New Interpretations," p. 337. Julius W. Pratt, *Cordell Hull*, 2 Vols. (New York: Coopers Square Publishers, Inc., 1964), Vol. I, Chaps. 3-5.

56. Beard, *The Open Door at Home,* pp. 316-17.

57. Ibid., p. vi. Beard (p. vii) writes that *The Open Door at Home* is "avowedly, an expression of my conception of national interest as a guide to future policy."

58. Kennedy, *Charles A. Beard and American Foreign Policy*, p. 73.

59. Parrini and Sklar, "New Thinking about the Market," pp. 559-78

60. Beard, *A Foreign Policy for America*, p. 69.

61. Norman Angell, *The Great Illusion: A Study of the Relation of Military Power in Nations to their Economic and Social Advantage* (New York: G. P. Putnam's Sons, 1912, Third Revised and Enlarged Edition). Angell's book was published simultaneously in English (London and New York), French, German, Danish, Spanish, Finnish, Dutch, Italian, Swedish, and Japanese. The English edition of the work went through four printings and three editions in only thirteen months. Angell was a British-born economist who grew up in the United States and became a Paris-based journalist for British and American newspapers. Angell embraced the ideas of John Maynard Keynes, beginning with Keynes' *The Economic Consequences of the Peace* (1922) and was awarded the 1933 Nobel Peace Prize

62. Angell, *The Great Illusion*, pp. 49, 50-51.

63. Cf. Joseph Schumpeter, *Imperialism and Social Classes* (New York: Augustus M. Kelley, 1951); V. I. Lenin, *Imperialism: The Highest Stage of Capitalism* (New York: International Publishers, 1939).

64. Charles A. Beard, "Forces Making for Peace," *Bulletin of the University of Georgia: Institute of Public Affairs and International Relations* 10, 2, Serial no. 466 (November 1929): 82-84. An earlier version of this essay is published as Charles A. Beard, "Prospects for Peace," *Harper's Magazine* 158 (January 1929): 320-29.

65. Charles A. Beard, "That Promise of American Life," *New Republic* (February 6, 1935): 352.

66. Cf. John P. Mallan, "Roosevelt, Brooks Adams, and Lea: The Warrior Critique of the Business Civilization," *American Quarterly*, 8 (Fall 1956): 216-30.

67. Alfred Thayer Mahan quoted in Angell, *The Great Illusion*, p. 19: "It is upon their national security (assured by naval supremacy) that their economic future —their food, clothing, and housing—depends."

68. Beard, *The Open Door at Home*, p. 38. For example, Claude G. Bowers, *Beveridge and the Progressive Era* (Cambridge, MA: Houghton-Mifflin, 1932), pp. 66-145. Albert Beveridge rose to the United States Senate in 1898 with an explicit

commitment to imperialism, based on the assumption that "American factories are making more than the American people can use; American soil is
producing more than they can consume. Fate has written our policy for us;
the trade of the world must and shall be ours" (quoted in 1898, p. 69); John
Braeman, *Albert J. Beveridge: American Nationalist* (Chicago: University
of Chicago Press, 1971), pp. 22-25. William E. Leuchtenburg, "Progressivism and Imperialism: The Progressive Movement and American Foreign
Policy, 1898-1916," *Mississippi Valley Historical Review* 39 (December
1952): 483-502, documents that most Progressives "ardently supported the
imperialist surge."

69. Beard, *The Idea of National Interest*, pp. 107, 167. Noble, *The Progressive Mind*, p. 21, seems to concur with Beard's interpretation.
70. Kennedy, *Charles A. Beard and American Foreign Policy*, p. 69.
71. Beard, *A Foreign Policy for America*, pp. 52, 54.
72. Ibid., p. 55. Beard's reference is to a passage from Shakespeare respecting a king's ability to divert "giddy minds" with "foreign quarrels." Charles A. Beard, *Giddy Minds and Foreign Quarrels* (New York: Macmillan, 1939), where Beard develops this thesis at greater length.
73. Beard, *A Foreign Policy for America*, p. 72. Ibid., pp. 71-72 emphasizes that: "...historical records do not support the proposition that American capitalists as a class or in large groups originated the idea of imperial expansion as a solution of the problem presented by cyclical disturbances or prolonged domestic depressions....The principal weight of 'Wall Street' was against the war on Spain in 1898. American bankers did not originate the movement to force American capital on China under the administration of President Taft; it is truer to say that they were 'dragooned' into it by the politicians. The detailed history of the process by which the imperialist idea attained popularity in wide circles of business enterprise has not been written; but enough is known to warrant the assertion that, on the whole, great capitalists were at first skittish about the brave, new world which imperialists were proposing to create and were followers rather than leaders in the revolution of foreign policy."
74. Beard, *The Idea of National Interest*, pp. 107, 167.
75. Beard, *A Foreign Policy for America*, p. 46.
76. Kennedy, *Charles A. Beard and American Foreign Policy*, p. 67; Cohen, "Revisionism Between World Wars," p. 145.
77. Angell, *The Great Illusion*, p. vii.
78. Ibid., pp. vii-viii, 62.
79. Ibid., pp. 61, 51, 66.
80. Cf. Benjamin Cohen, *The Question of Imperialism* (New York: Basic Books, 1973).
81. Angell, *The Great Illusion*, pp. 31-32, 60, 55. Cf. Charles E. Lindblom, "The Market as Prison," *Journal of Politics* 44 (May 1982): 324-32, concerning the market's automatic recoil mechanism; Claus Offe, "The Theory of the Capitalist State and the Problem of Policy Formation," in Leon Lindberg, ed., *Stress and Contradiction in Modern Capitalism* (Lexington, MA: D. C. Heath, 1975), pp. 125-44, on the dependency principle. Fred Block, "The Ruling Class Does Not Rule: Notes on the Marxist Theory of the State," *Socialist Revolution* 7 (May-June 1977): 6-28, on business confidence as the major structural mechanism for disciplining policy in capitalist states.
82. Beard, *Cross Currents in Europe Today*, p. 85.
83. Beard, "Prospects for Peace," p. 320. For this reason, even though Beard sup-

ported the Allies in World War I, as early as 1917, he opposed calls for indemnities and reparations. See Beard, "German Annexations and Indemnities."

84. Angell, *The Great Illusion*, p. 35, 107, 139, 143.
85. Ibid., pp. 83, 84.
86. Beard, *Cross Currents in Europe Today*, pp. 85-86.
87. Kennedy, *Charles A. Beard and American Foreign Policy*, p. 67.
88. Cordell Hull quoted in Williams, *The Contours of American History*, p. 414. Pratt, *Cordell Hull*, Chap. 6.
89. Nore, *Charles A. Beard*, p. 144.
90. Nor has that number changed substantially to this very day. See Paul Krugman, "Competitiveness: Does it Matter?," *Fortune* 129 (March 7, 1994): 109-15, finds that in 1992 exports were 10.6 percent of U.S. GDP, while imports were 11.1 percent. Also, Paul Krugman, *Peddling Prosperity: Economic Sense in the Age of Diminished Expectations* (New York: W. W. Norton, 1994).
91. Beard, *The Idea of National Interest*, p. 534. Cf. Paul Krugman, "Europe Jobless, America Penniless?" *Foreign Affairs* 95 (Summer 1994): 19-34, echoes Beard's theme with almost identical language: "Even today, U.S. exports are only 10 percent of the [gross national product] in the economy. That is, the United States is still almost 90 percent an economy that produces goods and services for its own use."
92. Beard, *The Open Door at Home*, pp. 48-49, 226.
93. Beard and Beard, *America in Mid-Passage*, p. 453.
94. Beard, *The Open Door at Home*, p. 225.
95. Beard, *A Foreign Policy for America*, p. 70.
96. Beard, "A Five-Year Plan for America," pp. 9-10.
97. Beard, *A Foreign Policy for America*, p. 9.
98. Beard, *The Idea of National Interest*, p. 545.
99. Beard, *The Open Door at Home*, p. 269.
100. Ibid., pp. 218-19, 213, 232, 287.
101. Beard, "A Five-Year Plan for America," p. 10.
102. Beard, *The Open Door at Home*, pp. 287-88.
103. Ibid., p. 288.
104. Ibid., p. 289.
105. Ibid., pp. 214-15, 221-24. Cf. Alfred Ruhl, *Zur Frage der internationalen Arbeitstilung* (Berlin: Reimar Hobbing, 1932).
106. Max Lerner, "Civilization and the Devils," *New Republic* 119 (November 1, 1948): 24; Beard, *The Open Door at Home*, p. 214.
107. Beard, *The Open Door at Home*, p. 290.
108. Beard, "A Five-Year Plan for America," p. 10.
109. Beard, *The Open Door at Home*, p. 261.
110. Charles A. Beard quoted in "Einstein Advocates Economic Boycott," *The New York Times*, February 28, 1932, p. 2.
111. Beard and Beard, *America in Mid-Passage*, pp. 452-53.
112. Kennedy, *Charles A. Beard and American Foreign Policy*, p. 92.
113. Beard, *The Open Door at Home*, p. 213; Beard, *Giddy Minds and Foreign Quarrels*, p. 95. Cf. Gary Clyde Hufbauer, and Jeffrey J. Schott, *Western Hemisphere Economic Integration* (Washington, DC: Institute for International Economics, 1993).
114. Beard, *A Foreign Policy for America*, p. 151.
115. Beard, *The Open Door at Home*, p. 297. Beard proposed that a Bureau of the Navy and a Bureau of the Army be established within the Division of National Defense and that each bureau be headed by civilian technical experts, rather than

military officers. As part of the same consolidation, Beard proposed to abolish the Department of Commerce and move its technical bureaus into the Export-Import Syndicate.

116. Ibid., p. 298.
117. Beard, *A Foreign Policy for America*, pp. 18, 152, emphasis added.
118. Beard, *The Open Door at Home*, p. 303.
119. Beard, *A Foreign Policy for America*, p. 19.
120. Beard, *The Open Door at Home*, p. 286.
121. Cohen, "Revisionism Between World Wars," p. 157.
122. Nore, *Charles A. Beard*, p. 182.
123. Williams, *The Contours of American History*, pp. 451, 454-55.
124. Ibid., p. 461, finds that as Roosevelt clarified his intentions to expand foreign trade, the United Steel Workers of America resolved that foreign policy should not be "formulated or made dependent upon the protection of the vested or property interests in foreign countries of the large corporations in this country." In the same year (1937), the CIO drew attention to the "still unsolved grave economic, social, and industrial maladjustments" in the United States. Likewise, John L. Lewis in 1940 continued to prefer a hemispheric trade zone that would link the U.S. and Latin America, rather than pursuing concerns in Europe or Asia.
125. Beard, *The Idea of National Interest*, p. 548.
126. Beard, *Economic Basis of Politics*, p. 85.
127. Beard, "National Politics and War," pp. 65-70.
128. Ibid., p. 65. Beard and Beard, *Rise of American Civilization*, Vol. 1, pp. 545 ff.
129. Beard, "National Politics and War," p. 66.
130. Ibid., p. 67.
131. Ibid., p. 69. Cf. Richard Bensel, *Yankee Leviathan: The Origins of Central State Authority in America, 1859-1877* (Cambridge: Cambridge University Press, 1990).
132. Hofstadter, *The Progressive Historians*, pp. 328, 324, emphasis added.
133. Beard, "National Politics and War," p. 69.
134. Ibid., pp. 69-70.
135. Ibid., p. 70.
136. Soule, "Beard and the Concept of Planning," in Beale, ed., *Charles A. Beard*, pp. 69-70.
137. Beard quoted in Hofstadter, *The Progressive Historians*, p. 324.
138. B, "National Politics and War," p. 70.
139. Strout, *The Pragmatic Revolt in American History*, p. 144. Cf. Charles A. Beard, "Going Ahead With Roosevelt," *Events* 1 (January 1937): 12; Charles A. Beard, "Roosevelt's Place in History," *Events* 3 (February 1938): 86.
140. Stourzh, "Charles A. Beard's Interpretations of American Foreign Policy," p. 140, fn. 75.
141. Kennedy, *Charles A. Beard and American Foreign Policy*, p. 74.
142. Stourzh, "Charles A. Beard's Interpretations of American Foreign Policy," pp. 139, 143. George R. Leighton, "Beard and Foreign Policy," in Beale, ed., *Charles A. Beard*, traces the escalation of Beard's attacks on Roosevelt.
143. Beard, *Economic Basis of Politics*, pp. 90-93. Cf. Bertram Gross, *Friendly Fascism* (New York: M. Evans Publishers, 1980).
144. Nore, *Charles A. Beard*, p. 222.
145. Hofstadter, *The Progressive Historians*, p. 324.
146. Nore, *Charles A. Beard*, p. 179.
147. Charles A. Beard, "Crisis in the Pacific: I—War With Japan?" *Events* 8 (Novem-

ber 1940): 323.

148. For background, see Morton Halperin, *The Lawless State* (New York: Penguin, 1976).

149. Counts, "Charles Beard, The Public Man," in Beale, ed., *Charles A. Beard*, p. 235. "Review of *President Roosevelt and the Coming of the War, 1941*, by Charles A. Beard," *Time* 51 (April 12, 1948): 12, observes that "historians will probably find it no great job to riddle the argument of Dr. Beard's book. It will not be so easy to ignore his emphatic conclusion."

150. See especially, Williams, *The Tragedy of American Diplomacy*; William Appleman Williams, *From Colony to Empire* (New York: J. Wiley, 1972).

7

The Legacy

The Ghost of Charles A. Beard

There is no question that Beard's final two books on foreign policy damaged his reputation among liberals and ultimately threw his whole life's work into question only months before his death. Beard's last two books were based largely on newspaper and magazine articles, press releases, and speeches, because they were the only sources available to him at the time. Beard did not have access to the intelligence or inside information that would have allowed him to correctly evaluate the intentions of Germany and Japan or the motives of President Roosevelt with respect to World War II. Unlike many of his progressive and liberal colleagues, Beard had spent much of the last twenty years isolated on his dairy farm in Connecticut, insulated from developments in academia and excluded from the inner circles of the new liberal regime in Washington, D.C. The dispute between Beard and the New Deal liberals became so vitriolic in the 1940s that Thomas Kennedy identifies his last two books as the fundamental reason for the decline of Beard's scholarly reputation. Indeed, the two books had a snowball effect on his reputation that continued to gain momentum over the following two decades.

Many of Beard's long-time critics, such as fellow historian Allan Nevins, condemned his economic interpretation of foreign policy because its "frigid indifference to moral considerations" can make "no appeal to any motive more elevated than self-interest."[1] The moral argument against Beard's continentalism was that it refused to recognize any non-economic component to the national interest and thus had little to offer at a time when the defense of liberal and democratic values seemed especially pertinent to American foreign policy. At a time when liberal democracy was being threatened by brutal regimes on both ends of the ideological spectrum, Beard's last two books—despite being published in 1946 and 1948—had little to say about Stalin's gulags, Hitler's extermination camps, or Japanese atrocities during World War II. The indictment of Roosevelt's intentions seemed petty, silly, and stubborn by comparison, particularly since the books were published after many of these facts were common knowledge to the American public.

Other critics dismissed Beard's *President Roosevelt* as the literature of embitterment, which had been authored by an aging scholar excluded from the centers of political power and who refused to admit being wrong about something as big as World War II. Scholars who had once been among his greatest admirers lined up to denounce Beard as the fallen angel of American liberalism, as a wayward liberal, and a liberal gone sour.[2] George McBundy dismissed Beard's last two books as the corroded Beard.[3] The books left many people shocked and wondering how the nation's most revered scholar could have been so misguided about World War II. However, the more significant question was that if Beard had erred about something so obvious was it because some fundamental flaw in his approach to history had led him to that conclusion?

The same question was also raised in an escalating debate with the Communist party, where Beard chastised American Marxists for abandoning radical economic reform in exchange for collective security arrangements and the Popular Front.[4] American Marxists reversed their previous endorsement of Beard's work in the mid-1930s and began citing his writings to illustrate the bankruptcy of vulgar Marxism and economic reductionism.[5] Needless to say, observers on the political right were jubilant to find that Beard was now "generally execrated and disavowed by the whole crew of his former Leftist idolaters."[6]

Beard was isolated politically and intellectually from the entire progressive movement when he died in 1948, and that isolation set the stage for a feeding frenzy on his economic interpretation of history during the Cold War. Forrest McDonald, who authored the most important challenge to Beard's *Economic Interpretation* during this time, denies that the anti-Beardian movement was part of a conservative ideological agenda, but he acknowledges that Cold War anti-Communism "made the atmosphere ripe for an attack on Beard," because many people confused his work with Marxism.[7] Conservatives had always considered Beard a Marxist, but during the 1930s and 1940s it was also becoming clear to liberals that his political thought was not liberal in the sense that Roosevelt's New Dealers understood that term.

During the 1930s and 1940s, Beard's criticism of New Deal liberalism became as sharp as his critique of laissez-faire capitalism had been during the 1910s and 1920s. At the peak of his intellectual influence in the 1930s, Beard's ideological differences with old progressives and new liberals were being clarified by the public policy debates on economic planning. Beard dismissed the New Deal as a minor gain for labor and instead called for a workers' republic that was uncomfortably similar in its program to Lenin's New Economic Policy.[8] Beard's attacks on Roosevelt in his last two books only widened the rift between himself and the New Deal liberals, who embraced an aggressive internationalism as most had done during World War I.

The liberals' nervousness with Beard was further exacerbated by the necessities of ideological warfare during World War II and the Cold War.[9] During the 1930s, Beard played a leading role, in conjunction with Carl Becker and John Dewey, in promoting the "relativism" of German historicists and the Italian Benedetto Croce. Shortly after his 1934 AHA presidential address, Allan Nevins charged Beard with embracing a theory of historical writing developed "under state pressure in Nazi Germany and Fascist Italy."[10] Anyone familiar with these writers would have known better and the charge did not resonate at the time, but with the onset of World War II historical relativism was not a comfortable foundation for reaffirming the self-evident moral certainties of America's liberal democracy.[11] To the extent that historical relativism was associated with cultural relativism and moral nihilism, Eric F. Goldman recalls that World War II "increased the psychological difficulty a thousandfold, for war admits of no relativism. There is only our side, which is good, and the other side, which is bad."[12] John G. Gunnell finds that "the increasingly pivotal issue of relativism was, at this time, grounded in a concrete concern about the defense of liberal democratic principles."[13] The work of Beard, Dewey, and Becker, which had fueled philosophical speculation about the relativist foundations of American historiography, became morally and politically suspect in an era where epistemological skepticism was no longer compatible with the dominance of a liberal regime under stress. A commitment to democracy and American liberalism seemed to require the rejection of Beardian (and progressive) historiography.

The advent of the Cold War led many intellectuals who had distanced themselves from Beard over the Roosevelt controversy to eventually reject the method of economic interpretation entirely, mainly because of its perceived affinity with Marxism and moral relativism. The postwar generation of liberal historians and political theorists began to reassess the previous generation of progressive scholarship in the context of America's confrontation with totalitarian regimes.[14] Cushing Strout called on liberals to abandon the progressive thesis, because it had "corrupted and confused" liberalism with "utopian views about reason, social planning, or historical progress."[15] Robert Allen Skotheim introduced his survey of American intellectual history with the caveat that he was sympathetic to progressivism, but that his interpretation of the progressive historians had "been modified by reactions to totalitarianism which have ramifications for our views of human nature and of social progress through planning."[16] This claim is still echoed by contemporary critics who blame Beard for America's cultural retreat from the transcendent truths and moral values at the core of the Western philosophical tradition.[17]

Thus, Beard's isolation from liberals and the left opened the door to a wide-ranging assault on his economic interpretation of American history. The most visible reaction to Beardian historiography was the blistering counter-offensive launched by scholars in the 1950s who sought nothing less than to refute Beard by using his own approach to explain the origins of the Constitution.[18] Robert Eldon Brown, who challenged Beard's *Economic Interpretation* virtually line by line, explained the ferocity of his rebuttal as the result of a Cold War mood that had made American scholars "especially sensitive to class structure in recent years because of the threat of communism in undeveloped areas."[19] The growing aversion of postwar liberals to anything that sounded Marxist made them sympathetic to the idea that Beard's emphasis on class divisions and state planning, whether wittingly or unwittingly, played into the hands of America's Communist enemies.[20]

Thus, Robert Eldon Brown challenged Beard with an analysis of wealth distribution in pre-Revolutionary America, which suggested contrary to Beard's theory of class struggle, that the United States had been a middle-class democracy at its founding.[21] Forrest McDonald's analysis of the Founders' property-holdings complemented Brown's findings by documenting a more pluralistic division of economic interests among the Founding Fathers.[22] Douglas Adair advanced the anti-Beardian movement by claiming that Beard was not only wrong in his empirical claims, but that he misconstrued the theory of Madison's *Tenth Federalist*, which was not an economic interpretation of politics, but a theory of interest group pluralism.[23] By using Beard's own method and sources, scholarly views of the founding were gradually transformed from a critique of the capitalist state into a defense of liberal pluralism.[24]

In the ideologically charged postwar and Cold War milieu, scholars were uncritically receptive to these critiques and often exaggerated their polemical significance. Contemporary scholars read about Beard, but they rarely read Beard except through the lens of his numerous critics and often "read" him through the lens of tertiary sources. In the backrooms of the Beard debate, Jackson Turner Main considered it "a little strange" that McDonald's critique "aroused scarcely a whimper of protest" after historians and political scientists had relied on Beard's economic interpretation for forty years. Main authored a detailed rejoinder to McDonald and concludes that "Beard has survived the attack."[25] Forrest McDonald was compelled to "entirely agree" with many of Main's rejoinders and noted that he "correctly pointed out some of my factual errors, though he missed others that I have discovered since publication."[26]

Yet, even as criticism of Beard's work gained momentum, Louis Hartz was terribly frustrated that "Beard somehow stays alive."[27] Indeed, during the recent state theory debates, Theda Skocpol again complained that the Beardian thesis seems to be an "unquenchable proclivity in American progressive historiography."[28] As a result, Henry Steele Commager has aptly described Beard as the King Charles' head of American scholarship: "You can't get away from him; he's always there and if he's not there as an influence he's there as a counterinfluence. First you have to dispose of him before you can get on with the job."[29]

Louis Hartz suggested that the only way to dispose of Beard was to ignore him and hope that future scholars would forget his work as it drifted into the dim mists of history. Unlike the historians, political scientists took Hartz's advice after Beard's American government textbook was published in its final 1948 edition. While historians waged an unrelenting siege against Beardian historiography, political scientists migrated away from history altogether.[30]

The behavioral revolution of the 1950s allowed political scientists to ignore the hand-to-hand combat among historians, because they were immigrating to a newly discovered territory where hypothesis testing, quantitative methodology, and mainframe computing substituted the certainties of positivism for the speculations of Universal History.[31] Unlike many progressive scholars, Beard continued to approach political science as a historical institutionalist even though he was aware of the positivist movement in the 1920s.[32] Beard developed a historicist critique of behavioral methodology in several of his books, but these critiques were ignored by the new generation of political scientists.[33]

A central feature of positivism and behavioralism was their analytic separation of facts and values. Political philosophers collaborated actively in this process by severing political philosophy from politics and history and retreating to the arid terrain of analytic and transcendental philosophy.[34] As the foundations of American political theory shifted from history to philosophy, Beard's status as a political theorist was also undermined by developments within political philosophy. As early as 1934, Harold Laski criticized Beard for failing to formulate a "consistent or systematic philosophy of politics."[35] Max Lerner sought to resist the dissociation of history and theory by suggesting that Beard "was a great historian...mainly because he was more than a historian. He was a political theorist, and a dabbler in philosophy." However, Lerner agrees that "Beard floundered about as a theorist."[36] Bernard Wishy concludes that Beard "never brought his single formulation into that precise, coherent, complex view of social process that could be recognized as a really significant intellectual achievement."[37]

As disciplinary conceptions of political theory changed in the 1950s and 1960s, a few political philosophers attempted to rectify the analytic disorder in Beard's political thinking by rendering it consistent with the central concepts of the new political philosophy. Almost against common sense, Bernard Borning's rendition of Beard's political thought asserts that its central core is not really economic factors but a conception of human nature.[38] John Patrick Diggins claims that Beard "started from the premise of moral choice and individual freedom," rather than economic factors because he "wanted to judge history by some standard other than the relentless activity of interests and power."[39] Fred Matthews extends this thesis by arguing that Beard called for a moral consensus to "supersede factional interests and allow the creation of a virtuous Republic."[40]

Therefore, the dominant view among political philosophers is that Beard was not a political philosopher or at best he was a mediocre one when judged by his contributions to our understanding of human nature and moral values. However, both judgments depend upon the analytic standards of traditional political *philosophy*, which insist that political theory must somehow transcend history and rise above ordinary politics to count as theory.[41] Beard was challenging this very conception of political theory by demonstrating that ideas emerge from within history and as a result of political conflict, rather than in spite of politics and above politics.

Between History and Theory

The enthusiasm to bury Beard under the scrap heap of history has resulted in a legacy of questioned motives, accusations of lying and habitual exaggeration, empirical challenges to his factual claims, and suggestions that he did not understand the theoretical underpinnings of his own writings. There is virtually no aspect of Beard's thinking that has not been subject to distortion and misrepresentation by ideological critics or equal misuse and misappropriation by ideological enthusiasts. The weight of these preconceptions was so heavy in his own day that Beard mused "perhaps no other book on the Constitution has been more severely criticized and so little read" as *An Economic Interpretation of the Constitution*.[42]

This book has attempted to meet Beard's challenge by reading his political and economic thought from the inside and in a way that accepts his intentional statements as valid touchstones of interpretation. In doing so, I have rejected the idea that there is an early and a later Beard, although his thought clearly developed over time as he grappled with methodological and political issues. In the 1930s, Beard's concern with historiography shifted from the method of economic interpretation to the historical sociology of knowledge, but he never abandoned one position for the other. Beard enunciated both positions simultaneously throughout the 1930s, because they are complementary positions when anchored in Mannheim's *Ideology and Utopia*.

In the 1910s and 1920s, Beard's main interest was *the application* of the method of economic interpretation to American history and this task was begun in 1913 with the publication of *An Economic Interpretation of the Constitution*. His general history was essentially complete by 1927 when he co-authored *The Rise of American Civilization* with his wife Mary Ritter Beard. For Beard, general history was the bridge between philosophy and politics, because the spirit of a people is manifested over the course of its history, while the normative trajectory immanent in that history engages the intellectual as a statesman without portfolio. Thus, the new history inextricably linked general history to political engagement, since the main purpose of historical writing was to extrapolate prescriptions for political action and contemporary public policy.

Beard made constant forays into public policy debates and politics throughout his career, although his ideological and political loyalties are not easily identified by conventional standards. Beard was a critic of laissez-faire capitalism, who was deeply influenced by the British Fabians and German Social Democracy. He embraced the ideal of a constitutional workers' republic and identified the Weimar Constitution as the closest approximation to its state form. He clearly favored a mixed economy with extensive public ownership and worker ownership of enterprises operating within a centrally planned market economy.

Beard would likely be identified as a market socialist in contemporary debates on political economy, which may partly explain why he was never comfortable with any of the existing political labels. Beard dismissed the economic proposals of Populists and New Freedom liberals as anachronistic yearnings for a small producer economy that were unrealistic in the age of corporate capitalism. He considered the Roosevelt Progressives (1912) a mouthpiece for the new middle class, which was wedged between the competing demands of corporate capitalists and industrial workers and who wanted a liberal state to mediate between these antagonistic social forces. Beard made it clear that he wanted a more radical restructuring of economic and social relations than Progressives were prepared to offer in 1912 and, in the 1930s, he refused overtures from the Democratic Party to run for Governor and U.S. Senator as the liberal candidate in Connecticut.

Beard maintained a close relationship with the social-democratic wing of the American Socialist Party into the 1920s, including support for the early campaigns of Morris Hillquit and the McNamara brothers defense fund. He maintained contact with the Rand School of Social Science until 1921, helped found the socialist leaning Workers' Education Bureau, and called for a British style labor party during this time. He even taught the "Economic Basis of Politics" at the Workers' (Communist) School for a few years in the late 1920s. Yet, Beard was neither a Marxist in theory nor a revolutionary in practice and, hence, he never joined the Socialist or Communist party. The party he wanted to join did not exist, except in Great Britain and Germany, and by the mid-1930s it was clear to Beard that not even the Great Depression would bring this agency into existence in America. The road he had mapped out for American political development was not being followed, so in the 1940s Beard turned to foreign policy to explain this diversion from the anticipated end of history.

It is remarkable, and perhaps unparalleled, that one of the nation's most respected and popular scholars of the first half of the twentieth century became one of the most debunked and reviled intellectual figures in the second half of the twentieth century. Yet, Beard's economic interpretation of the Constitution continues to resonate with scholars, students, and citizens because class-based political privilege and economic inequality are facts that stand in sharp contrast to constitutional mythology. Beard emphasized that regardless of the time or place, and regardless of the details, "where the configurations and pressures of economic interests are brought into an immediate relation to the event or series of events under consideration, an economic interpretation is effected."[43] Economic interpretations of American politics are routinely effected each day in the classroom, on network news, in bars and restaurants, and the living rooms of ordinary citizens. Beard's name is rarely invoked in these discussions, but his method of analysis and his major ideas continue to flow through numerous channels into the mainstream of American political culture.[44] If Communism was the specter that haunted Marx's Europe, Beard is the ghost that haunts Madison's constitution.

For this reason alone, Beard's political and economic thought should be taken seriously and indeed his most accomplished critics continue to recognize the power of his interpretive method. Regardless of how one judges the details of Beard's economic interpretation of American political development, its central core emphasizes the antagonism between capitalism and democracy and this topic remains an important theme in contemporary political theory.[45] Consequently, Gordon S. Wood suggests that even if Beard's economic interpretation of the Constitution has been dismantled *in a narrow sense* his general interpretation continues to be "the most helpful framework for understanding the politics and ideology surrounding the constitution."[46] Forrest McDonald, who has done more than anyone to challenge the details of Beard's economic interpretation, agrees that Beard's general analysis of the Constitution still pervades constitutional scholarship.[47]

Yet, there has been little effort to exactly define Beard's general framework and it is my conclusion that much of the previous scholarship has done more to obscure that framework than to clarify it. In particular, most scholars have failed to appreciate the importance of E. R. A. Seligman's methodological foundation to Beard's historiographic and political thought. Beard's *Economic Interpretation of the Constitution* was so quickly engulfed by the bitter polemics of ultra-conservatives and Marxists that proponents of both sides chose to ignore Beard's statements that he was not a Marxist. Yet, Seligman's treatise on *The Economic Interpretation of History* is an essential background to understanding Beard's writings.

There are numerous implications to reading Seligman as an integral component of Beard's own corpus. First, Seligman's *Economic Interpretation of History* gives substance to Beard's disclaimers about not being a Marxist. As a reading of Seligman indicates, Beard had very specific conceptions about what separated his method of economic interpretation from Marxian historical materialism. Moreover, these ideas were by no means peculiar in the late nineteenth and early twentieth centuries and were, in fact, commonly understood among European liberals and socialist revisionists. This clarification of Beard's methodology enables one to take seriously his claim that the theory of the state developed in *An Economic Interpretation* is essentially Madisonian in origins. Whether he read Madison correctly is debatable, but the predisposition to question Beard's honesty has suppressed the rather simple point that one can find a basis for economic interpretation in Madison's *Tenth Federalist*.[48]

Furthermore, reading Beard through Seligman's lens has signficiant implications for how we understand his *Economic Interpretation of the Constitution*. The implications for how we read this text fall along the three methodological dimensions addressed by Seligman. Beard suggests the rudiments of a non-Marxian theory of class struggle and the state that owes a great deal to the institutional economics of John R. Commons and Richard T. Ely. As I have pointed out, Commons' work especially evinces suggestive parallels to Madison in defining the relation between constitutional law, class interests, and property rights.

Once Beard's theory of class struggle is severed from Marx and situated in the larger context of his writings on American political development, it becomes evident that Beard approaches the ratification struggle as an illustration of the open-endedness of history and the contingency of its final outcome. In Beard's *Economic Interpretation of the Constitution*, the Federalists' victory is the result of politics, although its ideological meaning is determined by its relation to economic and class forces. Finally, Beard's methodological *relationism* leads him to claim far less for his economic interpretation than either detractors on the right or supporters on the left imputed to it.

In replying to critics who accused him of economic reductionism, Beard reiterates that he "never believed that 'all history' can or must be 'explained' in economic terms, or any other terms." It was never Beard's intention to claim that the form of government established by the Constitution and the powers conferred on that government "were 'determined' in every detail by the conflict of economic interests." In some ways, Beard anticipated the ideological school of constitutional interpretation—Douglas Adair, Bernard Bailyn, J. G. A. Pocock, and Gordon Wood—by cautioning scholars not to exclude the possibility that ideas and other cultural phenomena "may have been conditioned if not determined by economic interests and activities."[49] Indeed, Forrest McDonald suggests persuasively that in the final analysis the ideological school has not displaced Beard, but merely replicated "Beard's interpretation with the dollar signs removed."[50] When one examines the empirical and ideological critiques closely, they have tended to correct factual errors, refine the class analysis, and supplement Beard's economic explanation with political and ideological factors to provide a more comprehensive understanding of the Constitution's origins. When Beard is read with the appropriate complexity, and when one looks beneath ideas to their carriers, then the recent work by historians has actually built on Beard's foundation, rather than displaced it.

In the same way, it is important to recognize that Beard's frequent use of dialectical terminology was neither covert Marxism nor slip-shod rhetoric.[51] Beard utilized dialectics to conceptualize American political development throughout his career. Beard's students recall that he made frequent references to becoming reality, the becoming future, and constantly becoming situations in his lectures at Columbia University.[52] He continued using dialectical terms into the 1930s when he first proposed the idea of a realistic dialectics. Beard's idea of realistic dialectics is implicit in Marx's dialectical materialism once the latter's mechanical and positivistic overtones are jettisoned and this is clearly an aspect of Marxism that Beard rejected.[53] On the other hand, the same idea is implicit in Hegel's dialectical idealism once the latter's metaphysical state is translated into the history of actually existing constitutions.

It would be terribly misleading to claim that Beard was a compre-hensive or systematic philosophical thinker; yet, it is equally mistaken to charge Beard with superficial and confused thinking about the prob-lem of historical knowledge. Beard spent much of his career working through the problems of Hegelian dualism with Marx and Croce de-fining the two poles of that philosophical antinomy. Beard picked and chose his way through the problems of Hegelian dualism in a manner that appears excessively eclectic only to later scholars who have aban-doned Hegelianism for an analytic approach to philosophy or a posi-tivist approach to social science.

Like his economic interpretations of American history, Beard's philo-sophical forays achieve greater coherence when they are read against the background of neo-Hegelian and post-Hegelian thinkers who re-ceive little attention today from historians, political philosophers, or political scientists (i.e., Croce, Scheler, Mannheim). Croce's influence on Beard has long been recognized by intellectual historians, but rela-tively minor German figures, such as Kurt Riezler and Karl Heussi, have been identified as the dominant influences on Beard's philo-sophical thinking mainly due to Lloyd Sorenson's essay. Although Sorenson acknowledges Croce's influence on Beard, he was "con-cerned only with Beard's study of German historiography" and noted that "another article would be necessary if his indebtedness to Croce were to be dealt with adequately."[54] Neither Sorenson, nor anyone else has rectified this omission, but as if to compound the problem, Sorenson focuses almost exclusively on Heussi and Riezler, both fig-ures that he considers minor players in the German historiographical debates. Interestingly, Sorenson claims that it was Karl Heussi's *Die Krisis des Historismus* (1932) that first made Beard conscious of the subjective element in historical investigation. This claim is patently false, since Beard was introduced to Croce a decade before the publication of Heussi's book and thus Sorenson greatly overestimates Heussi's influence on Beard.

It is also quite astounding that Sorenson's essay has stood unchallenged for four decades when it does not even deal adequately with Beard's German sources, particularly Scheler and Mannheim, who play a far more significant role in Beard's theoretical development and who were far more important in founding the sociology of knowledge. Although Sorenson purports to assess the German influence on Beard, he fails to discuss Scheler and makes only a single reference to the fact that Beard had read Karl Mannheim. The failure to recognize Scheler's and Mannheim's influence on Beard would seem to explain Sorenson's rather puzzling assertion that Beard was unable to specify concrete manifestations of any schemes of reference.[55] Scheler's schemes of reference and Mannheim's styles of thinking were being reproduced in detail in Beard's methodological writings throughout the 1930s.

By adopting the sociology of knowledge to explain the different schemes of reference utilized by historians *and* political actors, Beard latched onto a more sophisticated economic interpretation of ideological phenomena than was found in Seligman's *Economic Interpretation of History*. Beard's discovery of Scheler and Mannheim should have enabled him to rebut the charges of economic reductionism with greater vigor, but he never utilized them to their full capacity and when he did cite them it was in his more obscure methodological writings of the 1930s. Moreover, as the Hegelian influence waned in American academia, American scholars lost the ability to comprehend the philosophical logic of Beardian historiography. Many of the alleged inconsistencies and ambiguities later attributed to Beard's realistic dialectics stem from a failure to read Beard in the broad intellectual context that frequently linked the Progressive historians to European currents of thought.[56]

Beard's immersion in the Continental tradition of Hegelian dialectics is most evident in his conceptualization of American political development. Beard was not unique in viewing American political development as the outcome of a dialectic between the Jeffersonian and Hamiltonian traditions. J. Allen Smith and Herbert Croly, among others, employed variants of this dialectic to explain American political development. Beard was also not alone in following Hegel to conceptualize constitutions as the spirit of a people. George Bancroft and John W. Burgess had employed the same idea to glorify the U.S. Constitution with the Hegelian metaphysics of Teutonic and Anglo-American superiority.

However, amid the backdrop of dialectical and neo-Hegelian histories, Beard did establish a unique position that differs significantly from Populist and Progressive historians, while challenging the ideological explanations of constitutional origins. Beard's analysis of constitutional origins, early state-building, and subsequent political development did not focus on a political division between aristocracy and democracy, but on the competing interests of capitalist and agrarian coalitions. Neither of these coalitions was exclusively aristocratic or democratic in Beard's reconstruction of the conflict and, hence, he considered the Constitution of 1789 to be anti-populist, but not inherently anti-democratic. What was more important in Beard's view is that the new constitutional structure, if used properly, could more readily promote capitalist development than the Articles of Confederation and that it was less amenable to long-term domination by agrarian regimes.

Since Beard placed this dialectic at the center of his analysis, he recognized that the spirit of the people was not a unity, but a difference based in class divisions. In contrast to interpreters who emphasize ideological consensus, Beard argues that the spirit of the Constitution is neither exclusively capitalist (Hamiltonian), nor exclusively democratic (Jeffersonian), but a unity of opposites. Beard's general history is a monumental effort to transcend the antinomies of American political thought through an immanent resolution of their contradiction in a workers' republic.[57] Thus, where Populists and Progressives saw American political development as a repetitive cycle of renewal (democracy) and decay (aristocracy),[58] Beard interpreted American political development as a dialectic of thesis (agrarian populism), antithesis (liberal capitalism), and synthesis (social democracy).[59] In the final chapter of *The Rise of American Civilization* (1927), entitled "Toward Social Democracy," Beard concludes that in America: "Hegel's theory of history had been illustrated once again."[60]

Beard's proclamation of a workers' republic was premature and it seems naively optimistic in the aftermath of our own neo-conservative counter-revolution against the welfare state. Yet, in Beard's defense, it is difficult to fully appreciate how close he thought he was to witnessing the birth of a workers' republic that would finally realize the promise of American life. By 1931, virtually every major American interest group, including big business, agreed that some type of macroeconomic planning was necessary to address the crisis of the Great Depression. Beard's own proposal for agricultural planning was taken directly from Franklin D. Roosevelt's New York Plan, while Senator Robert LaFollette introduced a bill into Congress to create a National Economic Council before Beard published his plan. Thus, when FDR was elected President in 1932, quick passage of the National Industrial Recovery Act and the Agricultural Adjustment Act seemed to provide an institutional framework for the type of planning and economic restructuring proposed by Beard. At the same time, the rise of the Congress of Industrial Organizations (CIO), with strong ties to the Socialist and Communist parties, promised a new type of militant social unionism in America.[61]

Beard was correct in recognizing the New Deal as a significant rupture with laissez-faire policies and institutions and he embraced the New Deal for that reason. However, Beard never saw the New Deal as anything more than a transitional form of state capitalism. Beard pointed approvingly to Lenin's New Economic Policy, which was based on the premise that "socialism is nothing but the next step forward from state-capitalist monopoly. In other words, Socialism is nothing but state-capitalist monopoly *made to benefit the whole people*; by this token it ceases to be capitalist monopoly."[62] Therefore, at the trough of the Great Depression, Beard admonished the revolutionary left that "in a similar situation," Lenin had not proposed the confiscation of property and immediate socialization, but an advanced form of state capitalism; namely, compulsory syndicalization, under workers' control, supplemented by heavy income and inheritance taxes.

Beard was convinced that the magnitude of the Great Depression would eventually move Congress and the unions toward more radical restructuring, including the nationalization of key industrial sectors. Thus, in Beard's view, the one missing element in this evolving historical trajectory was the workers' equivalent of an Alexander Hamilton or Thomas Jefferson who could articulate a world-historic vision of the workers' republic. During the early years of the New Deal, Beard thought that Roosevelt was groping toward a third conception of policy that would synthesize the Hamiltonian vision of a strong central government with the Jeffersonian vision of an egalitarian economic order. Beard was pleased that Roosevelt had rejected "the long-dominant conception that the so-called surpluses of American industry and agriculture are inexorable" and had embraced national planning as a solution to the Great Depression.[63] Similarly, Beard was convinced that Roosevelt's administration would strongly favor labor in the "struggle over the distribution of wealth, which arises from the conflict between private property and social need."[64] The last unforged link in the unfolding chain of events was that the Rooseveltian vision was still "too fragmentary to be characterized by a single word or phrase."[65]

Beard was convinced that economic forces would drive Roosevelt and the New Dealers toward ever more radical solutions to the economic crisis of the Great Depression. However, Beard exaggerated the necessity and inexorability of state-centered economic planning and socialization of the means of production. He overestimated the capacity of economists and engineers to centrally direct a large, complex, and growing economy and those difficulties have only become more pertinent in the intervening fifty years. Beard had overestimated the impulse to create an independent labor party in the 1920s because he projected the trends of the 1910s indefinitely into the future. In the 1930s, he again overestimated the transformative impulse of the social union movement because he projected the events of the early 1930s indefinitely into the future. When the combined agencies of social unionism and a labor party failed to materialize during the moment of world-historical crisis, Beard was left with only a Prince.

While preparing *The Open Door at Home* in October of 1933, Beard was invited to dine with President Roosevelt at the White House. While meeting with the President, Beard expressed his concern that Roosevelt and the New Dealers were pursuing contradictory policies with inconsistent goals, but that if Roosevelt could enunciate a vision as grand as that of Hamilton or Jefferson—a workers' republic—he would occupy an unsurpassed place in American history. Beard left the dinner believing that Roosevelt might follow the path of a bold political economist.[66] The final chapter of Beard's *The Open Door at Home* makes it clear that his blueprint for economic planning was aimed directly at FDR and his advisers. It is well documented that Roosevelt read *The Open Door at Home*, that he marked passages and jotted down marginal comments in the book, and even kept a copy of the book on his desk for three weeks to show people who entered the Oval Office.[67]

This was a better reception than Machiavelli received from Lorenzo de Medici, but Roosevelt considered Beard's book a novelty and he was never inclined to take Beard's recommendations seriously. Moreover, Beard's admiration of the Weimar Constitution discredited his restructuring proposals among the many advisors who blamed it for the German economic disorder and the rise of Hitler. Hence, like Machiavelli before him, Beard was disappointed by the Prince. Beard came to harbor a deep bitterness against the President for allowing a world-historical moment to slip past him without taking what Beard considered decisive action. By 1938, Beard had already dismissed Roosevelt's place in American history with the caustic observation that "the circumstances of 1933 were propitious for such a stroke of state, but he avoided it."[68]

In retrospect, Beard's proposals for economic planning are based on a concept of industrial technology that has been displaced in many ways by the decentralizing and deterritorializing impact of computer and information technology. The industrial capitalism described by Beard has clearly been superceded by post-industrial or post-modern capitalism. It is hardly controversial to note that Beard's proletariat has been supplanted by a new service class or neo-proletariat and that militant social unions have been weakened by declining union density. The rise of new social movements defined by non-economic identities has added a degree of complexity to the political landscape that Beard did not anticipate.

Thus, Beard's political economy may seem antiquated, particularly in a period when both neo-conservatives and neo-liberals have embraced market forces and the private sector. On the other hand, the American left has not been able to challenge neo-conservatism or neo-liberalism with anything more than a last ditch defense of a disintegrating welfare state. Beard spent most of his own life writing against the backdrop of a similar historical era, and he often warned Americans that the bizarre persistence of an anachronistic laissez-faire ideology in the United States would eventually "become a danger to society" if it sustained a continuing policy of muddle and drift.[69] Beard's political and economic thought is not unique in criticizing laissez-faire capitalism or in being to the left of New Deal liberalism, but it is one of the few attempts to develop a left-critique of American liberalism that is anchored in institutional economics and a historical conception of American political development. There are few other thinkers in the twentieth century—Veblen, Ely, and Commons—who occupy a comparable niche in American political thought. Beard's analysis of American political development opens the door to an institutionalist critique of both neo-conservative and neo-liberal economic policy. His concept of a workers' republic provides a vehicle for breaking with a welfare state philosophy that the democratic left in America never viewed as the long-term solution to inequalities of wealth, opportunity, and power. His critique of the cost of empire suggests that even if the United States is successful in asserting political and military dominance on a global scale, the inexorable economic drain on its resources will always ricochet back onto America's working class.[70]

Notes

1. Allan Nevins, "Two Views of America's Part: Mr. Buell Argues Our Responsibility—Professor Beard Upholds Isolation," *The New York Times Book Review* (May 26, 1940), Section 6, pp. 1, 20.
2. Levin, "Charles A. Beard: Wayward Liberal," pp. 36-40.
3. Quoted in Nore, *Charles A. Beard*, p. 222.
4. For example, Earl Browder and Charles A. Beard, "Collective Security—A Debate," *New Republic* 93 (February 2, 1938): 356-59, for a debate with Earl Browder, General Secretary of the Communist Party, U.S.A.; Earl Browder, "Concerning American Revolutionary Traditions," *The Communist* 17 (December 1938): 1079-85; Jonas, *Isolationism in America*, pp. 39-41.
5. Thomas C. Cochran, "Review of *The Open Door at Home* by Charles A. Beard," *The Modern Monthly* 8 (February 1935): 759-60. Similarly, Eugene D. Genovese, *In Red and Black: Marxian Explorations in Southern and Afro-American History* (New York: Pantheon Books, 1968), pp. 315-56, passim; Harry Frankel, "Three Conceptions of Jacksonianism," in Novack, ed., *America's Revolutionary Heritage*, pp. 170-80; George Novack, "Historians and the Belated Rise of American Imperialism," in Novack, ed., *America's Revolutionary Heritage*, pp., pp. 287-307; Herbert Aptheker, *Early Years of the American Republic* (New York: International Publishers, 1976), pp. 45-89.
6. Harold Lord Varney, "The Man Who Lived Twice," *American Mercury* 85 (August 1957): 148-50.
7. Forrest McDonald, "A New Introduction (1986)," in Charles A. Beard, *An Economic Interpretation of the Constitution of the United States* (New York: Free Press, 1986), p. xxiii-xxiv.
8. For example, see Beard, "Lenin and Economic Evolution," pp. 22-24.
9. See, Ellen Schrecker, *No Ivory Tower: McCarthyism and the Universities* (New York: Oxford University Press, 1986), for political background on the period.
10. Nevins, *The Gateway to History*, p. 43.
11. Donovan, *Historical Thought in America*, esp. Chap. 4, passim. For example, Roy F. Nichols, "Postwar Reorientation of Historical Thinking," *American His-*

torical Review 54 (October 1948): 78-89; Chester M. Destler, "Some Observations on Contemporary Historical Thinking," *American Historical Review* 55 (April 1950): 503-29; Lewis White Beck, "The Limits of Skepticism in History," *South Atlantic Quarterly* 49 (October 1950): 461-68.

12. Goldman, "A Historian at Seventy," p. 697.
13. Gunnell, "American Political Science, Liberalism, and the Invention of Political Theory," in Farr and Seidelman, eds., *Discipline and History*, p. 186; Breisach, *American Progressive History*, pp. 165-66.
14. Higham, ed., *The Reconstruction of American History*, esp. Chap. 1 and Chap. 9.
15. Strout, *The Pragmatic Revolt in American History*, p. 10.
16. Skotheim, *American Intellectual Histories and Historians*, p. ix. Commager, *The American Mind*, cautions that his interpretation owed "much to the officials of the Office of War Information and the United States Army who at one time and another sent me abroad" (p. ix).
17. Bloom, *The Closing of the American Mind*, pp. 147-48. Bloom's charge dates back to the Cold War. See, for instance, Hanley, "Christian History for America," p. 326, a Catholic theologian who complains that the great misfortune in Beard's writing is that his "philosophy of history has taken an historical starting point outside Christianity."
18. William C. Pool, "An Economic Interpretation of the Ratification of the Federal Constitution in North Carolina, Part 1," *North Carolina Historical Review* 27 (April 1950): 119-41; William C. Pool, "An Economic Interpretation of the Ratification of the Federal Constitution in North Carolina, Part 2," *North Carolina Historical Review* 27 (July 1950): 289-313; Robert E. Thomas, "The Virginia Convention of 1788: A Criticism of Beard's *An Economic Interpretation of the Constitution*," *Journal of Southern History* 19 (February 1953): 63-72; Brown, *Middle-Class Democracy and the Revolution in Massachusetts*; Brown, *Charles Beard and the Constitution*; McDonald, *We the People: The Economic Origins of the Constitution* (Chicago: University of Chicago Press, 1958).
19. Brown, *Reinterpretation of the Formation of the American Constitution*, p. 2.
20. Eidelberg, *The Philosophy of the American Constitution*.
21. Brown, *Middle-Class Democracy and the Revolution in Massachusetts*; Cf. Martin Diamond, "Democracy and *The Federalist*: A Reconsideration of the Framers' Intent," *American Political Science Review* 52 (1959): 52-68.
22. McDonald, *We the People*.
23. Adair, "The Tenth Federalist Revisited," pp. 48-67.
24. Hofstadter, *The Progressive Historians*, pp. 218-224.
25. Main, "Charles A. Beard and the Constitution," p. 86. Cf. Benson, *Turner and Beard*, who concludes that it is premature to jettison Beard's economic interpretation of the Constitution.
26. Forrest McDonald, "Forrest McDonald's Rebuttal," *William and Mary Quarterly* 17 (January 1960), p. 102.
27. Louis Hartz, *The Liberal Tradition in America* (New York: Harcourt, Brace, and World, 1955), pp. 28, 23.
28. Theda Skocpol, "A Reply [to G. William Domhoff]," *Politics and Society* 15, 3 (1986/87): 331.
29. Henry Steele Commager, "Panel Discussion," in Swanson, ed., *Charles A. Beard*, p. 118.
30. David Easton, *The Political System* (New York: Alfred A. Knopf, 1953); Dahl, *A Preface to Democratic Theory* (Chicago: University of Chicago Press, 1956); Eulau, *The Behavioral Persuasion in Politics*.

31. Robert K. Merton, *Social Theory and Social Structure* (Glencoe, IL: Free Press, 1957), pp. 5-10.

32. Charles Merriam tried to draw Beard into the "scientific movement" in political science by inviting him to participate more actively in the disciplinary association, but Beard rebuffed these overtures. See Ross, *Origins of American Social Science*, p. 460.

33. Beard, *A Charter for the Social Sciences in the Schools*; Beard, *The Nature of the Social Sciences*; Beard, *The Discussion of Human Affairs*.

34. Richard Ashcraft, "One Step Backward, Two Steps Forward: Reflections Upon Contemporary Political Theory," in John S. Nelson, ed., *What Should Political Theory Be Now?* (Albany, NY: SUNY Press, 1983), pp. 515-48; John G. Gunnell, *Between Philosophy and Politics: The Alienation of Political Theory* (Amherst: University of Massachusetts Press, 1986); Gunnell, *The Decline of Political Theory*, Chap. 11.

35. Harold Laski, "Review of Charles A. Beard and George E. Smith, *The Idea of National Interest*," *The Nation* (April 25, 1934): 479.

36. Lerner, "Charles Beard's Stormy Voyage," pp. 20-23; Lerner, "Charles Beard's Political Theory," in Beale, ed., *Charles A. Beard*, p. 45.

37. Bernard Wishy, "A New Appraisal of Charles Beard," *The New Leader* (March 23, 1959): 20-22.

38. Borning, *Political and Social Thought of Charles A. Beard*, p. 182.

39. Diggins, "Power and Authority in American History," pp. 724, 730. Diggins rests this claim on the premise that "Beard's mistake...was to translate conflicts that inhered in political principles into conflicts that supposedly divided social classes" (p. 703).

40. Fred Matthews, "The Attack on 'Historicism': Allan Bloom's Indictment of Contemporary American Historical Scholarship," *American Historical Review* 95 (April 1990): 437. Likewise, Ross, *Origins of American Social Science*, p. 460, asserts that Beard envisaged "a utopian transformation, in which moral ends would finally supersede economic ones."

41. Leo Strauss, "Political Philosophy and History," in Leo Strauss, *What is Political Philosophy? and Other Studies* (Glencoe, IL: Free Press, 1959), pp. 56-77, draws a sharp distinction between the disciplines of history and political philosophy, but the idea that political philosophy is concerned with reasoning about concepts in a timeless present remains the dominant approach in political theory even among academic practitioners who otherwise reject Straussianism. For a methodological critique of this approach, see Ashcraft, "On the Problem of Methodology and the Nature of Political Theory"; Ashcraft, "Political Theory and the Problem of Ideology."

42. Beard, "Introduction to the 1935 Edition," *Economic Interpretation of the Constitution*, p. viii.

43. Ibid., p. xii.

44. Genovese, "Beard's Economic Interpretation of History," p. 26.

45. Cf. Robert A. Dahl, *A Preface to Economic Democracy* (Berkeley and Los Angeles: University of California Press, 1985), esp. Chaps 1-2; Samuel Bowles and Herbert Gintis, *Democracy and Capitalism: Property, Community, and the Contradictions of Modern Social Thought* (New York: Basic Books, 1987); Claus Offe, *Contradictions of the Welfare State* (Boston: MIT Press, 1984), esp. Chaps. 5-6; Robert Lekachman, "Capitalism or Democracy," in Goldwin and Schambra, eds., *How Capitalistic is the Constitution?* pp. 127-47.

46. Gordon S. Wood, *The Creation of the American Republic, 1776-1787* (Chapel Hill: University of North Carolina Press, 1969), p. 626, my italics, C.W.B.

47. McDonald, "Charles A. Beard," in Cunliffe and Winks, ed., *Pastmasters*, p. 119; Forrest McDonald, "A New Introduction (1986)," in Charles A. Beard, *An Economic Interpretation of the Constitution of the United States* (New York: Free Press, 1986), pp. xxxiii-xxxiv.

48. McDonald, "A New Introduction (1986)," in Beard, *An Economic Interpretation of the Constitution*, p. xii.

49. Beard, "Introduction to the 1935 Edition," *Economic Interpretation of the Constitution*, pp., xii, xvi, x.

50. McDonald, "A New Introduction (1986)," in Beard, *An Economic Interpretation of the Constitution*, p. xxxii-xxxiv.

51. Nore, *Charles A. Beard*, p. 121.

52. MacMahon, "Charles Beard, the Teacher," in Beale, ed., *Charles A. Beard*, p. 217.

53. Berg, *Historical Thinking of Charles A. Beard*, p. 14.

54. Sorenson, "Charles A. Beard and German Historiographical Thought," p. 277, fn. 9.

55. Ibid., pp. 280-84.

56. James T. Kloppenberg, *Uncertain Victory: Social Democracy and Progressivism in European and American Thought, 1870-1920* (New York: Oxford University Press, 1986).

57. Seidelman, *Disenchanted Realists*, pp. vii-xvi, Chaps. 1, 3.

58. The theme of declension and renewal is a paradigmatic element of republican political thought. See J. G. A. Pocock, *The Machiavellian Moment: Florentine Political Thought and the Atlantic Republican Tradition* (Princeton, NJ: Princeton University Press, 1975). The idea of political cycles has been advanced more recently by Arthur Schlesinger, Jr., *The Cycles of American History* (Boston: Houghton-Mifflin, 1986).

59. Noble, *The Progressive Mind*, pp. 30-31, concurs that Beard "did not define a golden age of American democracy during the age of Jackson as had Turner....He did not have to describe the nineteenth century as a decline from the state of nature established by the Founding Fathers into a state of decadence....Beard was rewriting American history, so that the national identity as a democracy of free and equal producers lay in the future and not in the past."

60. Beard and Beard, *The Rise of American Civilization*, Vol. 2, p. 544.

61. Beard and Beard, *America in Mid-Passage*, pp. 531-33, praised the CIO as "more than a mere bargainer over hours and wages" that possesses a "broader view of politics, economics, and culture" than the AFL.

62. Lenin quoted in Beard, "Lenin and Economic Evolution," pp. 23-24.

63. In 1932, Roosevelt delivered several highly publicized speeches calling for the expansion of national planning and for other collectivist policies: most notably, the Jefferson Day speech (April 1932); a speech at Oglethorpe, Georgia (May, 1932); and the Commonwealth Club speech (September, 1932). See Graham, Jr., "The Planning Ideal," pp. 258-62.

64. Beard and Smith, *The Future Comes*, p. 162.

65. Beard, *The Open Door at Home*, p. 36. Elsewhere, Beard, "Roosevelt's Place in History," p. 83, reiterates that Roosevelt "does not appear to have any 'system' of thought for himself."

66. Nore, *Charles A. Beard*, p. 144.

67. Kennedy, *Charles A. Beard and American Foreign Policy*, pp. 73-74. Thus, Cohen, "Revisionism Between World Wars," p. 153, also notes that "Beard had high hopes for Franklin Delano Roosevelt as a man who would use the presidency to foster the national interest as Beard himself conceived it."

68. Beard, "Roosevelt's Place in History," p. 84. As the economy again turned dramatically downward in 1937, Beard predicted that whole sectors of the economy would have to be socialized and that democratic processes would be employed in the course of these socializations. The determinism of economic circumstances would force Roosevelt to socialize from necessity, rather than from inclination or vision. See Charles A. Beard, "Future of Democracy in the United States," *Political Science Quarterly* 8 (October 1937): 495-506. Similarly, in earlier Congressional testimony, Beard predicted that "public ownership may be forced upon the country," John F. Sinclair, "Power Issue Looms Large," *Los Angeles Times*, March 13, 1931, p. 15.
69. Beard, "Myth of Rugged American Individualism," p. 22; Beard, "The Contest Between Urban and Rural Economy," p. 73.
70. Cf. Seymour Melman, *The Permanent War Economy* (New York: Simon and Schuster, 1974)

Bibliography

Abernathy, Thomas P. *Western Lands and the American Revolution.* New York: D. Appleton-Century Co., 1937.

Adair, Douglass. "The Tenth Federalist Revisited." *William and Mary Quarterly* 8 (January 1951): 48-67.

Adams, Brooks. *The Law of Civilization and Decay.* New York: Macmillan and Co., 1896.

Adams, Willi Paul. 1980. *The First American Constitutions: Republican Ideology and the Making of the State Constitutions in the Revolutionary Era.* Chapel Hill: University of North Carolina Press.

Adler, Selig. "The War-Guilt Question and American Disillusionment." *Journal of Modern History* 23 (March 1951): 1-28.

Akin, William E. *Technocracy and the American Dream: The Technocrat Movement, 1900-1941.* Berkeley and Los Angeles: University of California Press, 1977.

Alchon, Guy. *The Invisible Hand of Planning: Capitalism, Social Science, and the State in the 1920s.* Princeton, NJ: Princeton University Press, 1985.

Ambler, Charles H. *Sectionalism in Virginia.* Chicago: University of Chicago Press, 1910.

Angell, Norman. *The Great Illusion: A Study of the Relation of Military Power in Nations to Their Economic and Social Advantage.* New York: G. P. Putnam's Sons, 1912, Third Revised and Enlarged Edition.

Ankersmit, F. R. *History and Tropology: The Rise and Fall of Metaphor.* Berkeley and Los Angeles: University of California Press, 1994.

Aptheker, Herbert. *Early Years of the American Republic.* New York: International Publishers, 1976.

Aristotle. *The Politics of Aristotle,* translated by Ernest Barker. Oxford: Oxford University Press, 1974.

Ashcraft, Richard. "On the Problem of Methodology and the Nature of Political Theory." *Political Theory* (February 1975): 5-25.

———. "Political Theory and the Problem of Ideology." *Journal of Politics* (August 1980): 687-705.

———. "One Step Backward, Two Steps Forward: Reflections Upon Contemporary Political Theory." In John S. Nelson, ed., *What Should Political Theory Be Now?* Albany, NY: SUNY Press, 1983, pp. 515-48.

———. *Revolutionary Politics and Locke's Two Treatises of Government.* Princeton, NJ: Princeton University Press, 1986.

———. "The Changing Foundations of Political Theory." In *Political Power and Social Theory,* Vol. 6. Greenwich, CT: JAI Press, 1987, 27-56.

———. "German Historicism and the History of Political Theory." *History of Political Thought* 8 (Summer 1987): 289-324.

Baldwin, Simeon E. *Modern Political Institutions*. Boston: Little, Brown, and Co., 1898.

Baltzell, E. Digby. "Religion and the Class Structure." In Seymour Martin Lipset and Richard Hofstadter, eds., *Sociology and History: Methods*. New York: Basic Books, 1968, 311-57.

Bancroft, George. *History of the Formation of the Constitution of the United States*, 2 Vols. New York: D. Appleton and Co., 1882.

Baran, Paul A., and Paul M. Sweezy. *Monopoly Capital*. New York: Monthly Review Press, 1966.

Barber, William J. "The Divergent Fates of Two Strands of 'Institutionalist' Doctrine During the New Deal Years." *History of Political Economy* 26:4 (1994): 569-87.

Barnes, Harry Elmer. *A History of Historical Writing*, 2nd Edition Revised. New York: Dover Publications, Inc., 1963.

——. *The New History and the Social Studies*. New York: The Revisionist Press, 1972.

Barrow, Clyde W. "Styles of Intellectualism in Weber's Historical Sociology." *Sociological Inquiry* 60 (February 1990): 47-61.

——. "Pedagogy, Politics, and Social Reform: The Philosophy of the Workers' Education Movement." *Strategies: A Journal of Theory, Culture, and Politics* 2 (Fall 1989): 45-66.

——. "Counter-Movement Within the Labor Movement: Workers' Education and the American Federation of Labor, 1900-1937." *Social Science Journal* 27 (October 1990): 395-417.

——. *Universities and the Capitalist State: Corporate Liberalism and the Reconstruction of American Higher Education, 1894-1928*. Madison: University of Wisconsin Press, 1990.

——. *Critical Theories of the State: Marxist, Neo-Marxist, Post-Marxist*. Madison: University of Wisconsin Press, 1993.

Beale, Howard K. "Beard's Historical Writings." In Howard K. Beale, ed., *Charles A. Beard: An Appraisal*. Lexington: University of Kentucky Press, 1954, pp. 255-312.

——. "Charles Beard: Historian," Howard K. Beale, ed., *Charles A. Beard: An Appraisal*. Lexington: University of Kentucky Press, 1954, pp. 115-59.

Beard, Charles A. *The Industrial Revolution*. New York: Greenwood Press, 1969. Reprint of 1902, 2nd Edition.

——. *The Office of the Justice of the Peace in England in Its Origins and Development*. Ph.D. Dissertation, Columbia University, 1904.

——. "A Socialist History of France." *Political Science Quarterly* 21, 1 (March 1906): 111-20.

——. *An Introduction to the English Historians*. New York: Macmillan Co., 1906.

——. "Review of *The Spirit of American Government* by J. Allen Smith." *Political Science Quarterly* (March 1908): 136-37.

——. "Review of *The American Constitution* by Frederic J. Stimson." *Political Science Quarterly* (June 1908): 340-43.

——. "The Constitution of Oklahoma." *Political Science Quarterly* (March 1909): 95-114.

——. *American Government and Politics*, 1st Edition. New York: Macmillan, 1910.

——. "Review of *The Constitution of the United States* by David K. Watson." *Political Science Quarterly* (September 1911): 549-51.

——. "Review of *The Records of the Federal Convention of 1787* by Max Farrand." *Political Science Quarterly* (September 1911): 551-53.

——. "The Supreme Court-Usurper of Grantee?" *Political Science Quarterly* 27 (March 1912): 1-35.

——. *American City Government*. New York: The Century Co., 1912.

——. *Politics: A Lecture Delivered at Columbia University in the Series on Science, Philosophy, and Art*, February 12, 1908. New York: Columbia University Press, 1912.

——. *The Supreme Court and the Constitution*. New York: Macmillan, 1912.

——. *An Economic Interpretation of the Constitution of the United States*. New York: Free Press, 1913.

——. "Review of *The New Freedom: A Call for the Emancipation of the Generous Energies of a People*, by Woodrow Wilson." *Political Science Quarterly* 29 (September 1914): 506-507.

——. "Jefferson and the New Freedom." *New Republic* 1 (November 14, 1914): 18-19.

——. *Contemporary American History, 1877-1913*. New York: Macmillan Co., 1914.

——. "Review of *Property and Contract in their Relation to the Distribution of Wealth* by Robert T. Ely." *Political Science Quarterly* (September 1915): 510-11

——. "Methods of Training for Public Service." *School and Society* 2 (December 25, 1915): 904-11.

——. *Economic Origins of Jeffersonian Democracy*. New York: Macmillan Co., 1915.

——. "Review of *Political Parties: A Sociological Study of the Oligarchical Tendencies of Modern Democracy* by Robert Michels." *Political Science Quarterly* (March 1917): 153-55.

——. "The Perils of Diplomacy." *New Republic* (June 2, 1917): 136-38.

——. "German Annexations and Indemnities." *New Republic* (July 14, 1917): 309-10.

——. "Political Science in the Crucible," *New Republic* 13 (November 17, 1917): 3-4.

——. "A Call Upon Every Citizen." *Harper's Magazine* 137 (October 19, 1918): 655-56.

——. "Review of *Popular Government* by William A. Taft." *Political Science Quarterly* (December 1918): 594-96.

——. "Review of *Political Thought in England from Locke to Bentham*, by Harold J. Laski." *New Republic* 24 (November 17, 1920): 303-04.

——. "A Constitution Before the Fact." *The Nation* 111 (December 8, 1920): 664-66.

——. "National Guilds." *New Republic* 25 (December 8, 1920): 50-51.

——. "The Frontier in American History," *New Republic* (February 16, 1921): 349-50.

——. "The Potency of Labor Education." *American Federationist* (July 1922): 500-502.

——. "The Economic Basis of Politics." *New Republic* 32 (September 27, 1922): 128-29.

——. *Cross Currents in Europe Today*. Boston: Marshall Jones Co., 1922.

——. "Foreword." In Rene Brunet, *The New German Constitution*. New York: Alfred A. Knopf, 1928, pp.v-ix.

——. *The American Party Battle*. New York: Macmillan Co., 1928.

——. "Prospects for Peace," *Harper's Magazine* 158 (January 1929): 320-29.

——. "Review of *Making the Fascist State* by Herbert W. Schneider." *New Republic* (January 23, 1929): 277-78.

——. "The Contest Between Rural and Urban Economy." *Bulletin of the University of Georgia: Institute of Public Affairs and International Relations* 30, 2, Serial No. 466 (November 1929): 70-78.

——. "Forces Making for Peace." *Bulletin of the University of Georgia: Institute of Public Affairs and International Relations* 30, 2, Serial No. 466 (November 1929): 82-84.

————. "Introduction." In Charles A. Beard, ed., *Toward Civilization*. London: Longman, Green, and Co., 1930, pp. 1-20.

————. "Summary—Planning of Civilization." In Charles A. Beard, ed., *Toward Civilization*. London: Longman, Green, and Co., 1930, pp. 297-307.

————. *American Government and Politics*, 5th Edition. New York: Macmillan Co., 1930.

————. "A 'Five-Year Plan' for America." *Forum* 86 (July 1931): 1-11.

————. "A Historian's Quest for Light." *Proceedings of the Association of History Teachers of the Middle States and Maryland 29 (1931): 12-21.*

————. "Address of Dr. Charles Beard." *Proceedings of a Conference of Progressives: To Outline a Program of Constructive Legislation Dealing with Economic and Political Conditions for Presentation to the First Session of the Seventy-Second Congress.* Washington, DC, March 11-12, 1931, pp. 70-73.

————. "The Myth of Rugged American Individualism." *Harper's Monthly Magazine* (December 1931): 13-22.

————. "Einstein Advocates Economic Boycott," *The New York Times*, February 28, 1932, p. 2.

————. "A 'Five-Year Plan' for America." In Charles A. Beard, ed. *America Faces the Future*. Boston: Houghton Mifflin Co., 1932, pp. 117-40.

————. "The Rationality of Planned Economy." In Charles A. Beard, ed., *America Faces the Future*. Boston: Houghton Mifflin, 1932, pp. 400-10.

————. *A Charter for the Social Sciences in the Schools*. New York: Charles Scribner's Sons, 1932.

————. "Lenin and Economic Evolution." *New Republic* 75 (May 17, 1933): 22-24.

————. "Introduction." In Graham A. Laing, *Towards Technocracy*. Los Angeles: The Angelus Press, 1933, pp. 5-8.

————. "Author's Preface to New Edition." In Charles A. Beard, *The Economic Basis of Politics*. London: George Allen & Unwin, 1935.

————. "Neutrality: Shall We Have Revision?" *Congressional Record*, 76th Congress, 1st Session, Vol. 84, pt. 11 (1940): 259-60.

————. "Written History as an Act of Faith." *American Historical Review* 39 (January 1934): 219-31.

————. "The World As I Want It." *Forum and Century* 91 (June 1934): 333-34.

————. "Property and Democracy." *The Social Frontier: A Journal of Educational Criticism and Reconstruction* 1 (October 1934): 13-15.

————. "The Blessed Profit System." *New Republic* (December 26), 1934): 188-190.

————. *The Nature of the Social Sciences in Relation to Objectives of Instruction*. New York: Charles Scribner's Sons, 1934.

————. *The Open Door at Home: A Trial Philosophy of National Interest*. New York: Macmillan Co., 1934.

————. "National Politics and War." *Scribner's Magazine* 97 (February 1935): 65-70.

————. "That Promise of American Life." *New Republic* (February 6, 1935): 350-52.

————. "Social Change v. the Constitution." *Current History* 42 (July 1935): 345-52.

————. "That Noble Dream." *American Historical Review* 41 (October 1935): 74-87.

————. "Jefferson in America Now." *Yale Review* (December 1935): 241-57.

————. "Industry's Attack on the New Deal." *Current History and Modern Culture* 43 (February 1936): 399-406.

————. "Minority Rule in America." *American Mercury* 37 (February 1936): 190-96.

————. *The Discussion of Human Affairs*. New York: Macmillan Co., 1936.

————. *Jefferson, Corporations, and the Constitution*. Washington, DC: National Home Library Foundation, 1936.

——. "Going Ahead With Roosevelt." *Events* 1 (January 1937): 9-12.

——. "The Rise of the Democratic Idea in the United States." *Survey Graphic* (April 1937): 201-203.

——. "Democracy and Education." *Social Research* 4 (September 1937): 391-98.

——. "Future of Democracy in the United States." *Political Science Quarterly* 8 (October 1937): 495-506.

——. "Roosevelt's Place in History." *Events* 3 (February 1938): 81-86.

——. "The Anti-Trust Racket." *New Republic* (September 21, 1938): 182-84.

——. "Monopoly in Fact and Fiction." *Events* 4 (November 1938): 383-87.

——. "By Charles A. Beard." *The Christian Science Monitor*, July 22, 1939, p. 5.

——. *Giddy Minds and Foreign Quarrels*. New York: Macmillan, 1939.

——. "Crisis in the Pacific: I — War With Japan?." *Events* 8 (November 1940): 321-23.

——. "Freedom in Political Thought." In Ruth Nanda Anshen, ed. *Freedom: Its Meaning*. New York: Harcourt, Brace and Co., 1940, pp. 288-304.

——. *A Foreign Policy for America*. New York: Macmillan, 1940.

——. *Public Policy and the General Welfare*. New York: Farrar and Rinehart, 1941.

——. "Grounds for a Reconsideration of Historiography." In Merle Curti, ed., *Theory and Practice in Historical Study: A Report of the Committee on Historiography*. New York: Social Science Research Council, 1946, pp. 1-14.

——. *American Foreign Policy in the Making, 1932-1940: A Study in Responsibilities*. New Haven, CT: Yale University Press, 1946.

——. *President Roosevelt and the Coming of the War, 1941: A Study in Appearances and Reality*. New Haven, CT: Yale University Press, 1948.

——. *The Enduring Federalist*. Garden City, NY: Doubleday and Co., Inc., 1948.

——. *The Economic Basis of Politics*. New York: Vintage Books, 1958.

Beard, Charles A., and Mary R. Beard. *American Citizenship*. New York: Macmillan Co., 1914.

——. *The Rise of American Civilization*, 2 Vols. New York: Macmillan, 1927.

——. *America in Mid-Passage*. New York: Macmillan, 1939.

——. *The American Spirit: A Study of the Idea of Civilization in the United States*. New York: Macmillan, 1942.

Beard, Charles A., and George H. Smith. *The Future Comes: A Study of the New Deal*. New York: Macmillan Co., 1933.

Beard, Charles A., and Alfred Vagts. "Currents of Thought in Historiography." *American Historical Review* 42 (April 1937): 460-83.

Beard, Mary Ritter. *The Making of Charles A. Beard*. New York: Exposition Press, 1955.

Beck, Lewis White. "The Limits of Skepticism in History." *South Atlantic Quarterly* 49 (October 1950): 461-68.

Beers, Forrest W. "A New Labor College." *American Federationist* (January 1901): 14.

Bellot, H. Hale. 1952. *American History and American Historians: A Review of Recent Contributions to the Interpretation of the History of the United States*. London: Athlone Press.

Bensel, Richard. *Yankee Leviathan: The Origins of Central State Authority in America, 1859- 1877*. Cambridge: Cambridge University Press, 1990.

Benson, Allan L. *Our Dishonest Constitution* New York: B. W. Huebsch, 1914.

Benson, Lee. "Achille Loria's Influence on American Economic Thought: Including His Contributions to the Frontier Hypothesis." *Agricultural History* 24 (October 1950): 182-99.

——. *Turner and Beard: American Historical Writing Reconsidered*. Glencoe, IL: Free Press, 1960.

Berg, Elias. *The Historical Thinking of Charles A. Beard.* Stockholm: Almqvist & Wiksell, 1957.

Bernstein, Eduard. *Evolutionary Socialism.* New York: Schocken Books, 1961.

Bernstein, Richard J. *Beyond Objectivism and Relativism.* Philadelphia: University of Pennsylvania Press, 1983.

Bimba, Anton. *History of the American Working Class.* New York: International Publishers, 1936.

Blau, Joseph L., ed. *Social Theories of Jacksonian Democracy.* New York: Liberal Arts Press, Inc., 1954.

Blinkoff, Maurice. *The Influence of Charles A. Beard Upon American Historiography.* Buffalo, NY: University of Buffalo Monographs in History, Vol. 12, 1936.

Block, Fred. "The Ruling Class Does Not Rule: Notes on the Marxist Theory of the State." *Socialist Revolution* 7 (May-June 1977): 6-28.

Bloom, Allan. *The Closing of the American Mind.* New York: Simon and Schuster, 1987.

Bloom, Allan, ed. *Confronting the Constitution.* Washington, DC: The AEI Press, 1990.

Borning, Bernard. *The Political and Social Thought of Charles A. Beard.* Seattle: University of Washington Press, 1962.

Boudin, Louis B. "Government by Judiciary." *Political Science Quarterly* (June 1911): 238-70.

——. *Government by Judiciary,* 2 Volumes. New York: William Goodwin, Inc., 1932.

Bourgin, Frank. The Great Challenge: The Myth of Laissez-Faire in the Early Republic. New York: George Braziller, 1989.

Bowen, Catherine Drinker. *Miracle at Philadelphia: The Story of the Constitutional Convention May to September 1787.* Boston: Little, Brown, and Co., 1966.

Bowers, Claude G. *Beveridge and the Progressive Era.* Cambridge, MA: Houghton-Mifflin Co., 1932.

Bowles, Samuel, and Herbert Gintis. *Democracy and Capitalism: Property, Community, and the Contradictions of Modern Social Thought.* New York: Basic Books, 1987.

Braeman, John. *Albert J. Beveridge: American Nationalist.* Chicago: University of Chicago Press, 1971.

Breisach, Ernest A. *American Progressive History: An Experiment in Modernization.* Chicago: University of Chicago Press, 1993.

Bright, John, and James E. Thorold Rogers, eds. *Speeches on Questions of Public Policy by Richard Cobden.* London: Macmillan, 1880.

Browder, Earl, and Charles A. Beard. "Collective Security—A Debate." *New Republic* 93 (February 2, 1938): 356-59.

Browder, Earl. "Concerning American Revolutionary Traditions." *The Communist* 17 (December 1938): 1079-85.

Brown, Robert E. *Middle-Class Democracy and the Revolution in Massachusetts, 1691-1780.* Ithaca, NY: Cornell University Press, 1955.

——. *Charles Beard and the Constitution.* Princeton, NJ: Princeton University Press, 1957.

——. *Reinterpretation of the Formation of the American Constitution.* Boston: Northeastern University Press, 1963.

Brunet, Rene. *The New German Constitution.* New York: Alfred A. Knopf, 1928.

Bryce, James. *The American Commonwealth,* 2 Vols. London: Macmillan Co., 1888.

Budish, Jacob M. *The New Unionism in the Clothing Industry.* New York: Harcourt Brace, 1920.

Burgess, John W. *Political Science and Comparative Constitutional Law*, 2 Vols. Boston: Ginn and Co., 1902.

Calhoun, Arthur W. *The Worker Looks at Government*. Katonah, NY: Brookwood Labor College, 1927.

Campbell, John L., and Leon Lindberg. "Property Rights and the Organization of Economic Activity by the State." *American Sociological Review* 55 (October 1990): 634-47.

Chasse, John Dennis. "John R. Commons and the Democratic State." In Marc R. Tool and Warren J. Samuels, ed., *State, Society, and Corporate Power*, 2nd Edition, Completely Revised. New Brunswick, NJ: Transaction Publishers, 1989, pp. 131-56.

Clark, Walter. "Some Defects in the Constitution of the United States." *Congressional Record* (July 31, 1911): 3374-77.

"Classes Open at Workers' School." *Daily Worker* (October 16, 1928): 2:2.

Clawson, Marion. *New Deal Planning: The National Resources Planning Board*. Baltimore, MD: Johns Hopkins University Press, 1981.

Coase, R. H. "The Nature of the Firm." *Economica* 4 (1937): 386-405.

——. "The Problem of Social Cost." *Journal of Law and Economics* 3 (1960): 1-44.

Cochran, Thomas C. "Review of *The Open Door at Home* by Charles A. Beard." *The ModernMonthly* 8 (February 1935): 759-60.

Cohen, Benjamin. *The Question of Imperialism*. New York: Basic Books, 1973.

Cohen, Warren Ira. *Revisionism Between World Wars: A Study in American Diplomatic History*. Ph.D. Dissertation, University of Washington, 1962.

Cole, Wayne S. *Roosevelt and the Isolationists, 1932-1945*. Lincoln: University of Nebraska Press, 1983.

Colwell, James L. "The Populist Image of Vernon Louis Parrington." *Mississippi Valley Historical Review* (June 1962): 52-66.

Commager, Henry Steele. *The American Mind: An Interpretation of American Thought and Character Since the 1880's*. New Haven, CT: Yale University Press, 1950.

——. "Panel Discussion." In Marvin C. Swanson. *Charles A. Beard: An Observance of the Centennial of His Birth*. Greencastle, IN: DePauw University, 1974, pp. 101-20.

Commons, John R. *The Distribution of Wealth*. New York: Macmillan, 1893.

——. *Proportional Representation*. New York: T. Y. Crowell, 1896.

——. *The Legal Foundations of Capitalism*. New York: Macmillan, 1924.

——. *Institutional Economics: Its Place in Political Economy*. New York: Macmillan Co., 1934.

——. *A Sociological View of Sovereignty*. New York: Augustus M. Kelley, 1965.

Conkin, Paul K. "Intellectual History." In William H. Cartwright and Richard L. Watson, Jr., eds., *The Reinterpretation of American History and Culture*. Washington, DC: National Council for the Social Studies, 1973, pp. 227-46.

Cooley, T. M. *Constitutional History of the United States*. New York: G. P. Putnam's Sons, 1889.

Corwin, E. S. "Review of *Economic Interpretation of the Constitution* of the United States, by Charles A. Beard." *History Teachers' Magazine* 5 (February 1914): 65-66.

Cott, Nancy F. "Two Beards: Coauthorship and the Concept of Civilization." *American Quarterly* 42, 2 (June 1990): 274-300.

Cowley, Malcolm, and Bernard Smith, eds. *Books That Changed Our Minds*. New York: Doubleday, Doran, and Co., 1940.

Counts, George S. "Charles Beard, The Public Man." In Howard K. Beale, ed., *Charles A. Beard: An Appraisal*. Lexington: University of Kentucky Press, 1954, pp. 231-53.

Critchlow, Donald T. "Is Political History Dead?" *Clio: Newsletter of Politics and History* 5 (Spring/Summer 1995): 2-3.

Croce, Benedetto. *Aesthetic as Science of Expression and Pure Linguistic.* London: Macmillan and Co., Ltd., 1909.

——. *Philosophy of the Practical: Economic and Ethic.* London: Macmillan and Co., Ltd., 1913.

——. *What is Living and What is Dead of the Philosophy of Hegel.* London: Macmillan and Co., Ltd., 1915.

——. *Logic as the Science of the Pure Concept.* London: Macmillan and Co., Ltd., 1917.

——. *The Theory and History of Historiography.* London: G. C. Harrap, 1921.

——. *History: Its Theory and Practice.* New York: Harcourt, Brace, and Co., 1921.

——. *Historical Materialism and the Economics of Karl Marx.* New Brunswick, NJ: Transaction Books, 1981.

Croly, Herbert. *Progressive Democracy.* New York: Macmillan Co., 1915.

——. *The Promise of American Life.* Boston: Northeastern University Press, 1989. Reprint of 1909 Edition.

Cunliffe, Marcus, and Robin W. Winks., eds. *Pastmasters: Some Essays on American Historians.* New York: Harper and Row Publishers, 1960.

Curti, Merle. "A Great Teacher's Teacher." *Social Education* 31 (October 1949): 263-66.

——. *The Growth of American Thought*, 3rd Edition. New York: Harper and Row, 1964.

Curtis, George Ticknor. *History of the Origin, Formation & Adoption of the Constitution of the United States, With Notices of Its Principal Framers*, 2 Vols. New York: Harper & Bros., 1854-1858.

——. *Constitutional History of the United States from the Declaration of Independence to the Close of the Civil War*, 2 Volumes. New York: Harper and Brothers, 1889-1896.

Dahl, Robert A. *A Preface to Democratric Theory.* Chicago: University of Chicago Press, 1956.

——. *A Preface to Economic Democracy.* Berkeley and Los Angeles: University of California Press, 1985.

Dahlberg, Jane S. *The New York Bureau of Municipal Research: Pioneer in Government Administration.* New York: New York University Press, 1966.

De Alessi, L. "Development of the Property Rights Approach." In Eirik G. Furubotn and Rudolf Richter, eds., *The New Institutional Economics.* College Station: Texas A&M University Press, 1991, pp. 45-53.

Dean, Howard E. "J. Allen Smith: Jeffersonian Critic of the Federalist State." *American Political Science Review* (December 1956): 1093-1104.

Deininger, Whitaker T. "The Skepticism and Historical Faith of Charles A. Beard." *Journal of the History of Ideas* 15 (October 1954): 573-88.

Dennis, Lawrence J. *George S. Counts and Charles A. Beard: Collaborators for Change.* Albany, NY: SUNY Press, 1989.

Derrida, Jacques. *Of Grammatology.* Baltimore, MD: Johns Hopkins University Press, 1976.

——. *Writing and Difference.* London: Routledge and Kegan Paul, 1978.

Destler, Chester M. "Some Observations on Contemporary Historical Thinking." *American Historical Review* 55 (April 1950): 503-29.

Diamond, Martin. "Democracy and *The Federalist*: A Reconsideration of the Framers' Intent." *American Political Science Review* 52 (1959): 52-68.

Dickerson, Oliver Morton. *The Navigation Acts and the American Revolution*. Philadelphia: University of Pennsylvania Press, 1951.

Diggins, John P. *Mussolini and Fascism: The View From America*. Princeton, NJ: Princeton University Press, 1972.

——. "Power and Authority in American History: The Case of Charles A. Beard and His Critics." *American Historical Review* 86 (October 1981): 701-30.

Divine, Robert A. *The Illusion of Neutrality*. Chicago: University of Chicago Press, 1962.

Donahue, Charles, Jr. "The Future of the Concept of Property Predicted From Its Past." In J. Roland Pennock and John W. Chapman, eds. *Property: NOMOS XXII*. New York: New York University Press, 1980, pp. 28-68.

Donovan, Timothy Paul. *Historical Thought in America: Postwar Patterns*. Norman: University of Oklahoma Press, 1973.

Dorfman, Joseph. *Institutional Economics: Veblen, Commons, and Mitchell Reconsidered*. Berkeley: University of California Press, 1963.

——. *The Economic Mind in American Civilization*, 5 Vols. New York: Augustus M. Kelley, 1969.

Douglas, Elisha P. *Rebels and Democrats*. Chapel Hill: University of North Carolina Press, 1955.

Draper, Theodore. *American Communism and Soviet Russia*. New York: Viking Press, 1960.

Ducharme, Raymond A., Jr. *Charles A. Beard and the Social Studies*. New York: Teachers College Press, 1969.

Dupree, A. Hunter. *Science in the Federal Government: A History of Policies and Activities to 1940*. Cambridge, MA: Harvard University Press, 1957.

Dutt, R. Palme. *Socialism and the Living Wage*. London: Independent Labour Party, 1926.

——. *Fascism and Social Revolution*. Chicago: Proletarian Publishers, 1974. Reprint of the 1934, 2nd edition.

Earnest, Ernest. *The Single Vision: The Alienation of American Intellectuals, 1910-1930*. New York: New York University Press, 1970.

East, Robert A. *Business Enterprise in the American Revolutionary Era*. New York: Columbia University Press, 1938.

Easton, David. *The Political System*. New York: Alfred A. Knopf, 1953.

Edman, Irwin. *Philosopher's Holiday*. New York: Viking Press, 1937.

Eggertsson, Thrainn. "The Role of Transaction Costs and Property Rights in Economic Analysis." *European Economic Review* 34 (1990): 450-57.

Ehrenreich, Barbara, and John Ehrenreich. "The Professional Managerial Class." *Radical America* 11 (March-April 1977): 7-31.

Eidelberg, Paul. *The Philosophy of the American Constitution: A Reinterpretation of the Intentions of the Founding Fathers*. New York: Free Press, 1968.

——. *A Discourse on Statesmanship: The Design and Transformation of the American Polity*. Urbana: University of Illinois Press, 1974.

Ely, Richard T. *Property and Contract in Their Relations to the Distribution of Wealth*, 2 Vols. New York: Macmillan, 1914.

Ernst, Joseph A. *Money and Politics in America, 1755-1775; a study in the Currency Act of 1764 and the Political Economy of the Revolution*. Chapel Hill: University of North Carolina Press, 1973.

Ethington, Philip, and Eileen McDonagh. "The Eclectic Center of the New Institutionalism: Axes of Analysis in Comparative Perspective." *Social Science History* 19 (Winter 1995): 467-77.

Eulau, Heinz. *The Behavioral Persuasion in Politics*. New York: Random House, 1963.

Evans, Peter B., Dietrich Rueschemeyer, and Theda Skocpol. "On the Road Toward a More Adequate Understanding of the State." In Peter Evans, Dietrich Rueschemeyer, and Theda Skocpol, eds., *Bringing the State Back In* (Cambridge: Cambridge University Press, 1985), pp. 347-66.

Fain, H. *Between Philosophy and History*. Princeton, NJ: Princeton University Press, 1970.

Fay, Brian. *Social Theory and Political Practice*. Boston: George Allen and Unwin, 1975.

Ferguson, Elmer James. *The Power of the Purse: A History of American Public Finance, 1776-1790*. Chapel Hill: University of North Carolina Press, 1961.

Fisher, Sydney George. *True History of the American Revolution*. Philadelphia: J. B. Lippincott Co., 1902.

Fiske, John. *The Critical Period of American History, 1783-1789*. Boston: Houghton-Mifflin Co., 1893.

Fiss, Owen M. *Troubled Beginnings of the Modern State, 1888-1910*. New York: Macmillan Publishing Co., 1993.

Fitzsimons, Matthew A., Alfred G. Pundt, and Charles E. Nowell, eds. *The Development of Historiography*. Port Washington, NY: Kennikat Press, 1967.

Foner, Philip S. *Labor and the American Revolution*. Westport, CT: Greenwood Press, 1976.

Frankel, Harry. "Three Conceptions of Jacksonianism." In George Novack, ed., *America's Revolutionary Heritage: Marxist Essays*. New York: Pathfinder Press, 1976, pp. 170-80.

Frankfurter, Felix. "Hours of Labor and Realism in Constitutional Law." *Harvard Law Review* (February, 1916): 353-73.

Freeman, Joseph. *An American Testament: A Narrative of Rebels and Romantics*. New York: Octagon Books, 1973.

Frooman, Jack, and Edmund David Cronon. "Bibliography of Beard's Writings." In Howard K. Beale, ed., *Charles A. Beard: An Appraisal*. Lexington: University of Kentucky Press, 1954, pp. 265-86.

Furner, Mary O. *Advocacy and Objectivity: A Crisis in the Professionalization of American Social Science, 1865-1905*. Lexington: University of Kentucky Press, 1975.

——. "The Republican Tradition and the New Liberalism: Social Investigation, State Building, and Social Learning in the Gilded Age." In Michael J. Lacey and Mary O. Furner, eds., *The State and Social Investigation in Britain and the United States*. Cambridge: Woodrow Wilson Center Press and Cambridge University Press, 1993, pp. 171-241.

Furubotn, Eirik G., and Rudolf Richter. "The New Institutional Economics: An Assessment." In Eirik G. Furubotn and Rudolf Richter, eds., *The New Institutional Economics*. College Station: Texas A&M University Press, 1991, pp. 1-32.

Galbraith, John Kenneth. *The New Industrial State*. Boston: Houghton-Mifflin Co., 1978.

Genovese, Eugene. *In Red and Black: Marxian Explorations in Southern and Afro-American History*. New York: Pantheon Books, 1968.

——. "Beard's Economic Interpretation of History." In Marvin C. Swanson. *Charles A. Beard: An Observance of the Centennial of His Birth*. Greencastle, IN: DePauw University, 1974, pp. 25-44.

Gideonse, Harry. 1935. "Nationalist Collectivism and Charles A. Beard." *Journal of Political Economy* 43 (December): 778-99.

Gilbert, James B. *Designing the Industrial State: The Intellectual Pursuit of Collectivism in America, 1880-1940*. Chicago: Quadrangle Books, 1972.

Ginger, Ray. *The Age of Excess: The United States From 1877 to 1914.* New York: Macmillan Co., 1965.

Gleason, Arthur. *Workers' Education: American and Foreign Experiments.* New York: Bureau of Industrial Research, 1921.

Goldman, Eric F. *John Bach McMaster; American Historian.* Philadelphia: University of Pennsylvania Press, 1943.

———. "J. Allen Smith: The Reformer and his Dilemma." *Pacific Northwest Quarterly* (July 1944): 195-212.

———. "A Historian at Seventy." *New Republic* 111 (November 27, 1944): 696-97.

———. "The Origins of Beard's *Economic Interpretation of the Constitution.*" *Journal of the History of Ideas* 13 (April 1952): 234-49.

———. *Rendezvous With Destiny: A History of Modern American Reform.* New York: Alfred A. Knopf, 1952.

———. "Charles A. Beard: An Impression." In Howard K. Beale, ed., *Charles A. Beard: An Appraisal.* Lexington: University of Kentucky Press, 1954, pp. 1-8.

Gonce, R. A. "The New Property Rights Approach and Commons' Legal Foundations of Capitalism." *Journal of Economic Issues* 10 (December 1976): 765-97.

Goodnow, Frank J. *Municipal Home Rule.* New York: Macmillan Co., 1895.

———. *Politics and Administration: A Study in Government.* New York: Macmillan Co., 1900.

———. *Social Reform and the Constitution.* New York: Macmillan, 1911.

Goodrich, Carter. "The Climate for Planning: Review of *America Faces the Future,* edited by Charles A. Beard," *New Republic* (March 9, 1932): 105.

Goodwyn, Lawrence. "Organizing Democracy: The Limits of Theory and Practice." *Democracy* 1 (January 1981): 41-60.

Graham, Otis L., Jr. "The Planning Ideal and American Reality: The 1930s." In Stanley Elkins and Eric McKitrick, eds. *The Hofstadter Aegis: A Memorial.* New York: Alfred A. Knopf, 1974, pp. 257-99.

———. *Toward a Planned Society: From Roosevelt to Nixon.* Oxford: Oxford University Press, 1976.

Grey, Thomas C. "The Disintegration of Property." In J. Roland Pennock and John W. Chapman, eds. *Property: NOMOS XXII.* New York: New York University Press, 1980, pp. 69-85.

Gross, Bertram. *Friendly Fascism.* New York: M. Evans Publishers, 1980.

Gruber, Carol. *Mars and Minerva: World War I and the Uses of the Higher Learning in America.* Baton Rouge: Louisiana State University Press, 1975.

Guerin, Daniel. *Fascism and Big Business.* New York: Monad Press, 1973, 2nd American Edition.

Gulick, Luther. "Beard and Municipal Reform." In Howard K. Beale, ed., *Charles A. Beard: An Appraisal.* Lexington: University of Kentucky Press, 1954, pp. 47-60.

Gunnell, John G. "American Political Science, Liberalism, and the Invention of Political Theory." In James Farr and Raymond Seidelman, eds., *Discipline and History: Political Science in the United States.* Ann Arbor: University of Michigan Press, 1993, pp. 179-97.

———. *The Descent of Political Theory: The Genealogy of an American Vocation.* Chicago: University of Chicago Press, 1993.

———. *Between Philosophy and Politics: The Alienation of Political Theory.* Amherst: University of Massachusetts Press, 1986.

Haber, Samuel. *Efficiency and Uplift: Scientific Management in the Progressive Era, 1890-1920.* Chicago: University of Chicago Press, 1964.

Hacker, Louis M. *The Triumph of American Capitalism*. New York: Simon and Schuster, 1940.

Halperin, Morton. *The Lawless State*. New York: Penguin, 1976.

Hanley, Thomas O'Brien. "Christian History for America." *Catholic World* 178 (February 1954): 326-31.

Hansome, Marius. *World Workers' Educational Movements: Their Social Significance*. New York: Columbia University Press, 1931.

Harrington, Fred Harvey. "Beard's Idea of National Interest and New Interpretations." *American Perspective* 4 (1950): 335-45.

Hart, Albert Bushnell. *Formation of the Union, 1750-1829*. London: Longman, Green and Co., 1892.

Harter, Lafayette. *John R. Commons: His Revolt Against Laissez-Faire*. Corvallis: Oregon State University Press, 1962.

Hartz, Louis. *The Liberal Tradition in America*. New York: Harcourt, Brace, and World, 1955.

Haskell, Thomas. *The Emergence of Professional Social Science: The American Social Science Association and the Nineteenth-Century Crisis of Authority*. Urbana: University of Illinois Press, 1977.

Hawley, Ellis J. "Herbert Hoover, the Commerce Secretariat, and the Vision of an 'Associative State', 1921-1928," *Journal of American History* 61 (1974): 116-40.

Hegel, George W. F. *The Philosophy of History*, translated by J. Sibree. Buffalo, NY: Prometheus Books, 1991.

Hendricks, Luther. *James Harvey Robinson: Teacher of History*. New York: King's Crown Press, 1946.

Herbst, Jurgen. *The German Historical School in American Scholarship: A Study in the Transfer of Culture*. Port Washington, NY: Kennikat Press, 1972.

Herring, Hubert. "Charles A. Beard: Freelance Among the Historians." *Harper's Magazine* (May 1939): 641-52.

Hicks, Granville. "The Critical Principles of V. L. Parrington." *Science and Society* (Fall 1939): 443-60.

Hicks, John D. *The Federal Union: History of the United States to 1865*. Boston: Houghton-Mifflin Co., 1937.

Higham, John, ed. *The Reconstruction of American History*. London: Hutchinson and Co., Ltd., 1962.

Higham, John. *Writing American History: Essays on Modern Scholarship*. Bloomington: Indiana University Press, 1970.

Higham, John, Leonard Krieger, and Felix Gilbert. *History: The Development of Historical Studies in the United States*. Englewood Cliffs, NJ: Prentice-Hall, 1965.

Hilferding, Franz. *Finance Capital*. Boston: Routledge and Kegan Paul, 1981.

Hill, David Jayne. "A Defense of the Constitution." *North American Review* (March 1917): 389-97.

Himmelberg, Robert F. *The Origins of the National Recovery Administration: Business, Government, and the Trade Association Issue, 1921-1933*. New York: Fordham University Press, 1976.

Himmelfarb, Gertrude. *The New History and the Old: Critical Essays and Reappraisals*. Cambridge, MA: Harvard University Press, 1987.

Hockett, Homer Carey. *The Critical Method in Historical Research and Writing*. New York: Macmillan Co., 1955.

Hohfeld, Wesley. "Some Fundamental Legal Conceptions as Applied in Judicial Reasoning." *Yale Law Journal* 23 (1913): 16-59.

Hofstadter, Richard. "Parrington and the Jeffersonian Tradition." *Journal of the History of Ideas* (October 1941): 391-400.

——. "Charles Beard and the Constitution." In Howard K. Beale, ed., *Charles A. Beard: An Appraisal.* Lexington: University of Lexington Press, 1954, pp. 75-92.

——. *The Age of Reform: From Bryan to F.D.R.* New York: Alfred A. Knopf, 1955.

——. *Anti-Intellectualism in American Life.* New York: Vintage Books, 1962.

——. *The Progressive Historians: Turner, Beard, Parrington.* Chicago: University of Chicago Press, 1968.

Horne, Roger. "John R. Commons and the Progressive Context." *Midwest Quarterly* 32 (Spring 1991): 324-37.

Horowitz, David A. "Senator Borah's Crusade to Save Small Business From the New Deal." *The Historian* 55 (1993): 693-708.

Horowitz, Morton J. *The Transformation of American Law, 1790-1860.* Cambridge, MA: Harvard University Press, 1977.

Hoxie, R. Gordon. *A History of the Faculty of Political Science, Columbia University.* New York: Columbia University Press, 1955.

Hufbauer, Gary Clyde, and Jeffrey J. Schott. *Western Hemisphere Economic Integration.* Washington, DC: Institute for International Economics, 1993.

Iggers, G. G. *The German Conception of History.* Middletown, CT: Wesleyan University Press, 1984.

Jacobsen, Jacob Mark. *The Development of American Political Thought.* New York: The Century Co., 1932.

Jay, Martin. *The Dialectical Imagination: A History of the Frankfurt School and the Institute of Social Research, 1923-1950.* Boston: Little, Brown, and Co., 1973.

Jensen, Merrill. *The Articles of Confederation: An Interpretation of the Socio-ConstitutionalHistory of the American Revolution, 1774-1781.* Madison: University of Wisconsin Press, 1948.

——. *The Making of the American Constitution.* Princeton, NJ: D. Van Nostrand and Co., 1964.

——. *The New Nation: A History of the United States during the Confederation 1781-1789.* Boston: Northeastern University Press, 1981.

Johnson, Alvin. "A Born Politician." *New Republic* 130 (May 3, 1954): 20.

——. *Pioneer's Progress: An Autobiography.* New York: Viking Press, 1957.

Jonas, Manfred. *Isolationism in America, 1935-1941.* Ithaca, NY: Cornell University Press, 1966.

Josephson, Matthew. "Charles A. Beard: A Memoir." *Virginia Quarterly Review* 25 (1949): 585-602.

Kallen, Horace M. "In Remembrance of Charles Beard, Philosopher-Historian." *Social Research* 18 (June 1951): 243-49.

Katznelson, Ira. "The State to the Rescue? Political Science and History Reconnect." *Social Research* 59 (Winter 1992): 719-37.

Kennedy, Thomas C. *Charles A. Beard and American Foreign Policy.* Gainesville: University Presses of Florida, 1975.

Kenyon, Cecelia M. "Constitutionalism in Revolutionary America." In J. Roland Pennock and

John W. Chapman, eds. *Constitutionalism.* New York: New York University Press, 1979, pp. 84-121.

Kloppenberg, James T. *Uncertain Victory: Social Democracy and Progressivism in European and American Thought, 1870-1920.* New York: Oxford University Press, 1986.

Knight, Melvin M. "Introduction to the American Edition." In Henri See, *The Economic Interpretation of History.* New York: Augustus M. Kelley, 1968, pp. 9-42.

Kohn, Hans. "A Historian's Creed for Our Time." *South Atlantic Quarterly* 52 (July 1953): 341-48.

Krugman, Paul. "Competitiveness: Does it Matter?" *Fortune* 129 (March 7, 1994): 109-15.

———. "Europe Jobless, America Penniless?" *Foreign Affairs* 95 (Summer 1994): 19-34.

———. *Peddling Prosperity: Economic Sense in the Age of Diminished Expectations*. New York: W. W. Norton, 1994.

LaFeber, Walter. *The New Empire: An Interpretation of American Expansion, 1860-1898*. Ithaca, NY: Cornell University Press, 1987.

Laidler, Harry. *The Concentration of Control in American Industry*. New York: Thomas Y. Crowell Co., 1931.

Laing, Graham A. *Towards Technocracy*. Los Angeles: Angelus Press, 1933.

Land, Aubrey C. "Economic Base and Social Structure: The Northern Chesapeake in the Eighteenth Century." *Journal of Economic History* (December 1965): 639-54.

Landon, Judson S. *The Constitutional History and Government of the United States*. Boston: Houghton-Mifflin Co., 1889.

Laski, Harold. "Review of *The Idea of National Interest*, by Charles A. Beard and George E. Smith." *The Nation* (April 25, 1934): 479.

———. "Charles Beard: An English View." In Howard K. Beale, ed., *Charles A. Beard: An Appraisal*. Lexington: University of Kentucky Press, 1954, pp. 9-24.

Lee, Frederic S. "From Multi-Industry Planning to Keynesian Planning: Gardiner C. Means, the American Keynesians, and National Economic Planning at the National Resources Committee." *Journal of Policy History* 2, 2 (1990): 186-212.

Leighton, George R. "Beard and Foreign Policy." In Howard K. Beale, ed. *Charles A. Beard: An Appraisal*. Lexington: University of Kentucky Press, 1954.

Lekachman, Robert. "Capitalism or Democracy." In Robert A. Goldwin and William A. Schambra, eds., *How Capitalistic Is the Constitution?* Washington, DC: American Enterprise Institute, 1982, pp. 127-47.

Lemisch, Jesse. "Jack Tar in the Streets: Merchant Seamen in the Politics of Revolutionary America." *William and Mary Quarterly* (July 1968): 371-407.

Lenin, V. I. *Imperialism: The Highest Stage of Capitalism*. New York: International Publishers, 1939.

———. *The State and Revolution*. New York: International Publishers, 1974.

Lerner, Max. *Ideas Are Weapons: The History and Uses of Ideas*. New York: Viking Press, 1939.

———. "Charles Beard's Stormy Voyage." *New Republic* (October 25, 1948): 20-23.

———. "Charles Beard: Civilization and the Devils." *New Republic* 119 (November 1, 1948):21-24.

———. "Charles Beard's Political Theory." In Howard K. Beale, ed., *Charles A. Beard: An Appraisal*. Lexington: University of Kentucky Press, 1954, pp. 24-45.

Leuchtenburg, William E. "Progressivism and Imperialism: The Progressive Movement and American Foreign Policy, 1898-1916." *Mississippi Valley Historical Review* 39 (December 1952): 483-502.

———. "The Pertinence of Political History: Reflections on the Significance of the State in America." *Journal of American History* 73 (December 1986): 585-600.

———. "The Uses and Abuses of History." *History and Politics Newsletter* 2 (Fall 1991): 6-7.

Levin, Peter R. "Charles A. Beard: Wayward Liberal." *Tomorrow* 8 (March 1949): 36-40.

Libby, Orin Grant. *The Geographical Distribution of the Vote of the Thirteen States on the Federal Constitution, 1787-1789*. Madison: University of Wisconsin Press, 1894.

———. "Review of *Economic Interpretation of the Constitution of the United States* by

Charles A. Beard," *Mississippi Valley Historical Review* 1, 1 (June 1914): 113-17.
——. "Review of *Economic Origins of Jeffersonian Democracy* by Charles A. Beard." *Mississippi Valley Historical Review*, 3, 1 (June 1916): 99-102.
Lindblom, Charles E. "The Market as Prison." *Journal of Politics* 44 (May 1982): 324-32.
Lippincott, Benjamin E. "The Bias of American Political Science." *Journal of Politics* 12 (1940): 125-39.
Longley, R. S. "Mob Activities in Revolutionary Massachusetts." *New England Quarterly* (March 1933): 98-130.
Loria, Achille. *The Economic Foundations of Society.* London: Swan, 1899.
Lowith, Karl. *Meaning in History.* Chicago: University of Chicago Press, 1949.
Lukacs, Georg. *History and Class Consciousness.* Cambridge: M.I.T. Press, 1971.
Lynd, Staughton. "The Mechanics in New York Politics, 1774-1778." *Labor History* (Fall 1964): 224-46.
Lyotard, Jean Francois. *The Postmodern Condition.* Minneapolis: University of Minnesota Press, 1984.
Manuel, Frank E. *Shapes of Philosophical History.* Stanford: Stanford University Press, 1965.
McCann, Michael W. "Resurrection and Reform: Perspectives on Property in the American Constitutional Tradition." *Politics and Society* 13 (1984): 143-76.
McClintock, Brent. "Institutional Transaction Analysis." *Journal of Economic Issues* 21, 2 (June 1987): 673-81.
McClintock, Thomas C. "J. Allen Smith: A Pacific Northwest Progressive." *Pacific Northwest Quarterly* (April 1962): 49-59.
McConaughy, John. *Who Rules America? A Century of Invisible Government.* New York: Longman, Green and Co., 1934.
McCorkle, Pope. "The Historian as Intellectual: Charles Beard and the Constitution Reconsidered." *American Journal of Legal History* 28 (1984): 314-63.
McDonald, Forrest. *We the People: The Economic Origins of the Constitution.* Chicago: University of Chicago Press, 1958.
——. "Forrest McDonald's Rebuttal." *William and Mary Quarterly* 17 (January 1960): 102-10.
——. "Charles A. Beard." In Marcus Cunliffe and Robin W. Winks, eds., *Pastmasters: Some Essays on American Historians.* New York: Harper and Row, 1969, pp. 110-41.
——. "The Constitution and Hamiltonian Capitalism." In Robert A. Goldwin and William A. Schambra, eds., *How Capitalistic Is the Constitution?* Washington, DC: American Enterprise Institute, 1982, pp. 49-74.
——. "A New Introduction (1986)." In Charles A. Beard, *An Economic Interpretation of the Constitution of the United States.* New York: Free Press, 1986, pp. vii-xl.
MacDonald, William. "American Interests in Foreign Affairs." *The Saturday Review of Literature* 10 (February 24, 1934), 1, 505-6.
McLaughlin, Andrew C. *The Confederation and the Constitution, 1783-1789.* New York: Harper and Brothers Publishers, 1905.
——. *A Constitutional History of the United States.* New York: D. Appleton-Century Co., 1935.
MacMahon, Arthur W. "Charles A. Beard." *American Political Science Review* (December 1948): 1208-209.
——. "Charles Beard, The Teacher." In Howard K. Beale, ed., *Charles A. Beard: An Appraisal.* Lexington: University of Kentucky Press, 1954, pp. 213-30.
McMaster, John Bach. *History of the People of the United States*, 8 Vols. New York: D. Appleton and Co., 1883-1892.

——. *With the Fathers: Studies in the History of the United States.* New York: D. Appleton and Co., 1897.

——. *The Acquisition of Political, Social, and Industrial Rights of Man in America.* Cleveland, OH: Imperial Press, 1903.

MacPherson, C. B. *The Life and Times of Liberal Democracy.* Oxford: Oxford University Press, 1977.

——. *Property: Mainstream and Critical Positions.* Toronto: University of Toronto Press, 1978.

Madison, James, John Jay, and Alexander Hamilton. *The Federalist Papers.* New York: New American Library, 1961.

Mahan, Alfred T. *The Influence of Sea Power Upon History, 1660-1783.* Boston: Little, Brown, and Co., 1890.

Maier, Pauline. "The Charleston Mob and the Evolution of Popular Politics in Revolutionary South Carolina, 1765-1784." *Perspective in American History* 4 (1970): 173-98.

Main, Jackson Turner. "Sections and Politics in Virginia, 1781-1787." *William and Mary Quarterly* (January 1955): 96-112.

——. "Charles A. Beard and the Constitution: A Critical Review of Forrest McDonald's *We the People.*" *William and Mary Quarterly* 17 (January 1960): 86-102.

——. *The Antifederalists: Critics of the Constitution, 1787-1788.* Chapel Hill: University of North Carolina Press, 1961.

——. *Political Parties Before the Constitution.* New York: W. W. Norton, Inc., 1973.

Mallan, John P. "Roosevelt, Brooks Adams, and Lea: The Warrior Critique of the Business Civilization." *American Quarterly* 8 (Fall 1956): 216-30.

Mandelbaum, Maurice. *The Problem of Historical Knowledge: An Answer to Relativism.* Freeport, NY: Liveright Publishing Corporation, 1938.

Mannheim, Karl. *Ideology and Utopia.* New York: Harcourt, Brace, Jovanovich, 1936.

Marcell, David. *Progress and Pragmatism: James, Dewey, Beard, and the American Idea of Progress.* Westport, CT: Greenwood Press, 1974.

March, James G., and Johan P. Olsen. "The New Institutionalism: Organizational Factors in Political Life." *American Political Science Review* 78 (1984): 734-49.

——. *Rediscovering Institutions: The Organizational Basis of Politics.* New York: Free Press, 1989.

Marks, Harry J. "Ground Under Our Feet: Beard's Relativism." *Journal of the History of Ideas* 14 (October 1953): 628-33.

Marx, Karl. *Capital,* Vol. I. New York: Modern Library, 1906.

——. *The German Ideology.* New York: International Publishers, 1970.

——. *A Contribution to the Critique of Political Economy.* New York: International Publishers, 1970.

——. "The German Ideology: Part I." In Robert C. Tucker, ed., *The Marx-Engels Reader,* 2nd Edition. New York: W. W. Norton Co., Inc., 1978, pp. 146-200.

Marx, Karl, and Freidrich Engels. *The Holy Family, or Critique of Critical Criticism.* Moscow: Progress Publishers, 1975.

Mathews, John M. "Review of *American Foreign Policy in the Making, 1932-1940; A Study in Responsibilities,* by Charles A. Beard." *American Political Science Review* (December 1948): 1189-191.

Matthews, Fred. "The Attack on 'Historicism': Allan Bloom's Indictment of Contemporary American Historical Scholarship." *American Historical Review* 95 (April 1990): 429-47.

Means, Gardiner C. *The Structure of the American Economy.* Washington, DC: Government Printing Office, 1939.

——. "Business Concentration in the American Economy." In Richard C. Edwards, Michael Reich, and Thomas Weisskopf, eds. *The Capitalist System.* Englewood Cliffs, NJ: Prentice-Hall, 1972, pp. 145-56.

Meiland, Jack. "The Historical Relativism of Charles A. Beard." *History and Theory* 12 (1973): 405-13.

Melman, Seymour. *The Permanent War Economy.* New York: Simon and Schuster, 1974.

Merriam, Charles E. *A History of American Political Theories.* New York: Macmillan Co., 1903.

——. "The National Resources Planning Board: A Chapter in American Planning Experience." *American Political Science Review* 38 (December 1944): 1075-88.

——. "Recent Advances in Political Methods." In James Farr and Raymond Seidelman, eds., *Discipline and History: Political Science in the United States.* Ann Arbor: University of Michigan Press, 1993, pp. 129-46.

Merton, Robert K. *Social Theory and Social Structure.* Glencoe, IL.: Free Press, 1957.

Michalak, Stanley J., Jr. *Competing Conceptions of American Foreign Policy: Worldviews in Conflict.* New York: Harper Collins, 1992.

Michelman, Frank. "Property as a Constitutional Right." *Washington and Lee Law Review* 38 (Fall 1982): 1101-109.

Miliband, Ralph. *The State in Capitalist Society.* New York: Basic Books, Inc., 1969.

Miller, Perry. "Charles A. Beard." *Nation* 167 (September 25, 1948): 344-46.

Miller, Spencer, Jr. "Workers' Education—Its Achievements and Failures." *American Federationist* (December 1922): 885-86.

Millett, John D. *The Process and Organization of Government Planning.* New York: Columbia University Press, 1947.

Moody, John. *The Truth About the Trusts: A Description and Analysis of the American Trust Movement.* New York: Moody Publishing Co., 1904.

Morais, Herbert M. "Artisan Democracy and the American Revolution." *Science and Society* (Summer 1942): 227-49.

Morris, James O. *Conflict within the AFL: A Study of Craft vs. Industrial Unionism.* Ithaca, NY: Cornell University Press, 1958.

Morris, Richard B. "Why the Constitution Was Adopted." *Saturday Review* (May 19, 1956): 33, 61.

Munz, P. *The Shapes of Time.* Middletown, CT: Wesleyan University Press, 1977.

Murray, Charles A. *Losing Ground: American Social Policy.* New York: Basic Books, 1984.

Myers, Gustavus. *History of the Supreme Court of the United States.* Chicago: Charles H. Kerr and Co., 1912.

Nash, Gary B. *The Urban Crucible: Social Changes, Political Consciousness, and the Origin of The American Revolution.* Cambridge: Cambridge University Press, 1979.

Nash, Gerald D. "Self-Education in Historiography: The Case of Charles A. Beard." *Pacific Northwest Quarterly* 52 (1961): 108-15.

Neibuhr, Helmut Richard. *The Social Sources of Denominationalism.* New York: Henry Holt and Co., 1929.

Nelson, Ralph. *Merger Movements in American Industry: 1895-1956.* Princeton, NJ: Princeton University Press, 1956.

Nevins, Allan. *The American States During and After the Revolution, 1775-1789.* New York: Macmillan Co., 1924.

————. *The Gateway to History*. New York: D. Appleton-Century Co., 1938.

————. "Two Views of America's Part: Mr. Buell Argues Our Responsibility – Professor Beard Upholds Isolation." *The New York Times Book Review*, May 26, 1940, Section 6, pp. 1, 20.

Nichols, Roy F. "Postwar Reorientation of Historical Thinking." *American Historical Review* 54 (October 1948): 78-89.

————. *A Historian's Progress*. New York: Alfred A. Knopf, 1968.

Noble, David W. *The Progressive Mind, 1890-1917*. Minneapolis: University of Minnesota Press, 1980 Revised.

Nore, Ellen. "Charles A. Beard's Act of Faith: Context and Content." *Journal of American History* 66 (March 1980): 850-66.

————. *Charles A. Beard: An Intellectual Biography*. Carbondale: Southern Illinois University, 1983.

"North Carolina Meeting of the American Historical Association." *American Historical Review* 35 (April 1930): 481-506.

North, Douglass C. "The New Institutional Economics." *Journal of Institutional and Theoretical Economics* 142 (1986): 230-37.

Novack, George. "Historians and the Belated Rise of American Imperialism." In George Novack, ed., *America's Revolutionary Heritage: Marxist Essays*. New York: Pathfinder Press, 1976, pp. 287-307.

Novack, George, ed. *America's Revolutionary Heritage: Marxist Essays*. New York: Pathfinder Press, 1976.

Offe, Claus. "The Theory of the Capitalist State and the Problem of Policy Formation." In Leon Lindberg, ed., *Stress and Contradiction in Modern Capitalism*. Lexington, MA: D. C. Heath, 1975, pp. 125-44.

————. *Contradictions of the Welfare State*. Cambridge: M.I.T. Press, 1984.

Ogg, Frederick, and Charles A. Beard. *National Governments and the World War*. New York: Macmillan Co., 1919.

Olton, Charles S. "Philadelphia Mechanics in the First Decade of the American Revolution, 1765-1775." *Journal of American History* (September 1972): 311-26.

Oneal, James. *The Workers in American History*. Terre Haute, 1910.

Orren, Karen, and Stephen Skowronek. "Editors' Preface." *Studies in American Political Development*, Vol. 1. New Haven, CT: Yale University Press, 1986.

Pancake, John S., ed. *Thomas Jefferson: Revolutionary Philosopher: A Selection of Writings*. Woodbury: Barron's Educational Series, Inc., 1976.

Pannekoek, Anton. *Workers' Councils*. Somerville, MA: Root and Branch, 1970. Reprint of 1945 edition.

Parrington, Vernon Louis. *Main Currents in American Thought*, 3 Vols. New York: Harcourt, Brace, and World, Inc., 1927-1930.

————. "Introduction." In James Allen Smith, *The Growth and Decadence of Constitutional Government*. New York: Holt, Rinehart, and Winston, 1930, pp. vii-xv.

Parrington, Vernon Louis, Jr., ed. "Vernon Parrington's Views: Economics and Criticism." *Pacific Northwest Quarterly* (July 1953): 97-105.

Parrini, Carl, and Martin J. Sklar. "New Thinking about the Market, 1896-1904: Some American Economists on Investment and the Theory of Surplus Capital." *Journal of Economic History* 43, 3 (September 1983): 559-78.

Pateman, Carole. *Participation and Democratic Theory*. Cambridge: Cambridge University Press, 1970.

Paul, Eden, and Cedar Paul. *Proletcult*. London: Leonard Parsons, 1921.

Perkins, Van L. *Crisis in Agriculture: The Agricultural Adjustment Administration and the New Deal*. Berkeley and Los Angeles: University of California Press, 1969.

Phillips, Clifton J. "The Indiana Education of Charles A. Beard." *Indiana Magazine of History* 55 (March 1959): 1-15.

Phillips, Harlan B. "Charles Beard, Walter Vrooman, and the Founding of Ruskin Hall." *South Atlantic Quarterly* 50, 2 (April 1951): 186-91.

———. "Charles Beard: The English Lectures, 1899-1901." *Journal of the History of Ideas* 14 (June 1953): 451-56.

Pixton, John E., Jr. "The Ghost of Charles Beard." *The Christian Century* (October 1, 1952): 1120-22.

Pocock, J. G. A. *The Machiavellian Moment: Florentine Political Thought and the Atlantic Republican Tradition*. Princeton, NJ: Princeton University Press, 1975.

———. *Politics, Language and Time*. New York: Atheneum Press, 1973.

Pool, William C. "An Economic Interpretation of the Ratification of the Federal Constitution in North Carolina, Part 1." *North Carolina Historical Review* 27 (April 1950): 119-41.

———. "An Economic Interpretation of the Ratification of the Federal Constitution in North Carolina, Part 2." *North Carolina Historical Review* 27 (July 1950): 289-313.

———. "An Economic Interpretation of the Ratification of the Federal Constitution in North Carolina, Part 3." *North Carolina Historical Review* 27 (October 1950): 437-61.

Poulantzas, Nicos. *Political Power and Social Classes*. London: New Left Books, 1973.

Porter, Glenn. *The Rise of Big Business, 1860-1910*. New York: Thomas Y. Crowell Co., 1973.

Porter, Michael E. *The Competitive Advantage of Nations*. New York: Free Press, 1990.

Pound, Roscoe. "Liberty of Contract." *Yale Law Journal* (May, 1909): 454-87.

Pratt, Julius W. *Cordell Hull*, 2 Vols. New York: Coopers Square Publishers, Inc., 1964.

President's Research Committee on Social Trends. *Recent Social Trends in the United States*. New York: Whittlesey House, 1934.

Radosh, Ronald. "Charles A. Beard and American Foreign Policy." In Ronald Radosh, ed., *Prophets on the Right*. New York: Simon and Schuster, 1975, pp. 17-37.

———. "Charles A. Beard: World War II Revisionist." In Ronald Radosh, ed., *Prophets on the Right*. New York: Simon and Schuster, 1975, pp. 39-65.

Ransom, William L. *Majority Rule and the Judiciary*. New York: Charles Scriber's Sons, 1912.

Recchiuti, John L. "The Rand School of Social Science During the Progressive Era: Will to Power of a Stratum of the American Intellectual Class." *Journal of the History of the Behavioral Sciences* 31 (April 1995): 149-61.

Reich, Charles. "The New Property." *Yale Law Journal* 73, 5 (April 1964): 733-87.

Reich, Robert B. *The Work of Nations: Preparing Ourselves for 21st Century Capitalism*. New York: Alfred A. Knopf, 1991.

"Review of *President Roosevelt and the Coming of the War, 1941*, by Charles A. Beard," *Time* 51 (April 12, 1948): 12.

Reynolds, R. Larry. "Institutionally Determined Property Claims." In Marc R. Tool and Warren J. Samuels, eds., *State, Society, and Corporate Power*, 2nd Edition, Completely Revised. New Brunswick, NJ: Transaction Publishers, 1989, pp. 237-45.

Ricci, David. *The Tragedy of Political Science*. New Haven, CT: Yale University Press, 1984.

Riezler, Kurt. "Idee und Interesse in de politischen Geschichte." *Dioskuren* (Munich) III (1924): 1-13.

Ripley, William Z. *Trusts, Pools, and Corporations.* New York: Ginn and Co., 1905.

Roberts, David D. "Croce in America: Influence, Misunderstanding, and Neglect," *Humanities* 8, 2 (1995): 3-34.

Robinson, James Harvey. *The New History.* New York: Macmillan Co., 1912.

Robinson, James Harvey, and Charles A. Beard. *The Development of Modern Europe: An Introduction to the Study of Current History*, 2 Vols. New York: Ginn and Co., 1908.

Roe, Gilbert. "Our Judicial Oligarchy." *LaFollette's Weekly Magazine* (June 24, 1911): 7-9.

———. "Why the People Distrust the Courts." *LaFollette's Weekly Magazine* (July 1, 1911): 7-9.

Rogers, James E. Thorold. *A Manual of Political Economy: for schools and colleges*, 3rd edition. Oxford: Oxford University Press, 1876.

———, ed. *Speeches on Questions of Public Policy by John Bright.* London: Macmillan, 1883.

———. *The Economic Interpretation of History.* New York: G. P. Putnam's Sons, 1888.

Ross, Dorothy. *The Origins of American Social Science.* Cambridge: Cambridge University Press, 1991.

Ruhl, Alfred. *Zur Frage der internationalen Arbeitstilung.* Berlin: Reimar Hobbing, 1932.

Rutland, Robert Allen. *The Ordeal of the Constitution: The Antifederalists and the Ratification Struggle of 1787-1788.* Norman: University of Oklahoma Press, 1965.

Schaper, William A. "Sectionalism and Representation in South Carolina." *Annual Report of the American Historical Association.* Washington, DC: Government Printing Office, 1901.

Schapsmeier, Edward L., and Frederick H. Shapsmeier. *Henry A. Wallace of Iowa: The Agrarian Years, 1919-1940.* Ames: Iowa State University Press, 1968.

Scheler, Max. *Mensch und Geschichte.* Zurich: Neuen Schweizer Rundschau, 1929.

———. *Philosophical Perspectives.* Boston: Beacon Press, 1958.

———. *Problems of a Sociology of Knowledge.* London: Routledge and Kegan Paul, 1980.

Schiesl, Martin J. *The Politics of Efficiency: Municipal Administration and Reform in America,1880-1920.* Berkeley and Los Angeles: University of California Press, 1977.

Schlesinger, Arthur M. *The Colonial Merchants and the Revolution.* New York: Columbia University Press, 1918.

Schlesinger, Arthur, Jr. *The Cycles of American History.* Boston: Houghton-Mifflin, 1986.

Schnitzer, Martin. *The Swedish Investment Reserve: A Device for Economic Stabilization?* Washington, DC: American Enterprise Institute, 1967.

Schrecker, Ellen. *No Ivory Tower: McCarthyism and the Universities.* New York: Oxford University Press, 1986.

Schumpeter, Joseph. *Imperialism and Social Classes.* New York: Augustus M. Kelley, 1951.

Schuyler, Robert Livingston. *The Constitution of the United States.* New York: Macmillan Co., 1923.

Scott, William B., and Peter M. Rutkoff. *New School: A History of the New School for Social Research.* New York: Macmillan, Inc., 1986.

See, Henri. *The Economic Interpretation of History.* New York: Augustus M. Kelley, 1968.

Seidelman, Raymond. *Disenchanted Realists: Political Science and the American Crisis 1884-1984*. Albany: State University of New York Press, 1985.

Seligman, E. R. A. "Economic Interpretation of History." *Political Science Quarterly* 16 (December 1901): 612-40.

——. "Economic Interpretation of History." *Political Science Quarterly* 17 (March 1902): 71-98.

——. "Economic Interpretation of History." *Political Science Quarterly* 17 (June 1902): 284-312.

——. *The Economic Interpretation of History*, 2nd Edition Revised. New York: Columbia University Press, 1924.

Shapiro, Martin. "The Constitution and Economic Rights." In M. Judd Harmon, ed., *Essays in the Constitution of the U.S.* Port Washington, NY: Kennikat Press, 1978, pp. 74-98.

Shefter, Martin. "History and Political Science." *Clio: Newsletter of Politics and History* 7 (Fall/Winter 1996-97): 1, 14.

Shoemaker, Robert W. "'Democracy' and 'Republic' as Understood in Late Eighteenth-Century America." *American Speech* 41 (1966): 83-95.

Simons, A. M. *Class Struggles in America*. Chicago: Charles H. Kerr and Co., 1903.

——. *Social Forces in American History*. New York: Macmillan Co., 1911.

Sinclair, John F. "Power Issue Looms Large." *Los Angeles Times*, March 13, 1931, p. 15.

Skinner, Quentin. "Meaning and Understanding in the History of Ideas." *History and Theory* 8 (1969): 3-53.

Skinner, Quentin. "Motives, Intentions, and the Interpretation of Texts." *New Literary History* 3 (Winter 1972): 393-408.

Sklar, Martin J. *The United States as a Developing Country: Studies in U.S. History in the Progressive Era and the 1920s*. New York: Cambridge University Press, 1992.

Skocpol, Theda. "Bringing the State Back In: Strategies of Analysis in Current Research." In Peter Evans, Dietrich Rueschemeyer, and Theda Skocpol, eds. *Bringing the State Back In*. Cambridge: Cambridge University Press, 1985, pp. 3-43.

——. "A Reply [to G. William Domhoff]." *Politics and Society* 15, 3 (1986/87): 331-32.

Skotheim, Robert Allen. *American Intellectual Histories and Historians*. Princeton, NJ: Princeton University Press, 1966.

Smith, James Allen. *The Spirit of American Government*. New York: Macmillan Co., 1907.

——. *The Growth and Decadence of Constitutional Government*. New York: Holt, Rinehart, and Winston, 1930.

Smith, Theodore Clark. "The Writing of American History in America, 1884-1934." *American Historical Review* 40 (April 1935): 439-49.

Sorenson, Lloyd R. "Charles A. Beard and German Historiographical Thought." *Mississippi Valley Historical Review* 42 (September 1955): 274-87.

Sosin, Jack M. *Agents and Merchants: British Colonial Policy and the Origins of the American Revolution, 1763-1775*. Lincoln: University of Nebraska Press, 1965.

Soule, George. "Beard and the Concept of Planning." In Howard K. Beale, ed., *Charles A. Beard: An Appraisal*. Lexington: University of Kentucky Press, 1954, pp. 61-74.

Spargo, John. *Applied Socialism: A Study of the Application of Socialistic Principles to the State*. New York: Macmillan, 1909.

Spengler, Oswald. *Decline of the West*. New York: Alfred A. Knopf, 1926.

Spitz, Elaine. *Majority Rule*. Chatham: Chatham House Publishers, Inc., 1984.

Staude, John Raphael. *Max Scheler, 1874-1928: An Intellectual Portrait.* New York: Free Press, 1967.

Stevens, C. Ellis. *Sources of the Constitution of the United States.* New York: Macmillan and Co., 1894.

Stimson, Frederick J. *The American Constitution.* New York: Charles Scribner's Sons, 1914.

Storing, Herbert J. *What the Antifederalists Were For.* Chicago: University of Chicago Press, 1981.

Stourzh, George. "Charles A. Beard's Interpretations of American Foreign Policy." *World Affairs Quarterly* 28 (July 1957): 111-48.

Straus, Oscar S. *The Origin of the Republican Form of Government in the United States of America.* New York: G. P. Putnam's Sons, 1885.

Strauss, Leo. "Political Philosophy and History." In Leo Strauss, *What is Political Philosophy? and Other Studies.* Glencoe, IL: Free Press, 1959, pp. 56-77.

Strout, Cushing. "In Retrospect: Charles Beard's Liberalism." *New Republic* 133 (November 17, 1955): 17-18.

———. *The Pragmatic Revolt in America: Carl Becker and Charles Beard.* Ithaca, NY: Cornell University Press, 1966. Reprint edition. Published originally by Yale University Press, 1958.

Stubbs, William. *The Constitutional History of England,* 3 vols. Oxford: Clarendon Press, 1878.

Sunstein, Cass R. "The Enduring Legacy of Republicanism." In Stephen L. Elkin and Karol Edward Soltan, eds., *A New Constitutionalism: Designing Political Institutions for a Good Society.* Chicago: University of Chicago Press, 1993, pp. 174-206.

Thayer, James Bradley. *Legal Essays.* Boston: Boston Book Co., 1908.

Thomas, Robert E. "A Reappraisal of Charles A. Beard's *An Economic Interpretation of the Constitution of the United States.*" *American Historical Review* 5 (January 1952): 370-75.

———. "The Virginia Convention of 1788: A Criticism of Beard's *An Economic Interpretation of the Constitution,*" *Journal of Southern History* 19 (February 1953): 63-72.

Thompson, Dennis L. "Introduction to the 1972 Edition." In Vernon Louis Parrington and James Allen Smith. *The Growth and Decadence of Constitutional Government.* New York: Holt, Rinehart, and Winston, 1930, pp. xvii-xxiv.

Thompson, Noel. "Hobson and the Fabians: Two Roads to Socialism in the 1920s." *History of Political Economy* 26 (Summer 1994): 203-20.

Thompson, Ralph. "Books of the Times." *New York Times,* May 15, 1940, p. 23.

Thurow, Lester. *Head to Head: The Coming Economic Battle Among Japan, Europe, and America.* New York: William Morrow and Co., 1992.

Thwing, Charles F. *The American and German University: One Hundred Years of History.* New York: Macmillan, 1928.

Tool, Marc R., and Warren J. Samuels, eds. *State, Society, and Corporate Power,* 2nd Edition, Completely Revised. New Brunswick, NJ: Transaction Publishers, 1989.

Trickett, Dean William. "Judicial Dispensation from Congressional Statutes." *American Law Review* (January 1907): 65-91.

Tridon, Andre. *The New Unionism.* New York: B. W. Huebsch, 1912.

Tully, James, ed. *Meaning and Context: Quentin Skinner and his Critics.* Princeton, NJ: Princeton University Press, 1988.

Utter, William T. "Vernon Louis Parrington." In *The Marcus W. Jernegan Essays in American Historiography.* Chicago: University of Chicago Press, 1937.

U.S. House Banking and Currency Committee. *Report of the Committee Appointed*

Pursuant to H.R. 429 and 574 to Investigate the Concentration of Money and Credit. 62nd Congress, 2nd Session. 1913.

Varney, Harold Lord. "The Man Who Lived Twice." *American Mercury* 85 (August 1957): 148-50.

Veblen, Thorstein. *The Engineers and the Price System.* New York: B. W. Huebsch, 1921.

———. *Absentee Ownership and Business Enterprise in Recent Times.* New York: B. W. Huebsch, 1923.

Virtue, George Olien. *British Land Policy and the American Revolution.* Lincoln: University of Nebraska Press, 1953.

von Ranke, Leopold. *Zur Kritik neuer Geschichtschreiber.* Leipzig: Duncker und Humbolt, 1874.

Wallace, Henry A. *America Must Choose.* New York: Foreign Policy Association, 1934.

———. "Beard: The Planner." *New Republic* 81 (January 2, 1935): 225-27.

Warren, Charles. *The Trumpeters of the Constitution.* Rochester, NY: University of Rochester Press, 1927.

———. *The Making of the Constitution.* Boston: Little, Brown, and Co., 1929.

Weber, Max. *The Protestant Ethic and the Spirit of Capitalism.* New York: Charles Scribner's Sons, 1958.

Weinstein, James. *The Corporate Ideal in the Liberal State: 1900-1918.* Boston: Beacon Press, 1968.

White, Morton. *Social Thought in America: The Revolt Against Formalism.* Boston: Beacon Press, 1957. Reprint edition. Published originally by the Viking Press in 1949.

———. *Philosophy, The Federalist, and the Constitution.* New York: Oxford University Press, 1987.

Wilkins, Burleigh J. "Charles A. Beard on the Founding of Ruskin College." *Indiana Magazine of History* 52 (September 1956): 277-84.

Wilkins, B. T. *Has History Any Meaning? A Critique of Popper's Philosophy of History.* Ithaca, NY: Cornell University Press, 1978.

Williams, William Appleman. "A Note on Charles Austin Beard's Search for a General Theory of Causation." *American Historical Review* 62 (October 1956): 59-80.

———. "Charles Austin Beard." In Harvey Goldberg, ed., *American Radicals: Some Problems and Personalities.* New York: Monthly Review, Inc., 1957, pp. 295-308.

———. *The Contours of American History.* New York: New Viewpoints, 1973.

———. *From Colony to Empire.* New York: J. Wiley, 1972.

———. *The Tragedy of American Diplomacy.* New York: Dell Publishing, 1972.

———. *Americans in a Changing World: A History of the United States in the Twentieth Century.* New York: Harper and Row, 1978.

Williamson, Chilton. *American Suffrage; From Property to Democracy, 1760 to 1860.* Princeton, NJ: Princeton University Press, 1960.

Wilson, Woodrow. *Division and Reunion, 1829-1889.* New York: Longman, Green, and Co., 1898.

———. *A History of the American People.* New York: Harper and Brothers, 1901.

———. *The New Freedom.* New York: Doubleday, Page and Co., 1913.

Wise, Gene. *American Historical Explanations: A Strategy for Grounded Inquiry.* Minneapolis: University of Minnesota Press, 1980.

Wish, Harvey. *The American Historian: A Social-Intellectual History of the Writing of the American Past.* New York: Oxford University Press, 1960.

Wishy, Bernard. "A New Appraisal of Charles Beard." *The New Leader* (March 23, 1959): 20-22.

Wolfe, Bertram D. *A Life in Two Centuries: An Autobiography.* New York: Stein and Day, 1981.

Wood, Gordon S. *The Creation of the American Republic, 1776-1787.* Chapel Hill: University of North Carolina Press, 1969.

Wood, Neal. *John Locke and Agrarian Capitalism.* Berkeley: University of California Press, 1984.

Woodburn, J. A. *The Causes of the American Revolution.* Baltimore, MD: John Hopkins University Press, 1892.

Index